Fodor's First Edition

D0091341

Nepal, Tibet, and Bhutan

The complete guide, thoroughly up-to-date

Packed with details that will make your trip

The must-see sights, off and on the beaten path

What to see, what to skip

Mix-and-match vacation itineraries

City strolls, countryside adventures

Smart lodging and dining options

Essential local do's and taboos

Transportation tips, distances and directions

Key contacts, savvy travel tips

When to go, what to pack

Clear, accurate, easy-to-use maps

Books to read, videos to watch, background essays

Fodor's Travel Publications • New York, Toronto, London, Sydney, Auckland
www.fodors.com

Fodor's Nepal, Tibet, and Bhutan

EDITORS: Amy Karafin, Melanie Sponholz

Editorial Contributors: Wendy Kassel, Laura Kidder, Michael Koeppel, Natasha Lesser, Lily Tung, Lara Wozniak
Production Editorial: Tom Holton
Maps: David Lindroth, *cartographer*; Mapping Specialists Ltd., *cartographers*; Rebecca Baer and Bob Blake, *map editors*
Design: Fabrizio La Rocca, *creative director*; Guido Caroti, *art director*; Jolie Novak, *photo editor*
Cover Design: Pentagram
Production/Manufacturing: Robert B. Shields
Cover Photograph: Peter Guttman

Copyright

First Edition

ISBN 0–679–00167–0

ISSN 1528–9222

Special Sales

Fodor's Travel Publications are available at special discounts for bulk purchases for sales promotions or premiums. Special editions, including personalized covers, excerpts of existing guides, and corporate imprints, can be created in large quantities for special needs. For more information, contact your local bookseller or write to Special Markets, Fodor's Travel Publications, 280 Park Avenue, New York, NY 10017. Inquiries from Canada should be directed to your local Canadian bookseller or sent to Random House of Canada, Ltd., Marketing Department, 2775 Matheson Boulevard East, Mississauga, Ontario L4W 4P7. Inquiries from the United Kingdom should be sent to Fodor's Travel Publications, 20 Vauxhall Bridge Road, London SW1V 2SA, England.

PRINTED IN THE UNITED STATES OF AMERICA

10 9 8 7 6 5 4 3 2 1

Important Tip

Although all prices, opening times, and other details in this book are based on information supplied to us at press time, changes occur all the time in the travel world, and Fodor's cannot accept responsibility for facts that become outdated or for inadvertent errors or omissions. So **always confirm information when it matters,** especially if you're making a detour to visit a specific place.

CONTENTS

Maps

ON THE ROAD WITH FODOR'S

THE TRIPS YOU TAKE this year and next are going to be significant trips, if only because they'll be your first in the new millennium. Acutely aware of that fact, we've pulled out all stops in preparing *Fodor's Nepal, Tibet, and Bhutan.* To guide you in putting together your experience, we've created multiday itineraries and neighborhood walks. And to direct you to the places that are truly worth your time and money in these important years, we've rallied the team of endearingly picky know-it-alls we're pleased to call our writers. Having seen all corners of the regions they cover for us, they're real experts. If you knew them, you'd poll them for tips yourself.

Nigel Fisher, the peripatetic writer and knowledgeable publisher of "Voyager International," a newsletter on world travel, wrote parts of the Tibet chapter. His particular interests are in telling his readers about art, about good places to stay, and about the most delicious food. He is currently living in Thailand.

A former resident of Manhattan, Bhutan writer **Wendy Kassel** worked for *Elle* magazine before giving up the urban life to join the Peace Corps. After finishing her assignment in Nepal, Wendy traveled extensively throughout Asia. She currently works in the travel business and lives in Kathmandu.

Michael Koeppel, co-author and updater of the Tibet chapter, divides his time between travel writing and photography and working for a disaster-relief organization. His work in the Pacific Rim includes writing about his travels through Cambodia, photographing Shanghai, and assisting with the response and recovery efforts in Guam and Saipan in the wake of Supertyphoon Paka.

Lily Tung, now a journalist and news producer living in San Francisco, was based in Shanghai, China from 1994 to 1999. She is the former editor of the city magazine *Shanghai Talk* and has worked with the *Wall Street Journal, Asiaweek, Newsweek, National Geographic Magazine, Asia Inc,* NBC News, Associated Press TV, and WGBH Boston. Lily cowrote and updated the Tibet chapter.

Lara Wozniak, a lawyer who worked as a business reporter for the *St. Petersburg Times* in Florida, packed in the traditional newspaper job to travel the world. She has contributed to international newspapers and magazines and written a novel on mountain climbing in the Himalayas. Lara wrote the Nepal sections of this edition.

We'd also like to thank Michael Burroughs, Christine Daniels, Tsering and family at the Double Dorjee, Alex Fell, the High Himalaya communications center, Sonam Jatso at Travel Bhutan, Namgyal Lhendup, Melissa McFerrin, Liam McMillan, Thuji D. Nadik and the Tourism Authority of Bhutan, Rabi Paudel, Roger Pfister, Suzie Robertson, Sheba and Rajiv Shrestha, Tibet Ningchi International Travel Co., Thopten's family in Boudha, Lea Wyler, and Dolores Wozniak.

Don't Forget to Write

Keeping a travel guide fresh and up-to-date is a big job. So we love your feedback—positive and negative—and follow up on all suggestions. Contact the Nepal, Tibet, and Bhutan editor at editors@fodors.com or c/o Fodor's, 280 Park Avenue, New York, New York 10017. And have a wonderful trip!

Karen Cure

Karen Cure
Editorial Director

The Himalayan Countries

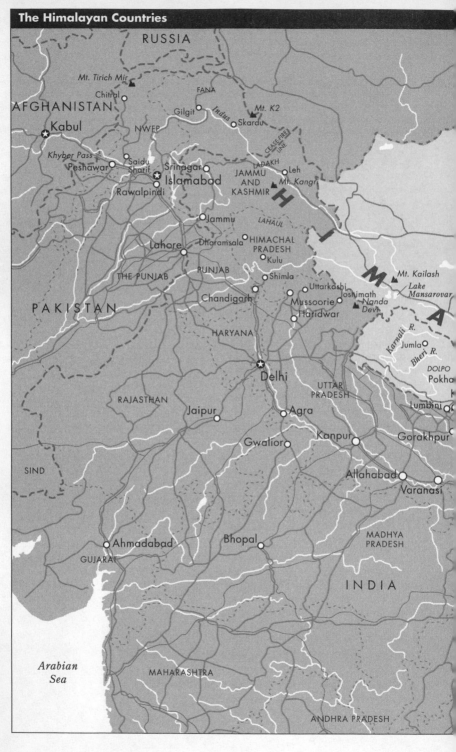

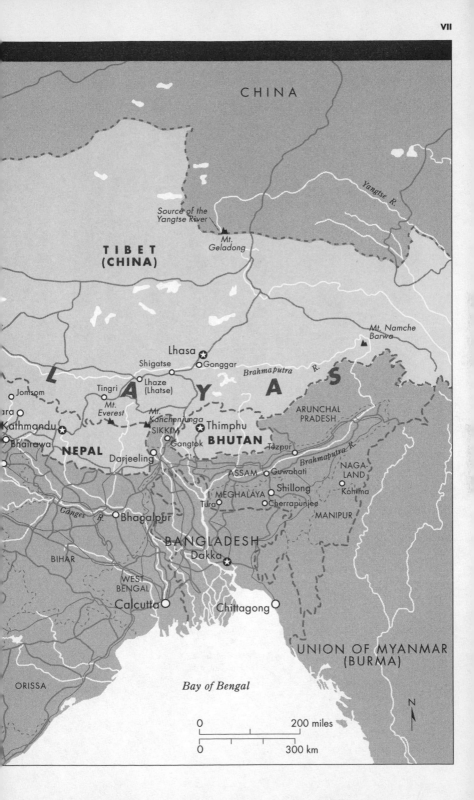

World Time Zones

Numbers below vertical bands relate each zone to Greenwich Mean Time (0 hrs.).
Local times frequently differ from these general indications,
as indicated by light-face numbers on map.

Algiers, **29**

Anchorage, **3**

Athens, **41**

Auckland, **1**

Baghdad, **46**

Bangkok, **50**

Beijing, **54**

Berlin, **34**

Bogotá, **19**

Budapest, **37**

Buenos Aires, **24**

Caracas, **22**

Chicago, **9**

Copenhagen, **33**

Dallas, **10**

Delhi, **48**

Denver, **8**

Dublin, **26**

Edmonton, **7**

Hong Kong, **56**

Honolulu, **2**

Istanbul, **40**

Jakarta, **53**

Jerusalem, **42**

Johannesburg, **44**

Lima, **20**

Lisbon, **28**

London
(Greenwich), **27**

Los Angeles, **6**

Madrid, **38**

Manila, **57**

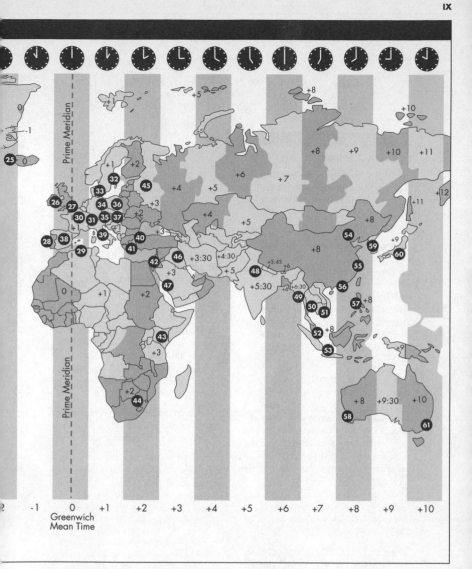

SMART TRAVEL TIPS A TO Z

Basic Information on Traveling in Nepal, Tibet, and Bhutan, Savvy Tips to Make Your Trip a Breeze, and Companies and Organizations to Contact

AIR TRAVEL

BOOKING YOUR FLIGHT

When you book **look for nonstop flights** and **remember that "direct" flights stop at least once.** Try to avoid connecting flights, which require a change of plane.

Currently, only Royal Nepal Airlines Corporation (RNAC) flies nonstop to Kathmandu from Frankfurt. Austrian Airlines flies nonstop from Vienna and Transavia from Amsterdam. All other major airlines flying from Europe, North America, Australia, and New Zealand use connecting flights from Bangkok, Singapore, or Delhi.

Note that two airlines may jointly operate a connecting flight to Nepal from an Asian hub, so **ask if your chosen airline operates every segment of your flight**—you may find that your preferred carrier flies only part of the way. For instance, if you purchased a ticket through an international carrier such as Northwest Airlines, you would fly to Bangkok on Northwest Airlines then fly to Kathmandu on a Royal Nepal Airlines Corporation or Thai Airways plane.

To get to Lhasa, Tibet, you will first have to fly to Hong Kong, Shanghai, or Beijing, China or Kathmandu, Nepal. Most travelers fly from Hong Kong, Shanghai, or Beijing to Chengdu, in Sichuan Province, where they stay overnight and then leave for Lhasa by plane the next morning. China Southwest Airlines offers two daily flights between Chengdu and Lhasa. There are only two weekly flights from Kathmandu to Lhasa.

There is only one airline that services Bhutan, Druk Air, the Royal Bhutanese national airline. Druk Air flies twice weekly to Delhi via Kathmandu and three times weekly to Bangkok via Calcutta.

CARRIERS

Several airlines offer direct flights to Shanghai and Beijing, including United Airlines, Northwest Airlines, Asiana, Korean Air, Canadian Airlines, Air France, British Airways, Virgin Atlantic, Japan Airlines, Lufthansa, Qantas, SAS, and Swissair. Although some Westerners are loath to fly China's own airline companies for service and safety reasons, Air China and China Eastern offer acceptable services for cheaper fares. Air China also has a partnership with Northwest, which means that it offers frequent flier miles on WorldPerks. Once in China, you'll most likely have to take a domestic flight to Chengdu, and then another one, on China Southwest Airlines, from Chengdu to Lhasa.

The above airlines also service Hong Kong, in addition to Hong Kong's primary carrier, Cathay Pacific.

Finally, if you're planning on going into Tibet via Kathmandu, *see* Chapter 2 for carriers from your home country to Kathmandu. From Kathmandu to Lhasa, you'll fly China Southwest Airlines.

➤ To and From China: **Air China** (☎ 415/392–2156). **Air France** (☎ 800/321–4538). **Asiana** (☎ 800/227–4262). **British Airways** (☎ 800/247–9297). **Canadian Airlines** (☎ 800/426–7000). **Cathay Pacific** (☎ 800/233–2742). **China Eastern Airlines** (☎ 800/200–5118). **Japan Airlines** (☎ 800/525–3663). **Korean Air** (☎ 800/438–5000). **Lufthansa** (☎ 800/645–3880). **Northwest Airlines** (☎ 800/255–2525). **Qantas** (☎ 800/227–4500). **SAS** (☎ 800/221–2350). **Swissair** (☎ 800/221–4750). **United Airlines** (☎ 800/241–6522).**Virgin Atlantic Airways** (☎ 800/862–8621).

➤ To and From Lhasa via Chengdu or Kathmandu: **China Southwest Airlines** (Contact **CAAC** at ☎ 800/

227–5118. In Lhasa: ✉ 1 Niangre Rd., Lhasa, ☎ 0891/683–3446).

➤ MAJOR AIRLINES: **Aeroflot Russian Airlines** (☎ 800/995–5555), **Air France** (☎ 800/237–2747), **Austrian Airlines** (☎ 800/843–0002), **British Airways** (☎ 800/247–9297), **Delta Air Lines** (☎ 800/221–1212), **Japan Airlines** (☎ 800/525–3663), **Lufthansa** (☎ 800/645–3880), **Northwest Airlines** (☎ 800/225–2525), **Singapore Airlines** (☎ 800/742–3333), **Thai Airways** (☎ 800/426–5204).

➤ FROM THE U.K: There are no direct flights to Kathmandu from the United Kingdom. New Delhi, Bangkok, and Singapore are the easiest connection points, from which there are daily connecting flights to Kathmandu. **Air India** (☎ 01753/684–828), **British Airways** (☎ 0345/222–111), **Thai Airways** (☎ 0171/491–7953).

➤ SMALLER AIRLINES: **Gulf Air** (☎ 800/553–2824), **Indian Airlines** (☎ 091/11–548–3327), **Qatar Airways** (☎ 0171/896–3636), **Royal Nepal Airlines Corp. (RNAC)** (☎ 020/7494–0974).

CHECK-IN & BOARDING

Assuming that not everyone with a ticket will show up, airlines routinely overbook planes. When everyone does, and that happens, airlines ask for volunteers to give up their seats. In return these volunteers usually get a certificate for a free flight and are rebooked on the next flight out. If there are not enough volunteers, the airline must choose who will be denied boarding. The first to get bumped are passengers who checked in late and those flying on discounted tickets, so **get to the gate and check in as early as possible,** especially during peak periods.

Always **bring a government-issued photo I.D. to the airport.** You may be asked to show it before you are allowed to check in.

CUTTING COSTS

The least expensive airfares to Nepal, Tibet, and Bhutan are priced for round-trip travel and usually must be purchased in advance. It's smart to **call a number of airlines, and when you are quoted a good price, book it**

on the spot—the same fare may not be available the next day. Always **check different routings** and look into using different airports. Prices for international flights are sensitive to the season: **plan to fly in the off-season** for the cheapest fares. Travel agents, especially low-fare specialists (☞ Discounts & Deals, *below*), are helpful.

Consolidators are another good source. They buy tickets for scheduled international flights at reduced rates from the airlines, then sell them at prices that beat the best fare available directly from the airlines, usually without restrictions. Sometimes you can even get your money back if you need to return the ticket. Carefully read the fine print detailing penalties for changes and cancellations, and **confirm your consolidator reservation with the airline.**

When you **fly as a courier** you trade your checked-luggage space for a ticket deeply subsidized by a courier service. There are restrictions on when you can book and how long you can stay.

Courier companies often have flights to Hong Kong. Check your local newspaper. Most likely you will not be able to fly to mainland China by courier.

➤ CONSOLIDATORS: **Cheap Tickets** (☎ 800/377–1000). **Up & Away Travel** (☎ 212/889–2345). **Discount Airline Ticket Service** (☎ 800/576–1600). **Unitravel** (☎ 800/325–2222). **World Travel Network** (☎ 800/409–6753).

ENJOYING THE FLIGHT

For more legroom **request an emergency-aisle seat.** Don't sit in the row in front of the emergency aisle or in front of a bulkhead, where seats may not recline. If you have dietary concerns, **ask for special meals when booking.** These can be vegetarian, low-cholesterol, or kosher, for example. On long flights, try to maintain a normal routine, to help fight jet lag. At night **get some sleep.** By day **eat light meals, drink water** (not alcohol), and **move around the cabin** to stretch your legs.

THE GOLD GUIDE / SMART TRAVEL TIPS

FLYING TIMES

Most flights to Nepal include stopovers, so the length of time you spend in the air depends on where you stop. For example, it could take from 11 to 14 hours to travel from London to Kathmandu, depending on whether you stop in Delhi or Frankfurt and then Dubai. Similarly, it can take 11 to 14 hours to reach Nepal from Sydney, depending on whether you stop in Bombay or Bangkok. From the United States, it also depends on your point of departure and, of course, where in Asia you stop off. On average, the trip from the United States takes about 17 hours.

It takes about 12 hours to fly from the west coast of the United States to Beijing, Shanghai, or Hong Kong, China. From there, it's another 2 hours to Chengdu, and another 2 to Lhasa. Flights from the east take a bit longer and usually include a stop. From London, a nonstop flight to Shanghai takes 10 hours. You can also go through Kathmandu, which is a one-hour flight from Lhasa.

Flights to Bhutan also include stopovers. It can take from 14 to 17 hours to travel from Amsterdam to Paro, depending on whether you stop in Delhi or Calcutta and then Kathmandu. Flying time from Sydney can be 12 to 15 hours, depending on whether you stop in Dhaka or Bangkok. The trip from the United Kingdom, the United States, Canada, Australia, or New Zealand takes about 14 hours.

HOW TO COMPLAIN

If your baggage goes astray or your flight goes awry, complain right away. Most carriers require that you **file a claim immediately.**

➤ AIRLINE COMPLAINTS: U.S. Department of Transportation **Aviation Consumer Protection Division** (✉ C-75, Room 4107, Washington, DC 20590, ☎ 202/366–2220). **Federal Aviation Administration Consumer Hotline** (☎ 800/322–7873).

RECONFIRMING

Always **reconfirm your flights,** even if you have a ticket and a reservation. If you are flying out of Hong Kong, you should reconfirm your flight 72 hours in advance. It's a good idea to confirm both domestic and international flights out of Kathmandu at least 24 hours in advance, particularly since weather often causes delays and cancellations of domestic flights.

AIRPORTS

China's major airports include Beijing International Airport, Shanghai Pudong International Airport, and Hong Kong International Airport. Chengdu Airport services Chengdu, and Lhasa Airport serves Tibet.

Flights to Shanghai and Beijing may be slightly cheaper than to Hong Kong, but there are often special deals to Hong Kong, so check all three destinations. Hong Kong is by far the most convenient of the three cities to travel to—accommodation and amenities are more modern; transportation is more convenient; things are generally more organized; and almost everyone speaks English.

AIRPORTS & TRANSFERS

➤ AIRPORT INFORMATION: The major gateway to Nepal is Kathmandu's **Tribhuvan International Airport** (☎ 01/471933).

Lhasa's airport is **Gongkar Airport,** 95 kilometers south of Lhasa in the village of Gongkar.

Paro International Airport (✉ Paro, ☎ 08/2–71401) is the main gateway into Bhutan.

DUTY-FREE SHOPPING

Hong Kong International Airport has a large duty-free shopping center that carries a wide range of goods, including fashion, cosmetics, alcohol, cigarettes, local arts and crafts, and CDs. Shanghai and Beijing International airports both have much less flashy duty-free shopping and carry mostly Chinese arts and crafts.

The Duty Free Shop at the Tribhuvan International Airport is small and expensive. It has a limited number of curios, alcohol, and tobacco. It does not accept credit cards and is only open from 7 AM to 6 PM, although the liquor shop stays open until 8 PM.

BIKE TRAVEL

You can get around Lhasa fairly easily by bicycle. Outside of Lhasa, biking is only recommended for very experienced bikers who are willing to put up with Tibet's bad roads and permit hassles. The high altitudes also make strenuous exercise difficult. If you do want to bike through the country, you must join a tour; independent biking through Tibet is not permitted. A mountain bike is a must if you take on the rough Tibetan roads.

In Pokhara, Nepal, biking is a convenient way to get around town. Many people also bike in Kathmandu. However, because of the smog and heavy traffic, you might want to wear a mask over your mouth and nose when biking in the capital. It will be black when you take it off. You can rent locally built bikes or mountain bikes from Europe and America. The cost is $3 to $10 per day in Kathmandu, slightly less in Pokhara (☞ Kathmandu A to Z *and* Pokhara A to Z *in* Chapter 2). **Make sure the bike has an attached wheel lock.** There are no bike racks, so ask for permission to lock your bike to a railing. Some people pay locals to watch their bike. A few tour operators organize bike trips across Nepal (☞ Special-Interest Tours *in* Kathmandu A to Z *in* Chapter 2). Don't consider biking in the Royal Chitwan National Park. Rhinos aren't too keen on bikes.

BIKES IN FLIGHT

Most airlines accommodate bikes as luggage, provided they are dismantled and boxed. For bike boxes, often free at bike shops, you'll pay about $5 (at least $100 for bike bags) from airlines. International travelers can sometimes substitute a bike for a piece of checked luggage at no charge; otherwise, the cost is about $100.

BUS TRAVEL

In Nepal, the best company to use for trips between Pokhara, Chitwan, and Kathmandu is **Greenline Tours** (☞ Nepal A to Z *in* Chapter 2). It takes 5½ hours to go from Kathmandu or Pokhara to Chitwan. Book reservations at least one day in advance.

It is difficult to travel through Tibet by bus. Travel to many areas requires special permits that cannot be obtained by independent travelers. Thus, most travel must be done as part of an organized tour, and your transportation will be arranged by your tour operator. You're not missing much: buses in Tibet are overcrowded, old, rattly, and rarely on time.

CAMERAS & PHOTOGRAPHY

In Nepal, photography is not permitted at some religious sites and events. Guards are usually quick to inform you. Many Nepalis, particularly in the hills, believe photographs steal their souls. They also think that Westerners have made a fortune on the sale of photos of Nepalis. Ask before you take a picture of a local.

Many monasteries in Tibet charge a fee for taking interior photographs, although you can take as many outside shots as you please. As in most locations, it is polite to ask local people for permission to take photos of them.

➤ PHOTO HELP: **Kodak Information Center** (☎ 800/242–2424). *Kodak Guide to Shooting Great Travel Pictures,* available in bookstores or from Fodor's Travel Publications (☎ 800/533–6478; $16.50 plus $4 shipping).

EQUIPMENT PRECAUTIONS

Always **keep your film and tape out of the sun.** Carry an extra supply of batteries, and **be prepared to turn on your camera or camcorder** to prove to security personnel that the device is real. Always **ask for hand inspection of film,** which becomes clouded after successive exposures to airport X-ray machines, and **keep videotapes away from metal detectors.**

VIDEOS

If you plan on doing any videotaping in Bhutan, you must abide by the *Bhutan Filming Regulations,* available from the Tourism Authority of Bhutan (☞ Bhutan A to Z *in* Chapter 4). Applications for a filming permit must be submitted to the Tourism Authority at least 30 days in advance.

THE GOLD GUIDE / SMART TRAVEL TIPS

CAR RENTAL

In all three countries, the only travel by car is arranged through tour operators and includes a hired driver (☞ individual country A to Z sections).

CHILDREN IN NEPAL, TIBET, AND BHUTAN

More and more people are bringing children to Nepal. Be sure to plan ahead and **involve your children in planning your trip.** If you are going hiking with your children, you might want to "train" at home, to see how long your they are prepared to walk before getting tired or asking to be carried. Most treks require people to be able to walk up and downhill for four to five hours a day. If you plan a trip to the Royal Chitwan National Park or Royal Bardia National Park do not go on a walking tour, as you might have to climb a tree to flee a charging rhino. Many hotels in Nepal offer free or inexpensive baby-sitting service.

Tibet is probably not the most ideal place to travel with young children, especially if you plan to leave Lhasa and its environs. The terrain is rugged, and amenities are scarce.

FLYING

If your children are two or older **ask about children's airfares.** As a general rule, infants under two not occupying a seat fly at greatly reduced fares or even for free. When booking **confirm carry-on allowances** if you're traveling with infants. In general, for babies charged 10% of the adult fare, you are allowed one carry-on bag and a collapsible stroller; if the flight is full the stroller may have to be checked or you may be limited to less.

Experts agree that it's a good idea to use safety seats aloft for children weighing less than 40 pounds. Airlines set their own policies: U.S. carriers usually require that the child be ticketed, even if he or she is young enough to ride free, since the seats must be strapped into regular seats. Do **check your airline's policy about using safety seats during takeoff and landing.** And since safety seats are not allowed just everywhere in the plane, get your seat assignments early.

When reserving, **request children's meals or a freestanding bassinet** if you need them. But note that bulkhead seats, where you must sit to use the bassinet, may lack an overhead bin or storage space on the floor.

LODGING

Most hotels in Nepal allow children under a certain age to stay in their parents' room at no extra charge, or for half the cost. Still others charge them as extra adults; be sure to **ask about the cutoff age for children's discounts.**

PRECAUTIONS

Any precautions recommended for adults are doubly recommended for children. Only drink bottled water; be prepared for changes in food preparation; and watch closely for altitude sickness.

SUPPLIES & EQUIPMENT

Pack things to keep your children busy while traveling. For children of reading age, **bring books from home;** locally, literature for kids in English is hard to find.

COMPUTERS ON THE ROAD

Dust is a problem in Nepal for sensitive electronic equipment. Keep delicate equipment under wraps when it is not in use. If you're bringing a laptop, you should consider carrying a spare battery and a spare adapter: New batteries and replacement adapters are expensive and can be hard to find in Nepal. **Never plug your computer into any socket before asking about surge protection.** Some hotels do not have built-in current stabilizers, and the extreme electrical fluctuations and surges are sure to short your adapter and likely destroy your computer. IBM sells a pen-size modem tester that plugs into a telephone jack to check if the line is safe to use. This is an invaluable gadget for Nepal where telephone lines are not always reliable and could destroy your modem. Outside of Kathmandu and Pokhara you will not find hotels with built-in current stabilizers.

In Lhasa, Tibet, you'll be able to find electrical outlets and phone jacks in all rooms of the more modern hotels. Guest houses have electrical outlets in noneconomy rooms and either private or public telephone lines you can plug into. Bring any equipment you may need, including batteries and adapters—you won't be able to find it in Tibet.

CONSUMER PROTECTION

Whenever shopping or buying travel services, **pay with a major credit card** so you can cancel payment or get reimbursed if there's a problem. If you're doing business with a particular company for the first time, **contact your local Better Business Bureau and the attorney general's offices** in your state and the company's home state, as well. Have any complaints been filed? Finally, if you're buying a package or tour, always **consider travel insurance** that includes default coverage (☞ Insurance, *below*).

➤ LOCAL BBBs: **Tibet Tourism Bureau** (✉ 18 Yuanlin Lam, Lhasa, ☎ 0891/683–4315 (information); 0891/683–4193 (to register complaint)). **Council of Better Business Bureaus** (✉ 4200 Wilson Blvd., Suite 800, Arlington, VA 22203, ☎ 703/276–0100, ℻ 703/525–8277).

CUSTOMS & DUTIES

When shopping, **keep receipts** for all purchases. Upon reentering the country, **be ready to show customs officials what you've bought.** If you feel a duty is incorrect or object to the way your clearance was handled, note the inspector's badge number and ask to see a supervisor. If the problem isn't resolved, write to the appropriate authorities, beginning with the port director at your point of entry.

IN NEPAL

Apart from used personal belongings, you can bring into Nepal, free of duty, 200 cigarettes or 50 cigars, a 1.15-liter bottle of distilled liquor and 15 rolls of film. You can bring binoculars, a movie or video camera, still camera, laptop computer, and portable music system, but only on condition that you take them back with you when you leave.

Nepal has a vested interest in protecting its valuable artwork. According to Nepali law, it is illegal to export objects over 100 years old (sacred images, paintings, manuscripts, etc.). If you buy something that looks old, you need to get a certificate from the **Department of Archaeology** (☎ 01/250687). This certificate will prove to airport security that the item is allowed to leave the country. Handicraft dealers and travel agents should be able to assist you in this process.

IN TIBET

Travelers arriving and leaving China are not required to go through customs. When departing, be sure to go through the green channel; don't get caught in the red. One caveat: only items dated after 1797 can be legally exported.

IN BHUTAN

The Bhutanese authorities strictly prohibit the export of antiques of any type. Travelers should be cautious when purchasing old and used items. Cameras, video cameras, computers, and personal electronic equipment may be brought into the country, but they must be listed on the customs form provided on arrival at Paro and will be checked on departure.

IN AUSTRALIA

Australia residents who are 18 or older may bring home $A400 worth of souvenirs and gifts (including jewelry), 250 cigarettes or 250 grams of tobacco, and 1,125 ml of alcohol (including wine, beer, and spirits). Residents under 18 may bring back $A200 worth of goods. Prohibited items include meat products. Seeds, plants, and fruits need to be declared upon arrival.

➤ INFORMATION: **Australian Customs Service** (Regional Director, ✉ Box 8, Sydney, NSW 2001, ☎ 02/9213–2000, ℻ 02/9213–4000).

IN CANADA

Canadian residents who have been out of Canada for at least 7 days may bring home C$500 worth of goods duty-free. If you've been away less than 7 days but more than 48 hours, the duty-free allowance drops to C$200; if your trip lasts 24–48 hours, the allowance is C$50. You may not pool allowances with family members. Goods claimed under the C$500 exemption may follow you by mail;

those claimed under the lesser exemptions must accompany you. Alcohol and tobacco products may be included in the 7-day and 48-hour exemptions but not in the 24-hour exemption. If you meet the age requirements of the province or territory through which you reenter Canada, you may bring in, duty-free, 1.14 liters (40 imperial ounces) of wine or liquor *or* 24 12-ounce cans or bottles of beer or ale. If you are 16 or older you may bring in, duty-free, 200 cigarettes and 50 cigars. Check ahead of time with Revenue Canada or the Department of Agriculture for policies regarding meat products, seeds, plants, and fruits.

You may send an unlimited number of gifts worth up to C$60 each duty-free to Canada. Label the package UNSOLICITED GIFT—VALUE UNDER $60. Alcohol and tobacco are excluded.

➤ INFORMATION: **Revenue Canada** (✉ 2265 St. Laurent Blvd. S, Ottawa, Ontario K1G 4K3, ☎ 613/993–0534; 800/461–9999 in Canada).

IN NEW ZEALAND

Homeward-bound residents 17 or older may bring back $700 worth of souvenirs and gifts. Your duty-free allowance also includes 4.5 liters of wine or beer; one 1,125-ml bottle of spirits; and either 200 cigarettes, 250 grams of tobacco, 50 cigars, or a combination of the three up to 250 grams. Prohibited items include meat products, seeds, plants, and fruits.

➤ INFORMATION: **New Zealand Customs** (Custom House, ✉ 50 Anzac Ave., Box 29, Auckland, New Zealand, ☎ 09/359–6655, FAX 09/359–6732).

IN THE U.K.

You may bring home, duty-free, 200 cigarettes or 50 cigars; 1 liter of spirits or 2 liters of fortified or sparkling wine or liqueurs; 2 liters of still table wine; 60 ml of perfume; 250 ml of toilet water; plus £136 worth of other goods, including gifts and souvenirs. Prohibited items include meat products, seeds, plants, and fruits.

➤ INFORMATION: **HM Customs and Excise** (✉ Dorset House, Stamford St., Bromley Kent BR1 1XX, ☎ 0171/202–4227).

IN THE U.S.

U.S. residents who have been out of the country for at least 48 hours (and who have not used the $400 allowance or any part of it in the past 30 days) may bring home $400 worth of foreign goods duty-free.

U.S. residents 21 and older may bring back 1 liter of alcohol duty-free. In addition, regardless of your age, you are allowed 200 cigarettes and 100 non-Cuban cigars. Antiques, which the U.S. Customs Service defines as objects more than 100 years old, enter duty-free, as do original works of art done entirely by hand, including paintings, drawings, and sculptures.

You may also send packages home duty-free: up to $200 worth of goods for personal use, with a limit of one parcel per addressee per day (and no alcohol or tobacco products or perfume worth more than $5); label the package PERSONAL USE and attach a list of its contents and their retail value. Do not label the package UNSOLICITED GIFT or your duty-free exemption will drop to $100. Mailed items do not affect your duty-free allowance on your return.

➤ INFORMATION: **U.S. Customs Service** (inquiries, ✉ 1300 Pennsylvania Ave. NW, Washington, DC 20229, ☎ 202/927–6724; complaints, ✉ Office of Regulations and Rulings, 1300 Pennsylvania Ave. NW, Washington, DC 20229; registration of equipment, ✉ Resource Management, 1300 Pennsylvania Ave. NW, Washington, DC 20229, ☎ 202/927–0540).

DINING

You will encounter two types of restaurants in Nepal: upscale Western-style restaurants (including hotel restaurants), which can be surprisingly elegant and hip, serving Nepalese, Chinese, Indian, Tibetan, and Continental cuisines; and trekker restaurants, which cater primarily to budget travelers, serving the same fare in big quantities but of mediocre quality. There are a number of hole-in-the-wall joints that look dirty, and many are; unless you see other travelers in them, stay away. Usually the only restaurants that accept credit cards and perhaps traveler's checks are the more upscale places. However, if you do pay with plastic, these places may add a 4% or 5% service charge to your bill.

It's important to **be careful of what you eat and drink** in Nepal. The vegetables and fruit here are particularly tasty, but leafy vegetables are known to carry parasites, so avoid those of dubious origin or those likely to have been washed in tap water. Also, try to eat only fruit that has a peel.

It is imperative that you **avoid drinking tap water as well as beverages with ice,** which often is made of local water. Most good restaurants either make their own ice using boiled water or buy ice in bulk from huge freezer warehouses.

Dairy is not pasteurized in Nepal. Many people have no problems; others get quite sick. Try a little at a time or avoid it.

With the explosion of tourism in Tibet over the past few years, the quality and variety of food available in the region has improved greatly. In Lhasa, Tibetan and Chinese fare is supplemented by a competitive market of Western restaurants offering fast food, Italian, Nepali, and Indian cuisines. Variety is not nearly as good outside the capital city. Fussy eaters should order a picnic from their Lhasa hotel before going off for trips into the countryside. Beer and soft drinks are available nearly everywhere. The local drink is *chang* (a fortified barley ale). Local water is not potable; it must be boiled or treated with iodine before it passes your lips.

MEALTIMES

Nepalis usually have a steaming cup of tea first thing in the morning. They have their first big meal around 10 AM, then don't eat again until around 6 or 7 PM.

Tibet and Bhutan follow typical three-meal schedules.

RESERVATIONS & DRESS

Reservations are always a good idea: we mention them only when they're essential or are not accepted. Book as far ahead as you can, and reconfirm as soon as you arrive. We mention dress only when men are required to wear a jacket or a jacket and tie.

DISABILITIES & ACCESSIBILITY

Travelers with disabilities or using wheelchairs may find it difficult to get around. Roads are often uneven or unpaved. Most sights and establishments do not offer wheelchair access.

Very few places in Nepal, Tibet, and Bhutan, including hotels, restaurants, and sites, are fully wheelchair accessible. For example, many luxury hotels have ramps, but few bathrooms are designed for use by people with disabilities. Disembarkation from planes in the region is by stairs.

LODGING

When discussing accessibility with an operator or reservations agent **ask hard questions.** Are there any stairs, inside *or* out? Are there grab bars next to the toilet *and* in the shower/tub? How wide is the doorway to the room? To the bathroom? For the most extensive facilities meeting the latest legal specifications **opt for newer accommodations.**

TRANSPORTATION

➤ COMPLAINTS: **Disability Rights Section** (✉ U.S. Department of Justice, Civil Rights Division, Box 66738, Washington, DC 20035-6738, ☎ 202/514–0301; 800/514–0301; 202/514–0301 TTY; 800/514–0301 TTY, ℻ 202/307–1198) for general complaints. **Aviation Consumer Protection Division** (☞ Air Travel, *above*) for airline-related problems. **Civil Rights Office** (✉ U.S. Department of Transportation, Departmental Office of Civil Rights, S-30, 400 7th St. SW, Room 10215, Washington, DC 20590, ☎ 202/366–4648, ℻ 202/366–9371) for problems with surface transportation.

TRAVEL AGENCIES

In the United States, although the Americans with Disabilities Act requires that travel firms serve the needs of all travelers, some agencies specialize in working with people with disabilities.

➤ TRAVELERS WITH MOBILITY PROB-LEMS: **Access Adventures** (✉ 206 Chestnut Ridge Rd., Rochester, NY 14624, ☎ 716/889–9096), run by a former physical-rehabilitation coun-selor. **Accessible Vans of the Rockies, Activity and Travel Agency** (✉ 2040 W. Hamilton Pl., Sheridan, CO 80110, ☎ 303/806–5047 or 888/837–0065, FAX 303/781–2329). **Flying Wheels Travel** (✉ 143 W. Bridge St., Box 382, Owatonna, MN 55060, ☎ 507/451–5005 or 800/535–6790, FAX 507/451–1685). **Hinsdale Travel Service** (✉ 201 E. Ogden Ave., Suite 100, Hinsdale, IL 60521, ☎ 630/325–1335).

DISCOUNTS & DEALS

Be a smart shopper and **compare all your options** before making decisions. A plane ticket bought with a promo-tional coupon from travel clubs, coupon books, or direct-mail offers may not be cheaper than the least expensive fare from a discount ticket agency. And always keep in mind that what you get is just as important as what you save.

DISCOUNT RESERVATIONS

To save money on flights and tours booked in your home country, **look into discount-reservations services** with toll-free numbers, which use their buying power to get a better price on hotels and airline tickets.

When shopping for the best deal on hotels and car rentals **look for guar-anteed exchange rates,** which protect you against a falling dollar. With your rate locked in, you won't pay more, even if the price goes up in the local currency.

➤ AIRLINE TICKETS: ☎ **800/FLY–4–LESS.**

➤ HOTEL ROOMS: **Travel Interlink** (☎ 800/888–5898).

PACKAGE DEALS

Don't confuse packages and guided tours. When you buy a package, you travel on your own, just as though you had planned the trip yourself. Fly/drive packages, which combine airfare and car rental, are often a good deal.

ELECTRICITY

To use your U.S.-purchased electric-powered equipment **bring a converter and adapter.** The electrical current in Tibet is 220 volts. The current in Bhutan is 230 volts, 5 cycles alternat-ing current (AC). The electrical current in Nepal is 220 volts, 50 cycles AC.

If your appliances are dual-voltage you'll need only an adapter. Don't use 110-volt outlets, marked FOR SHAVERS ONLY, for high-wattage appliances such as blow-dryers. Most laptops operate equally well on 110 and 220 volts and so require only an adapter. Make sure the electricity has either a built-in stabilizer or there is a surge protector box in your room. Black-outs are not uncommon in these countries, but many hotels have back-up generators. Ask your hotelier if the generator kicks in immediately.

EMBASSIES AND CONSULATES

The following embassies and con-sulates are in Kathmandu, Nepal: **Australian Embassy** (✉ Bansbari, ☎ 01/371678), **British Embassy** (✉ Lainchaur, ☎ 01/410583), **Cana-dian Embassy** (✉ Lazimpat, ☎ 01/415193), **New Zealand Consulate** (✉ Dilli Bazaar, ☎ 01/412436), **United States Embassy** (✉ Panipokhari, Lazimpat, ☎ 01/411179).

The only consulate in Tibet is the **Nepalese Consulate** (✉ 13 Norbul-ingka Lu, Lhasa, ☎ 0891/632–2881).

GAY & LESBIAN TRAVEL

Nepal is a sexually conservative country. No hotel will object to two people of the same sex sharing a bedroom; but you may want to **avoid public displays of affection.** Although it is common to see people of the same gender walking hand in hand, this is a reflection of friendship. Knowing that Westerners generally don't hold hands, some Nepalis may be suspicious when they see Western-ers of the same gender touching. The Tibetans and Bhutanese are also conservative people; discretion is advised.

➤ GAY- AND LESBIAN-FRIENDLY TRAVEL AGENCIES: **Different Roads Travel** (✉ 8383 Wilshire Blvd., Suite 902, Beverly Hills, CA 90211, ☎ 323/

651–5557 or 800/429–8747, FAX 323/
651–3678). **Kennedy Travel** (✉ 314
Jericho Tpke., Floral Park, NY
11001, ☎ 516/352–4888 or 800/
237–7433, FAX 516/354–8849). **Now
Voyager** (✉ 4406 18th St., San Francisco, CA 94114, ☎ 415/626–1169
or 800/255–6951, FAX 415/626–8626).
Yellowbrick Road (✉ 1500 W. Bal-
moral Ave., Chicago, IL 60640,
☎ 773/561–1800 or 800/642–2488,
FAX 773/561–4497). **Skylink Travel
and Tour** (✉ 1006 Mendocino Ave.,
Santa Rosa, CA 95401, ☎ 707/546–
9888 or 800/225–5759, FAX 707/546–
9891), serving lesbian travelers.

HEALTH

A first-aid kit with antacids, antidiar-
rheal, cold medicine, Band-Aids,
antiseptics, aspirin, a thermometer
(that can also read low temperatures
for hypothermia), moleskin (for
blisters) and other medical items you
may need is a good idea. Also, know
your blood type and **bring enough
medication to last the entire trip.** It
also makes sense to **bring an extra
pair of eyeglasses or contact lenses.**

FOOD & DRINK

In Nepal, Tibet, and Bhutan, the
major health risk is traveler's diarrhea, caused by eating contaminated
fruit or vegetables or drinking contaminated water. Traveler's diarrhea
can also be caused simply by a change
of diet. It usually only lasts a few
days; **if symptoms persist or worsen,
seek medical assistance.**

So **watch what you eat.** Stay away
from ice, uncooked food, and unpasteurized milk and milk products, and
drink only bottled water or water that
has been boiled for at least 20 minutes,
even when you're brushing your teeth.
Mild cases may respond to Imodium
(known generically as loperamide) or
Pepto-Bismol (not as strong), both of
which can be purchased over the
counter. Drink plenty of purified water
or tea. In severe cases, rehydrate
yourself with a salt-sugar solution
(½ teaspoon salt and 4 tablespoons
sugar per quart of water). **Avoid eating
unpeeled fruit and uncooked vegetables,** drinking unbottled, untreated
water, and using ice made from unbottled, untreated water.

MEDICAL PLANS

No one plans to get sick while traveling, but it happens, so **consider sign-
ing up with a medical-assistance
company.** Members get doctor referrals, emergency evacuation or repatri-
ation, hot lines for medical
consultation, cash for emergencies,
and other assistance.

➤ MEDICAL-ASSISTANCE COMPANIES:
International SOS Assistance (✉
8 Neshaminy Interplex, Suite 207,
Trevose, PA 19053, ☎ 215/245–4707
or 800/523–6586, FAX 215/244–9617;
✉ 12 Chemin Riantbosson, 1217
Meyrin 1, Geneva, Switzerland, ☎
4122/785–6464, FAX 4122/785–6424;
✉ 331 N. Bridge Rd., 17-00, Odeon
Towers, Singapore 188720, ☎ 65/
338–7800, FAX 65/338–7611).

OVER-THE-COUNTER REMEDIES

Western medicine is not largely available, so bring your own cold reme-
dies, aspirin, acetaminophen, and
ibuprofen.

PESTS & OTHER HAZARDS

Malaria has been by-and-large eradicated in the Terai region of Nepal,
where it was once a problem. It still
doesn't hurt to take preventive measures. Wear mosquito repellent and
sleep under mosquito nets.

Leeches can be a problem in the
summer. Usually, they attack your
legs and climb into your boots. Use
insect repellent—generously—to ward
them off. If they do attack, don't pull
them off, the bite is more likely to
become infected if you do. Instead,
burn them off by holding a lighter
close to the leech.

SHOTS & MEDICATIONS

As with any trip to a developing
country, you should **check with the
Centers for Disease Control and your
physician** about current health risks in
Nepal, Tibet, and Bhutan and recommended vaccinations before you go.

**Consider bolstering your tetanus and
polio vaccinations.** If you have never
contracted measles, mumps, or
rubella, you should also be immu-
nized against them. Also note: **Immunizations for hepatitis A, meningitis,
and typhoid fever are advised.**

➤ HEALTH WARNINGS: **National Centers for Disease Control** (CDC, National Center for Infectious Diseases, Division of Quarantine, Traveler's Health Section, ✉ 1600 Clifton Rd. NE, M/S E-03, Atlanta, GA 30333, ☎ 888/232–3228, FAX 888/232–3299).

INSURANCE

The most useful travel insurance plan is a comprehensive policy that includes coverage for trip cancellation and interruption, default, trip delay, and medical expenses (with a waiver for preexisting conditions).

Without insurance you will lose all or most of your money if you cancel your trip, regardless of the reason. Default insurance covers you if your tour operator, airline, or cruise line goes out of business. Trip-delay covers expenses that arise because of bad weather or mechanical delays. Study the fine print when comparing policies.

If you're traveling internationally, a key component of travel insurance is coverage for medical bills incurred if you get sick on the road. Such expenses are not generally covered by Medicare or private policies. U.K. residents can buy a travel-insurance policy valid for most vacations taken during the year in which it's purchased (but check preexisting-condition coverage). British and Australian citizens need extra medical coverage when traveling overseas.

Always **buy travel policies directly from the insurance company**; if you buy it from a cruise line, airline, or tour operator that goes out of business you probably will not be covered for the agency or operator's default, a major risk. Before you make any purchase **review your existing health and home-owner's policies** to find what they cover away from home.

If you plan on trekking or river rafting, make sure your policy does not bar coverage for "dangerous activities." If it does, find out what constitutes a dangerous activity and make sure trekking and river rafting are not included. Also consider emergency evacuation insurance. If you contract a serious illness at high altitude, you may need to evacuated

by helicopter, which costs $2,500 to $3,000. Some special insurances can cover this expense for an additional modest premium.

➤ TRAVEL INSURERS: In the United States **Access America** (✉ 6600 W. Broad St., Richmond, VA 23230, ☎ 804/285–3300 or 800/284–8300), **Travel Guard International** (✉ 1145 Clark St., Stevens Point, WI 54481, ☎ 715/345–0505 or 800/826–1300). In Canada **Voyager Insurance** (✉ 44 Peel Center Dr., Brampton, Ontario L6T 4M8, ☎ 905/791–8700; 800/668–4342 in Canada).

➤ INSURANCE INFORMATION: In the United Kingdom the **Association of British Insurers** (✉ 51–55 Gresham St., London EC2V 7HQ, ☎ 0171/600–3333, FAX 0171/696–8999). In Australia the **Insurance Council of Australia** (☎ 03/9614–1077, FAX 03/9614–7924).

LANGUAGE

Nepali, written in the Devanagiri script, is the national language of Nepal. It is also the lingua franca for Nepal's diverse communities. Numerous languages and dialects are spoken in the Kingdom. English and Hindi are widely understood in Kathmandu and Pokhara. Most restaurant workers and store owners will know some English; taxi drivers will know a few basic words.

With the exception of tour agents and guides, Public Security Bureau alien division officers, and some hotel staff, Tibetans generally do not speak English. Besides Tibetan, many residents also speak Chinese.

The official language of Bhutan is Dzongkha, which is similar to Tibetan, from which it was originally derived. A growing proportion of the people, especially in the urban areas, speak English. Currently, English is the language of instruction in schools, so most educated people speak it fluently. Throughout the kingdom, signs, books, menus, road signs, and even government documents are written in both Dzongkha and English.

LODGING

The quality of lodging in Nepal runs the gamut. The upscale hotels in

Kathmandu can compete the world over. Similarly, Pokhara is developing a high-standard hotel system. But when you go to the jungle and the mountains expect rustic conditions. The upmarket lodgings in these areas are long on charm, but don't expect to soak in a Jacuzzi while watching CNN in the Terai.

While there are no true luxury hotels in Tibet, Lhasa does have several large hotels that are more than adequately comfortable. Most offer rooms of varying quality and price. Outside Lhasa, in the major towns, there are bland Chinese hotels, about half of which have hot running water. You may prefer to seek a Tibetan guest house, many of which are quite clean, where the hospitality is warm and welcoming. However, be forewarned that the shared bathing facilities in these guest houses are primitive.

All travelers visit Bhutan through a licensed tour operator and are placed in a government-approved hotel. All hotels listed in this guide are government approved and are very clean and well maintained, ranging from plush to basic. Most have private bathrooms that are reasonably modern, with 24-hour hot water. However, if you are traveling to eastern Bhutan, facilities are more limited, with very basic accommodations that lack hot water and Western toilets.

In all three countries, trekking accommodations are usually rustic at best. They can range from the teahouses of Nepal to yak-skin tents in Tibet.

The lodgings (all indicated with 🏠) that we list are the cream of the crop in each price category. We always list the facilities that are available—but we don't specify whether they cost extra: When pricing accommodations, always ask what's included. All hotels listed have private bath unless otherwise noted. Properties indicated by ✕🏠 are lodging establishments whose restaurant warrants a special trip.

CAMPING

Most travelers to Nepal, Tibet, and Bhutan camp and trek as part of their tour. Your tour operator can provide details on the campsites, and the equipment provided.

HOSTELS

➤ ORGANIZATIONS: **Hostelling International—American Youth Hostels** (✉ 733 15th St. NW, Suite 840, Washington, DC 20005, ☎ 202/783–6161, FAX 202/783–6171). **Hostelling International—Canada** (✉ 400–205 Catherine St., Ottawa, Ontario K2P 1C3, ☎ 613/237–7884, FAX 613/237–7868). **Youth Hostel Association of England and Wales** (✉ Trevelyan House, 8 St. Stephen's Hill, St. Albans, Hertfordshire AL1 2DY, ☎ 01727/855215 or 01727/845047, FAX 01727/844126). **Australian Youth Hostel Association** (✉ 10 Mallett St., Camperdown, NSW 2050, ☎ 02/9565–1699, FAX 02/9565–1325). **Youth Hostels Association of New Zealand** (✉ Box 436, Christchurch, New Zealand, ☎ 03/379–9970, FAX 03/365–4476). Membership in the United States is $25, in Canada C$26.75, in the United Kingdom £9.30, in Australia $44, in New Zealand $24.

HOTELS

China has a star-rating system, from one to five stars. Three-star hotels can be compared to nicer American motels. There are no five-star hotels in Tibet. Hotels offer singles and doubles with air-conditioning, TV, electrical outlets, telephone, and bathrooms with shower and tub. In Lhasa, you can find rooms at higher-end hotels with queen-size beds. Outside of Lhasa, doubles have two twin beds.

Swimming pools, exercise facilities, multiple upscale restaurants, bars, business centers, and valet service is typical in most of the international standard hotels in Kathmandu and Pokhara. Most of the guest rooms have central-heating/air-conditioning, satellite TV, IDD telephones, minibars, and bathtubs. Be sure to ask if your hotel will pick you up and drop you off at Tribhuvan International Airport.

MAIL & SHIPPING

See each country's A to Z sections for post office information.

OVERNIGHT SERVICES

International express mail companies operating out of Nepal include Federal Express, DHL, and UPS. DHL also operates in Bhutan. There are international and domestic express mail services at the Lhasa General Post Office in Tibet.

POSTAL RATES

In Nepal, the cost of an airmail letter (weighing 20 grams) is 20 Rs. for the United States and Canada, 18 Rs. for the United Kingdom and Europe. Aerograms cost 17 Rs. for the United States and Canada and 12 Rs. for the United Kingdom and Europe. Air mail postcards cost 15 Rs. for the United States and Canada and 10 Rs. for the United Kingdom and Europe.

From Tibet, international letters cost RMB6.40. Postcards cost RMB4.20.

The International Postage Rate for postcards, aerograms, and letters (up to .75 oz) sent from Bhutan is Nu 20.

RECEIVING MAIL

Considering there are no street numbers and not all places use P.O. Boxes, it is amazing that any mail reaches Nepal. Most Nepalese business owners urge people who are trying to contact them to use fax and e-mail. The main post office in Kathmandu has a Poste Restante where you can have mail sent to you from abroad. Mail to Poste Restante should be addressed: Your name, Poste Restante, GPO, Kathmandu, Nepal.

The only reliable place to receive general mail in Tibet is at the poste restante at the Lhasa General Post Office. You can freely shuffle through the poste restante box that is organized alphabetically. As postal employees generally don't speak or read English, your letters may be randomly alphabetized under you first or last name.

In Bhutan, you can arrange to have mail sent to the post office box of either your tour operator or your hotel.

MONEY MATTERS

CREDIT CARDS

Throughout this guide, the following abbreviations are used: **AE**, American Express; **DC**, Diner's Club; **MC**, MasterCard; and **V**, Visa.

➤ REPORTING LOST CARDS: When in Nepal, if you need to replace a lost or stolen American Express or Thomas Cook card/traveler's check contact the offices at **Yeti Travels** on Durbar Marg (☎ 01/221234). The **American Express** office is in Hotel Mayalu (☎ 01/227635). In Bhutan, visit American Express's representative, Chhundu Travels & Tours in Thimphu (✉ 39/40 Norzin Lam, ☎ 975/22592 or 975/23586).

CURRENCY

Nepalese currency is the rupee (abbreviated Rs.), which is divided into 100 paisa. Banknotes come in denominations of 1, 2, 5, 10, 20, 25, 50, 100, 500, and 1,000 rupees. There are 1-, 2-, and 5-rupee coins, but they are rarely used. Paisa rates are rounded up to the nearest rupee.

The currency used in Tibet is the Chinese Renminbi (RMB). RMB comes in Y1, 2, 5, 10, 50, and 100 notes and Y1, 1-mao, 5-mao, and 1-fen, 2-fen, and 5-fen coins. All denominations of bills and coins are different in size.

Bhutan's unit of currency is the ngultrum (Nu), although the Indian rupee is also legal tender in the kingdom. The ngultrum is divided into 100 cheltrum.

CURRENCY EXCHANGE

The approximate exchange rate from the Nepal Rastra Bank at press time was U.S.$1 = Rs. 67; Euro 1 = Rs. 72; £1 = Rs. 108; A$1 = Rs. 42; and C$1 = Rs. 44.

The Nepal Rastra Bank sets the exchange rate. Private banks usually offer about the same rate. Both the *Kathmandu Post* and the *Rising Nepal* publish the rate daily. There are exchange counters at the airport and throughout Kathmandu and Pokhara. There are now two exchange services in the Royal Chitwan National Park area. In the rest of the country it's best to carry small denominations of rupees. Teahouses will not be able to change 1,000 Rs. notes for a 5 Rs. cup of tea. Note that at many places you may get a better exchange rate using higher-denomination bills. The black market does not offer a substantially better rate, and it's dangerous.

The approximate exchange rate in Tibet at press time was U.S.\$1 = RMB8; Euro 1 = RMB8.15; £1 = RMB13.3; A\$1 = RMB5.23; and C\$1 = RMB5.7.

In Tibet, it's best to exchange your money in Lhasa, since it can be difficult to change money in the countryside. All of the larger Lhasa hotels offer foreign exchange service. The main branch of the **Bank of China** (✉ Dekyi Linghor Lam) will exchange traveler's checks or cash into RMB and also process credit card cash advances. For a nominal fee you can even change traveler's checks into U.S. currency. A smaller branch office in the Barkhor area (✉ Dekyi Shar Lam, 1 block west of Banak Shol hotel) exchanges traveler's checks and U.S. cash. You can also change traveler's checks at the Bank of China branches in Zhigatse, Zhangmu, and Shiquanbe.

The money exchange counters at the airport, larger hotels, and guest houses, and the banks in Thimphu, Bhutan, can exchange cash and traveler's checks. Some banks in the smaller towns can exchange money for you, but be prepared for delays, since it will probably be a lengthy process. It is highly advised to change money before you travel east or leave for a trek. At press time, exchange rates were: U.S.\$1 = Nu 43.4; Euro 1 = Nu 42.7; £1 = Nu 69.8; A\$1 = Nu 27.4; and C\$1 = Nu 30.

TRAVELER'S CHECKS

Do you need traveler's checks? It depends on where you're headed. If you're going to rural areas and small towns, go with cash; traveler's checks are best used in cities. Lost or stolen checks can usually be replaced within 24 hours. To ensure a speedy refund, buy your own traveler's checks—don't let someone else pay for them: irregularities like this can cause delays. The person who bought the checks should make the call to request a refund.

PACKING

Since you never know where you will have to lug your bags, it is always a good idea to **pack light.** Bring luggage that is easy to carry and makes the most sense for your travel plans, whether that means a backpack (especially ones that double as a bag), rolling suitcase, or duffle bag. If you go trekking, a backpack is the best option. Be sure to leave room in your suitcase or bring expandable totes for all your bargain purchases. A lock for your suitcase is wise.

For warm weather, bring cotton, linen, and any other natural-fiber clothing that allows your skin to breathe and is easy to wash. If you visit during the summer, rain gear is essential. If you visit during the winter, or plan to hike to high altitudes, heavy winter clothing is necessary. The trick to assembling your cold-weather wardrobe is triple layering. The layer next to your skin (long johns) should be made of synthetic fabrics or silk that carry moisture away from the skin to the outer surface of the garment. Cotton soaks up perspiration and will make you wet. For the second layer, wool, fleece or a synthetic fabric knitted into thick pile is best. For the third layer, bring a well-made, generously sized parka insulated with a small amount of down and made of Gore-Tex (or an equivalent fiber), which not only allows moisture to escape but is waterproof, not merely water-repellent.

Trekkers should bring a day pack that will hold a sweater, a camera, a plastic quart-size water bottle, and a small medical kit. Consider bringing along a good pair of binoculars and sunglasses that block out ultraviolet rays. Hiking boots and sports sandals (for forging rivers) are recommended.

Dress in Nepal is informal but conservative; dress modestly. Furthermore, **shorts, short skirts, and revealing tops put women at risk** of encountering unflattering remarks and, increasingly, unwanted touching.

Just to be safe, bring your own amenities. You'll be able to find toothpaste, shampoo, tampons, and other needs in Lhasa, but you may not have much choice concerning brand. Bring your own contact lens supplies, birth control pills, and other medication.

In your carry-on luggage **bring an extra pair of eyeglasses or contact lenses** and **enough of any medication you take** to last the entire trip. You may also want your doctor to write a spare prescription using the drug's generic name, since brand names may vary from country to country. In luggage to be checked, **never pack prescription drugs or valuables.** To avoid customs delays, carry medications in their original packaging. You may also want to bring extra toiletries, including toothpaste and shampoo. Such items are only available in more cosmopolitan areas, such as Lhasa and Kathmandu, and even then you won't have much choice concerning brands. Finally, don't forget to copy down and carry addresses of offices that handle refunds of lost traveler's checks.

CHECKING LUGGAGE

How many carry-on bags you can bring with you is up to the airline. Most allow two, but not always, so make sure that everything you carry aboard will fit under your seat, and get to the gate early. Note that if you have a seat at the back of the plane, you'll probably board first, while the overhead bins are still empty.

Baggage allowances on international flights are usually determined not by piece but by weight—generally 88 pounds (40 kilograms) in first class, 66 pounds (30 kilograms) in business class, and 44 pounds (20 kilograms) in economy.

Airline liability for baggage is limited to $1,250 per person on flights within the United States. On international flights it amounts to $9.07 per pound or $20 per kilogram for checked baggage (roughly $640 per 70-pound bag) and $400 per passenger for unchecked baggage. You can buy additional coverage at check-in for about $10 per $1,000 of coverage, but it excludes a rather extensive list of items, shown on your airline ticket.

Before departure **itemize your bags' contents** and their worth, and label the bags with your name, address, and phone number. (If you use your home address, cover it so that potential thieves can't see it readily.) Inside each bag **pack a copy of your itinerary.** At check-in **make sure that each bag is correctly tagged** with the destination airport's three-letter code. If your bags arrive damaged or fail to arrive at all, file a written report with the airline before leaving the airport.

PASSPORTS & VISAS

When traveling internationally **carry a passport even if you don't need one** (it's always the best form of I.D.), and **make two photocopies of the data page** (one for someone at home and another for you, carried separately from your passport). If you lose your passport, promptly call the nearest embassy or consulate and the local police.

ENTERING NEPAL, TIBET, AND BHUTAN

See individual chapter A to Z sections for specific passport and visa requirements.

PASSPORT OFFICES

The best time to apply for a passport or to renew is during the fall and winter. Before any trip, check your passport's expiration date, and, if necessary, renew it as soon as possible.

➤ AUSTRALIAN CITIZENS: **Australian Passport Office** (☎ 131–232).

➤ CANADIAN CITIZENS: **Passport Office** (☎ 819/994–3500 or 800/567–6868).

➤ NEW ZEALAND CITIZENS: **New Zealand Passport Office** (☎ 04/494–0700 for information on how to apply; 04/474–8000 or 0800/225–050 in New Zealand for information on applications already submitted).

➤ U.K. CITIZENS: **London Passport Office** (☎ 0990/210–410) for fees and documentation requirements and to request an emergency passport.

➤ U.S. CITIZENS: **National Passport Information Center** (☎ 900/225–5674; calls are 35¢ per minute for automated service, $1.05 per minute for operator service).

REST ROOMS

Nepal has very few public rest rooms. There are even fewer that you would want to enter. Try to stick with hotel and restaurant rest rooms in Kathmandu and Pokhara. On the trails, try to avoid polluting streams and rivers. In the monsoon season, beware of leeches when you squat.

Tibet is not a pretty place for rest rooms. Although the higher-end hotels and some of the restaurants have clean Western-style toilets, the majority of Tibetan toilets are merely a slab of concrete with slatted squat holes placed over a large ditch. Carry your own toilet paper and don't breathe. Some toilets are cleaner than others. But there have been times when travelers have opted to brave the wilderness rather than go into a W.C.

SAFETY

Tibet, Nepal, and Bhutan are all generally safe places for travelers. Of course, you should take general precautions with your valuables and protect yourself from pickpocketing, which has become more popular in Nepal, especially on local public transportation and in big crowds. Keep an eye on your personal belongings at all time. You also may want to **remove any jewelry that stands out.** Avoid leaving passports, cameras, laptop computers, and other valuables in your hotel room, except if the room has a safe. If it doesn't, consider leaving your valuables in the hotel's safe. A lock for your luggage is also a good idea.

WOMEN IN NEPAL, TIBET, AND BHUTAN

Women travelers are welcome in the area and generally don't have to worry about special precautions—but use common sense. If you are traveling alone, you should never get into a taxi or rickshaw if there's a second man accompanying the driver. Also, avoid wandering the streets alone at night. In your hotel room, chain lock the door; hotel staff often knock and come right in.

In Nepal, beware that many men, particularly the Tibetan refugees who have no passports, are looking for foreign women to marry. While the attention can be flattering, be cautious of the underlying motives.

SENIOR-CITIZEN TRAVEL

To qualify for age-related discounts **mention your senior-citizen status up front** when booking hotel reservations (not when checking out) and before you're seated in restaurants (not when paying the bill). When renting a car ask about promotional car-rental discounts, which can be cheaper than senior-citizen rates.

➤ EDUCATIONAL PROGRAMS: **Elderhostel** (✉ 75 Federal St., 3rd fl., Boston, MA 02110, ☎ 877/426–8056, FAX 877/426–2166). **Interhostel** (✉ University of New Hampshire, 6 Garrison Ave., Durham, NH 03824, ☎ 603/862–1147 or 800/733–9753, FAX 603/862–1113). **Folkways Institute** (✉ 14600 Southeast Aldridge Rd., Portland, OR 97236-6518, ☎ 503/658–6600 or 800/225–4666, FAX 503/658–8672).

SHOPPING

In Nepal and Tibet, bargaining is the norm. Start by slashing the price in half and negotiate your way up. There are so many shops selling the same goods, you can easily price items in other stores before committing yourself to a purchase. It's important, however, to keep the bargaining process good-natured: shopkeepers generally don't respond kindly to aggressive haggling. Don't make an offer unless you are seriously interested in the item. Shopkeepers are not fond of "testing" the price—if you name a price, be prepared to honor it if or when they agree to sell. The final price generally ranges from 10% to 40% off the original price.

WATCH OUT

When purchasing antiques, be careful. More often than not, they're not as old as they look. Antiques dating before 1797 cannot be legally exported from China, and those over 100 years old can't leave Nepal.

STUDENTS IN TIBET

Generally, student discounts are not common in the area. However, there are a number of organizations that run special programs for students.

➤ I.D.s & SERVICES: **Council on International Educational Exchange** (CIEE, ✉ 205 E. 42nd St., 14th fl., New York, NY 10017, ☎ 212/822–2600 or 888/268–6245, FAX 212/822–2699) for mail orders only, in the United States. **Travel Cuts** (✉ 187 College St., Toronto, Ontario M5T 1P7, ☎ 416/979–2406 or 800/667–2887) in Canada.

TELEPHONES

For details on making calls to, within, and from each country, *see* individual chapter A to Z sections.

INTERNATIONAL CALLS

AT&T, MCI, and Sprint access codes make calling long distance relatively convenient, but you may find the local access number blocked in many hotel rooms. First ask the hotel operator to connect you. If the hotel operator balks, ask for an international operator, or dial the international operator yourself. One way to improve your odds of getting connected to your long-distance carrier is to travel with more than one company's calling card (a hotel may block Sprint, for example, but not MCI). If all else fails call from a pay phone or communication shop.

TIME

Tibet observes Beijing standard time, which is eight hours ahead of Greenwich mean time and 13 hours ahead of U.S. EST. Nepal is five hours and 45 minutes ahead of GMT, 10 hours and 45 minutes ahead of U.S. EST, and Bhutan is just 15 minutes ahead of Nepal.

TIPPING

Tipping in everyday restaurants is not common in Nepal, although many upscale places are starting to add a service charge and/or 10% gratuity to bills or they simply expect you to tip their staff. Ten percent is reasonable.

You might also consider tipping taxi drivers a few rupees extra if they do not haggle too aggressively about

their price or about using the meter. You could simply round up the fare by approximately 5 or 10 Rs.

For camping treks, consider tipping 200 Rs. per group member, per day. Give this to the guide in the presence of other staff for a later ceremonious distribution to all staff. If you are not camping and just have a single guide, consider 100 Rs. per person trekking, per day for the guide and about 50 Rs. per day for your porter.

Tipping is not a Tibetan custom. Taxi drivers and waitstaff will not expect it. Higher-end hotels may add a 15% service charge to your total bill.

TOURS & PACKAGES

Because a prepackaged tour or independent vacation everything is prearranged you'll spend less time planning—and often get it all at a good price.

BOOKING WITH AN AGENT

Travel agents are excellent resources. But it's a good idea to collect brochures from several agencies because some agents' suggestions may be influenced by relationships with tour and package firms that reward them for volume sales. If you have a special interest, **find an agent with expertise in that area**; ASTA (☞ Travel Agencies, *below*) has a database of specialists worldwide.

Make sure your travel agent knows the accommodations and other services of the place they're recommending. Ask about the hotel's location, room size, beds, and whether it has a pool, room service, or programs for children, if you care about these. Has your agent been there in person or sent others whom you can contact?

Do some homework on your own, too: Local tourism boards can provide information about lesser-known and small-niche operators, some of which may sell only direct.

BUYER BEWARE

Each year consumers are stranded or lose their money when tour operators—even large ones with excellent reputations—go out of business. So **check out the operator.** Ask several travel agents about its reputation, and try to **book with a company that has a consumer-protection program.** (Look for information in the company's brochure.) In the United States, members of the National Tour Association and United States Tour Operators Association are required to set aside funds to cover your payments and travel arrangements in case the company defaults. It's also a good idea to choose a company that participates in the American Society of Travel Agent's Tour Operator Program (TOP); ASTA will act as mediator in any disputes between you and your tour operator.

Remember that the more your package or tour includes the better you can predict the ultimate cost of your vacation. Make sure you know exactly what is covered, and **beware of hidden costs.** Are taxes, tips, and transfers included? Entertainment and excursions? These can add up.

➤ TOUR-OPERATOR RECOMMENDATIONS: **American Society of Travel Agents** (☞ Travel Agencies, *below*). **National Tour Association** (NTA, ✉ 546 E. Main St., Lexington, KY 40508, ☎ 606/226–4444 or 800/ 682–8886). **United States Tour Operators Association** (USTOA, ✉ 342 Madison Ave., Suite 1522, New York, NY 10173, ☎ 212/599–6599 or 800/ 468–7862, 𝔽𝔸𝕏 212/599–6744).

TRAIN TRAVEL

Although trains are uncommon in the area, Nepal does have one line. The 51-km/31.6-mi-long route runs from Lewri via Janakpur to Jayanagar in India. However, at press time, visitors could not cross the border here as there was no immigration office.

TRAVEL AGENCIES

A good travel agent puts your needs first. Look for an agency that has been in business at least five years, emphasizes customer service, and has someone on staff who specializes in your destination. In addition **make sure the agency belongs to a professional trade organization.** The American Society of Travel Agents (ASTA), with 27,000 agents in some 170 countries, is the largest and most influential in the field. Operating under the motto "Integrity in Travel," it maintains and

enforces a strict code of ethics and will step in to help mediate any agent-client disputes if necessary. ASTA also maintains a Web site that includes a directory of agents. (Note that if a travel agency is also acting as your tour operator, *see* Buyer Beware *in* Tours & Packages, *above*.)

➤ LOCAL AGENT REFERRALS: **American Society of Travel Agents** (ASTA, ☎ 800/965–2782 24-hr hot line, 𝔽𝔸𝕏 703/684–8319, www.astanet.com). **Association of British Travel Agents** (✉ 55–57 Newman St., London W1P 4AH, ☎ 0171/637–2444, 𝔽𝔸𝕏 0171/ 637–0713). **Association of Canadian Travel Agents** (✉ 1729 Bank St., Suite 201, Ottawa, Ontario K1V 7Z5, ☎ 613/521–0474, 𝔽𝔸𝕏 613/521– 0805). **Australian Federation of Travel Agents** (✉ Level 3, 309 Pitt St., Sydney 2000, ☎ 02/9264–3299, 𝔽𝔸𝕏 02/9264–1085). **Travel Agents' Association of New Zealand** (✉ Box 1888, Wellington 10033, ☎ 04/499– 0104, 𝔽𝔸𝕏 04/499–0786).

VISITOR INFORMATION

➤ TOURIST INFORMATION: The **Nepal Tourism Board** (✉ Bhrikuti Mandap, ☎ 01/256909, 𝔽𝔸𝕏 01/256910, ntb@mos.com.np, ☉ daily 9–5:30). **Tibet Tourism Bureau** (✉ 18 Yuanlin Lam, Lhasa, ☎ 0891/683–4315 information; 0891/683–4193 to register complaints). **Tourism Authority of Bhutan** (✉ Doebom Lam, Thimphu, ☎ 02/3–23251, or 02/3– 23252, 𝔽𝔸𝕏 02/3–23695, TAB@druknet.net.bt).

➤ U.S. GOVERNMENT ADVISORIES: **U.S. Department of State** (✉ Overseas Citizens Services Office, Room 4811 N.S., 2201 C St. NW, Washington, DC 20520; ☎ 202/647–5225 for interactive hot line; 301/946–4400 for computer bulletin board; 𝔽𝔸𝕏 202/ 647–3000 for interactive hot line); enclose a self-addressed, stamped, business-size envelope.

WEB SITES

Do check out the World Wide Web when you're planning. You'll find everything from up-to-date weather forecasts to virtual tours of famous cities. Fodor's Web site, www.fodors.com, is a great place to start your online travels. For more information specifically on Nepal, Tibet, and Bhutan, visit:

www.info-nepal.com This site gives general information about the country, including transportation and some accommodation and dining information.

www.nepalonline.net/hra The Himalaya Rescue Association posts information about mountain safety, hazards, and conditions. It updates weekly reports on the passes in the Annapurna and Everest region and provides a ton of information on acute mountain sickness.

www.tibet-tour.com The official site of the Tibet Tourism Bureau has a government slant, but has good information about the region and tour packages.

www.tibet.ca/wtnnews.htm The World Tibet Network News site is run by the Canada Tibet Committee. It has an archive of Tibet-related news stories from news agencies all over the world.

www.tibet.com The Government of Tibet in Exile Web site posts a comprehensive set of articles about Tibet's political situation and culture.

www.kingdomofbhutan.com The Bhutan Tourism Corporation's site has photographs of the country as well as general information, including a link to an American company that arranges trips to the region.

WHEN TO GO

The best touring weather is from mid-April through June, with September to mid-November a close second. But with pleasant weather comes hordes of tourists. Summers are too wet and winters too cold for most travelers, although because of this, there are good deals at these times. Summer rain often closes roads to popular tourist destinations, including Everest Base Camp. Wintertime is frightfully cold, but at least the climate is dry and the skies perpetually blue. Late

January and early February is usually when Losar, or the Tibetan New Year, rings in. This is an especially busy time in Boudhanath and Swayambhunath in Nepal where there is a large Tibetan refugee population. Travel is also less restrictive in winter as police monitoring checkpoints are more concerned with keeping warm than turning back curious tourists.

You can also arrange your trip surrounding Tibetan festivals, which are colorful and culturally fascinating. (☞ Festivals and Seasonal Events *in* Chapter 1 for more information.)

CLIMATE

From September until the beginning of December, the weather is warm and the air is clear in Nepal. From December to mid-February high-altitude inns and trekking routes sometimes get snowed in. In the Kathmandu Valley and in the Lake District of Pokhara it remains cool during the day and rarely snows. Mornings can be damp and misty in Kathmandu. It is not too hot in the Terai, and there aren't too many visitors, so it's a good time to check out the national parks in peace. Spring usually begins around the last week of February when the whole country is temperate. Once the monsoon arrives with daily doses of heavy rain, the mountains take refuge behind the clouds, landslides make roads impassable, and leeches attach themselves to unsuspecting passersby.

Tibet is a land of extremes. In winter, temperatures can sink to −23°C (−10°F), but in summer the thin mountain air permits the sun to penetrate, to heat the days to 30°C (high 80°s F). There can, however, be drops in temperature, especially at night. Look out for dust storms in May and June, and for rain in July and August. Fall can be clear and quite warm.

➤ FORECASTS: **Weather Channel Connection** (☎ 900/932–8437), 95¢ per minute from a Touch-Tone phone.

1 DESTINATION: NEPAL, TIBET, BHUTAN

A WORLD OF DREAMS

THE HIMALAYAS ARE A MYSTICAL LAND of swooping valleys, towering mountains, and lush jungles. It is a land far more diverse than most travelers imagine. You can encounter tigers and rhinos in the jungles of the Terai region of Nepal, or snow leopards in the frosty highlands of Tibet and Bhutan.

These are places of startling contrast. You may find yourself in a modern hotel in cosmopolitan Kathmandu or in a yak-hide tent beside a mountain trail. Reverent monks, little different from their predecessors of centuries past, mingle with karaoke swingers in Tibet, henna-haired hippies in Nepal, and video-obsessed teens in Bhutan. What may at first glance seem to be a land and culture the West has left behind is full of jarring reminders that the 21st century is encroaching. All three countries are struggling to incorporate the new with the tried and true, all the while coping with invading Western influences.

WHAT'S WHERE

Nepal

Central Nepal

Nepal's two biggest cities are in the center of the country, with Pokhara slightly to the west and Kathmandu to the east. Kathmandu wears its past like a proud diva showing off a string of pearls: it is home to dozens of shrines and temples and a citizenship rightly proud of their glorious, artistic past. Artisans still create beautiful woodwork, metalwork, and handicrafts using ancient tools and techniques. Pokhara itself seems a work of art. With an emerald-colored lake in town and the halo of the mighty Himal around its perimeter, the city is breathtaking. The two cities are connected by the Prithvi Highway. Along that route, you will see farmers whose way of life has changed little for hundreds of years.

The Terai

The southern portion of Nepal is a sun belt of tall grasses and abundant wildlife. Big-game hunters have been lured here for decades, enticed by adventure and trophies. These days, you can hunt with your camera for scenes of rhinos and other wildlife that you might have thought were only found in Africa. Like central Nepal, this southern region is as full of man-made treasures as it is of nature's gifts. Lumbini and Janakpur have shrines and temples dedicated to major figures from Buddhism and Hinduism.

The Himal

The mountains that have inspired, crushed, awed, and subdued mountaineers from around the world are perhaps Nepal's greatest asset. Home to eight of the world's ten highest peaks, the Himal dominate Nepal. They fill the rivers with life-supplying water, yet crush villages with the landslides that often follow storms. When clouds shroud the peaks, locals seem to slump into a depression, as if a faithful friend has gone away. When the weather is clear, visitors who curse at alarm clocks at home are up before dawn, awaiting the sun's first beams to give them a glimpse of the stone giants.

Tibet

Lhasa

There's no doubt that the entirety of Tibet, the plateau and the people, has a beating heart and a common soul that is Lhasa. The dusty, old-world city that seems farther from home than any other may have lost some of its reputed magic and mysticism to the sterile modernity of Communist China, but it remains the hub for travelers to the region and the most important pilgrimage destination for Tibetan Buddhists. Impoverished pilgrims with nothing but the clothes on their backs traverse Tibet's rugged roads to prostrate themselves at the feet of their culture's heavenly treasures—Jokhang Temple and the surrounding Barkhor, the most holy and active temple and circumambulation route on the plateau; the majestic yet eerie Potala Palace, home of the Dalai

Lamas; and a garden of sprawling monasteries. It may seem odd that they must often do so amidst polluting traffic and jarringly modern buildings, their colorful robes trailing on the uncompromising pavement. Still, the deep color of Lhasa succeeds at softening the harsh Chinese grey, almost making it an otherworldly hue.

Central Tibet and the Road to Kathmandu

Unfolding from Lhasa's locus is a verdant yet rugged land full of narrow roads to monasteries like Tsurphu, Ganden, and Samye. East of Samye is the town of Tsetang, the gateway to the historical birthplace of Tibetan culture—the Yarlung and Chongye Valleys. To the north of the city lie grasslands ringed by peaks, and the saltwater lake of Namtso, with waters the color of the sky. To the west of this land that once made up the Tibetan province of Ü, is a dusty and brown horizon, growing more severe as it rises towards the pinnacles of the Himalayas. The former Tibetan province of Tsang chaperones the journey west on the jolting Friendship Highway towards Kathmandu. Out of Lhasa, a spidery lake with turquoise tentacles threads through mountain passes. The road out of Yamdrok-Tso then passes through the spiritual towns of Shigatse and Gyantse and other villages the color of dust that seem to rise spontaneously out of the earth. Life and land grow more severe, and finally, before the road descends into verdant Nepal on the south side of the mountain, the Himalayas appear, not on the horizon, but looming from another atmospheric layer, with Mt. Everest the tall one in the family picture.

Ngari

Out past the truck-stop town of Lhatse, before the turn towards Nepal, the Friendship Highway meets another path that leads to one of the most remote parts of Asia called Ngari. Western Tibet is long, long ago, and far, far away—where the land is isolated, the roads are bad if existent at all, travel is like the terrain (rough), and the beauty is magnificent. Few Westerners make it out here, but the ones who do enjoy the experience of one of the holiest, most culturally intriguing, and most stunning lands in the world. Pilgrims from both sides of the border come to Ngari to rid their life of sin, completing the one- to three-day kora of majestic Mt. Kailash

and perhaps an extended four- to five-day jaunt around the vast, breathtaking Lake Manasarovar.

Bhutan

Bhutan is located on the slopes of the eastern Himalayas, east of Nepal and west of the Indian state of Arunachal Pradesh. To the north lies the Tibetan region of China and in the south, the Indian territories of Assam and West Bengal.

A small land-locked country surrounded by high Himalayan mountain ranges, Bhutan is sparsely populated with just over 600,000 people. Bhutan is often compared to Switzerland because of its size, isolation, and stunning scenery. Approximately 90% of the population are hill farmers who live in small villages spread over rugged mountain country and subtropical terrain. The nation contains many ethnic groups and nomadic hill tribes who have very little contact with Western civilization and trade only in bartered goods.

Bhutan is the only surviving Buddhist kingdom of the Himalayan region. Dzongs dot the countryside and the people's deep faith permeates all aspects of secular life. The Bhutanese have long lived in harmony with nature and the kingdom's environment remains pristine. The scenery is spectacular, with jungles and rugged hills, rhododendron forests and long sweeping valleys.

NEW AND NOTEWORTHY

Nepal

Nepal '98 was a big tourism campaign that, depending on whom you asked, was a grand success or a total flop. The big push was largely done within the domestic press, so while Nepalis all knew about it, much of the rest of the world did not. Nonetheless, many of the roads and the communication systems have improved as a result of the tourism effort. Some of the repaving and new Web sites took all of 1998 to be completed, so they were unveiled after the grand year had passed. Several hotels were built or expanded to attract more affluent travelers.

Tour agents, hoteliers, and restaurateurs really want your business. There are deals to be had: just shop around. The deluxe, international hotels offer a high standard of service. Many of the resorts will pamper you and treat you like royalty.

Sadly, once you arrive, you can't help but see the extreme poverty that still plagues Nepal, which is among the poorest and least developed countries in the world. More than half of its 23 million people live below the poverty line. Only 3% of the population is 65 or older. In fact, the average Nepali only lives 57 years. Nearly 42% of the population is under 14, and many children start working at age 5.

To make matters worse, approximately 90,000 Bhutanese refugees, 90% of whom are in seven United Nations Office of the High Commissioner for Refugee camps, are living in Damak in southeastern Nepal. They are awaiting a resolution to be hammered out between Nepal, Bhutan, and India over their status. Since the late 1800s, Lhotshamapas (people of Nepali origin) have been immigrating to the southern regions of Bhutan in search of farmland. Throughout the years, the Lhotshampas settled in Bhutan but retained their Nepali culture, language and religious traditions, which differed from the ruling Drukpas of Bhutan. For years, the two groups coexisted. However, tensions surfaced in 1985 with legislation that required Lhotshampas to adopt Drukpa culture, language and religion. Furthermore, a large portion of the Lhotshampas were classified as illegal immigrants. Protests ensued, followed by arrests, violence and then a mass exodus into Nepal and southern India. Between 1988 and 1994 it is estimated that more than 100,000 refugees fled Bhutan.

At press time, Nepal's political situation was becoming increasingly tense, with frequent demonstrations in Kathmandu. The U.S. government instituted more stringent control checks to locate American expat residences. Check with the Department of State for an update before you go.

Tibet

The last decade has seen many changes in tourism at the Roof of the World. Tibet emerged from martial law in the early 1990s, when foreigners could fly into Tibet on expensive tours. Meanwhile, others dressed up in hooded Chinese clothing and crossed the Tibetan border on local trucks and buses; many succeeded and were rewarded with a Tibetan experience virtually untouched by tourism.

Today things are different. While many still prefer to book a tour in their home countries, independent travelers are entering Tibet from Chengdu, Sichuan Province, China and Kathmandu, Nepal. Over the last few years, the Chinese have loosened restrictions on getting into the region—as long as you're not a journalist or a filmmaker.

Chengdu and Kathmandu are swimming with travel agencies eager for a buck. For permit reasons, you still have to go in with a "tour," but you can also leave your tour behind in Lhasa and stay in Tibet as long as your Chinese visa will allow.

With all the changes, don't expect to find yourself in an "untouched" Lhasa. With improving infrastructure and increased tourism, there are more options for the traveller. The hotel and restaurant industry in the capital city has grown steadily, with more hotels in both budget and luxury classes. In the past, you could only find Tibetan or Chinese food in Lhasa; today you can find a taste of home in a multitude of quaint restaurants.

There are also more locations in Tibet open to travelers. Foreigners are not asked to limit themselves to Lhasa any longer. With the proper permits, you can go as far as remote Western Tibet. Although some places are still only reachable by excruciating dirt roads, in the mid-1990s the Friendship Highway connecting Lhasa and Shigatse to Kathmandu was completed, making journeys easier.

However, permits are still necessary for regions outside of Lhasa and its environs. The Shigatse Public Security Bureau (PSB) often grants permits to several destinations, but the only way to get a permit in Lhasa is through a travel agent. As a result, crooked agents are everywhere—so many in fact that the Tourism Bureau has a hotline reserved for complaints. Ironically, China's tourism administration is also profiting from permit-granting and travel-agent license fees.

The most important thing to remember about traveling to Tibet is that things are always changing. The Tibetan political tide is unpredictable, and to complicate matters, China's situation contributes to the volatility, as the incident in Tiananmen Square showed in 1989. Chinese oppression remains concretely felt—in permit checkpoints; in Chinese architectural, social, and economic infringement; in increasing numbers of Chinese being persuaded by government perks to move there; and in over 2,000 Tibetan refugees fleeing to India every year.

Last December, Tibet's third-highest lama behind the Dalai and Panchen Lamas—the 14-year-old 17th Karmapa—fled to Dharamsala. When the Karmapa was chosen, there was conflict concerning whether he or another boy in New Delhi was the rightful reincarnation, but the Chinese officially backed him. Now that their approved heir has blatantly turned his back on them after their efforts to groom him as a "patriotic" Chinese figure, they've felt a slap in the face. His departure seriously undermined China's efforts to enforce their authority in Tibet.

Bhutan

On June 2, 1999, the Kingdom of Bhutan celebrated the 25th anniversary of the reign of His Majesty the King, Jigme Singye Wangchuck. In conjunction with this special occasion, several dramatic developments took place, virtually throwing this isolated kingdom into the 21st century overnight: the first live broadcast took place over national radio, national television was introduced, and Bhutan went online, gaining access to the Internet. Simultaneously, city bus service in the capital city was launched, the country's first Royal Botanical Gardens opened, and the new terminal complex was inaugurated at the Paro International Airport. Lastly, there was a rededication of the country's policy of Gross National Happiness. His Majesty declares that this policy is more important than the Gross National Product.

In 1998, His Majesty introduced the election of Council of Ministers by the National Assembly and granted full executive powers to the Council of Ministers. This constituted the first step towards a "self-constrained" monarchy.

GREAT ITINERARIES

The itineraries that follow suggest ways destinations can be combined and give an idea of reasonable (minimum) amounts of time needed at various sites. Other suggested itineraries are in every chapter.

Temples & Fortresses

TWO-WEEK TOUR➤ This whirlwind tour includes the cultural and religious highlights of all three countries: Nepal, Tibet, and Bhutan. Use Kathmandu as your base and take two five-day trips, one to Tibet where you will tour Lhasa, the other to Bhutan, where you will tour Paro and Thimphu. On the first day, click close-up photos of the icy peaks of the Himalayas during your flight to Tibet that passes eight of the fourteen 8,000-m (26,240-ft) peaks. Spend the next three days sightseeing in the Lhasa area. Visit the 1,000-room Potala Palace, which was the former seat of the Dalai Lama. On the next day see the Sera Monastery, a 1419 temple about 5 km (3 mi) north of Lhasa, and then venture on to the largest temple in Tibet, Drepung Monastery, built in 1416 and only about 10 km (6 mi) from the capital. Finally, see the old city, which centers on the seventh-century Jokhang Temple, perhaps the holiest Buddhist shrine in Tibet. Then wander the quaint surrounding Barkhor market. On the fifth day, fly back to Kathmandu.

Now spend two days in Nepal. In the morning drive to Bhaktapur Durbar Marg where you can spend your day visiting ancient temples and monuments in this historic city filled with metal- and woodworking artisans. In the early afternoon, drive to Changu Narayan, less than a half hour away, to see the Hindu temple where a pillar with a 4th-century inscription has the earliest example of writing in Nepal. Then drive to Nagarkot before sunset, to watch the sun rest behind the Himalayas. Spend the night for the sunrise over the Himal. Dawdle the rest of the next day at this hill station and drive back to Kathmandu after sunset or drive back to Kathmandu and spend some time shopping.

Now, take your second small trip, flying Druk Air to Paro, Bhutan. On the next day, see the ruined Drugyal Dzong (fortress) set on a spur above the Paro Chu (river), where on a clear day you can view Mt. Chomolhari and the surrounding lush valley. In the afternoon, sightsee at the Rinpung Dzong (or Paro Dzong), which was built in 1646 by Bhutan's great unifier Ngawang Namgyal. This is approached by a gentle sloping flagstone road and a beautiful wooden bridge roofed with shingles and abutted by two guard houses. You will also visit the National Museum, which was converted from a 17th-century watchtower to a museum in 1968. Day three, a driver takes you along the winding Paro/Thimphu River to Thimphu. In the morning, visit the Memorial Chorten of His Majesty the late Jigme Dorjee Wangchuck and the National library, where ancient manuscripts are preserved. Then stroll downtown to the Handicraft Development Corporation for some shopping. In the afternoon, you see the Simtokha Dzong, which was built in 1627 and now houses one of the largest monastic schools in the country. Then visit Tashichho Dzong, which is a government building and houses the state monastic body. On the fourth day you drive to Dochula Pass for Himalayan views en route to Paro. Finally, on the fifth day you fly from Paro back to Kathmandu.

For your last two days, take it easy in the Kathmandu area. Tour Kathmandu Durbar Square where dozens of ancient temples and monuments fill a square in the central section of the city. Shop in Old Kathmandu afterward, soaking up the rich scenery of the ancient alleys. Visit Pashupatinath temple and the ghats where Hindus take ritual baths and cremate the dead on the sacred Bagmati River, which flows to the Ganges in India. A short walk or taxi ride away, spend your sunset at Boudhanath where Tibetan exiles pray. Dine out at one of the numerous upscale Kathmandu restaurants. On the second day, do all your last-minute shopping in Thamel, Babar Mahal, or Durbar Marg or visit Patan Durbar Marg and Swayambhunath to round out seeing all seven of the UNESCO World Heritage sites in the Kathmandu Valley.

THREE-WEEK TOUR (OR LONGER)➤ If you have 21 days, you can do the first twelve days of the above tour, visiting Tibet and Bhutan. But then, when you re-turn to Kathmandu, go for a week-long hike, finishing up with the same last two days in Kathmandu.

During your seven-day trek, you could either hike in Helambu or Langtang. You can set foot on the Helambu circuit after an hour of driving from your Kathmandu hotel. It takes about seven days to walk the loop. The maximum altitude is only 2,800 m (9,184 ft) along a roller coaster trail. On the upswings you get good Himalayan views, plus the route is along a rhododendron-lined ridge.

If you opt to walk in the Langtang area, you spend about two days walking northwest through rhododendron toward Kyanjin Gompa (3,479 m/11,411 ft), where you will get a picture-perfect view of Langtang Lirung (7,246 m/23,771 ft). You can wander up a glacier on one day, then spend a full day hiking up the valley where the views of Langtang Lirung are stunning. On the next day, you begin your backtrack to Kathmandu.

GETTING AROUND➤ Travel by air to and from Tibet and Bhutan. Schedule your Tibet trip first, because usually there are only two flights a week to and from Lhasa. Use a hired car with a driver to get around all the cities. Contact travel agents several months in advance to guarantee availability of flights to Bhutan and arrange visas to Tibet and Bhutan. Five-day tours to both countries are standard fare from Kathmandu, but they still should be booked well in advance to get the best accommodations. Hire a guide to take you to the Langtang or Helambu area for a seven-day trek in the region north of Kathmandu.

Tigers and Temples

TWO-WEEK TOUR➤ Another alternative is to consider spending the first five days in either Bhutan or Lhasa on the above tours and then spend the last nine days in Nepal. This reduces the likelihood of snafus caused by canceled flights, blocked roads, or a bureaucratic boo-boo that runs afoul of the schedule.

For the first five days, pick either Bhutan or Tibet and tour Paro/Thimphu or Lhasa (☞ *above*).

When you are back in Nepal, visit Patan Durbar Square for a taste of the Kathmandu Valley temples and palaces, as a comparison to those in Tibet or Bhutan. On the seventh day, drive to Pashupatinath and Boudhanath to see a Hindu temple, followed by a Buddhist stupa.

Then spend three days in the Terai. Drive to Chitwan and stay in one of the upscale hunting-style lodges. Take a jeep safari in search of rhinos and tigers. Go canoeing in the crocodile-laden rivers and ride an elephant while listening to the chirping birds and searching for more wildlife before driving back to Kathmandu.

Finally, visit Kathmandu's Durbar Square for one last look at temples and shrines and spend your last day shopping in Thamel or at Durbar Marg or Babar Mahal.

GETTING AROUND➤ Fly to either Paro or Lhasa and spend five days touring the major cities. Then return to Kathmandu and drive to Chitwan National Park for a taste of the Terai.

FODOR'S CHOICE

Comforts

★ **Dwarika's Hotel, Battisputali, Kathmandu, Nepal.** A breathtaking, museumlike complex, Dwarika's showcases traditional Nepali art. Check out the oversize bathrooms with sunken baths—almost the size of many other hotels' rooms. *$$$$*

★ **Fulbari Resort, Pokhara, Nepal.** This luxury hotel brings Durbar Square to your hotel room, with hidden courtyards, temple-styled windows, a dragon-spouted fountain, and masterfully carved furniture. *$$$$*

★ **Hotel Druk, Thimphu, Bhutan.** One of the largest hotels in Thimphu, the Druk is Western-style and considered one of the best. Even the restaurant is run in a modern way: it's the only place that caters to a business crowd by offering a set lunch. *$$$$*

★ **Hotel Yak & Yeti, Durbar Marg, Kathmandu, Nepal.** A former palace filled with traditional art and modern comforts, this is a landmark that attracts the rich and famous. *$$$$*

★ **Radisson Hotel Kathmandu, Lazimpat, Kathmandu, Nepal.** Carved Nepali wooden tables and local pottery distinguish this Radisson from those at home, while trademark amenities like a tea/coffee maker on a marble table, an electric safe, and an ironing board and iron in your closet provide the comfort of familiarity. *$$$$*

★ **Shangri-La Village Pokhara, Nepal.** Private balconies overlook the garden, Koi-fish pond, and waterfall pool that reflects the snow-tipped Himalayas. Enjoy the Tibetan, Newari, and Nepali artwork in the rooms. *$$$$*

★ **Kichu Resort, Paro and Chuzomsa, Bhutan.** Although these resorts look dissimilar—Paro is more traditionally designed, Chuzomsa more modern—the architecture of both is unusual and stunning. Ceilings are arched, and whitewashed walls and fresh linens are complemented by light wood trim. Both resorts have cottages along the river. *$$$–$$$$*

★ **Lhasa Fandian, Lhasa, Tibet.** The Lhasa Fandian has solidified its position as the premier Western-style hotel in Lhasa, with all the standard trappings, right down to in-house movies. *$$$–$$$$*

★ **Hotel Zangthopelri, Punakha, Bhutan.** On a sprawling estate high above the valley, Hotel Zangthopelri is one of the most luxurious hotels in Bhutan, with the only hotel swimming pool and tennis courts in the country. *$$$*

★ **Pinewood Hotel, Thimphu, Bhutan.** This small hotel is across the river with a spectacular view of the valley. Each room is designed with different colors and decorations, right down to the bathrooms. At night, the dining room has beautiful views of the lights of Thimphu. *$$$*

★ **Himalaya Hotel, Lhasa, Tibet.** With its new nine-story building, the Himalaya Hotel provides accommodations ranging from fine luxury suites to budget triples, complete with a new lobby lavishly appointed with four grand columns, a marble floor, and a chandelier. *$$*

★ **Kechu Hotel, Lhasa, Tibet.** This small, charming hotel in the heart of the Tibetan Quarter veers away from the modern sterility of the other hotels in its class. Hallways with ornate ceilings and old black-and-white Tibetan photographs lead to rooms with hardwood floors and traditional door frames and furniture. $$

★ **Mirabel Resort Hotels, Dhulikhel, Nepal.** This mountainside resort offers service that would meet the highest Kathmandu standards in a quiet, fresh-aired setting in the hills, with stunning views of the Himal that the Kathmandu hotels can't match. $$

★ **Summit Hotel, Kupondol Height, Patan, Nepal.** Evocative of a Raj-era hunting lodge, this hotel overlooking the Himal has rooms with comfortable, madras-covered bamboo chairs, marble baths, and terracotta and tile artwork. $$

★ **Banak Shol, Lhasa, Tibet.** This ain't no Shangri-La, but it's a favorite among the backpacker crowd, who like its monastery setting, free laundry facilities, and unbelievably friendly staff. $

★ **Hotel Fewa, Pokhara, Nepal.** Check out the cottages with terra-cotta-colored mud and clay walls, fireplaces, and sleeping lofts reached by ladder, with views of Lake Phewa. $

★ **Kathmandu Guest House, Thamel, Kathmandu, Nepal.** Colonial architecture, expansive gardens, and first class service for a fraction of the cost. $

Flavors

★ **Kilroy's of Kathmandu, Jyatha, Kathmandu, Nepal.** Visit for the culinary delight as well as the opportunity to tell your friends you dined on French onion soup and Irish stew at a restaurant that also specializes in Indian cuisine and fine pastries. $$$$

★ **Wunjala Moskva, Naxal, Kathmandu, Nepal.** If you can't decide whether you are craving caviar or boar, dine at this restaurant specializing in Russian and Newari cuisine. $$$$

★ **Mike's Breakfast, Naxal, Kathmandu; Mike's Restaurant, Lakeside, Pokhara, Nepal.** Those in the know consider the Kathmandu restaurant a landmark: generous servings of healthy, fresh vegetables served in omelets or burritos, with real coffee, classical music, flowers, and chirping birds in the background. The newer Pokhara restaurant is equally delightful. $$$

★ **Utse Restaurant and Bar, Jyatha, Kathmandu, Nepal.** This is the place to get authentic Tibetan dishes, beyond the usual momos and rice fare. $$$

★ **Restaurant Rabten, Thimphu, Bhutan.** Relax on comfortable couches while dining in the capital city's only pure Bhutanese restaurant. The food is delicious, carefully prepared and beautifully presented in traditional wooden bowls. It's known for using unusual spices and natural foods; don't forget to ask to see the spice basket. $$

★ **Plum's Café, Thimphu, Bhutan.** Plum's serves a variety of Asian food in a bistro-like setting. Ask the owner what the fresh catch of the day is; it's always prepared with savory seasonings. $$

★ **Third Eye, Thamel, Kathmandu, Nepal.** This Indian restaurant would have succeeded on ambience alone—pillows, low tables, dim lighting, and Indian and Nepali art—but it's also renowned for its zesty Indian cuisine. $$

★ **Crazy Yak, Lhasa, Tibet.** You'll be treated to a full Tibetan banquet here in a traditional atmosphere. Although the food may be no more than "interesting," it is accompanied by a performance of Tibetan opera and folk dance. $

★ **Makye Ame, Lhasa, Tibet.** Right at a corner of Barkhor Square, this charming second-story restaurant allows you to sip on carrot soup and chomp on yak burgers while watching the dizzying crowds of pilgrims stroll by below. Don't forget to grab a brownie. $

★ **Snowlands, Lhasa, Tibet.** It will never be an international highlight, but Snowlands is consistent (especially for Tibet) in turning out good food for tired sightseers, including Western and Indian dishes. Try the chicken sizzler with mashed potatoes, a delicious order of garlic naan bread, and a cinnamon roll from the pastry counter. $

FESTIVALS AND SEASONAL EVENTS

WINTER

JAN.➤ **Magh Sankranti** in Nepal is the first day of the winter solstice and thus one of the rare holidays not governed by the lunar calendar. During Magh Sankranti, many Nepalis dip in the ice-cold holy rivers for ritual bathings. More bathing, particularly at the Narayani river in Devghat in the Terai, occurs on Tribeni Mela, which is the first day of the new moon after Magh Sankranti. Nepal's **Basant Panchami** falls on the fifth day after the new moon and celebrates the Goddess of Learning, Saraswati. Events are held at the shrine to Saraswati at Swayambhunath in the Kathmandu Valley. In Tibet, Shigatse holds a **New Year Festival.**

FEB.➤ **Shivaratri** is a Hindu holiday in honor of Lord Shiva's birthday; it's on the new moon of February. Thousands of pilgrims from all over India and Nepal flock to the Pashupatinath temple complex, east of Kathmandu, where they believe a dip in the Bagmati river will absolve all past sins. Orange-robed sadhus (holy men) smoking marijuana, naked ascetics with rings in their genitals, and half-clad, ash-covered yogis make it a must-see cultural event. In Lhasa during **Mönum** (the Great Prayer Festival), the image of Maitreya is paraded from the Jokhang around Barkhor, and during the Lantern Festival (the Day of Offerings), huge sculptures made of yak butter are placed on the Barkhor pilgrimage route.

FEB. OR MAR.➤ **Losar,** the Tibetan New Year Festival, is Tibet's most colorful celebration, with performances of Tibetan drama, traditional dance and other festivities, and pilgrims flocking into Lhasa from all over the region, donning their monastery best. Immediately before and during the Year End Festival, monks dance at the monasteries to frighten away the evil spirits of the former year. Visit Nepali monasteries in Boudhanath to hear chanting and see monks dressed as dragons and spirits while performing ritual dances. It is a time for family gatherings and partying; fireworks crackle throughout the nights.

SPRING

MAR.➤ **Holi,** or the Festival of Colors, is an eight-day Hindu festival that celebrates spring. Revelers throw water balloons and shoot high-powered water guns all week long in Nepal. On the eighth day they splatter pedestrians and even vehicles with colored dyes, usually red, which is a color of rejoicing. Wear old clothes, protect your camera, and watch out for torrents of water tossed from pranksters on balconies. **Sweta Macchendranath Rath Jaatra** is a four-day festival in Patan that honors the White Macchendranath (Shiva to the Hindus, Avalkitesvara to the Buddhists). The image of the white Macchendranath is removed from Kel Tole temple and then drawn in a huge chariot through the streets of Kathmandu.

APR.➤ **Bisket Jatra** is the festival in Bhaktapur in the Kathmandu Valley celebrating the Nepali New Year. It starts in mid-April when processions carry a variety of images of sacred gods drawn in chariots. A 25-m/80-ft-high mask is erected on New Year's Eve and then knocked down the next day to chase away evil spirits. This is the only other major Nepali holiday (besides Magh Sankranti) governed by the solar, rather than lunar calendar. On **Rato Macchendranath Jaatra** the image of the rain-bringing god Rato (red) Macchendranath is drawn through Patan by a chariot. It is only carried on astrologically auspicious days, so it takes several weeks to complete the festival, by which time the monsoon is normally looming.

SUMMER

MAY➤ **Buddha Jayanti** is the anniversary of the Buddha's birth, enlightenment, and death. In the Kathmandu Valley it's celebrated at Boudhanath and Swayambhunath on the full moon of May.

MAY–JUNE➤ **Saga Dawa** (Buddha's Enlightenment Day) draws many pilgrims to Tibet, and there are outdoor opera performances in Lhasa. Pilgrims also come in crowds to complete the kora around Mount Kailash. The **Birth of Sakyamuni** is celebrated by pilgrims at holy sights all over Tibet, including the Lhasa, Ganden, Samye and Tsurphu Dgon Monasteries. **Tsurphu Dgon Festival,** held at the monastery, includes traditional dancing and lots of drinking. The Karmapa used to do his annual dance during this festival, but since his crossing to Dharamsala, he most likely won't be appearing again in the near future.

JULY–AUG.➤ **Janai Purnima** is on the full moon of the Nepali month of Saaun. Hindus of the Brahman and Chhetri castes exchange the Janai, or holy thread that they wear across their left shoulder and tied under their right arm. Young men first receive the cord, which symbolizes body, language, and understanding, during a ritual that initiates them into their religion. Celebrations are held at Gosainkund Lake, north of Kathmandu and in Patan. **Gai Jatra** honors cows who are said to use their tails to guide those who died the year before to the underworld. It occurs immediately after Janai Purnima. Be on the lookout for real cows or young boys dressed as cows guiding their relatives and friends through the streets.

AUG.–SEPT.➤ Tibet's **Drepung Zöton** (Yogurt Festival) takes place at Drepung Monastery in Lhasa, with dances by the

monks and the hanging of a monumental thangkha. **Zöton,** two days after Drepung Zöton, is known as the Popular Yogurt Festival; it starts at the Drepung Monastery and moves to Norbulingka, where operas and dances are held. Go to Patan, Nepal, to see the oil lamps illuminating the Hindu temples and hear the singing during the celebrations of **Krishna Jayanti,** Krishna's birthday. This holiday falls on the seventh day after the full moon of the Nepali month of Bhadra.

AUTUMN

AUG.–SEPT.➤ During the three-day holiday of **Teej,** Hindu women honor their husbands with a feast on the first day, a fast and a ritual dip in Nepal's polluted Bagmati River at Pashupatinath Temple on the second day. The women usually wear their red-and-gold wedding saris. On the third day of the festival, the women offer food to their husbands, after first offering it to the gods.

SEPT.➤ **Indra Jatra** is a lively eight-day festival that honors the recently deceased and the god Indra. The event begins with a parade of images of the gods and animal sacrifices. In Kathmandu's Durbar Square, devotees carry the Royal Kumari (the Living Goddess) in her gold chariot. There are masked dances, singing, and plenty of beer.

SEPT.–OCT.➤ **Dassain,** a Hindu festival embraced

by all of Nepal, celebrates the victory of Durga, Shiva's consort, over the buffalo demon Mahishasur. In commemoration, thousands of animals are slaughtered. Blood is smeared on vehicles (even planes) to ensure safety. The holiday lasts for up to 15 days, ending on the full moon of late September or early October. Be warned, buses are crowded with locals heading home and many offices close during this period.

Tibet's **Festival of Horse-Racing** is held north of Lhasa around Lake Nam-Tso, where the nomads celebrate life with traditional competitions of archery and horsemanship.

NOV.➤ Nepal's festival of **Tihar** or **Diwali** honors Yama, the god of death, and Laksmi, the goddess of wealth and prosperity. During these five days dogs, cows, and bulls are decorated with garlands. Candles and oil lamps light homes throughout the country in the hopes of attracting Lakshmi. This is another holiday marked by fireworks. On the final day, sisters give their brothers sweets.

In the Solu Khumbu region near Mt. Everest, Sherpas celebrate **Mani Rimdu** with masked dances marking the victory of Buddhism over the Bon religion in 8th-century Tibet. **Labab Düchen** commemorates the deities' coming to earth and attracts numerous pilgrims to Lhasa. **Paldren Lhamo** honors the protective deity of Jokhang, whose image is paraded around Lhasa's Barkhor.

2 NEPAL

Stand on the roof of the world in the abode of gods. Raft a raging river emptying from the Himal into the plains where rhinoceros are shrouded by towering grass. Ride an elephant in search of Royal Bengal tigers who reign supreme in the lowlands of mugger crocodiles and wild boars. Or find yourself lost in an incense-filled world of saris, half-naked holy men, and Tibetan monks. Once you visit Nepal, you will never leave. Nepal will live on within you.

By Lara
Wozniak

NEPAL'S 22 MILLION PEOPLE represent 40 ethnic groups, each living in different regions, wearing unique traditional dress, and speaking 70 different languages, not to mention hundreds of dialects. Sandwiched between India and China, the kingdom extends approximately 885 km (548 mi) east to west, and about 193 km (120 mi) north to south. It is the world's only declared Hindu country, with 90% of the population espousing the religion. Yet, unlike in its neighboring countries, there is religious tolerance in Nepal. One reason is that throughout the land there is a fusion of Hinduism, Buddhism, and remnants of animism. For example, Avalokitesvra (Buddha of Compassion) is worshiped as a manifestation of Shiva by Hindus; Ganesh, the elephant-headed god, and Sarasvati, Brahma's consort, are Hindu deities that often appear in Buddhist sanctuaries; and animal sacrifices remain a lively part of daily life.

The people in the northern, remote mountains are usually Buddhist and speak Tibetan dialects. Around Mt. Everest, you encounter the Sherpas, intrepid mountaineers and often the indispensable lifeline for a successful climbing expedition. In the towering peaks to the west of Mt. Everest and due north of Annapurna reside the Lo-pa, the yak-traders of the ancient kingdom of Mustang. Not far away are the Thakali, successful traders and farmers. Inhabiting the area near Mt. Dhaulagiri are the people of Dolpa, who cultivate barley. Gorkhas include a variety of tribes—the Garung, Magar, Raj, Limbu, and Sunwar—either Buddhist or Hindu, and reside primarily within the Annapurna district of central Nepal.

The Newar in the Kathmandu Valley are predominantly Hindu and claim their ancestors were the original inhabitants of Nepal. On the valley fringe, you come across Buddhists called the Tamang, Tibetan for "Horse Trader," who once dealt in horses but now cultivate the land. In the tropical southern belt, called the Terai, are Hindu tribes, including the Tharu, who migrated north from the Tharu Desert in India's Rajasthan.

The first known inhabitants were Ahirs, most likely Tibeto-Burman migrants, who occupied the Kathmandu Valley as early as the 8th century BC. The second wave of inhabitants were the Middle-Eastern Kirats, with a succession of kings who ruled for centuries. Before the 6th century BC, the Shakyas, a Rajput clan from north India, settled in the Terai, where they founded the city of Kapilvastu. Here in Lumbini, Prince Siddhartha Gautama, who became Buddha, was born in 563 BC.

The Licchavis, who most likely migrated from India and took control around AD 300, introduced the caste system and an artistic age of prosperity to Nepal.

The 13th century saw the rise of the Malla dynasty, whose members were considered descendants of Vishnu. Great patrons of the arts, the Mallas constructed most of the beautiful temples and palaces of the Kathmandu Valley. King Yaksha Malla, who ruled until 1482, extended the Malla domain into parts of Tibet and India, but he forgot to watch over his own backyard. Family fighting left the dynasty vulnerable. In 1768, a Gorkha army, under the rule of Prithvi Narayan Shah, stormed across Nepal, conquering nearby rival kingdoms to create a buffer against the British threat ensconced in India. Prithvi Narayan Shah thus unified Nepal.

In 1846 palace intrigues erupted into a bloody massacre, which put an end to the Shah dynasty and marked the beginning of the Age of the Ranas. Acting as prime ministers, the Ranas ushered in a period of fragile peace, not to mention secrecy, since they closed Nepal's borders to outsiders. After World War II, fighting between the Ranas, helped along by pressure for meaningful reforms from newly independent India, set in motion their downfall. In 1950, the titular king, Tribhuvan, took refuge in India and the Nepalese revolted against the Rana government. A year later, King Tribhuvan returned to Nepal and recaptured the throne, putting an end to more than a century of Rana rule. But King Tribhuvan died in 1955, leaving the throne to his son Mahendra.

Political unrest led to a new constitution, which called for a parliamentary system of government and ushered in B.P. Koirala of the Nepali Congress as the prime minister in 1959. But in 1960, King Mahendra had the cabinet arrested, banned political parties, and took control. In 1962, he introduced a *panchayat* (council) system of government, which on the surface seemed fair. The reality, however, was quite different. The king still banned political parties, retained executive power, and chose nearly half of the 35-member National Panchayat party.

In 1972, King Mahendra died and was replaced by his son Birendra Bir Bikram Shah Dev (who is married to a descendent of the Rana family). Increasing discontent, corrupt officials, and inflation caused tension that erupted in violent riots in the late 1970s. Such tension marks contemporary politics in Nepal. In February 1990, a nonviolent protest was met with bullets and arrests, followed by riots and curfews. But eventually the people won their demand for multiple political parties. In May 1991, 20 parties vied for the 205 seats of parliament; the Nepali Congress won 110 seats, the Communist Party of Nepal-United Marxist-Leninist (CPN-UML) took 69 seats. The result is a parliamentary democracy headed by a constitutional monarchy.

Political unrest, economic insecurity, and official corruption still plague the country. Power regularly flip-flops, corruption is rampant, poverty prevails despite an astonishing amount of international aid, and strikes and protests have become the norm. Since 1996, more than 600 people have been killed in the "People's War" primarily waged by Maoists and the police in the western portion of the country where visitors rarely wander. It has, thus far, had little effect on tourism. However, it is always wise to ask your travel agent if any strikes are scheduled (yes, they are scheduled) during your visit.

In the spring of 1999, new elections brought a new wave of protests and demonstrations. Some critics question the degree of fairness to the elections: votes were counted even though they did not have signatures from polling officers; allegations of police harassment of voters were countered by allegations of Maoist coercion of votes. Each side accused the other of vote buying. Scores of people were injured during the elections, and six were killed. Yet the *Kathmandu Post* said in a post-election editorial that the "elections were largely free." The Nepali Congress won 110 seats, and the CPN-UML won 68 seats. Thus, the Nepali Congress remains in power, and the Communist Party remains the second most powerful party, in a prime position to continue to criticize the ruling government.

Pleasures and Pastimes

Dining

Daal baht—lentils, rice, and mixed vegetables—is the Nepali staple. For years, most visitors had no other choice. Now, you can visit Nepal and never taste daal baht. Not only are there scores of Indian, Tibetan, and Chinese restaurants, but Continental cuisine of the highest standard is easy to find in Kathmandu. Outside the capital, in Pokhara and

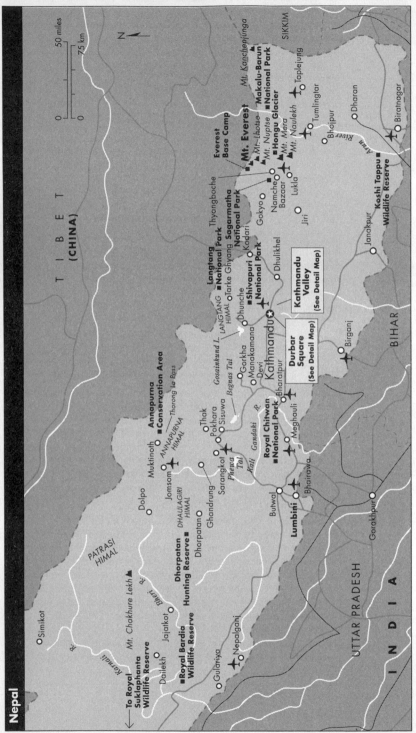

50 miles
75 km

N

T I B E T
(CHINA)

SIKKIM

Mt. Kanchenjunga

Taplejung

Makalu-Barun
National Park

Tumlingtar

Dharan

Biratnagar

Mt. Lhotse
Everest
Base Camp
Mt. Everest
Mt. Nuptse
Hongu Glacier
Mt. Mera

Mt. Naulekh
Bhojpur

Arun River

Koshi Tappu
Wildlife Reserve

Namche
Bazaar
Lukla

Thyangboche
Langtang
National Park
Sagarmatha
National Park
Tarke Ghyang
Kodari
Gokyo

Jiri

Janakpur

LANGTANG
HIMAL
Dhunche
Shivapuri
National Park
Dhulikhel

Kathmandu
Valley
(See Detail Map)

Gosainkund L.

Kathmandu

Durbar
Square
(See Detail Map)

BIHAR

Birganj

Bagnas Tal

Gorkha
Manakamana
Devi
Bharatpur

Annapurna
Conservation Area

Thak
Pokhara
Sisuwa

Thorong la Pass
ANNAPURNA
HIMAL

Muktinoth

Jomsom
DHAULAGIRI
HIMAL

Sarangkot
Phewa
Tal
Ghandrung

Seti R.
Gandaki
Kali

Royal Chitwan
National Park

Meghauli

Dolpo

Dhorpatan
Hunting Reserve

Dhorpatan

PATRASI
HIMAL

Buwal

Bhairawa

Lumbini

Gorakhpur

Mt. Chakhure Lekh

Simikot

Jajakot

Royal Bardia
Wildlife Reserve

Dailekh

Karnali R.

Bheri R.

To Royal
Suklaphanta
Wildlife Reserve

Gularia

Nepalganj

UTTAR PRADESH

I N D I A

the National Park areas, you won't have as many upscale restaurants to choose from, but you can still get quality fare at the expensive hotels and lodges. You will quickly discover a typical trekkers' Western menu of pizza, spaghetti, chow mein, and eggs at the lower-priced restaurants. If you go farther afield, make room for daal baht.

Daal baht is healthy and filling. It can be spicy, but usually you can work your way around the chilies. It is traditionally served on a *thali*, a shiny silver platter divided into compartments. To eat Nepali style, use your right fingertips to mix the lentils and vegetables with the rice into tablespoon-size servings that you scoop into your mouth. Typically, your thali is refilled until you cannot eat another bite.

During the high season make reservations. Dress is casual.

CATEGORY	COST*
$$$$	over $10
$$$	$5–$10
$$	$3–$5
$	under $3

per person, excluding drinks and service

Lodging

You will find superb hotels in Kathmandu and Pokhara, while Nagarkot and Dhulikel have some remarkably high-standard resorts. Inside Royal Chitwan National Park, you will find charming, luxurious hunting lodges. As for the rest of the country, more and more "resorts" are popping up. Unfortunately, many of them advertise what they plan to build; read the fine print on their brochures.

CATEGORY	COST*
$$$$	over $150
$$$	$120–$150
$$	$50–$120
$	under $50

All prices are for a double room, excluding tax and service.

Trekking

Trekking is one of the biggest draws to Nepal. You can either camp or stay in local teahouse accommodations. You can walk as fast or as slow as you like; travel agents will tailor trips to any level of fitness. The Annapurna and Everest ranges attract the most trekkers and can be extremely crowded during high season. Consider the Langtang region for a quieter hike.

Exploring Nepal

Once you arrive at the Tribhuvan International Airport, the best way to get around the Kathmandu Valley is by hired car or taxi. The most convenient way to travel around the country is to fly and then go by Land Rover, foot, or raft. For example, if you want to trek in the Everest region, you should fly to Lukla, then start your trek. Similarly, a half-hour flight to Pokhara is more convenient than the four- to six-hour road journey; and from there you can head out to the Annapurna range. If you take road trips, try to book air-conditioned, four-wheel-drive vehicles.

While it may sound adventurous to wander alone, it is safer and a valuable contribution to the country's economy to use a guide. It will add comparatively little to your budget to employ a guide who is likely supporting a family.

Great Itineraries

If just visiting the Kathmandu Valley is enough, three days will allow you to see Durbar Square, Swayambhunath, Boudhanath, Patan, and Bhaktapur, in a whirlwind tour that might leave you loathing the sight of yet another temple. A practical minimum stay for really absorbing the greatness of Nepal is 10 days, in which time you can take in the above sites, Pokhara, and either a one- or two-day-long trek, river rafting trip, or visit to a hill station to be amid the grandeur of the mountains. You might want to skip Kathmandu and its pollution altogether by transferring to the domestic terminal on arrival in Kathmandu and heading straight for Pokhara and the mountains, giving you time for a longer hike. To see Kathmandu and Pokhara and go on a serious trek or river rafting trip, you really need to plan on staying for a minimum of two weeks.

IF YOU HAVE 3 DAYS

If you have three days, consider visiting **Patan's Durbar Square** in Kathmandu in the morning, followed by **Boudhanath** and **Pashupatinath** in the afternoon. Or you can flip-flop the order. **Boudhanath** is a good place to get a bite to eat, or stop for a drink, so you can plan your touring accordingly. On the second day, visit **Patan** and **Swayambhunath;** the latter site is particularly beautiful at sunset, as you have a view of the whole valley from the hilltop. Spend your third day at **Bhaktapur,** making sure to visit the pottery-making section. If you are "templed out" after the first day, you might want to take a mountain flight so you can experience Everest in the warmth of an airplane.

IF YOU HAVE 10 DAYS

Six to eight days is the minimum amount of time you will need for a serious **trek,** so go hiking and then spend two or three days visiting some of the above sites. Always leave at least two days in the Kathmandu vicinity after a trek; that way if you get snowed in at some point while hiking, you won't spend the whole time worrying about missing your flight home. If you only have two days to tour the Kathmandu Valley before or after a trek (or river rafting trip), consider visiting **Patan's Durbar Square;** it gives you a good sampling of historic temples and is a relatively low-key, quiet section of the valley, where you will not be swarmed by touts trying to sell you things or guide you about. Then visit **Boudhanath** and **Pashupatinath** for a taste of Buddhism and Hinduism. In 10 days, you could also opt for a two-day **river rafting** trip that ends up in the **Royal Chitwan National Park** region, allowing you to spend two to three days in the Terai. Then drive or fly to **Pokhara** and spend two to three days hiking before flying back to Kathmandu. You could also replace any of those sites with a night in **Nagarkot** or **Dhulikhel** to watch the sun set and rise over the Himal. It would be best to book such a fast-paced trip through a travel agent, so that you don't spend all your time making arrangements.

IF YOU HAVE 2 TO 3 WEEKS

Most people who have two to three weeks go to Nepal for major walks, like a 15- to 21-day **Everest Base Camp** trek, or a similar hike in the **Annapurna** range. These long treks let you experience the area's stunning beauty and cultural diversity. Even if you stay a month, you may end up rushed to see the sites in the Kathmandu Valley. Returning from a long trek, your interest in hot baths and fine dining may keep you in the immediate Kathmandu area. That makes **Durbar Square** an appealing touring site, since it is in the center of the city. You might want to take a tour to this site, as men passing themselves off as "guides" will approach anyone carrying a guidebook and walking alone. Many climbers visit the stupa at **Boudhanath** or **Swayambhunath** to pray before they leave on their adventures.

The peak season is from September through December. Nonetheless, each season has distinct advantages.

From September until the beginning of December, the weather is warm, the air crisp and clear, and the mountains seem to sparkle in the fresh post-monsoon air. But during this high season inns are full, restaurants are packed, and river rafting trips book up. Trekking routes are so crowded that hikers sometimes walk up steep bits in single file, which detracts from the heady dream of retracing Maurice Herzog's or Sir Edmund Hillary's footsteps up to the great Himalayas.

From December to mid-February, high-altitude inns and trekking routes like the Thorung La pass on the Annapurna Circuit sometimes get snowed in. But for the intrepid hiker (with time to spare) this is the season to go. The trekking routes are quiet, and the experience is far more intense, although visibility is not as clear as in the fall. In the Kathmandu Valley and the Lake District of Pokhara it remains cool during the day and rarely snows. Mornings can be damp and misty in Kathmandu. It is not too hot in the Terai, and there are not too many visitors, so it is a good time to check out the national parks in peace.

Spring usually arrives around the last week of February, when it is suddenly T-shirt and sandals weather in Kathmandu, and the air is perfumed by flowers. The rhododendron burst onto the scene in April, but due to haze and dust (particularly if it does not rain much), it is often difficult to see the mountains. However, locals cut the grass in the Terai in late February, exposing the rhinos and making it the best time to go and view wildlife.

Once the monsoon arrives in June, with daily doses of heavy rain, the mountains take refuge behind the clouds, landslides make roads impassable, and leeches attach themselves to unsuspecting passersby. But once again, the numbers of visitors drops along with prices. Hoteliers, restaurateurs, and shopkeepers attend to clients with painstaking respect. Many of the rivers roar with white water, attracting expert rafters; although they are (or should be) off-limits to beginners during this time.

Great River Rafting Trips

Most rafting adventures start in either Kathmandu or Pokhara. They can be booked in either city. You can choose from one- to 12-day excursions on some of the wildest rivers that cut through the highest walls in the world. However, it's not all rough and tumble: the rivers also gently drift past ethnic villages, where you get to see the people and the countryside as you float downstream. The class (roughness rating) of a river depends on the amount of water running in the bed and varies with time as rainfall and weather change; the range is I–V, with V being the roughest.

The cost of a rafting trip usually includes camping equipment, meals (camp setup and cooking are handled by the guides), a helmet, and a life preserver. You often have a choice between an oar boat and a paddle boat, and on some rivers you can kayak. In an oar boat, the guide does the work. Paddling requires teamwork and often bonds a group of travelers.

It is very important to shop around and ask pertinent questions: Will you have to paddle all day? Or will you feel like you are in a pinball machine? Make sure the rafting company has high-standard life preservers and helmets that fit. Do not just take the guide's word for it. Try the equipment on before leaving Kathmandu or Pokhara. Agencies do not sell liability insurance, and there have been rafting fatalities in Nepal.

River rafting is the latest rage in Nepal, but it is stressing the environment. Try to leave nothing but footprints behind on the beaches.

Make sure you pack T-shirts, shorts or light cotton trousers, rubbersole sandals, a swimsuit, a sun hat, sunglasses with a string, and sunscreen. Many rafting companies serve instant coffee at breakfast, so if you are a coffee fiend, bring your own ground coffee; reusable filters are available in any grocery shop in Kathmandu. Chocolate or sweets are another lightweight goodie to bring along.

KARNALI

This 11- to 12-day trip through western Nepal can start in either Kathmandu or Pokhara. It takes about 14 hours by jeep to get to the put-in point from either of the two cities. The river trip is sometimes combined with a trekking trip. The Karnali River springs from the base of Mt. Kailash in Tibet, flowing south into Nepal to form the major drainage system of the western districts. The starting point is usually around Sauli, where there are powerful, high-volume, white-water rapids amid the canyons. You can get world-class, white-water adventure here. Toward the end of the trip, the river gradient eases as the Karnali leaves the mountains and flows into the Ganges. The finishing point is around Chisopani. Expect a 12-hour drive back to Kathmandu or Pokhara. The river is Class IV–V.

KALI GANDAKI

This trip is through mid-western Nepal, near Pokhara. The three- to five-day journey is on the Kali Gandaki River, which originates in Mustang, close to the Tibet border. It tumbles between the Dhaulagiri and Annapurna ranges, creating the world's deepest river gorge. Most trips depart from Pokhara and put in at a spot about a three-hour drive away, near Nayapul/Baglung. They finish near the Kali Hydroelectric dam, a five-hour drive from to Pokhara. Some trips continue to Narayanghat, near the Royal Chitwan National Park. The river grade is Class III–IV.

MARSYANGDI

This river runs through central Nepal, north of Pokhara. Marysyangdi means "raging," which says it all. The river, which drains the northern slope of the Annapurnas, was only opened to rafting in 1996, and yields some of the most exciting white water in Nepal. It is a whiteknuckle trip that requires your full attention and skill, as the river jostles you around like the ball in a pinball machine. The put-in point is near Nagdi, and the finish is near Bimal Nagar. Expect a bumpy fourhour (or longer) ride from Pokhara, plus a trek, to the put in, then five or six days of rafting. The river is Class IV–V.

SETI

This is a trip in central Nepal. You start out by driving 1½ hours west of Pokhara to the put-in point. The rafting trip is usually three to five days. It's a good trip for beginners and families; it's relaxing, with plenty of small, friendly rapids. You get to see some of the lowlands of Nepal in the background along the way. The Seti is only rated Class II–III.

TRISHULI

Another river in central Nepal, the Trishuli is one of the most popular for rafting (followed by the Sunkosi), because of its accessibility by road and because there are trips here that are as short as two days. Like the Seti, this is not a very challenging river, so it is excellent for beginners. You can also continue as far as Royal Chitwan National Park, so a Trishuli trip can end where a wildlife tour begins. The put-in point is about a two-hour drive west of Kathmandu. The river is Class II–IV.

This trip is in eastern Nepal. This big-volume, high-adrenaline Sunkosi River rises near Shishma Pangma in Tibet and runs eastward, draining the Himalayas before joining the Ganges. The most common put-in points are Baseri and Dolaghat, three hours east of Kathmandu. Expect to raft for 8 to 10 days, then drive the 14 hours back to Kathmandu. The waters here are usually Class IV–V. Be warned: some of the rapids actually have nicknames like Meat Grinder, High Anxiety, Jaws, and Big Dipper.

The Bhote Koshi provides an action-packed, short, white-water run, just a short bus ride to the north of Kathmandu. This is a steep, technically demanding river (Class IV–V) that requires a reactive crew. There are stretches of water that are expert only. Expect boulder gardens, small waterfalls, steep chutes, and 90-degree bends. The trip is five hours out and three back.

KATHMANDU

Kathmandu is in the eastern portion of the country. For hundreds of years it was one of three rival royal cities: Bhaktapur and Patan rounded out the triangle. But when Prithvi Narayan Shah unified the country in 1768, he declared Kathmandu the capital.

Today, Kathmandu is home to 700,000 people: a painter's palette of brilliant, colorful saris, and a cacophony of languages and dialects holding trading matches at top pitch, while motorcycles, trucks, buses, and cars zoom past, pouring out clouds of dust and fumes. Each street smells of a different curry, a new incense. It is a vibrant valley of life, where you can stand on any city street and watch a hundred minidramas unfold around you in surround sound.

Everything Western is here—from the latest flick bootlegged on laser disc to the newest outrageous fashion. You will see kids displaying more pierced jewelry than a Tiffany's store window. Teenagers are as cutting-edge here as anywhere else in the world, while their grandparents invariably still wear the traditional costumes of their origin. CNN blares out of 15th-century homes, just down the lane from ancient temples and palaces. Land Rovers inch their way down streets only to be stopped by a sleeping water buffalo or cow in the middle of the road. You may find the most interesting part of visiting Nepal is wandering the streets and watching this confusing, complex world unfold amid the backdrop of incredibly artful, if decaying, architecture.

Sadly, despite leaps and bounds of advances in just a half century of openness to the West, Kathmandu remains an exceedingly poor city that teeters on the edge of widespread disease at the least threat—a water shortage, a flu, a crop failure.

The hotels are primarily in Durbar Marg, Lazimpat, and Thamel. Durbar Marg is an upscale street geared toward Westerners: It has expensive restaurants and shops conveniently nearby. Lazimpat is a more sedate area of town, where many of the embassies are situated. It has a Nepali flavor to it, as parts of middle-class Nepali neighborhoods intersect there. Despite some nice hotels in Thamel, it is the backpackers' haven. That has turned it into a tourist trap, where hawkers try to sell you last week's creation as an antique, and young men try to get you to use the black market or blatantly push "hashish? marijuana?" as you breeze by. (Responding, loudly, "No I do not want drugs" usually shuts them up.) While it can be a bit like a carnival and give you a headache, Thamel is one of the best places to shop for handicrafts. If you want to see traditional culture, you must wander away from the hotel-every-100-feet sections of town, and venture through the narrow lanes.

According to legend, Kathmandu was founded by King Gunakama Deva in the latter half of the 10th century. In a dream, the goddess Mahalakshmi told the king to build a city where the Vishnumati flows into the Bagmati. The new city was named Kantipur and built in the shape of a *kharg* (the goddess' sword), which was a symbol of enlightenment. The king moved his palace from Patan to Kathmandu and established the city. The Mallas would later build temples in this city, but it was not until Prithvi Narayan Shah came along that Kathmandu really took charge. A wide street, Kantipath, was constructed, with palaces, schools, and barracks built off this road. More palaces were built by the Ranas in the 1900s, but many were destroyed in the massive 1934 earthquake. New Road was constructed after the earthquake, linking Kantipath with Old Kathmandu, a route taxi drivers still use to get to Durbar Square.

Exploring Kathmandu

You can start from Durbar Marg or Thamel. Pick any lane heading southwest, and walk toward **Durbar Square.** To and fro—you will wander through the walkways of **Old Kathmandu.** There are almost always four or five routes to the same site, so trust your instincts and follow the sites, sounds, and scents of Kathmandu. Do not worry about getting lost; bicycle rickshaw drivers abound. They can take you back to familiar routes or your hotel if you find yourself spun around in a maze of alleyways. The driver probably will not speak English, but he will understand if you simply signal with your hands that you want to go around the Durbar Square area, or if you read off the names of the sites from your map. You might prefer this conversational struggle to hiring a guide, because in these alleys you really want to be able to spend as much or as little time as you like lingering. Many people hire a guide for **Durbar Square** but then spend hours on their own wandering the surrounding area.

Durbar Square

Durbar means "palace," and a walking tour of Durbar Square in Kathmandu is well worthwhile. It is here that the kings of Nepal are crowned. There are more than 50 statues, temples, and monuments in the area. Aside from the grandeur of the temples, there are monkeys, goats, hundreds of pigeons, *sadhus* (holy men) begging for money, local vendors selling fragrant garlands of marigolds and fruit, along with souvenir stalls.

There are numerous touts who try to take you around on tour, particularly if you are carrying a guidebook. You may want to photocopy these pages, so you appear less touristy, or read up beforehand. You can also go ahead and hire a guide, just to keep the others away. Reputable tour agents will keep the local "guides" at bay.

Admission to the Square is free, but donations of a few small-note or coin rupees are gladly accepted.

Numbers in the text correspond to numbers in the margin and on the Durbar Square Kathmandu map.

A GOOD WALK

Begin at **Kashthamandap** ① in the southwest corner of the square; it is one of the easier temples to identify because it has a signpost out front. Just north of the temple is the small but exceedingly important

Maru Ganesh shrine ② (also called **Ashok Binayak**). Behind this shrine, across the courtyard, at the junction of Durbar and Basantapur squares, is **Kumari Chowk** (or **Kumari Bahal**) ③, the weatherworn house of the **Kumari** (**Living Goddess**). Across Basantapur Square from Kumari Chowk is the **Gaddi Baithak** ④, a neo-Grecian building constructed in 1908. Now turn to the middle of the Square, to the huge, three-tiered **Maju Deval** ⑤; climb the steps for a good view of the area. From Maju Deval you can look out at the statues of Shiva and Parvati, peering down from an upper window of the two-story **Shiva Parvati Temple** ⑥. Beyond the Shiva Parvati Temple, walk past the salesmen selling masks, shawls, and statues to **Hanuman Dhoka Square** ⑦, the cultural and religious center of Old Kathmandu.

The central point here is the **Royal Palace** (**Hanuman Dhoka**) ⑧, which is to your right once you enter the square known as Nassal Chowk. The dominant building in this courtyard is the nine-story **Basantapur Tower** ⑨. From here, you get a good view of Kathmandu, including the unusual round-roof pagoda, **Pancha Mukhi Hanuman Temple** ⑩. Dedicated to the monkey god, this temple is at the opposite end of the courtyard. When you leave the palace, check out the huge masked face behind a grill. It is the **Seto (White) Bhairav** ⑪, and it is on the corner of the courtyard if you are heading back toward Durbar Square. Across from it, atop a pillar, is a bronze **statue of King Pratap Malla** ⑫ sitting on a lotus-shape pedestal and surrounded by his four sons. All of the images are facing the **Degu Taleju Temple** ⑬. On a plinth near the pillar is the many-tiered, 17th-century **Jaganath Temple** ⑭. Next to it is the octagonal **Krishna Mandir.** ⑮. On the north wall of the square is the revered 17th-century **bas-relief of Kalo (black) Bhairav** ⑯. Nearby is the 17th-century temple **Indrapur** ⑰, with an open balcony on the second tier. The 16th-century **Taleju Temple** ⑱, guarded by a pair of stone lions, is east of Indrapur.

TIMING

The best time to go to the Square is early morning, when locals visit to offer prayers and the surrounding local marketplaces begin to wake up, but visiting anytime before sunset is interesting. Tour guides tend to fly through this site in an hour, but you should allot a minimum of two hours to linger if you are on your own. Give yourself another hour, at least, if you also plan to walk north of Durbar Square in **Old Kathmandu.** Ask your travel agent if there are any special events or religious ceremonies going on in the area.

SIGHTS TO SEE

⑨ **Basantapur Tower.** Constructed by King Prithvi Narayan Shah, this nine-story tower with struts of erotic carvings was restored prior to King Birendra's coronation. Climb the steps for excellent view of the palace and the valley, and on a clear day, of the Langtang Himal in the distance. ⊠ *Durbar Square, Kathmandu.*

⑯ **Bas-relief of Kalo (Black) Bhairav.** Here you see the dreaded aspect of Shiva, with fangs and a necklace of human skulls, trampling his father-in-law, who had insulted him. This image reminds devotees of the inevitability of justice. Legend claims that it once served as a lie detector: Anyone who stood before it and spoke dishonestly bled to death. ⊠ *Durbar Square, Kathmandu.*

⑬ **Degu Taleju Temple.** Once the Malla's private shrine, this is the tallest shrine in Hanuman Dhoka, with its gilded roofs rising high above the square. Its sacred idol, Taleju, is a manifestation of Parvati and was the guardian deity of the dynasty. ⊠ *Durbar Square, Kathmandu.*

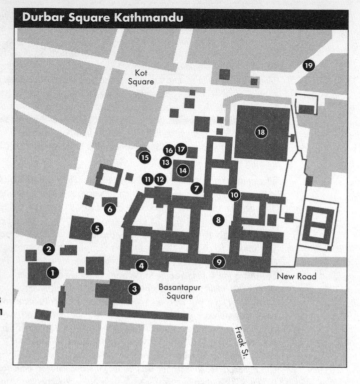

Durbar Square Kathmandu

❹ **Gaddi Baithak.** Architecturally, this neo-Grecian building looks mis-placed, but it is part of the Malla history, when royalty traveled to Europe, but foreigners were by and large barred from entering Nepal. It was constructed in 1908, after Jung Bahadur Rana visited England. Today the government uses the building for state functions. ⊠ *Durbar Square, Kathmandu.*

❼ **Hanuman Dhoka Square.** Hanuman Dhoka means "Gate of Hanuman," the monkey god of Ramayana fame. Today dozens of monkeys call this square home, although they seem to be particularly adept at avoiding the camera lens. Hanuman performed Herculean tasks on behalf of the other gods. The Malla dynasty's kings put Hanuman's image on their battle flags, and in 1672 placed his statue outside the Royal Palace to ward off evil spirits and disease. Hanuman's statue, dressed in a red cloak, is an object of devotion. For years, the faithful have dabbed on gobs of mustard oil and cinnabar (vermilion), which have faded away the face of the statue. ⊠ *Durbar Square, Kathmandu.*

⓱ **Indrapur.** Though this temple is dedicated to Indra, the god of rain, who saved Nepal from a destructive drought, the inner sanctum contains a Shiva lingam. ⊠ *Durbar Square, Kathmandu.*

⓮ **Jaganath Temple.** Dedicated to Jaganath (Krishna) and Guheshwari (Parvati), this 17th-century temple has erotic carvings on its wood struts. There are many explanations for the carvings. Some say they were created as instructional tools. Some say they were meant to test the willpower and concentration of worshippers. Still others claim that the carvings were created as protection against the goddess of lightning, whose prudish nature would keep her from approaching a structure decorated with such explicit figures. Maybe this explanation is true. After all, the temple has yet to be struck by lightning!

❶ **Kashthamandap.** This spacious, wooden temple is said to be one of the oldest temples in Kathmandu. Legend says it was built from the wood of one tree as ransom for a kidnapped god—a remarkable claim, given its 68-ft width and 60-ft height, hence, its name, Kashthamandap, or "Pavilion of Wood." Some historians say it was first built in the 12th century and restored in the 16th century, while others say it was built by King Laxmi Narsingha Malla in the beginning of the 16th century. Images of Ganesh, the elephant-headed god of good fortune, are in all four corners.

For years this pagoda-roof temple in the Maru Tole section of town was a stop for salesmen on the India–Tibet trade route. It is still a market for fruits and vegetables in season, a hawking ground for rickshaw drivers, and a good place to purchase the marigold garlands that hang from the picket fence around the temple. These garlands are auspicious offerings. ⊠ *Durbar Square, Kathmandu.*

⓯ **Krishna Mandir.** This octagonal temple built in the 1600s has a typical Nepalese first floor, but note the white plaster second floor, which is actually more commonly found in north India.

❸ **Kumari Chowk** (or Kumari Bahal). This is the weatherworn palace of the *Kumari* (Living Goddess). The building is easily identified by its numerous balconies and wooden screens. The Kumari is a virgin girl worshiped as a living incarnation of the Hindu goddess Durga. The last Malla king of Kathmandu built this temple for her in 1757. Non-Hindus are not allowed past the interior courtyard, but you still might get a glimpse of the Kumari. When she feels like it, or when her handlers collect enough *baksheesh* (tip or bribe money), she may show her kohl-lined eyes out her window. Photography in the courtyard is okay, but it is strictly forbidden to take a picture of the Living Goddess.

The young girl who lives here is not allowed to smile; her feet never touch ground. She leaves her palace only when she is honored in a festival, and then she travels in a gold chariot. Although she is supposed to be a Hindu goddess, candidates for the post of the Royal Kumari must be about five years old and a member of the Buddhist Sakya sect, which is just one example of the interconnectedness of Hinduism and Buddhism in Nepal. A Royal Kumari's horoscope must be compatible with that of the King, and her body must be flawless, conforming to 32 requirements, including no body odors, perfect white teeth with no gaps, a small tongue, and the voice of a sparrow. The would-be Kumari must also witness, without flinching, the midnight sacrifice of 108 goats and 108 buffalo (108 is a sacred number for Hindus), and she must spend the night in the temple with the carcasses. Only then is she named the Kumari, a title she keeps until she reaches puberty or cuts herself: if she sheds any blood, her reign is over. ⊠ *Durbar Square, Kathmandu.*

❺ **Maju Deval.** This is a Shiva temple built in the 1690s by the mother of Bhupatindra Malla of Bhaktapur. The supporting beams have cornices with animal heads, the roof struts are covered with erotic carvings, and the pinnacle is shaped like a Buddhist stupa. ⊠ *Durbar Square, Kathmandu.*

NEED A BREAK? **Maju Deval** seems to dominate the square. You can buy a soda from any of the nearby stalls for 10 Rs.–15 Rs., then climb the steps, sit back, and watch the sadhus and touts approaching all the Westerners. Young boys will likely ask to bring your empty soda back to the storekeeper, earning themselves a few rupees for the returned bottle. Older boys will want to shine your toes if you are wearing sandals, and fix your unbeknownst-to-you broken hiking boots.

② **Maru Ganesh shrine** (also called Ashok Binayak). In the morning, Hindus leave offerings at this small pagoda-style shrine. Maru means nonexistent, and may refer to the unusual lack of a spire on the gilded roof. This is the first place people make an offering—royalty included—before praying at any of the nearby temples. Hindus also recommend a visit to this shrine before embarking on any long journey.

Ganesh is supposed to bring good luck. Legend says that Ganesh and his brother Kumari, the god of war, were the sons of Shiva and Parvati. One day Shiva held a contest to see which son could circle the universe first. Kumari, tasting victory, flew off. Sad, fat Ganesh discussed his predicament with his rat, who told him to circle his parents and tell them they were the universe. Shiva was so impressed, he blessed Ganesh with the title "God of Auspicious Beginnings." The faithful start each day with an offering to Ganesh, and each King of Nepal comes to this temple to make a gift before he is crowned. ⊠ *Durbar Square, Kathmandu.*

⑩ **Pancha Mukhi Hanuman Temple.** Only the priests may enter this temple, distinguished by its stack of five circular roofs. Each of the three royal cities has a five-storied temple; the most spectacular one is Nyatapola Temple in Bhaktapur. However, there are often good monkey photo-ops at this temple, which is not surprising, considering it is dedicated to the monkey god. ⊠ *Durbar Square, Kathmandu.*

❽ **Royal Palace or Hanuman Dhoka.** Before entering the Royal Palace, notice the two guardian lions near Hanuman. Shiva (the male force) sits on one side, and Shakti (the female force) sits on the other. Just inside the Royal Palace, you come to a statue of Narsingha (an incarnation of Vishnu) killing the demon Hiranyakashipu. Vishnu turned himself into Narsingha, half-man and half-lion, stretched the demon across his lap, and tore open its stomach with his claws. This image appears throughout the valley.

The palace wraps around several courtyards, with the Golden Door leading into Nasal Chowk, where coronations take place. A gilded fish on a pole at the northern end is another avatar (in Hindu religion this is a god's coming in bodily form to earth) of Vishnu and can swim through the world's waters. It is an auspicious sign that represents peace, prosperity, and transcendental wisdom. On the eastern side of this courtyard is a small whitewashed shrine that contains a statue of Nasaleshwar (Dancing Shiva), which gives the square its name. You will have to leave your camera with the gallery guards before entering the palace. ⊠ *Durbar Square, Kathmandu.* ▦ *250 Rs. for foreigners.* ⊙ *Feb.–Oct., Wed.–Mon. 10:30–4; Nov.–Jan., Wed.–Mon. 10:30–3 (Fri. until 2). Closed Tues. and on government holidays.*

⑪ **Seto (White) Bhairav.** This wrathful aspect of Shiva was placed on the wall by a Rana in 1769 to protect his kingdom from evil and ignorance. During the Indra Jatra festival, the screen is opened, a big pot of *chang* (rice beer) is placed behind the mask's mouth, and the faithful drink the chang through a long bamboo straw—a gift from Seto Bhairav. ⊠ *Durbar Square, Kathmandu.*

❻ **Shiva Parvati Temple.** This is a rare domestic-style temple, resembling a house. Most other temples have a pagoda design. It is a relatively new temple, as it was built in 1790. ⊠ *Durbar Square, Kathmandu.*

⑫ **Statue of King Pratap Malla.** In this statue, the famous Malla king surveys the square as he sits cross-legged atop a stone pillar. This is fitting, since he was responsible for the construction of many of the temples and monuments in the area. Note that all of the images of this statue, erected in 1670, are facing the Degu Taleju Temple.

⑱ **Taleju Temple.** This four-story temple has a gold pinnacle and a gold umbrella atop its gilded roofs. Large bronze faces of the goddess Taleju gaze from upper-floor windows. Except for during the ninth day of the autumn Durga Puja festival, the interior is off-limits to everyone but the royal family and a few priests. ✉ *Durbar Square, Kathmandu.*

Old Kathmandu

The typical Newari houses of Old Kathmandu were built as early as 1400. You might notice the doorsills studded with bits of metal; each year a new piece is added to ward off evil spirits. The buildings are more than beautiful—they're manifestations of Nepal's religious beliefs. On many temples, window sills, and frames in Old Kathmandu, you see images of the male and female sexually united. This is an artistic rendering of the tantric concept that salvation comes from the union of the male and female forces.

Shakti, the consort of Shiva, is an example of the female force. She has numerous manifestations. Like Shiva, she can be benign (as Parvati) or destructive (as Devi, Durga, and Kali). Kali represents her most terrifying form: black, half naked, wearing a garland of human skulls, with her red tongue hanging from her mouth. Often you see Kali standing on a motionless Shiva. This image represents the universe, where everything is relative—static and dynamic. Shiva without Kali is incomplete, lethargic.Tantrics believe that through meditation; through a series of mysterious rituals; and, above all, through the mystical power of sexual union, you can realize nirvana. They compare human existence to the lotus. The root comes from mud; the flower represents perfect beauty. You cannot achieve nirvana without emerging from the dark. A six-sided star on a temple represents the union of the female and male forces. The female triangle points down; the male triangle points up. Their union represents nirvana and the cosmos. The points on the male triangle also stand for Brahma, Vishnu, and Shiva—the Hindu trinity. The points on the female triangle symbolize the consorts Sarasvati, Lakshmi, and Parvati.

The pagoda style of the temples has meaning, too. The two roofs represent the female triangle moving up to merge with the male. The stanchion in the center of each triangle points the way to enlightenment and stands above the temple's inner sanctum, which enshrines the sacred idol. The Nepalese flag also has two triangles. The one on top with the crescent moon represents the female energy; the lower triangle with the sun is the male.

The erotic art on many Hindu temples also depicts the tantric division of the human body into seven *chakras* (centers of energy). One must master the sexual urge at the site of the lowest chakra before one obtains enlightenment. Erotic art is always outside a shrine. Each female image stands for a vowel; each male represents a consonant. If you line up the figures on a temple, they spell out a prayer to the deity in the inner sanctum. Inside the shrine, you usually find a carving of a lotus.

The swastika, a symbol associated so irrevocably with Nazism, is actually Sanskrit for "well-being" or "doing good for all." Its four arms stand for pure love, compassion, happiness, and indifference, the qualities that lead both Buddhists and Hindus to salvation.

A GOOD WALK

This is a circular walk through Old Kathmandu, although you may find yourself sidetracked along the way by the lively market. Start at **Makhan Tole,** a street heading diagonally northeast of Hanuman Dhoka Square. Walk to the first of three squares, **Indra Chowk.** This is a shoppers' paradise. Four stone lion–styled dragons on a second-story balcony guard the tile-covered **Akash Bhairav Temple** (the ground floor has shops). En route to the second square, Kel Tole, you will pass numerous salesmen of brass ornaments, saris, sweaters, and shawls for both the local and tourist markets. In Kel Tole you will find the **Seto Macchendranath Temple** set behind a massive gate guarded by two dragons and small Buddha on a pillar. Pigeons are fed here, and their cooing fills the air like chanting. Keep walking down the street to get to Asan Tole, the third and busiest of the squares. It has numerous small temples. The most interesting is the three-story **Annapurna Temple,** dedicated to the benign aspect of Durga. Take a sharp left turn, and head due west for Bangemudha Square (there is a sign for the square), where you will find **Vaisha Dev,** a tree to cure toothaches. If you turn left at the tree and continue walking down this street, you will return to Indra Chowk.

TIMING

Give yourself an hour. If shopping, you could easily spend two hours wandering the streets.

SIGHTS TO SEE

Akash Bhairav Temple. The yellow and blue tile inlay on the front of this building makes it look like a pizzeria, but it is really a temple dedicated to the wrathful aspect of Shiva. Non-Hindus can go inside but are not allowed into the inner sanctum, which contains a silver head of Yalambar, a king whom legend claims Krishna beheaded during the Great Battle described in the Hindu epic *Mahabharata*. The head of the fallen king, whose eyes look up to the sky (the meaning of "Akash"), was enshrined here and he soon assumed the status of a god, called Akash Bhairav. ⊠ *Indra Chowk, Old Kathmandu.*

Annapurna Temple. Hindus say this goddess of abundance lived in the Indian plains and longed to see the mountain named in her honor. A priest offered to take her to Kathmandu. She turned herself into a *kalash* (sacred vessel), and he placed her here by a tree. Parts of the tree and kalash are enshrined in the inner sanctum. ⊠ *Asan Tole, Old Kathmandu.*

Indra Chowk. Here street vendors sell everything from *Pashmina* shawls to *pote*, which are colorful glass bead necklaces. Throw in some fresh flowers and garish plastic ones, live dogs and barking stuffed dog toys, and you have the marvelous hodgepodge of Indra Chowk. It is named in honor of the Hindu king of the gods, Indra, who is revered as a rainmaker. ⊠ *Old Kathmandu.*

OFF THE
BEATEN PATH

Store owners in Thamel or Durbar Marg will try to sell you overpriced pote, but it is much more fun to buy these necklaces in the colorful market where the locals purchase them. There are numerous stalls, mainly owned by Muslim descendants of Kashmiri traders who worked the trade circuit here 300 years ago. The **Pote Pasal** is a small market area on the southeast section (to the right of the road heading toward Thamel) of Indra Chowk. Pote are worn by married women in the hill areas of Nepal. You can also buy *dhaago*, or tassels, here. These are woven into long hair; red is the color that indicates a woman is married.

Makhan Tole. The ancient trade route to Tibet ran through this square, and *Makhan*, which means butter, was once sold here. Now you will find everything from fruit to *thangkas* (Buddhist scroll painting). Many consumers say this is one of the best places to price and learn about thangkas. ⊠ *Old Kathmandu.*

Seto Macchendranath Temple. This is one of Nepal's holiest and most ornate temples. Inside are bronze statues of the goddess Tara holding a lotus. The temple has metal banners hanging from the pinnacle of its gilded roof. Called *dhvajas*, these banners, which decorate many temples, provide a pathway to heaven. Behind the gilded doorway is the inner sanctum, which holds an image of the Seto Macchendranath. Buddhists revere this idol as Avalokitesvara, Hindus, as a manifestation of Shiva. And so, it is draped with *katas* (white scarves) by Buddhists and orange or yellow garlands by Hindus. ⊠ *Kel Tole, Old Kathmandu.*

Vaisha Dev (Toothache Tree). There are hundreds of coins nailed into this tree, which protrudes from the side wall of a corner shop. According to local lore, those who hammer in an offering are cured of their dental sufferings. The tree is hard to spot, you might have to ask locals to point it out. Bits of metal nearly obscure the tree and the golden statue of the deity that sits on an altar beside it. ⊠ *Bangemudha Square, Old Kathmandu.*

NEED A BREAK?

If you are craving sweets as a reward for all your walking, consider stopping by at **Kilroy's of Kathmandu** (⊠ Box 10542, Jyatha, Thamel, ☎ 01/250440). Thomas Kilroy, the chef, has made desserts for Bill Clinton, George Bush, Princess Diana, and Queen Elizabeth II, not to mention a host of models, rock stars, and movie stars. The butterscotch caramelized bananas with local rum and chocolate ice cream should be banned or labeled "diet destroyer," it is so good.

Dining

All of the major hotels have Western and Nepali restaurants. Outside the hotels, chefs range from internationally renowned gourmets to trekking guides who know how to bake cakes on open flames. You can dine on the familiar or indulge in boar, quail, duck, and buffalo. Avoid the side-alley dives: the kitchens are as dirty as the dining halls.

It is difficult to describe the exact locale of each restaurant, because there are no numbered streets and, often, there are sections of towns without named streets. Don't worry, taxi drivers know where nearly all of the major restaurants are located; and if they don't know the exact address, they'll usually go out of their way to find it for you; just give them the phone number.

Asian and Indian

$$$$ ✕ **Bhanchha Ghar.** For Nepali cuisine, go to this three-story Newari house, east of Durbar Marg in Kamaladi. Dinner includes rice, mixed vegetables, pickled tomatoes, and chicken served with a rich gravy. What makes the meal special is the black lentils, or *calo daal*, prepared with purified butter and Tibetan herbs. The most exotic offering, though, is the wild boar dish, popular among meat eaters for its rarity. The restaurant can seat more than 200 people, so it is great for big groups. Diners sit on cushions on the floor and watch a cultural dance show. Head south on Durbar Marg to Kamaladi. Turn left before you reach the clock tower. Bhanchha Ghar is on the right; there is a prominent sign out on the busy street. ⊠ *Box 3011, Kamaladi,* ☎ *01/225172. Dinner reservations essential. MC, V.*

$$$$ ✕ **Koto Restaurant.** There are two Koto restaurants in Kathmandu, one is on Durbar Marg near the Hotel De L'Annapurna, the other is in Thamel. The Durbar Marg restaurant is more expensive. Both are simply appointed with bamboo and kimonos, and both serve up startlingly delicious sushi, despite Nepal's landlocked geography. Another surprising delight is the boiled salmon and vegetable soup served in a pot. The salmon is shipped in and it is fresh. Even the miso soup is perfectly seasoned. If you are a vegetarian, the cook will make any of the dishes without meat. The Nepali waiters speak English and Jap-

anese. Perhaps the best recommendation for this restaurant is that it is frequented by repeat customers from Japan. ⊠ *Box 1137, Durbar Marg,* ☎ *01/226025 Durbar Marg, 01/256449 Thamel. Dinner reservations essential for Durbar Marg restaurant. MC, V.*

$$$$ ✕ **Krishnarpan.** You can choose between 6-, 9-, 12-, and 16-course Nepali meals at this restaurant in the artwork-laden Dwarika's Hotel. The six-course meal of three starters, a soup, lentils, vegetables, and pickles, plus dessert and tea is a nice mix, particularly favored by vegetarians. Plan to spend at least four hours for the 16-course meal, which includes various meats, fish, fruit, and dessert. Don't plan on eating anything else that day. Dining here in the hotel's beautifully carved interior is an experience. You can pretend you are royalty. ⊠ *Box 459, Dwarika's Hotel, Batisputali,* ☎ *01/470770. Dinner reservations essential. AE, MC, V. No lunch.*

$$$$ ✕ **Naachghar.** In 1885, Bir Shumsher-Jung Bahadur Rana, one of the more powerful Rana Maharajahs, created this fanciful Nepalese neoromantic theater, with cherubs and columns of plaster work, gilt mirrors, red velvet, and marble imported from Italy to India then transported on porters' backs to Nepal. Now there are nightly performances of Nepali folk and classical dances that enthrall diners and make this restaurant a must-visit. Dinner is pure vegetarian, made up of Indian and Nepali dishes collected from the Rana's own palace cookbooks. The spices are toned down a bit to appeal to Western taste buds, but nonetheless, Nepalis rave about the curries. ⊠ *Hotel Yak & Yeti, Durbar Marg,* ☎ *01/248999. Dinner reservations essential. AE, DC, MC, V.*

$$$$ ✕ **Nanglo Chinese Room.** Opened in 1978, this was the first upscale, independent Chinese restaurant in Kathmandu. The room is red and dim, and somehow the paper shades and fans are not tacky. Call at least two hours before dinner if you want to try their specialty: *jacok,* a shared dish of chicken, duck, pork, meatballs, prawn, soybean curd, mushroom, and vegetables served with boiled rice. Usually, even the pickiest of eaters can find something in the pot they like. (Then go to the Utse Restaurant [☞ *below*] to try the Tibetan version of this dish.) Known as Nanglo's, this restaurant is near Yeti Travels (☞ Contacts and Resources, *below*), and is often cited as a landmark on Durbar Marg. ⊠ *Box 3904, Durbar Marg,* ☎ *01/222636. Dinner reservations essential. AE, MC, V.*

$$$ ✕ **Baan Thai Restaurant.** This quiet, simple restaurant on the second floor, across from the Yak & Yeti entranceway on Durbar Marg, serves Thai food as good as you will find in Bangkok. The curries are spicy, but some say the best you will find in town. The fried chicken, pork, and tenderloin are good choices if you do not want to incinerate your mouth. The service is friendly. ⊠ *Box 5196, Durbar Marg,* ☎ *01/243271. AE, MC, V.*

$$$ ✕ **Utse Restaurant and Bar.** One of Kathmandu's oldest restaurants,
★ this Jyatha landmark has been serving Tibetan dishes to regular customers for more than 25 years. Diners are treated to specialties, beyond the usual *momos* (vegetable- or meat-filled dumplings that are fried or steamed) and rice fare. Try the Gacok for two: a mixed pot of mutton, eggs, shrimp, chicken, carrots, peas, cauliflower, and black mushrooms, served with fried rice, noodles, and steamed, meatless momos. For this dish, call and order two hours in advance. (Go to Nanglo Chinese Room [☞ *above*], and try the Chinese version of this dish.) The Utse is in Jyatha, on the left if you are walking from the Thamel taxi stand. It is past Kilroy's restaurant (☞ *below*). ⊠ *Utse Hotel, Jyatha, Thamel,* ☎ *01/226946. Dinner reservations essential. MC, V.*

$$ ✕ **Third Eye.** The Third Eye specializes in Tandoori and Muglai dishes
★ and is a favorite among overland travelers fresh from India. The Tandoori chicken has a kick; it will clear sinuses blocked by Kathmandu

smog. If you order the whole chicken, you might think you are going to take some home with you, but you will probably end up devouring it all. The setting is dark and decorated with local art: thangkas, paper lights, and handicrafts. You can choose from regular tables, or take off your shoes and enter the multilevel room with low tables and thick, soft cushions. You might want to take the beautifully cut wooden tables with you, if only you could carry them on the plane. If you do not want Indian food, they also serve steaks, chicken, and spaghetti dishes. ⊠ *Thamel,* ☎ *01/260478. AE, MC, V.*

$$ ✕ **Yin Yang Restaurant.** In the heart of Thamel, across from the Third Eye restaurant, Yin Yang offers tables set in a quiet garden outside the kitchen. For a more formal dinner, you can sit upstairs, inside the pitched-roof restaurant, with dim lights and linen tablecloths. The *Phad Thai,* fried noodles with tofu, is authentic; but if you are arriving from Thailand, you might find the curries are not spicy enough. Entrées usually include a cup full of rice and a bowl of vegetables, curries, or meats; your plate will be full but not overflowing. The chef is Thai, but the waitresses wear saris. You can also go here for buffet breakfast, and get real coffee, but do not order it later in the day, when it's often stale leftovers from the morning. ⊠ *Thamel,* ☎ *01/425510. AE, MC, V.*

International

$$$$ ✕ **Kilroy's of Kathmandu.** This 1998 addition to the restaurant scene ★ is a jewel that raises the level of dining in Kathmandu. The Irish co-owner, Thomas Kilroy, does not look like he needs to shave yet, but then again, when he was 21, he was the youngest pastry chef ever to be employed at Mosimann's Dining Club in Belgravia. He left the upscale European restaurant world after a trek in the foothills of Everest. Now, Kathmandu diners can delight in tuna salad Niçoise with a citrus vinaigrette, new potatoes, quail eggs, and crunchy green beans. If you are homesick, try Granny Maddens' Irish Stew, with perfectly softened potatoes and onions. The French onion soup is unmatched in Kathmandu, and you would be hard-pressed to find a better bowl in Paris. If you do not want Continental, check out the Indian restaurant. There is an entirely separate kitchen cooking up these delights. Kilroy's is on the left-hand side of the street, halfway down the road from the Thamel taxi stand. ⊠ *Box 10542, Jyatha, Thamel,* ☎ *01/ 250440. Dinner reservations essential. MC, V.*

$$$$ ✕ **Wunjala Moskva.** This exquisite restaurant defies categorization, as ★ its specialties are Newari *and* Russian, ranging from caviar to boar. You can start with the *zakuski,* a platter of assorted Russian salads with cheese and an egg topped with caviar. Then switch cultures and try duck meat cooked with ginger, which is a popular dish served during wedding receptions. This is a particularly appropriate meal at the restaurant, given that "Wunjala" means "Welcome the bride." For dessert, do not miss the *duru mari,* a saffron-flavored milk cake, a favorite among Newari royalty. The key to this restaurant is to order a variety of dishes, as servings are rich but small. The fixed dinners are the best way to sample the food, but you need to make reservations for them a day in advance. The serene seating is either in *bhatis,* individual brick patio-type houses, or inside the main building, overlooking the garden. The food is authentic (there is a Russian cook), and the women owners are attentive, making you feel like a welcomed guest to a party, rather than a mere customer. It's opposite the police headquarters, near Mike's Breakfast, in Naxal. ⊠ *Naxal,* ☎ *01/415236. Dinner reservations essential. MC, V.*

$$$ ✕ **The Coffee Shop.** Part of the Hotel De L'Annapurna, on Durbar Marg, this is a good, safe restaurant. It is crowded at breakfast, when you can order the normal Western selection of cereals, eggs, and yogurt, or something more substantial, like grilled lamb chops served with grilled

30

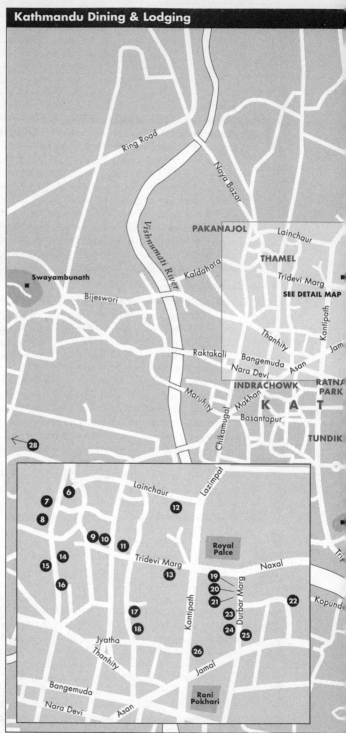

Kathmandu Dining & Lodging

tomatoes and hash browns. For the Indian palate, order stuffed paratha, which is Indian bread with a stuffing of potatoes, cottage cheese, or lentils, and served with yogurt and pickles. It is a good restaurant to start with, as you get acclimated to Nepali food. ⊠ *Box 140, Durbar Marg,* ☎ *01/221711. AE, DC, MC, V.*

$$$ ✕ **Nanglo Café & Pub.** A *nanglo* is a flat round tray, woven from bamboo, used for sifting grain. You will probably see it in the countryside, because it is an indispensable part of every Nepali kitchen. Hence the name of this restaurant that opened in 1976. Favored by wealthy expats and the Nepalese and Tibetan elite of Kathmandu, the restaurant has lovely garden seating. The pizzas are pan-pizza thick; a small one fills a cake plate and, at 80 Rs., is a great deal for lunch. Try the steak Italian with french fries and egg. The tangy Italian sauce is flavorful, the beefsteak is filling, and the bar fries may look as thin as fast-food fries but they are very tasty. The fixed Nepali lunch is served with a Sagarmatha-size pile of rice, and favored by the Nepali clientele. Service is fast and friendly. The café is near Yeti Travels, on the Hotel De L'Annapurna side of Durbar Marg. ⊠ *Durbar Marg, Box 3904,* ☎ *01/222636. AE, MC, V.*

Western

$$$$ ✕ **Kokonor.** Walk up the wooden spiral staircase in the Shangri-La Kathmandu Hotel to the airy room overlooking the garden. Sink into the comfy chairs, listen to the soft piano music in the background, and you might not want to leave. The fettuccine with cream and garlic is nicely blended, and the spinach, mushroom, and cheese crepes are rich. Meat eaters should try the roast leg of lamb, perfectly spiced with garlic and rosemary. ⊠ *Shangri-La Kathmandu Hotel, Box 655, Lazimpat,* ☎ *01/412999. Dinner reservations essential. AE, MC, V. No lunch.*

$$$$ ✕ **Simply Shutters.** After you are finished shopping at Babar Mahal
★   or a long day sightseeing, kick back and read the latest regional newspapers and magazines (there are always multiple copies) while you wait for your liver paté, followed by spiral pasta in hot olive oil, with well-browned garlic cloves and sautéed spinach and mushrooms. Or perhaps you prefer herb-roasted quail, or chicken legs and thighs flame-cooked in red wine with mushrooms and bacon. The ingredients always seem to be of the highest caliber and flavorful, but delicately balanced so as not to overpower one another. This is a restaurant that would flourish in the toughest of markets anywhere in the world. Leave room for dessert, particularly the rich chocolate terrine served with raspberry sauce. In fact, it is worth a trip just for dessert. ⊠ *Box 1166, Babar Mahal shopping complex,* ☎ *01/253337. MC, V.*

$$$ ✕ **Fire and Ice.** Opposite the old immigration building on Tridevi Marg, by the taxi stands of Thamel (ask a taxi driver, if you do not see the sign), this restaurant is one of the few in town that is frequented by locals, travelers, families, lovers, and expats. It serves thin Italian pizza that is delicious plain or with the meat, olive, and vegetable toppings. The ice cream is soft, but imported from Italy, and in season it is served with strawberries. With Pavarotti playing in the background, an unfailingly friendly waitstaff (despite working seven days a week), and birds chirping along the garden side of the restaurant, this is a relaxing lunch or dinner stop. ⊠ *Sanchaya Kosh Bldg. 219, Tridevi Marg,* ☎ *01/250210. No credit cards.*

$$$ ✕ **Mike's Breakfast.** Despite its name, go anytime to this garden-oasis
★   restaurant with relaxing classical music. The Mike's Special will fill you up: two eggs scrambled with onions, mushrooms, potatoes, cheese, and herbs, served with good toast (from real bread, not the local, thin stuff) or big muffins. For a lighter start, try the granola, fruit, and yogurt. The vegetables and fruit are incredibly fresh and, whenever possible,

organically grown. The coffee is real and generously refilled. Despite the fact that Mike hails from Minneapolis and not Mexico City, the burritos overflow with hot and tangy salsa. Opposite the police headquarters in Naxal, it is about a 15-minute walk from Durbar Marg. Most taxi and rickshaw drivers know the way to Mike's. ⊠ *Naxal,* ☎ *01/424303. No credit cards.*

$$$ ✕ **Northfield Café.** The nice garden and mellow music are signs of this restaurant's original affiliation with Mike Frame of Mike's Breakfast (☞ *above*). These days, the café is no longer connected with Mike, but it is still a good place for breakfast, lunch, cocktails, or dinner. The tostadas with beans and chicken are tasty; the enchiladas are huge. Try the generous country breakfast of two eggs, any style, with home-fried potatoes, toast, butter, jam, and a choice of fried mushrooms, sausage, ham, or liver and onions. As at Mike's, the bread is flavorful, not the dry local variety, and the coffee is real (not instant) and refilled frequently without extra charge. ⊠ *Box 8978, Thamel, next to Pilgrim's Book House,* ☎ *01/424884. No credit cards.*

$$$ ✕ **Old Vienna Inn.** Walk past the delicatessen counter to the back, which looks like an Austrian ski chalet. A favorite is the Hungarian goulash served with bread dumplings and topped with fried eggs and sausage. Or try the Farmer's Feast, a plate of various pork dishes served with sauerkraut and bread dumplings. The Inn is also well known for its bratwurst and Bavarian leberkaese. It is at the entrance to Thamel, just past the taxi stands. ⊠ *Chha-1-705 Thamel Chowk,* ☎ *01/419183. AE.*

$ ✕ **Gourmet Vienna.** There are two main branches of this restaurant, one in Thamel and another in Kantipath. The latter is three-fourths of the way down the street, on the left side, if your back is to the palace. The Thamel branch is in the **Old Vienna Inn** (☞ *above*), halfway between the taxi-stand area and the rickshaw stands. It is on the right if you are walking from Tridevi Marg. Both restaurants are self-service but worth the effort. Try the fried eggs with ham and New York–size bagels with cream cheese or imported butter. For sausages, don't miss the bratwurst and imported salami. Plus, the coffee is real. Both shops are good places to pick up box lunches, if you are headed out for a day of sightseeing or on a long bus journey to Pokhara or the Terai. ⊠ *Chha-1-705 Thamel Chowk,* ☎ *01/419183 Old Vienna, 01/247900 Delicatessen Center. No credit cards.*

$ ✕ **Helena's Restaurant.** Nicknamed "Samsara Place," or place of desire, for the chocolate cake, apple pie, and brownies displayed in the window, this restaurant is a favorite with budget trekkers who have subsisted on nothing but rice and lentils for weeks on end. The spinach quiche takes up three-fourths of a dinner plate, plus it is served with salad and garlic bread. The salads are fresh—crunchy greens, carrots, and tomatoes, all washed with iodinized water, so you do not have to worry about Montezuma's revenge. At any time during the day, try the steak breakfast; it is not top-quality sirloin, but it is tasty. ⊠ *Box 2301, Thamel,* ☎ *01/412135. No credit cards.*

$ ✕ **Pumpernickel Bakery.** This 12-year-old institution always has lines snaking outside and up the side alley, away from the hut where you order your freshly baked breads. The garden is usually teeming with birds and backpackers. The whole-wheat rolls and yak-cheese sandwiches make for good packed lunches. They also serve excellent jasmine tea. ⊠ *Thamel,* ☎ *01/259185. No credit cards.*

Lodging

The options range from hundreds of guest houses to expensive, international hotels. Currently, there is a price war going on in Kathmandu, because more and more high-end establishments have been built in re-

cent years. That means you can bargain when booking rooms, sometimes getting the rate down to nearly half the listed price. Hotels in
the Durbar Marg, Lazimpat, and Thamel areas are all central, so you
will have an easy time hailing taxis at night. But also consider hotels
in Boudhanath and Patan; the air is cleaner than in central Kathmandu, and you are still within 20 minutes of most areas of the city.
The only downside is that taxis will cost slightly more.

In the fall and spring, reserve well in advance. Highly recommended
lodgings are indicated by a star (★). Prices are for a standard double
room, excluding taxes and service charges.

Hotels in Kathmandu have business centers with faxing and computer
service, international telephone service, air-conditioning, television,
free transportation to the airport, travel information, laundry service,
currency exchange, and room service.

$$$$ ⊞ **Dwarika's Hotel.** This hotel is a breathtaking, museumlike complex
★   showcasing traditional Nepali art. It won the prestigious Pacific Area
Travel Association Heritage Award for cultural conservation efforts and
has attracted clients like Prince Charles. The bedrooms are huge, and
the custom-designed furniture, particularly the four-poster king-size
beds, are pieces of art. The bathrooms, with deluxe sunken baths, are
the size of many other hotels' rooms. Near national Heritage sites,
Pashupatinath, and Boudhanath, it is in the heart of the "real" Kathmandu of barbers, tailors, cows in the street, and busy shoppers rush-
ing here and there. This can be an interesting touring experience in and
of itself. Room service here offers only tea, coffee, and snacks, and there
are no TVs in the rooms. ⊠ *Box 459, Battisputali,* ☎ *01/470770,* 𝔽𝔸𝕏
*01/471379. 71 rooms, 1 presidential suite, 2 normal suites. 2 restaurants,
bar, breakfast room, massage, library, meeting room. AE, MC, V.*

$$$$ ⊞ **The Everest Hotel.** Around the corner from the Birendra International
Convention Centre, with an hourly shuttle to center city, this hotel in
New Baneswor is particularly convenient for business travelers meeting at the Centre. At first glance you might be worried: the traffic on
the street is hustle and bustle, and the air is very polluted. Don't fret.
The building is set far enough back from the road to reduce the noise
level and dust. On clear days, you can see all of Kathmandu, Patan, and
Bhaktapur. Ask for a room on one of the higher floors (there are seven)
to get the best view. The carpets are lush, the bedrooms are furnished
with comfortable beds and have marble bathrooms with standard-size
tubs. ⊠ *Box 659, New Baneswar,* ☎ *01/488100; 0800/44–UTELL
U.S.A./Canada; 44/71–413–8877 U.K.; 008/221–176 Australia; 0800/
656–666 New Zealand,* 𝔽𝔸𝕏 *01/490288 or 01/488130. 162 rooms, 6 suites.
9 restaurants and bars, pool, beauty salon, sauna, 2 tennis courts, exercise room, casino, dance club, meeting rooms. AE, DC, MC, V.*

$$$$ ⊞ **Hotel Yak & Yeti.** This former Rana palace is now perhaps Nepal's
★   most well-known five-star hotel. Set back off of Durbar Marg, it is a
quiet oasis with a helpful, friendly staff. Look for the 200-year-old
wooden balcony window in the Durbar Hall. For ambience, choose
the older rooms in the Newari wing, they feature carved wood and local
textiles and look more like bedrooms than hotel rooms. The deluxe
rooms in the Durbar wing are well appointed and more modern. For
sheer decadence, visit the restaurants in the century-old palace wing
with fanciful cornices, chandeliers, and ceilings. If you have $600 a night
to spend, stay in one of the two presidential suites, nicknamed by the
staff as the Richard Gere and Steven Seagal suites for their famous occasional residents. One is Tibetan style, the other Nepali style; both
have incredible woodwork. Perks for business travelers include secre-
tarial and valet service and free airport transfers for guests staying in

an executive suite. ✉ *Box 1016, Durbar Marg,* ☎ *01/248999,* FAX *01/ 227781. 270 rooms, 12 executive suites, 5 junior suites, 1 club junior suite, 2 presidential suites. 3 restaurants, bar, piano bar, 2 pools, hot tub, massage, sauna, steam rooms, 2 tennis courts, exercise room, jogging, casino, convention center. AE, DC, MC, V.*

$$$$
★ 🏨 **Radisson Hotel Kathmandu.** In Lazimpat, near the Royal Palace and many of the embassies and consulates, is this eight-story, redbrick building. The chain was still finishing some rooms at press time, although the hotel was open and already bustling with visitors. You enter a modern, spacious lobby, typical of many hotels around the world. Take the elevator to the plush, carpeted hallways that lead to softly lit rooms (that also have overhead, stronger lighting). Well-carved, Nepali art-influenced wooden tables and local pottery distinguish this Radisson from those at home. Touches like a tea/coffee maker on a marble table, an electric safe, and an ironing board and iron in your closet provide the comfort of familiarity. If you want a suite, consider the Plaza Club Room. It has similar amenities to the Junior Suites, plus a walk-in closet, but it costs $50 less. ✉ *Box 2269, Lazimpat,* ☎ *01/411818 or 800/333–3333,* FAX *01/411720. 172 rooms, 5 junior and garden suites, 2 presidential suites, 22 Plaza Club rooms. Restaurant, 2 cafés, bar, pool, hot tub, massage, sauna, exercise room, convention center, meeting rooms, free parking. AE, DC, MC, V.*

$$$$ 🏨 **Soaltee Crowne Plaza Hotels-Resorts Kathmandu.** Set on 11 acres in Tahachal, a fresh-air suburb of Kathmandu, this spacious, shiny, modern hotel, with marble floors, piped music, and mirrors galore, is Kathmandu's biggest hotel. The rooms are large and furnished with traditional Nepali woodwork. There is intricately latticework on the windows and beautifully carved dark-wood cabinets, writing tables, and headboards. Floor and bedside lamps cast atmospheric lighting. The hotel also has an independent complex with two huge conference halls and a fully trained conference support team that makes it an attractive convention site in South Asia. There's a regular downtown shuttle. ✉ *Box 97, Tahachal,* ☎ *01/272555; 800/465–4329 U.S.A./Canada; 0800/897– 121 U.K.; 800/221–066 Australia,* FAX *01/272205. 283 rooms, 15 suites. 3 restaurants, coffee shop, outdoor café, bar, pool, beauty salon, sauna, Turkish bath, tennis court, exercise room, casino, convention center, meeting rooms. AE, MC, V.*

$$$ 🏨 **Hotel De L'Annapurna.** From the outside, this is a 1960s-era, architecturally uninspiring building, but inside, it is back to the princely past. The luxuriousness of this hotel is definitely in its dark-wood lobbies, lounges, and bars, all designed with fanciful roofs, intricate carved wood, marble fountains, and huge chandeliers. Most of the sitting areas look out onto one of the city's largest swimming pools. The rooms are a bit garish, in a Rana-era, almost Victorian way, which can be viewed as grand or not, depending on your taste. They have intricate cornices, gilded wall fixtures, and blond furnishings. The cushioned bedroom window seats are soft and comfortable—they seem to beg for you to kick back and rest. ✉ *Box 140, Durbar Marg,* ☎ *01/221711; 800/ 458–8825 USA and Canada; 0800/282–699 U.K.,* FAX *01/225236. 156 rooms, 71 standard, 81 deluxe, 3 suites, 1 deluxe suite. 2 restaurants, bar, coffee shop, pool, beauty salon, massage, sauna, 2 tennis courts, exercise rooms, billiards, casino, convention center. AE, DC, MC, V.*

$$$ 🏨 **Malla Hotel.** In Lekhnath, near the Royal Palace and bustling Thamel, this hotel has an enviable front garden of birds-of-paradise. Inside, you can relax in a lounge decorated with art deco–esque lamps and modern, curving couches. The bedrooms are decorated in shades of mauve, with massive theater-style curtains. The furnishings are standard hotel-style, but comfortable and in good condition. You can choose a room overlooking the garden or a room overlooking the pool.

✉ *Box 787, Leknath,* ☎ *01/418383,* FAX *01/418382. 125 rooms, 50 executive rooms, 20 suites. 3 restaurants, bar, coffee shop, pool, beauty salon, hot tub, sauna, steam room, exercise room, convention center. AE, MC, V.*

$$$ ⊞ **Shangri-La Kathmandu.** With an expansive fragrant garden, exquisite pool fashioned after a 16th-century royal bath, and a cozy fireplace bar, the Shangri-La lives up to its ethereal namesake. The establishment is known for its friendly staff and fastidious cleanliness (you can usually smell the polish and spy the staff shining their brass nameplate). The well-lit, modern rooms secure the hotel's top-notch reputation in Kathmandu. Rooms overlooking the garden are the best. The hotel is close to the Japanese and American embassies. ✉ *Box 655, Lazimpat,* ☎ *01/412999,* FAX *01/414184. 72 rooms, 4 suites. 2 restaurants, bar, outdoor café, pool, beauty salon, health club, sauna. AE, MC, V.*

$$ ⊞ **Bluestar Hotel.** Near the bridge across the Bagmati River to Patan, this hotel is in a very polluted section of town, and the exterior is in need of a paint job. Inside, it has decor that beautifully blends Hinduism and Buddhism; copper statues, prayer wheels, and wooden pillars fill the white marble lobby. The rooms are large, but the halls are dark and, in many areas, are also in need of a paint job. The service is sometimes slow. ✉ *Box 983, Tripureshwar,* ☎ *01/228833,* FAX *01/243473. 100 rooms, 5 suites. 3 restaurants, bar, indoor pool, exercise room, squash, convention center. AE, MC, V.*

$$ ⊞ **Hotel Marshyangdi.** A location on the outskirts of Thamel lets you stay close to the busy center without being bothered by street noise. The staff is friendly and helpful, which is one reason why many travelers return. The rooms are small and furnished with a simple vanity desk, two upholstered chairs, a cocktail table, and a bed with an upholstered headboard. The place is not fancy and looks a bit like a highway hotel. Still, the backyard garden café, rooftop restaurant, and bar are all peaceful getaways. The hotel is around the corner from the Kathmandu Guest House, toward Kekhnath Marg, which leads to the Royal Palace. ✉ *Box 13321, Paknajol, Thamel,* ☎ *01/414105,* FAX *01/410008. 55 rooms, 4 minisuites. Restaurant, bar, outdoor café, babysitting, meeting room. AE, MC, V.*

$$ ⊞ **Hotel Sherpa.** You will not forget you are in Kathmandu if you stay here. Buddha eyes are painted on the elevator doors, and the red-velvet-covered headboards have Buddhas carved into their wooden moldings. The rooms have Formica desks and television stands, but the mirrors have dragon heads and Buddha images on their frames. To round out the garish decorating scheme, the cornices are gold trimmed. Once criticized for not having a pool, the hotel now has one with a waterfall on its second-floor roof. The staff is friendly, and the rates are lower than those of neighboring establishments on Durbar Marg. ✉ *Box 901, Durbar Marg,* ☎ *01/227000,* FAX *01/222026. 87 rooms, 9 suites. 3 restaurants, bar, pool, beauty salon, sauna, exercise room, baby-sitting, meeting rooms. AE, DC, MC, V.*

$$ ⊞ **Hotel Sunset View.** Snuggled on a hill, down a winding street from the bustling, dusty New Baneswor road, this deceptively small hotel is a relaxing paradise of ponds and Japanese gardens tucked into nooks and crannies. The hallways to the rooms are a bit cold in the winter, but the rooms themselves are well heated and simply furnished with small beds. You can ask for a room with a minikitchen. Management caters to a 50% Japanese, 50% American clientele and is very helpful with tourism advice, directions, and hotel services. The hotel shop is not overpriced and has some unique Nepali arts and crafts for sale. ⊠ *Box 1174, New Baneswor,* ☎ *01/482172,* FAX *01/482219. 28 rooms, 2 suites. 2 restaurants. AE, MC, V.*

$ ⊞ **Hotel Utse.** When you walk into this warm hotel on Jyatha Road in the Thamel area, one of the first things you see are huge murals of Tibet. The thick carpets and polished woodwork create a rich country-club atmosphere. The staff treat their clients like old friends, greeting and sending off guests with a white kata, or scarf, which is a traditional Tibetan custom. Staying at Hotel Utse is like living with a loving family who change the linen daily. Stay in the deluxe rooms: they have televisions and bathtubs. There's satellite TV in the lobby, and a rooftop garden that provides a nice spot to relax. ⊠ *Jyatha, Thamel,* ☎ *01/257614,* FAX *01/257615. 50 rooms, 8 with bath. Restaurant, library, laundry service, business services, airport shuttle. AE, MC, V.*

$ ⊞ **Kathmandu Guest House.** This Thamel institution, with its colonial-★ style architecture, is a second home to mountain climbers, business-people, social workers, and vacationers. The best rooms are in the south wing, overlooking the ever-blooming garden. The staff is very helpful and will treat you like you are staying in a far more expensive hotel, which is amusing since the place got its start serving hippie, overland travelers. Very basic rooms with attached bath are available in the old wing for less than $15. Rooms with air-conditioning are double the standard price. Unexpected perks at such an inexpensive place include laundry service, currency exchange, and a travel desk. It is almost always busy during the high season, so book well in advance. ⊠ *Box 2769, Thamel,* ☎ *01/413632,* FAX *01/417133. 120 rooms. Restaurant, 2 outdoor café-bars, beauty parlor, laundry service, business services, meeting room, travel services. AE, MC, V.*

Nightlife and the Arts

The Arts

There are free cultural shows, which usually include traditional dancing and costume-and-mask performances, at 8 PM every night at the **Bhanchha Ghar** restaurant (⊠ Kamaladi, ☎ 01/225172). Head south on Durbar Marg to Kamaladi. Turn left before you reach the clock tower, Bhanchha Ghar is on the right, and there is a prominent sign on the street. Also at 8 PM daily are shows at the **Naachghar** restaurant (⊠ Hotel Yak & Yeti, Durbar Marg, ☎ 01/248999). There are also shows at the **Hotel Sherpa,** next door to the Yak & Yeti (⊠ Durbar Marg, ☎ 01/227000).

You can also watch Nepali dancing at the **Hotel Marshyangdi** (⊠ Paknajol, Thamel, ☎ 01/414105), every night at 7:30. The hotel is around the corner from the Kathmandu Guest House, toward Kekhnath Marg, which leads to the Royal Palace. Of course, at all of these places you are encouraged to eat dinner as well. **Wunjala Moskva** (⊠ Naxal, ☎ 01/415236) has a nice, candlelit, outdoor stage for music and costumed dances. When there are large crowds, the owners book performances, so call and inquire. The restaurant is near Mike's Breakfast and the police station, in Naxal.

Nightlife

Most bars open at 4 PM. Prices at the luxury hotels are reasonable by
Western standards, but expensive by Nepali standards. If you go to the
Thamel area bars, be careful heading back to your hotel after 10:30
PM. There is technically a curfew at this hour, which is why late-night
bars will often close their front doors, but let customers in and out
through back doors. In reality, the curfew is imposed on Nepalis as
opposed to foreigners, but the result is desolate streets at night. Anec-
dotal evidence suggests that assault after dark is still rare but on the
increase. If you are not staying in the Thamel area, it is probably wiser
to drink at your hotel bar after 11 PM.

Along the walls of **The Rum Doodle** (⊠ Thamel, ☎ 01/414336) are cutout
"Yeti" footprints signed by travelers and mountain climbers who have
visited the bar over the years. Look for the signatures of Sir Edmund
Hillary, Reinhold Messner, and even Jimmy Carter. The restaurant section opens at 10 AM, but drinking begins at 4 and lasts until 10. **Tom
& Jerry** (⊠ Thamel, across the street from Pilgrim's Book House, ☎
01/262956) is a smoky, two–pool table, cable-sports-airing "bar" bar.
Happy hour is every day from 5 to 8, with free salted popcorn to make
you thirstier. If you ever wanted to fall out of a saddle, check out the
saddle-seat bar stools at the **Rodeo Express** (⊠ 15–6 Babar Mahal Revisited, ☎ 01/264074), a saloon-style bar at the Babar Mahal Revisited shopping complex. It's open daily, 11:30 AM–10 PM.

Casinos

Just think "easy" if you want to remember the names of the hotels housing the big casinos. They are in the Everest Hotel, the Hotel De L'Annapurna, the Soaltee Crowne Plaza Hotels-Resorts Kathmandu, and
the Hotel Yak & Yeti. Frequented primarily by Indian travelers, the
casinos let you gamble around the clock to the accompaniment of Indian and Nepali pop music. **Casino Anna** (⊠ Durbar Marg, ☎ 01/
228650) opened in 1992 in the Hotel De L'Annapurna. The **Casino
Everest** (⊠ New Baneswor, ☎ 01/488100), in the Everest Hotel, is nearest the airport, if you need a quick getaway. **Casino Nepal** (⊠ Tahachal,
☎ 01/270244), in the Soaltee, is the oldest of the bunch, open since
1968. **Casino Royale** (⊠ Durbar Marg, ☎ 01/228481) is the smallest
but the classiest; it is in the Yak & Yeti.

Shopping

You can buy handicrafts from Nepal, Tibet, India, and Thailand in Kathmandu. Traditionally, shops are open six days a week, from 10 to 6,
and closed on Saturday. However, more and more tourist-oriented
stores are open on Saturday.

Ask about what you are interested in purchasing at several places to
get a general bargaining price. While shopkeepers usually do not double the price of an item, it is never a bad idea to counter with half the
proffered price, just to make sure.

Markets

For basic Nepali handcrafts, Thamel has a good selection. You can find
some incredible buys here on quality jewelry as well. But as a rule of
thumb, for jewelry, the quality and price go up on Durbar Marg,
where there are dozens of stores surrounding the upmarket hotels. **Babar
Mahal Revisited** is a former Rana era palace complex of seven historic
courtyards and lanes that has been turned into a shopping and dining
paradise: it is upscale, but not overpriced. Best of all, the sales pitches
are low key and low pressure. Unlike Thamel and Durbar Marg, which
are within walking distance from one another and from most hotels,

you need to take a taxi to Babar Mahal Revisited (about 100 Rs. from Durbar Marg). Many taxi drivers know where it is, but you might want to take a map of Kathmandu with you to show the driver.

Specialty Stores

ARTWORK

The **Bamboo Gallery** (✉ Maharajgunj, ☎ 01/412507), across from the American embassy, exhibits and sells paintings, drawings, and sculptures by local and internationally known artists. You can also buy artistic greeting cards, flowering plants, and (but, of course?) fresh strawberries. You will find unique Nepalese, Tibetan, and Oriental art at **Avanti at Babar Mahal Revisited** (✉ Babar Mahal Revisited complex, ☎ 01/262454).

CARPETS

If you want Tibetan carpets, visit **Tsering's Carpets** (✉ Tsering Ngokhang, ☎ 01/215271, FAX 01/523391), opposite the Tara Guest House in Thamel. Tsering is usually open in the afternoon, but it's a good idea to call or fax ahead to let him know you are coming. He only deals in quality carpets and will take the time to honestly explain to you why a carpet is valuable or why it is not.

CLOTHES AND JEWELRY

For high-fashion, designer women's clothing, go to **Yasmine** (✉ Durbar Marg, ☎ 01/227864), across from the Hotel Yak & Yeti entrance way on Durbar Marg. For hand-painted silk garments try either **Green Tara Boutique** (✉ Tridevi Marg, ☎ 01/423466), across from Fire and Ice restaurant (☞ Dining, *above*), near where the taxis drop you off in Thamel, or **Mandala Art & Boutique** (✉ Thamel, ☎ 01/419523), on the corner before the Kathmandu Guest House (☞ Lodging, *above*). These sister shops also sell leather goods, exquisite jewelry, and perfume oils. Both shops are open Sunday–Friday 9:30–7:30 and Saturday 11:30–7:30.

HANDICRAFTS

A good place to find and price local handicrafts—from jewelry to statues to clothing—is **Amrita Craft** (✉ Thamel, ☎ 01/240757), near the Kathmandu Guest House (☞ Lodging, *above*). If you cannot find exactly the size and style of what you want in this fixed-price store, at least you will get an idea of how much to bargain it down to in the dozens of surrounding shops.

HANDMADE PAPER

There are some unique lamp shades, books, and stationary at **Paper Moon** (✉ Babar Mahal Revisited complex, ☎ 01/416968), where the designs are far more artistic than the typical examples displayed in the Thamel area. Also consider the **Calligrafic Print Gallery** (✉ Chha-2-68 Thahiti, Kwabahal, ☎ no phone). This tiny shop, entered by climbing a ladder to the second floor, is next to a bangle and bindi shop. It's near the end of the road, on the right, and has handmade paper goods hanging from its shuttered windows.

Outdoor Activities and Sports

Ballooning

Take a one-hour hot-air balloon flight to see the red-tile rooftops of houses, the spires of temples, and the domes of stupas in the Kathmandu Valley. The season is from September through April. You can reserve a flight on **Balloon Sunrise Nepal** (☎ 01/424131) through a travel agent, or directly, at the booking office in Lazimpat, near the American Embassy. The cost is $195 per person, per flight (they accept major credit cards), including hotel transfers, breakfast after the flight, and the all-important balloon flight certificate.

Golf

The **Gorkarna Forest Golf Resort** (☎ 01/450444, E-mail: gorkarna@mos.com.np) has an 18-hole, par-72 course designed by Gleneagles Golf Developments. Greens fees are $40 on weekdays, $50 on weekends. You can hire clubs for $10, shoes for $5, and a caddy for $3. Your hotel should be able to direct taxi drivers to this exclusive golf club that is beyond Boudhanath, in Rajnikuni Forest, Thali. The **Royal Nepal Golf Club** (☎ 01/472836) is adjacent to the airport, so you are not going to get a quiet round of 18. It charges $18.50 for greens fees, $7.50 to rent clubs, and $2.25 for a caddie. There is a one-stroke penalty for monkeys stealing your golf ball.

Mountain Flights

Many of the domestic airlines operate mountain flights that take you right up next to the summit of Everest, so you can reach the top of the world without ever breaking a sweat. Weather permitting, **Buddha Air** (☎ 01/542494) makes nine flights daily from Kathmandu, between 7 and 10 AM. The usually clear morning skies are best for viewing the mountain. A one-hour flight costs $99. You can book through a travel agent or the airline; book two to three days in advance during high season. The copilots sometimes duck their heads, so you can photograph over and around them. Helicopter flights can cost as much as $1,000 an hour but are an exciting way to get extremely close to the summits. Contact **Karnali Air Service** (☎ 01/488553).

Yoga

Breath control and yoga therapy classes are offered three mornings a week at the **Pilgrim's Book House auditorium** (✉ Thamel, ☎ 01/424942, FAX 01/424943), next to the Kathmandu Guest House (☞ Lodging, *above*). The classes cost about $3 per person; stop by for schedule information. The **Himalayan Buddhist Meditation Centre** (✉ Kamaladi, ☎ 01/221875) also has weekly yoga and meditation courses. Call for schedules and directions. The **Kopan Monastery** (☞ Boudhanath, *below*) also offers yoga classes.

Kathmandu A to Z

Arriving and Departing

BY PLANE

You will arrive at the **Tribhuvan International Airport** (☎ 01/471933) in Kathmandu, which is the only international airport in Nepal. It is about 7 km (4½ mi) from the Royal Palace, in the hub of Kathmandu. Do not be alarmed by the broken-down airplanes and helicopters on the side of the runway. They have been there for years. Domestic flights also leave from this airport.

When reconfirming your flight, do not call between 1 and 2:15 PM; it is lunch hour until 2, then the phone is usually busy until 2:15. The main airlines servicing Nepal are: **Aeroflot Russian Airlines** (☎ 01/227399), **Air France** (☎ 01/223339), **Austrian Airlines** (☎ 01/241470), **British Airways** (☎ 01/222266), **China Southwest Airlines** (☎ 01/419770), **Delta Air Lines** (☎ 01/220759), **Gulf Air** (☎ 01/430456), **Indian Airlines** (☎ 01/410906), **Japan Airlines (JAL)** (☎ 01/222838), **Lufthansa** (☎ 01/223052), **Necon Air** (☎ 01/480565), **Northwest Airlines** (☎ 01/410089), **Qatar Airways** (☎ 01/256579), **Royal Nepal Airlines Corp. (RNAC)** (☎ 01/220757), **Singapore Airlines** (☎ 01/220759), **Thai Airways** (☎ 01/224387), and **Transavia Airlines** (☎ 01/247215).

Domestic airlines are: **Buddha Air** (☎ 01/418864), **Cosmic Air** (☎ 01/246882), **Gorkha Airlines** (☎ 01/435121), **Lumbini Airways** (☎ 01/483381), **Necon Air** (☎ 01/480565), **Royal Nepal Airlines Corp. (RNAC)** (☎ 01/226574), and **Yeti Airways** (☎ 01/421215).

Domestic helicopter charters: **Asian Airlines Helicopter** (☎ 01/423273), **Cosmic Air** (☎ 01/246882), **Dynasty Aviation** (☎ 01/414625), **Fishtail Air** (☎ 01/485186), **Gorkha Airlines** (☎ 01/487033), and **Karnali Air Service** (☎ 01/488553).

Between the Airport and City: Most hotels provide complimentary airport transfers. Ask your travel agent if someone will meet you at the airport. No Western-style limousines are available in Nepal. If you want a Mercedes-Benz to transfer you to and from the airport, make arrangements with your hotel or travel agent; basic rates range from $4 to $12.

The Airport Queue Taxi Service Management Committee operates a fixed-rate (200 Rs.) taxi service from the airport to the city. The stand is on the left, once you exit the airport doors. If you are a patient, hard bargainer, you might be able to convince a taxi driver to take you to center city (Durbar Marg, Lazimpat, Kantipath, or Thamel areas) for 150 Rs. This is still more than it would cost by meter. You could try to convince the driver to take you by meter, but you probably will not succeed. Even if you do, he will likely drive the long, scenic way.

Be warned: throngs of anxious taxi drivers will try to lure you to their taxi and their brother's hotel. Hopeful children will try to load your bags into a taxi for a few rupees or foreign coins. If your travel agent or hotel service is meeting you at the airport, these guides will try to shield you from this aggressive behavior.

Getting Around
BY AUTO RICKSHAW
Most are polluting, uncomfortable, three-wheel rides called Tempos, although there are a few electronic, environmentally friendly, automated rickshaws. While the vehicles have meters that start at 5 Rs., the drivers will usually only negotiate fixed prices with visitors. The fixed price will be cheaper than a taxi, but the massage you will need afterwards will cost more.

BY BICYCLE RICKSHAW
These are fun for short distances. Like auto rickshaws, they can be bumpy rides, but it is worth the experience. From the higher vantage point of your slippery leather seat, you can see more of the hustle and bustle than you can in a car or auto rickshaw. They are great for the downtown alleys (around Durbar Square, for example). As a norm, when bargaining beforehand, you can offer half of what the bicycle rickshaw driver asks you to pay. If he absolutely says no, your offer is too low. Remember, though, these guys pedal for a living.

BY BICYCLE
As traffic and pollution continue to increase in the city, biking is becoming less viable. Nonetheless, sometimes it is still faster than public transportation. Be aware that although there are no bike racks in town, you have to find places to lock your bike, otherwise it will be stolen. Fences and railings are the best bet. **Bikeman** (✉ Jyatha-Thamel area, near Kilroy's restaurant [☞ Dining, *above*], ☎ 01/240633) rents bikes, from basic wheels to mountain models, for $3 to $10 a day.

BY BUS
The local buses do not have fixed schedules, but instead leave when they are overflowing with people. The services are fairly frequent from

dawn to 8 PM. City buses leave from the **City Bus Park** at the eastern side of Tundikhel Parade Ground. In addition to being overpacked and extremely polluted, these buses are notorious pick-pocketing grounds.

BY CAR

Do not even think of renting your own car. In Kathmandu you are not allowed to rent and drive your own vehicle. Although, technically you can drive outside of the valley, you need nerves of iron and a sixth sense for what other Nepali drivers are doing to drive in Nepal. Horns are signals. Brakes are optional. You must compete with cars, motorcycles, bicycles, rickshaws, tractors, cows, elephants, goats, dogs, porters carrying towering loads strapped across the forehead that are balanced on their backs, and pedestrians, all of whom think they have the right of way around the craters on the rubble-strewn roads. Traffic police speed up and seem to congest the roundabout areas, and in arguments, traffic rules apply after the fact. It is better to take public transportation; these drivers know the roads are horrendous, but at least it is all normal to them.

BY HIRED CAR WITH DRIVER

Travel agents will arrange hired cars to drive you around Kathmandu and nearby sites. Prices vary from $20 to $65 for a full day of sightseeing. After 6 PM, though, agencies will charge more. Some charge as much as $1 per kilometer (½ mi), others $5 per hour, others an extra flat fee. Shop around. Also, ask if the driver speaks English and in the spring and summer, ask if the car has air-conditioning. While taxis are cheaper, hired cars are often more comfortable vehicles.

BY TAXI

Taxis in Kathmandu as a whole are affordable by Western standards. By day, metered taxis start at 7 Rs. and then charge 2 Rs. for every 200 meters. At night, the rate starts at 9 Rs., plus 4 Rs. for every 200 meters. Some meters suspiciously seem to run faster than others. For sightseeing, it is best to negotiate a fixed price. Ask a local how much a trip should cost. Usually (although there are always exceptions) the drivers of the green taxis will not argue about using their meters for shorter trips, and you will probably find it is easier to bargain a reasonable fixed price with them. The white taxis and bigger cars seem to have the most overpriced fares.

Taxis are available at hotels and at taxi stands in shopping areas and can be flagged down from the street. To flag an empty cab down, extend your arm at chest level and wiggle your fingers, palm down. Do not whistle or yell. Theoretically, you can phone the **Night-Taxi Service** (☎ 01/224374), but you will be hard-pressed to reach an English-speaking attendant. At night, or by day (if you are going off the beaten path), simply ask a driver to wait for you. Definitely do this at night, if you are visiting a restaurant that's not at a $$$$ hotel or if you travel outside the Durbar Marg, Jyatha, and Thamel areas. About 400 Rs. for a four-to-five-hour wait is a reasonable fare for traveling within the city; 300 Rs. to 600 Rs. for a full day of taxi driving is a reasonable fare for traveling within the city.

BY TEMPO

These eight-seat, three-wheeled, minitrucks are cheap (2–5 Rs.) but dangerous. The pickpockets are professional.

Contacts and Resources

CURRENCY EXCHANGE

You can exchange money in the airport's international arrivals terminal, at the **Himalaya Money Exchange** (☎ 01/491313); the counter is to the right, after you enter the customs area. When departing Kathmandu, you can reconvert your currency in the international terminal at the **Nabil Bank counter** (☎ 01/228538), to your right, just inside the main entrance. It is next to the counter where you must pay your departure tax.

Your hotel will probably have a foreign-exchange desk. However, the rates may be more favorable in Thamel. Among the numerous stalls that exchange cash and traveler's checks in Thamel, **Zenith Money Exchange** (☎ 01/411676), across the street from the Vienna Inn, is open daily 8:30 AM–10 PM, and **Kantipur Money Exchange** (☎ 01/428876), near the Third Eye and Yin Yang restaurants, is open daily 8:30–8. **Nepal Grindlays Bank Ltd.** (☎ 01/22933), around the corner from Tridevi Marg, about 100 meters onto Kantipath, is open Sunday–Thursday 9:45–3:30, and until 12:45 on Friday. It handles cash advances on credit cards and charges no commission.

If you need to replace a lost or stolen **American Express** or **Thomas Cook** card or traveler's check, contact the offices at **Yeti Travels** (✉ Durbar Marg, ☎ 01/221234). They're open Sunday–Friday 10–1 and 2–5. The American Express division is not in the main office but in **Hotel Mayalu** (☎ 01/227635), around the corner on Jamal; hours are the same.

EMBASSIES AND CONSULATES

The **Australian Embassy** (✉ Bansbari, ☎ 01/371678) is beyond Ring Road on Maharajganj Road. It's open weekdays 8:30–1 and 1:30–5 (no afternoon hours on Fri.). The **British Embassy** (✉ Lainchaur, ☎ 01/410583) is next to the Indian Embassy on the road that juts to the left from the base of the Lazimpat street. It's open weekdays 8:15–12:30 and 1:30–5 (Fri. only until 3:15). The **Canadian Embassy** (✉ Lazimpat, ☎ 01/415193) is near the Shangri-La hotel and is open weekdays 8:30–12:30 and 1:30–4:30. The **New Zealand Consulate** (☎ 01/412436) is on Dilli Bazaar. It has no set hours, so call before visiting. The **United States Embassy** (✉ Panipokhari, Lazimpat, ☎ 01/411179) is on Lazimpat, past the Japanese Embassy. It's open weekdays 8–12:30 and 1:30–5.

EMERGENCIES

Ambulance: ☎ 01/228094. **Fire brigade:** ☎ 01/101. **Police:** ☎ 01/100.

For a medical emergency, the **Teaching Hospital** (✉ Maharajgunj, ☎ 01/412303) has a 24-hour emergency room. Taxi drivers know the way. **CIWEC Travel Medicine Center** (☎ 01/242779, E-mail: advice@ciwecpc.mos.com.np), which focuses on the health needs of foreigners in Nepal, is open weekdays by appointment, from 9 to 4, and has a doctor on call 24 hours a day. Emergency visits are available on weekends or after hours for an additional charge. CIWEC is on the road to the Yak & Yeti hotel in Durbar Marg. The **Himalayan International Clinic** (☎ 01/254172), next to Koto's in Thamel, is open daily 9–5 and will provide day-care service for very sick patients and give World Health Organization recommended vaccinations. If you lose or break your glasses, or just want to get a second pair, a good place to go for excellent, inexpensive (under $10) copies of your old lenses and a wide choice of frames is the **Nepal Eye Program Tilganga Eye Centre** (☎ 01/493684, E-mail: tilganga@mos.com.np), in Gaushala near the Bagmati Bridge.

ENGLISH-LANGUAGE BOOKSTORES

Pilgrims Book House (☎ 01/424942, E-mail: info@pilgrims.wlink.com.np), is open daily from 8 to 10. It's to the left of the driveway to the Kathmandu Guest House, if the house is at your back. Pilgrims stocks a huge selection of Himalayan titles and general reading. **Mandala Book Point** (☎ 01/245570, E-mail: mandala@ccsl.com.np) is on the left-hand side of the street, three-fourths of the way up the block, if your back is to the Royal Palace. It has a large selection of regional interest books and is open daily 10 to 7:30 (5 on Sat.). **Tibet Book Store** (☎ 01/415788, E-mail: nepcar@paljor.wlink.com.np), on the outskirts of Thamel, across from the Fire and Ice restaurant on Tridevi Marg, specializes in books on Buddhism and Tibetology. It's open Sunday–Friday 9:30–7. There are also dozens of secondhand bookstores in Thamel worth perusing. In these shops you can find anything from hard-to-find, out-of-date titles to current best-sellers, all for a fraction of the usual cost.

POST OFFICE, TELECOMMUNICATIONS, AND E-MAIL

The **General Post Office** (☎ 01/227499) is open Sunday–Friday 7–5 (only until 3 on Fri.); poste restante is only available until 4. The office is near the Dharahara Tower in lower Kantipath. Mail to poste restante should be addressed: Your name, Poste Restante, GPO, Kathmandu, Nepal. The lines at the GPO can be exceptionally long, hot, and frustrating. Most hotels and telecommunications service shops have mailing facilities. **American Express** at Yeti Travels (☞ Currency Exchange, *above*) will also handle mail sent to you care of American Express. You need to present a traveler's check or American Express card to collect the mail. The address is: Your name, American Express, C/O Yeti Travels Pvt. Ltd., Hotel Mayalu, Ground Floor, Jamal, Kathmandu, Nepal.

If your hotel does not have E-mail facilities, there are many shops in Kathmandu providing Internet service, with a standard price of 6 Rs. per minute. **Cyber Communications Service Centre** (☎ 01/258399) is in Thamel Mall in Jyatha, in the alley next to the side entrance of Kilroy's restaurant (☞ *Dining, above*). It has fast-moving Internet service and a knowledgeable staff, but at press time, only two computers. **Surf Internet Café** (☎ 01/265368) has a friendly staff who work in the Arcadia Complex, upstairs from the Casablanca restaurant, in Thamel. They have six computers.

Guided Tours

The best place to book any trip in the country is in Kathmandu. The capital is home to the most professional and trustworthy agencies. The following companies with multilingual guides provide a full range of services, from booking rooms, to hiring drivers, to setting up trekking and rafting trips. Most agencies are loath to quote prices, because costs vary with the number of people and days and the level of comfort required, not to mention your bargaining skills. Use the listed prices as benchmarks. The agents accept major credit cards, although you may get a better price if you pay cash.

Green Hill (✉ Box 5072, Lazimpat, ☎ 01/428326, ℻ 01/419985, E-mail: ghill@wlink.com.np) has an office to the right of the driveway to the Kathmandu Guest House, if you are facing the entrance. You can sightsee in the Kathmandu Valley for $25 per person, per half day; $35 per person, per full day. Trekking costs $20–$30 a day per person, with stays at teahouses, which are the Nepalese version of B&Bs. Rates are $40–$60 a day for a full-service camping trip, which includes tents, meals, porters, and guides.

Himalayan Journeys (✉ Box 989, Kantipath, ☎ 01/226138, ℻ 01/227068, E-mail: hjtrek@mos.com.np) is in Kantipath, before the Mandela Book Point shop, three-fourths of the way up the street on the left side, if your back is to the Royal Palace. This 21-year-old agency will charge from $545 to $640 for two people on a six-day trip (transportation and luxury accommodation included) touring Kathmandu City, Patan, Swayambhunath, and Bhaktapur, then flying to touring Pokhara, before returning to Kathmandu.

Natraj Tours & Travels (✉ Box 495, Kamaladi, ☎ 01/222906, for Kathmandu Guest House office, or 01/417083, FAX 01/227372, E-mail: natraj@vishnu.ccsl.com.np) was established in 1967 in Kamaladi but also has an office in the Kathmandu Guest House (☞ Lodging, *above*). Expect to pay about $14 a person to tour Kathmandu Valley sites for a half day, $25 for a full day. If you have a group of four to nine people, the price drops to $7 for a half day and $10 for a full day. A six-day, full-service, tented trekking trip for one or two people is about $65 a person. The price drops to $50 a person on 21-day or longer trips. Be warned: land transportation is in public buses.

Saiyu Travel Pvt. Ltd. (✉ Box 3017, Durbar Marg, ☎ 01/221707, FAX 01/226430, E-mail: saujai@mos.com.np) is a 17-year-old, established, full-service travel agency that will arrange tours around the city, book flights, and make hotel reservations. Expect to pay about $20 per person for a half-day tour and $40 per person for a full-day tour in the Kathmandu Valley. This agency's trekking company, staffed with professional guides, is called **Jai Himal Trekking Pvt. Ltd.** Rates are about $60 a day for a full-service, tented trekking trip, and $40 a day for a teahouse trip, not counting park fees. The company also owns **Safari Adventure Lodge**, a luxurious resort just outside of Royal Chitwan National Park. A two-night stay including all meals, transportation, and wildlife activities is a relative bargain at $175 per person.

Special-Interest Tours
BIKING
Bikeman (✉ Box 3380, Jyatha, Thamel, ☎ 01/240633, E-mail: bikeman@singnet.com.sg) is near Kilroy's restaurant (☞ Dining, *above*). It's run by professional, nice guides who will rent you anything from a $3-a-day local bike to a $10-a-day imported mountain bike. Tours include guides, meals, and accommodations.

Himalayan Mountain Bikes Tours & Expeditions (✉ Box 12673, ☎ 01/434560, FAX 01/419237, E-mail: bike@hmb.wlink.com.np), in the Northfield Café complex in Thamel, provides anything from half-day city tours for $18 to all-inclusive 21-day trips to the Tibet border, ranging in price from $995 to $2,000. Established in 1988 by an Australian, the company uses 1997-model Bianchi mountain bikes. It provides helmets, guides, mechanics, accommodations, and meals on its package trips.

TREKKING AND RIVER RAFTING COMPANIES
Equator Expeditions (✉ Box 8404, ☎ 01/424944, FAX 01/425801, E-mail: equator@mos.com.np) has two Thamel offices, to the left and right of the Kathmandu Guest House (☞ Lodging, *above*). The company provides a minimum of two safety kayakers on all river trips, plus one Western guide in peak season, with first-aid and EMT qualifications. Expect to pay anywhere from $65 to $110 for a two-day Bhote Kosi trip, depending on the number of people in your group and where you book it. (It is considerably cheaper to book your trips with this company in Nepal, rather than internationally.) If you want to hire a trekking guide, expect to pay $35 to $53 per person, per day, depending on the number of people and the mountain range.

Exodus Outdoor Enthusiast (✉ Box 5041, Thamel, ☎ 01/251753, FAX 01/259244, E-mail: exodus@visitnepal.com) maintains an office in Thamel, across the street from the DHL office. The guides-owned rafting company, established in 1995, will not let you raft or kayak unless you attend their safety lecture the night before. They raft all the major rivers, with guides who have 5 to 15 years of experience on Nepal's rivers. Expect to pay $100 per person for a three-day rafting trip on the Kali Gandaki, $400 per person for a 12-day Karnali float.

Himalayan Encounters (✉ Box 2769, Thamel, ☎ 01/417426, FAX 01/417133, E-mail: raftnepl@himenco.wlink.com.np) maintains an office in the Kathmandu Guest House compound. Originally connected to London-based Encounter Overland, this rafting and trekking company with 40 full-time staff members who speak English, was one of the first to forge the rivers in Nepal. You can book trips as diverse as a three-day rafting adventure on the Seti for $130 per person, or an eight-day Machhapuchhare and Mardi Himal trek for $325 per person. If you want to climb a trekking peak, consider Mera Peak, which costs about $965 per person, with a group of six climbers, not including domestic flights or climbing and regional permits. If you just want to hire a trekking guide, expect to pay $23 to $27 a day, depending on the region.

Ultimate Descents (✉ Box 6720, Thamel, ☎ 01/419295, FAX 01/411933, E-mail: rivers@ultimate.wlink.com.np) is at Northfield Café, in Thamel. Running rafting trips for more than 14 years, this veteran white-water rafting company has explored and led some of the first descents on rivers in Nepal. A six-day trip on the white-water Marsyangdi, which means "raging river," is $220. If you want an action-packed challenge in just two days, try the Bhote Kosi for $70; the company has a base up near the border of Tibet. Or you can take a four-day kayak clinic for $150.

Travel Agencies

Himalayan Travel & Tours Pvt. Ltd. (✉ Box 324, ☎ 01/223045, FAX 01/224001, E-mail: bks@htt.mos.com.np) is on Durbar Marg, on the left-hand side if your back is to the Royal Palace.

Yeti Travels (☞ Contacts and Resources, *above*) is on Durbar Marg, on the right-hand side if your back is to the Royal Palace.

Trekking Permits and Visa Extensions

Trekking permits, once an integral part of the adventure, are no longer required except for treks to the restricted areas of Dolpo and Kanchenjunga. For these treks, you can get your permit at the **Department of Immigration** (☎ 01/494273) in Kathmandu. Note that you must have a valid visa for the entire length of your stay; a trekking permit does not replace a visa. For a small fee ($10–$15), most travel agencies will handle this bureaucratic hassle for you.

You can also extend your visa at the Kathmandu immigration office. Payment for visa extensions and permits must be in Nepalese rupees; the exchange rate is in accordance to the rate published by the Nepal Rastra Bank, which is published daily in the *Kathmandu Post*.

The Department of Immigration office is no longer on the outskirts of Thamel. It has moved to New Baneswar. Taxis know the way. Visa extension applications are accepted Sunday–Thursday from 10 to 1:30, and Friday from 10 to noon. You can pick up your passport Sunday–Thursday from 3 to 5, or Friday between 2 and 3. It's a good idea to get to the office before it opens, because the lines snake out the door as the day wears on. Do not expect the officials to actually begin work at 10 AM—they usually sip their tea first. It is also better to pick up your passport closer to closing time, otherwise you might end up waiting at the office again, while the bureaucrats complete the forms and drink more tea. During high season, bring a novel or a newspaper to pass the time on the queue. Tasty Hot Bread's Gourmet Vienna deli across the street sells good bagels, bread, beverages and snacks. It is open during Immigration office hours.

Visitor Information

The **Himalayan Rescue Association** (✉ Jyatha, Thamel, ☎ 01/262746, E-mail: hra@aidpost.mos.com.np) gives lectures Sunday–Friday from

2 to 3 on altitude sickness and trekking safety. They also give good weather updates for the high mountain passes and outlying areas. They are on the second floor of Thamel Mall in Jyatha, across the street from the side entrance of Kilroy's restaurant (☞ Dining, *above*).

The **Nepal Tourism Board** (✉ Bhrikuti Mandap, ☎ 01/256909, FAX 01/256910, E-mail: ntb@mos.com.np) has general information on Nepal. The office is at the exhibition ground, off Exhibition Road, across from the city bus park. If you are coming from Durbar Marg, head south; you will pass the clock tower on your left, then Ratna Park on your right, followed by Tudikhel. Exhibition Road is then on your left; the office is in an impressive, huge red building. At press time, most of their brochures were general information from the Nepal '98 tourism campaign, and the agency had no maps to offer. The travel director at your hotel may be of more assistance. Also, check out *Travellers' Nepal,* which is distributed for free at the airport, major hotels, and embassies. The Tourism Board maintains an information counter at the Tribhuvan International Airport, which is open every day from 9 to 5 (☎ 01/470537). It also has an office at Basantapur, near Durbar Square (☎ 01/220818), that is open Sunday–Thursday 9–6, Friday until 4.

Phone numbers change frequently in Kathmandu, to everyone's eternal frustration. However, local **directory assistance** is relatively helpful. Simply dial **197.**

AROUND KATHMANDU VALLEY

The Kathmandu Valley is often labeled a "living museum." There is certainly plenty to see. In the poorest sections, where you would expect life to be drab, you will find houses with potted plants set along the ledges, a pride and beauty that brightens life. Brilliant, jewel-color saris cascade down from window sills, drying in the wind. If you are wondering what all the posters and hand-painted signs of suns and trees are that cover everything from banks to homes to rocks and trees, they are the symbols of political organizations, leftover billboards from campaigning. Some question why locally produced mailing envelopes do not have the same heavy-duty glue as these slogan-laden posters.

In the mornings, little boys and girls walk single file along the road, dressed in school uniforms, the boys' hair freshly watered down to their foreheads, the girls' onyx locks tied in pigtails with big grosgrain ribbon bows. Children are often tucked between mom and dad on motorbikes, or they ride in front of dad as if they are driving the bike. Usually the kids have wacky, neon-color sunglasses to block the dust from getting in their eyes. The women, wearing *saris* or Tibetan *chubas* (wraparound dresses that are a uniquely practical ethnic costume) ride sidesaddle on the motorbikes, a balancing act only outmatched by the huge piles carried on peoples' heads. A funny sight for sure: men walking ducks or goats on a rope lead, weaving their way around the free-roaming cows who choose to sleep in the road, trucks or not.

This lively backdrop is also home to seven UNESCO-listed World Heritage sites. You can easily visit the stupas at **Swayambhunath** and **Boudhanath,** where there are also large Tibetan populations, then stop down at the *ghats* (platforms) in **Pashupatinath** to see one of the holiest Hindu temples in the region. For a look at centuries-old lifestyles, inspect the architecture at **Patan** or **Bhaktapur Durbar margs,** both are quieter than the **Kathmandu Durbar Marg.** To round out the big sites, make sure to see another Hindu temple, **Changu Narayan,** a favorite for some simply because very few people visit. While touring these im-

Kathmandu Valley

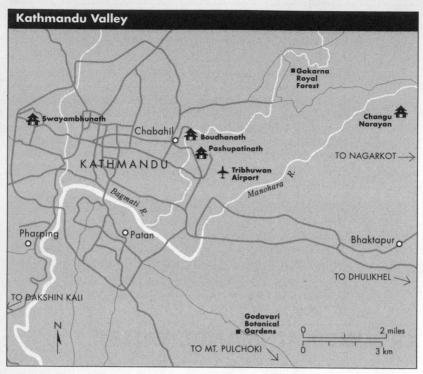

portant architectural landmarks you should also try to get away to a hill station to check out nature's architecture.

Dhulikhel and **Nagarkot** are relaxing weekend escapes from the pollution of Kathmandu, or an excellent place to visit if you have a few days left before going home and do not want to stay in the city. Some tour operators suggest flying into Kathmandu and driving straight out to either of these hamlets. You can reach most sites in Kathmandu in a one-hour drive—enabling you to tour the city without having to live under its cough-inducing cloud. The best time to visit Dhulikhel and Nagarkot is from October through April, when the soaring peaks of the Himalaya are almost always visible. Mountain views are less reliable from May through September, but the monsoon countryside is usually a lush, emerald green, and the spring blooms dot the land in rainbow clusters that attract fluttering butterflies in rival brilliant hues.

It is difficult to squeeze all the sites in, but well worth the effort.

Swayambhunath

2 km (1 mi) west of Kathmandu.

On a hill east of Old Kathmandu stands Swayambhunath, literally "Place of the Self-born," or as called affectionately by the Nepalese, the Monkey Temple, after the swarms of critters who scavenge for food left by devotees. To reach the top, walk up the 365 steps (benches are placed at frequent intervals) on the east side of the hill. You can also drive up the road from the southwest.

After walking through a colorful arch, you head up the steps past statues of the Dhyani Buddhas (Five Cosmic Buddhas) and their animal vehicles, plus small *chaityas* (spires). You walk in the footprints of Manjushri, Tibetan refugees, pilgrims, and the ever-mischievous monkeys. Watch your belongings, these animals are fast.

At the top, crowds of pilgrims circle the 2,000-year-old Swayambhunath and its monastery, which belong to the Nyngma (Old Sect). The large white hemisphere is made of brick and earth; it is called *garbha* (womb) and represents the cosmos. On the top, the gilded copper spire has 13 concentric circles; these represent the steps to enlightenment, here symbolized by an intricate metal umbrella above the circles. Below the all-knowing eyes that look out in each cardinal direction, is what looks like a nose but is really the Nepali numeral *"ek,"* or one. It reminds the devout that they are one with Buddha.

Numbers in the text correspond to numbers in the margin and on the Swayambunath map.

A Good Walk

Swayambhunath is virtually cluttered with historic religious monuments. Start your tour of the complex at the large 17th-century **vajra** ① (thunderbolt). It is placed on a plinth decorated with the 12 animals of the Tibetan calendar. The two white, bullet-shape monuments on either side are the **Pratapura shikhara** and the **Anantaupural shikhara** ②.

Now, focus on the stupa. The small shrine in the wall of the stupa, in front of the vajra, contains the first of the five **Dhyani Buddhas** ③ whose temples encircle the large stupa. It is the Aksobhya (Undisturbed Buddha and Buddha of the East). Walking clockwise, the direction you should always walk in when circling Buddhist monuments, you will find four other Buddhas. Whenever you come to a stupa, if you spot these Dhyani Buddhas, and recognize them by their hand positions or animal vehicles, you will know which direction they are facing, as if the stupa is one giant compass. Next is **Vairocana**, then **Ratnasambhva**, **Amitabha**, and finally **Amoghasiddhi.**

Walking clockwise around the stupa again, but looking at the monuments surrounding it, you will find the **temples of the elements** ④, dedicated to the air, water, fire, ether, and earth that make up the cosmos. First is **Vasupura**, for earth, then **Vayupura**, for air. Continuing around the stupa, you will come to a monastery, the **Devadharma Mahavihara** ⑤. To the right of the monastery, nearly directly opposite the staircase you walked up, you will find the very important **Harati Temple** ⑥.

Now stop your second circumnavigation of the stupa to continue into the northwest courtyard. You will find a platform where once stood another of the temples of the elements, the temple dedicated to the element of fire, **Agnipura**. Continue northwest to the farthest temple away in the compound, this is **Shantipura**, the temple for the sky or space. Now return to circling the stupa and you will find **Nagapura**, the pit temple dedicated to water and the serpents that, according to legend, originally lived in the lakes of the valley. The building on the far northeastern corner, is the **Karmaraja Mahavihara** ⑦, a Tibetan Kargyupa sect monastery built in 1954. Before leaving the compound, note the lookout views from both the northeast and southeast corners; on a clear day you can see all of Kathmandu.

If you leave from the southwest corner instead of from the front steps, there are dozens of shopping stalls set up along the walkway out.

TIMING
Give yourself an hour to circle the stupa twice and spend time viewing the Kathmandu Valley from the lookout areas. Sunset and clear days are the best times to go for an unrivaled view from this hilltop site.

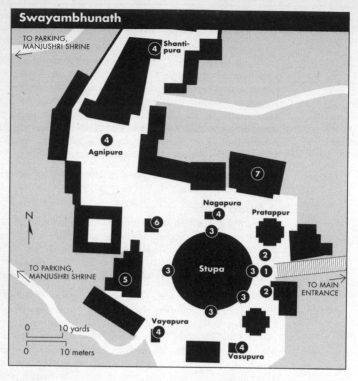

Sights to See

5 **Devadharma Mahavihara.** Founded around 1780, the current monastery is from the Rana period, when it was rebuilt after a fire. Bhutanese Buddhists use this monastery. ⊠ *Swayambhunath.*

3 **Dhyani Buddhas.** The **Aksobhya Buddha** always faces east. His right fingers touch the earth, and his vehicle is the elephant, which is carved into the base of the stupa. **Vairocana** is the Buddha of Resplendent Light and the Buddha of the Eternal. He holds his hands up like a teacher. He is usually in the center of a stupa and not seen, so do not let his absence throw you off at other stupas, when you are trying to figure out the direction. When he is shown, as at Swayambhunath, he usually faces the southeast. His animal vehicle is the lion. His consort, Mamki, is in a shrine to his right. **Ratnasambhava** is the Buddha of Precious Birth and Buddha of the south. His palm is open, and a horse, his vehicle, is carved into his pedestal. Pandara, his consort, is in the shrine to his right. **Amitabha,** Buddha of Boundless Light and Buddha of the west, rests his palms on his lap, as though he is meditating. His vehicle is the peacock, and his consort, Tara, is to his right. **Amoghasiddhi,** Buddha of Infallible Power and Buddha of the north, holds his right hand up, and has the winged Garuda, his man-bird vehicle, set in his base. Locana, his consort, brings you full circle, back to the vajra. ⊠ *Swayambhunath.*

6 **Harati Temple.** Dedicated to the goddess Harati according to Buddhists, and Ajima according to the Newars, this two-tiered temple attracts worshipers for the protection of children against disease. Harati or Ajima is the primal mother and responsible for fertility. This temple is yet another of the many that show an intertwined relationship between important Buddhist and Hindu figures. Saturday and Tuesday are special days when worship here is a crowded event. ⊠ *Swayambhunath.*

❼ Karmaraja Mahavihara. Inside this temple there are hundreds of butter lamps before a large meditating Buddha statue. Usually there are multicolored lights flashing lights around the Buddha, a bit like a Christmas tree. ⊠ *Swayambhunath.*

❷ Pratapura and Anantaupural shikhara. Dedicated to the Vajrayana deities, the two temples on the northeast and southeast of the stupa are in the Indian shikhara style. Both were built by King Pratap Malla in the mid-17th century and were named after himself and his consort Anantaypriya. ⊠ *Swayambhunath.*

❹ Temples of the elements. Vasupura, the goddess of wealth and abundance, adorns this building dedicated to the element earth. The current structure was rebuilt in 1982. **Vayupura** is dedicated to the air. **Shantipura,** also known as Akashapura, is the temple dedicated to the sky. It's named after Shantikar Acharya, a famous monk who worshiped inside. The sanctum, without an image, is accessible only to the Buddhist priests who have learned the tantric practices. Only the platform remains of the **Agnipura** temple dedicated to fire. **Nagapura,** the pit temple, is dedicated to *nagas* or serpents, the original lords of water. ⊠ *Swayambhunath.*

❶ Vajra. The big hourglass-shape structure is supposed to represent a thunderbolt that belonged to the Hindu god Indra, and symbolizes boundless power. It was installed by King Pratap Malla, in the middle of the 17th century. ⊠ *Swayambhunath.*

When you are heading back to Kathmandu, you might consider stopping at the **National Museum & Art Gallery.** Check out the dancing Ganesh, scroll paintings, and bronze statues. ⊠ *Chhauni,* ☎ *01/ 271478.* 🎟 *5 Rs., plus 20 Rs. for cameras.* ☉ *Wed.–Mon. 10–5.*

Or visit the **Museum of Natural History,** west of the stupa (visible from the hill, if you walk down the southwest steps). It has exhibits of stuffed animals, birds, crocodiles, and butterflies. ⊠ *Swayambhunath,* ☎ *01/271899.* 🎟 *10 Rs., plus 20 Rs. for cameras.* ☉ *Sun.–Fri. 10–5.*

Pashupatinath

5 km (3 mi) east of Kathmandu.

Dedicated to Shiva, Pashupatinath (Temple of Living Beings) is the oldest and most holy Hindu temple in Nepal. It is set on the banks of the sacred, but polluted, Bagmati River, a tributary to the Ganges. Historians believe people worshiped here as early as the 3rd century, and there are signs that there was a temple structure here as early as the 5th century. However, much of the present complex was built in 1696.

Legend says that Shiva wanted to escape his heavenly work, so he turned himself into a stag and escaped to the forest here. When the other gods chased him down here, they broke off his horn, which became the Pashupatinath *lingam* (phallus). It is said the lingam was discovered by a cow.

Pashupatinath is an important ritual bathing and cremation site, since the water flows to the Ganges. The ghats (platforms) in front of the temple are reserved for royalty. If you are cremated here, Hindus believe you will be released from the cycle of rebirths. Husbands and wives who bathe together at Pashupatinath will find one another again, and be remarried, in their next lives. For centuries, women committed *sati* here, throwing themselves on their husband's funeral pyres. This practice was outlawed in 1920 by the Ranas.

During Shiva Rati (February or March), pilgrims from all over India and Nepal flock here. If you visit during this festival, which celebrates

Lord Shiva's birthday, you will see half-dressed holy men with dread-locked hair, women in festive, auspicious red saris, and thousands of people stoned on ganja, which Shiva favored. Throughout the year, devotees come to Pashupatinath on pilgrimage. They take ritual baths, or bring cows, goats, and dogs to the shrine. The animals are not sacrificed, but honored with a *tika* (red dot on the forehead), which gives them the right to live undisturbed in the complex, as befits the temple's name.

Although the main temple is open only to Hindus, you can get a good look from the far side of the narrow river. Cross the bridge; as you climb the path, take the first set of stairs on the left. At the end of the terrace, notice the head of Shiva (its nose is missing) carved on a 5th- or 6th-century lingam. From this terrace you can see the walls and the intricate metalwork of the silver doors surrounding the lower level of the two-tier Pashupatinath, which is crowned with gilded roofs. Within the building is a huge Shiva lingam, and outside stands an equally large gilded bull, Nandi, Shiva's mount.

Continue up the path, accompanied by as many monkeys as wandering sadhus (Hindu holy men), and look at the numerous old shrines and small stone lingams. (This is the route to follow if you want to walk to Boudhanath.)

Returning to the far side of the river, head left along the bank, so you are directly across the water from the pyres. The actual cremations are remarkably matter-of-fact. Still, try not to be a voyeur of other peoples' grief. At the end of the walkway, look at the 7th-century head of the Buddha. Its presence supports the theory that this temple was also a Buddhist shrine.

TIMING

You can spend an hour here or a half day sitting on the banks, watching life and death unfold. Many people talk about an overwhelmingly calm energy here.

If you like, you can walk to or from Boudhanath from Pashupatinath. Simply follow the path back up the hill to where all the small shrines are situated. From the top of the hill you can see the Boudhanath stupa. Go beyond the Hindu shrine, and you will come across a few vendors selling garlands. Pass them to cross the suspension footbridge. Follow the path through pastoral settings with scattered hamlets. If you stroll, it will take about 20 minutes to reach the busy street. The path will dump you onto the main road, just left of Gemini Supermarket. Cross the street, and you will be standing in front of the stupa gates of Boudhanath.

Boudhanath

6 km (4 mi) east of Kathmandu.

Called Boudha by locals, this is an important section of the valley, both for its stupa and for the large Tibetan community that has taken refuge here since the Chinese invaded their country.

After you enter the stupa gates, which are flanked by salesmen and beggars, you approach the massive white dome that dates back to AD 600. It is bigger than Swayambhunath and not cluttered with other monuments. You can climb up onto its base and sit and look out at the mountains or the devout doing *kora*, walking round the stupa praying. Their chants are an ever-present murmur in the background of life in Boudha. (Be warned though, the whitewash on the stupa dome sometimes wipes off on your clothes.)

As with most Buddhist structures, the stupa's base is shaped like a *mandala,* a symbol of the universe that serves as an aid to meditation. The five elements appear in its design. The base, earth; the dome, water; the central tower, fire; the umbrella, air; the pinnacle on top, ether. There are 13 rings from the base to the pinnacle, symbolizing the steps to enlightenment, or "Bodhi," hence the stupa's name. There are 147 niches around the outer wall; each one houses four or five prayer wheels. There are also 108 forms of Buddha sculpted into the base.

The exact origin of the stupa is unknown. But, of course, there are legends. One claims that a daughter of Indra stole flowers from heaven and was sent to earth to repent. She arrived as a low-caste poultryman's daughter, but she prospered and built the stupa to honor Buddha. This tale is attributed to Guru Padma Sambhava, who was a well-loved Tibetan evangelist. He also predicted an invasion by a huge enemy which would send the Tibetan people into exile.

The Newaris believe that drought struck Kathmandu during the reign of one of the early Licchavi kings, Dharmadeva. He asked the court astrologers how to end the drought. They said that if a virtuous nobleman sacrificed himself, there would be rain. So the king commanded his son to go to the royal well one moonless night and decapitate the shrouded man he would meet there. When the son found out he killed his own father, he built the stupa to pay homage. This legend is perhaps most interesting for the fact that it is embraced by Newaris, suggesting that they once considered the stupa holy grounds for their own religious purposes.

A third tale says a prostitute asked the king to give her a piece of land the size of a buffalo hide so that she could build a shrine. He consented. She painstakingly shredded the hide and pieced it together in strips, then laid it out to form the huge circumference. The king grudgingly kept his promise and donated the land.

Whatever its origin, today the site is sacred to Buddhists, in particular Tibetan Buddhists. You will see hunched-over, elderly women in *chubas.* You can easily climb mountainsides or forge rivers in this full-skirted dress, without ever flashing your legs to the elements. Men and women wear large, chunky, turquoise or coral necklaces, usually family heirlooms and sometimes the only wealth the refugees were able to take out of Tibet. Many also wear Reeboks or Nikes on their feet, beneath all of this ethnic garb. The braided-haired men with red headbands are likely from the Kham or Dolpo-pa regions, and those walking with ski poles probably recently trekked from Tibet. The teenaged girls wear their chubas as frequently as they wear Western clothes, and more and more frequently henna their hair and cut it short, evidence of the changes occurring in this Tibetan community.

Many of the shopkeepers and hoteliers in the area have been here for nearly a half century and are wealthy and successful. But for all their money, they have no country, no passport, and no right to vote. Juxtaposed with this wealth are refugees who arrived last week, Hindu beggars reliant on the alms of the holy, and hundreds and hundreds of monks. Many of the monks are extremely devout. Some are young boys who were sent to monasteries because their families could not afford to educate them any other way. Amid this are dozens of Westerners flocking to Boudhanath to study Buddhism. The resulting melting pot is well worth watching from a café window or the stupa itself.

If you want to take part in the life of this community, it is easy to do. Chokyi Nyima, abbot of Ka Nying Shedrup Ling Monastery, teaches free courses on Buddhism, open to the public, every Saturday morning. He has a wry sense of humor and an excellent command of English. To get to his monastery, known locally as "the big white one," turn left up the first alley you reach at the stupa after entering the main gate. Walk up the alley until it makes a "Y." Bear right; you will pass a small stall selling soft drinks and several stalls employing children as metalworkers. The first right you can take, turn, and on the left you will see the massive monastery. There are usually a beggar or two out front. In the winter, sometimes Trangu Rinpoche is on hand for teachings at his monastery, the Trangu Tashi Choko Ling. This monastery is also up that first lane, on the first alley jutting off from the stupa to the right. It is a big red monastery. In front of it, on a garbage pit, you might see a huge blue tarp, if you visit between late December and the first week of March. This is the Rokpa International soup kitchen, run by volunteers and financed through donations. It serves nearly 800 hungry people a day, providing breakfast and lunch to anyone who needs it; Rokpa also runs a medical tent, with Western doctors providing free care. Throughout the year it runs a women's workshop, employing women who were previously beggars, and a children's home.

NEED A BREAK?   Stop by one of the stupa-side restaurants for ringside stupa seating. The **Original Stupa View** (☏ 01/480262) is just before the second alley jutting off from the stupa, about one-third of the way around the monument. Food here is slightly pricy for what you get: typical Western, Nepali, and Tibetan trekkers' cuisine. The **Three Sisters** (☏ no phone) café is three-fourths of the way around the stupa and has no phone. The sign says THREE SISTER; the owners recently learned it should be "Three Sisters," but good grammar isn't necessary to make an excellent apple pie. Be sure to sit on the first or second floor; if you go to the roof it can take as long as 30 minutes to get a cup of tea. The coffee at both restaurants is real. If you want authentic Tibetan food and interesting conversation, go to the **Double Dorjee** (☞ Dining and Lodging, *below*).

Try to schedule your visit for sunset, when the locals come out and pray. It is the best time to see how the stupa is still an integral part of community life here. Most tour guides come at noon, when only the shopkeepers and beggars seem to be out on the slate grounds around the stupa. If you do go at dusk, remember that people are praying, not posing for your lens. If you go on a full-moon evening, butter lamps are set up on the walkway, and some of the street kids are employed to oversee the candles. For two to three rupees, you can light one. The absolute best time to be here is during Losar, Tibetan New Year, which usually falls in February or March. Then it's crowded not just with celebrating local Tibetans and their families who have come to visit, but also with other pilgrims to this auspicious site. Tibetan women wear their finest silk chubas. The men wear their best traditional chubas (for men, this is a sheep or yakskin coat) over trousers and silk blouses, although you increasingly see them dressed in Western suits, as well. Not to be outdone, it seems the local Hindu women always don their brightest and most beautiful saris at Losar, too.

From Boudha, you can walk or bike to **Kopan Monastery,** which is 3 km (2 mi) due north of the stupa. The monastery is home to about 260 monks, and a place of study for 150 nuns from many parts of Tibet, Nepal, and India. The nuns live at the Khachoe Ghakyil Ling Nunnery. Meditation courses are held throughout the year at Kopan. ✉ *Box 817, Kathmandu,* ☏ *01/481268,* FAX *01/481267, E-mail: franz@komonpc.mos.com.np.*

Five kilometers (3 miles) to the northeast is **Pulahari Monastery,** where there is a stupa with the remains of the abbot Jamyung Kongtrol Rinpoche. It is another pilgrimage site. Farther afield, about another 9 km

(5½ mi), is **Nagi Gompa,** a beautiful nunnery from which there is an excellent view of the Kathmandu Valley. Locals can direct you to these sites, as well as to the Kopan Monastery. Visitors are sometimes greeted with cups of tea and biscuits. Bring water if you hike to Nagi Gompa: the last stretch is uphill, and there are no teahouses.

Dining and Lodging

$ ✕ **Double Dorjee.** This is where many of the expats living in Boudha eat their regular meals. Tsering, the *amala* (mother) who runs the restaurant, sometimes serves more than a dozen plates of french fries in an hour, arguably the best chips in town. Dimly lit and styled after the comfortable corner eateries that locals dine at, the difference is this is a kitchen accustomed to feeding Westerners. So if you want to try classic Tibetan dishes, like *thukpa*, vegetable noodle soup, or momos, this is a good place to do it. The expats here can also tell you who is teaching what and where. If you walk through the front gate of Boudha, turn down the second alley jutting off the kora circle; the Double Dorjee is the restaurant on the first corner on the right. It is next to a bright-yellow Kodak shop. ✉ *Phulbari Road,* ☎ *01/488947. No credit cards.*

$$$$ 🏨 **Hyatt Regency Kathmandu.** At press time, this hotel planned to open its doors by April 2000. It will have an excellent view of the stupa from its vantage point just down the road, but it should be far enough away from the monasteries to allow for peaceful sleep in the early morning hours. Set on 37 acres of land, it is the biggest, most modern hotel in Boudhanath and brings with it the upscale amenities you expect. All rooms will have hair dryers, safes, minibars, satellite cable television, direct-dial international telephone systems, data ports, and individually controlled air-conditioning and heating. ✉ *Box 9609, Boudha, Kathmandu,* ☎ *01/491234,* FAX *01/490033. 284 rooms, 4 junior suites, executive suite, presidential suite. 3 restaurants, pub, air-conditioning, in-room modem lines, in-room safes, minibars, room service, pool, wading pool, beauty salon, sauna, spa, 2 tennis courts, health club, babysitting, dry cleaning, laundry service, meeting rooms. AE, MC, V.*

$ 🏨 **Happy Valley.** Next to Trangu Gompa in Boudhanath, this gated hotel is run by a very friendly staff who seem to be on a first-name basis with all of their customers. The restaurant, on the roof of the six-story building, provides a perfect vantage point for taking photographs of the stupa. For a room with the best views, ask for one on the fourth floor or above. The two suites are massive, long-windowed rooms, with basic furniture but perhaps one of the best views in all of the Kathmandu Valley. Although you cannot see it from within the sparkling clean hotel, you can't miss the fact when you are entering the hotel: The building is situated across from a garbage dump, which is slowly getting built upon. Don't worry, the scent doesn't waft up to the hotel. As is typical of all of Boudha, you must accept the horns and chants coming from the neighboring monastery. There are no TVs in the rooms, but there's a satellite TV in the spacious lounge. ✉ *Box 1012, Boudha, Kathmandu,* ☎ *01/471241,* FAX *01/471876, E-mail: happy@mos.com.np. 30 rooms, 2 suites. Restaurant, room service, laundry service, airport shuttle. AE, MC, V.*

$ 🏨 **Hotel Padma.** Facing the Boudhanath stupa, this clean, modern-style hotel particularly attracts people interested in Tibetan Buddhism, which flourishes in Boudhanath. The rooms are spacious and decorated in light colors; all have attached bath, television, and telephone. Obviously the best ones are in the front, facing the stupa. Be prepared for the sound of chanting coming from the neighboring monastery early in the morning. ✉ *Box 13823, Boudha, Kathmandu,* ☎ *01/479052,* FAX *01/481550. 12 rooms. Restaurant, room service, laundry service, airport shuttle, car rental. MC, V.*

Shopping

If you are interested in buying a chuba, consider having one tailored for you. **Dorge's Tailoring** is an excellent option. Dorge doesn't speak English or have a telephone, but you can hand-signal your description or ask a Tibetan to help translate. Don't fret about the language barrier; who better to make your chuba than a Tibetan whose expertise is making chubas? He usually can finish clothes in two or three days, so stop by before you take off for trekking, rafting, or a meditation course. From the Double Dorjee restaurant (☞ Dining and Lodging, *above*), continue walking up the road toward Pulahari (away from the stupa) about 1½ city blocks. Dorge's shop is on your left. People in the Double Dorjee can give you directions to the Kailash Hotel, which is directly across the street from the tailor. You will spot Dorge easily: he's the tall, thin, Tibetan hunched over a Singer sewing machine and smiling.

Chabahil

6 km (4 mi) east of Kathmandu.

Chabahil is easy to miss, and unless you absolutely need to see another stupa, you might not opt to stop here. However, if you are wondering what the little stupa on the same side of the street as Boudha is (just 3 km/2 mi to the west), it is Chabahil stupa, or Dhando Chaitya. This site was once the crossing of two major trade routes from India to Tibet, one via Kathmandu, the other via Patan.

Built by King Ashoka's daughter Charumati, the original stupa predated Boudha. According to legend, Charumati saw an iron arrowhead transformed to stone at the site. The stupa that is here today was probably built in the 17th century and seems to be a miniature of Boudha. When the old stupa was opened, ancient manuscripts and statues were found. They were sealed back up into the 17th-century stupa. There are several small chaityas here from the 5th to the 8th centuries. In the southwest corner, there is a 6th-century, 39-inch-high statue of Buddha Shakyamuni, carved in black stone. Perhaps one of the most surreal elements of the Chabahil stupa is that life—in its full zest of honking horns, meandering cows, boys hawking dusters or trying to shine your shoes, men carrying loads, and women shopping for food—continues all around this shrine, as if it were just another building.

Patan

5 km (3 mi) south of Kathmandu.

Tibetan traders once called Patan "Ye Rang" (Eternity Itself). Also known as Lalitpur, it is the oldest of the three ancient city-kingdoms in Kathmandu Valley that were ruled by the Mallas, who created most of the old structures. However, it even predates the Mallas, who ruled from 1200 to 1768. A community was founded by Bir Deva around AD 650.

Records of the early Mallas are scarce. The city was sacked by the Moslems in 1346, and then ruled by Kathmandu kings for several generations. In 1618, under King Siddhinarasimbha, the city became independent. The temples in Durbar Square today date back to his successors Srinivasa and Yoganarendra. As many as 50 Buddhist monasteries were constructed during these kings' rules. However, the Gorkhas captured the city in 1768, and the Hindu conquerors plundered many of the treasures in the Buddhist temples.

Throughout history, the kingdom was linked to Tibet through trade. Today Patan is populated by Newars—two-thirds of them Buddhists—

who are talented artisans who continue to turn out traditional fine arts. Tibetan refugees have settled in the suburb of Jawalkhel.

As in Kathmandu and Bhaktapur, Patan has a Durbar Marg and a maze of winding lanes. Patan's Durbar Square is the quietest of the three in the valley. You can actually walk around it with maps open and mouth agape, and you won't be too hassled by locals trying to pass themselves off as guides.

In addition to the square and surrounding lanes, you can visit the valley's **Central Zoo.** If you have never been to an Asian zoo, this animal jail could be depressing. The cages for the big cats are the size of compact cars. The deer and antelope get relatively spacious, if sparsely planted grounds, more like courtyards than the wild. The rhinos (which tree people in Chitwan) stand at the edge of their stark compound and beg for food; a sorry sight. But there are up sides. There is a lovely green lake, and you can rent paddle boats and tool around the water. Children can take elephant rides (100 Rs. for a 200-meter ride within the park; 3,000 Rs. for a ride outside of the compound) and play at the playground. The zoo is also one of the few places in town where you might see young lovers cuddled next to each other on park benches or walking hand-in-hand. There are more than 106 species of birds, and at least 665 different animals, so you are sure to see plenty. Still, the overriding image may be of the people rattling the lions' cage, despite several signs over cages in the park that ask, "Do you like to be teased? I don't." ☏ *01/521467.* ✒ *60 Rs.* ☻ *Tues.–Sun. 10–5.*

The lodging in Patan is in the quiet, cleaner-aired neighborhood of Kopundol Height, which is close to the sights in Patan and downtown Kathmandu. The backroads leading to the Hotel Greenwich Village and the Summit Hotel are curving, winding roads that seem to turn taxi drivers into Mario Andretti.

Numbers in the text correspond to numbers in the margin and on the Durbar Square Patan map.

A Good Walk
You will probably be dropped off at the Taxi Stand area, so begin your walk there. Circle Durbar Square, checking out the monuments on the left first, then visiting the palace on the loop back. The first temple on your left is the octagonal-shape **Krishna Temple** ①, also known as Chyasim Deval. Farther along is the **Taleju Bell** ②. Behind the temples, beyond the stands selling spices and teas, in the western corner of the square, is the square-shape **Bhai Dega Temple** ③. Moving north on the main walkway of the square, you reach the **Hari Shanker Temple** ④, which you can identify by its three roofs and two stone elephants out front. Due north of it is **King Yoganarendra Malla's statue** ⑤. To the right of the statue is the small **Vishnu Temple** ⑥ and its Narsingha statue. Continuing north, you come to the oldest temple in the square, the two-story, brick **Jagan Narayan Temple** ⑦, also known as the Charnarayan Temple. North of it is the Indian-influenced **Krishna Mandir** ⑧, which has a **Garuda statue** ⑨ on a column in front of it. The two-story temple farther north is the **Vishwanath Temple** ⑩. Finally, at the top of the square, is the well-maintained, gold-roof, three-story **Bhimsen Temple** ⑪, which you will also find in Bhaktapur.

You have completed one half of the square; now, turn around and begin heading south. On the left is the royal coronation pavilion, **Mani Mandap** ⑫. Next to it is the sunken water tap known as **Manga Hiti** ⑬. Now you have reached the beginning of the Royal Palace complex. The first courtyard is the **Mani Keshab Narayan Chowk** ⑭ and is the entrance to the **Patan Museum** ⑮. Snuggled between this courtyard and the

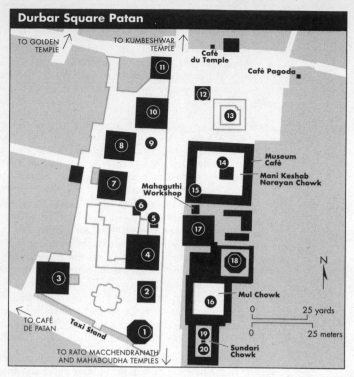

next is the Mahaguthi Workshop. The second courtyard is **Mul Chowk** ⑯, where you can view both the **Taleju Temple** ⑰ and the **Degutalle Temple** ⑱. Finally, the last courtyard is the **Sundari Chowk** ⑲, which houses the **Tusha Hiti** ⑳. Before you enter the courtyard, notice three statues on the front wall, moving from north to south you have: Narsingha ripping open the demon Hiranyakashipu, then the elephant, Ganesh, and last, Hanuman, wearing his familiar red coat with his hand raised.

NEED A
BREAK?

Need some tea? Perhaps lunch? Consider the **Patan Museum Café** (☎ 01/526271), in the museum complex of the Mani Keshab Narayan Chowk, for some excellent vegetable burgers or ham and eggs. If you are on the north side of Durbar Square, and just want a drink with a view, consider the **Café du Temple** (☎ 01/527127) or the **Café Pagoda** (☎ no phone). If you are on the other side of the square, stop by at the **Café De Patan** (☎ 01/537599), southwest of the square. This rooftop restaurant serves a refreshingly spicy (many restaurants in tourist areas serve food with no zip) dish of vegetable chow mein, and large but light momos.

TIMING

Give yourself an hour to wander through Durbar Square. You will need another hour to see the museum; then plan time for a break at either the **Museum Café** or the **Café de Patan** (☞ *above* for both) Finally, you could easily spend another hour wandering the alleys around the Square, where you will find hidden treasures of shrines and monuments.

Sights to See

❸ **Bhai Dega Temple.** Despite its simplicity, this box-shape temple base with a dome on top is supposed to house a valuable lingam. Therefore it is an important place of worship. ⊠ *Durbar Marg, Patan.*

⓫ **Bhimsen Temple.** Dedicated to the gods of trade and business, this three-story brick temple is lined with, appropriately enough, traders selling souvenirs. It is guarded by lions and has a gilded roof and gold dhvaja (banner) on the first floor. Elaborately carved balconies have images of Shiva, Parvati, and Ganesh. It is unknown when it was first built, but according to an inscription it was restored in the mid-1600s. It took a battering during the 1934 earthquake, then was restored and received a face-lift yet again in 1967. Merchants continue to bestow gifts to ensure the temple is well maintained, hence some of the garish "improvements," like the marble facade on the first floor. ⊠ *Durbar Marg, Patan.*

⓲ **Degutalle Temple.** This temple is on the northeastern side of Mul Chowk and has a circular roof. It was originally built in about 1600, destroyed by fire in 1663, and rebuilt to its original specifications. Look for the figures of Ganga and Yamuna (which are also in Mul Chowk) on the carved roof struts. ⊠ *Royal Palace complex, Durbar Marg, Patan.*

❾ **Garuda statue.** This man-bird is Krishna's animal vehicle, so it is fitting that he sits before Krishna's temple. Since Krishna is the eighth incarnation of Vishnu, Garuda is sometimes referred to as Vishnu's vehicle. The statue, which depicts Garuda sitting on a lotus pedestal, was erected in 1647 and is one of Nepal's finest sculptures. ⊠ *Durbar Marg, Patan.*

❹ **Hari Shanker Temple.** This typical Nepali-style, pagoda-shape temple was built in the early 1700s by the daughter of King Yoganarendra Malla and is dedicated to Shiva and Vishnu. It has roof struts with images of tortured creatures—not for the queasy. ⊠ *Durbar Marg, Patan.*

❼ **Jagan Narayan Temple** (Charnarayan Temple). This is the oldest temple in the square, built as early as 1566. It is dedicated to Narayan, an incarnation of Vishnu. It has two large stone lions, Ajaya and Vijaya, on the front steps, which head up to the first plinth. There, two more lions guard the passage up to the second platform, which leads to the inner sanctum. Inside is a lingam supported by four images of Narayan. Erotic carvings on the roof struts apparently depict 84 different positions for sexual intercourse. ⊠ *Durbar Marg, Patan.*

❺ **King Yoganarendra Malla's statue.** This gilded statue of the king, with a cobra looming over his head, and a bird on top of the cobra's head, is the basis of legends. One story says that King Yoganarendra Malla was kidnapped by the King of Bhaktapur, and later killed. But while Yoganarendra was still alive, he sent word to his people that he would continue to live until the bird on the statue flew away, the two elephants guarding the Hari Shanker temple walked off to drink from the Manga Hiti watertap, and a statue of a man with a gun fired it once. To this day, people leave Yoganarendra plates of food and prepare his *hookah* (water pipe).

Another legend says that following the death of the king's son, the king renounced his noble life and became a wandering ascetic. Before leaving, he said that as long as the face of the statue remained untroubled, and the bird remained on the cobra's head, the king would continue to live. That is why his bed was made up for a long time after his departure, and his water pipe is still prepared. Look up at the palace, and you will see a window is left open in case the king returns. Sadly, today the stone base of the statue pillar is marred by political posters. ⊠ *Durbar Marg, Patan.*

❽ **Krishna Mandir.** It took six years to build this temple, commissioned by King Siddhinarasingh Malla in 1637 and dedicated to Krishna. Like the octagonal-shape Krishna Temple, this building is influenced by the Indian shikhara-style temples, with graceful designs cut into the peaked roofs. Inside the shrine stands a black stone image of Krishna with his two consorts, Radha and Rukmani. The second story has sculptures of the nine incarnations of Vishnu. The third story has an image of Shiva. An inscription says that the temple is akin to the sacred Mount Meru, Shiva's home. ⊠ *Durbar Marg, Patan.*

11 **Krishna Temple** (Chyasim Deval). Built by King Vishnu Malla in 1823, note this temple's octagonal shape, which is more like the North Indian shikhara temples than the traditional pagoda-shape Nepali-style temples. ⊠ *Durbar Marg, Patan.*

13 **Manga Hiti.** This sunken water tap shaped like a lotus pool has *makara* (hybrid crocodile-elephant) head–shape spigots. Locals come here to gather cooking, drinking, and washing water—a great spot for a local color photograph. ⊠ *Durbar Marg, Patan.*

14 **Mani Keshab Narayan Chowk.** This courtyard is the northernmost point of the Royal Palace complex. It is also the newest part of the complex, built in 1734, and the location of the Patan Museum. The Golden Gate entrance is a Patan treasure, with three carved windows and a dazzling torana, covered with images of Shiva and Parvati, directly above the gate. In the center window is an image of Vishnu. It is from this window that the king would make appearances. ⊠ *Royal Palace complex, Durbar Marg, Patan.*

12 **Mani Mandap.** This 1700 pavilion is used for royal crownings. ⊠ *Durbar Marg, Patan.*

16 **Mul Chowk.** This second main courtyard of the Royal Palace complex was completed in 1660 by Srinivasa Malla. Its two temples are dedicated to the goddess Taleju. On the right, when you walk into the courtyard, Yamuna (goddess of the sacred Yamuna River) stands on a tortoise, her vehicle. To the left, the goddess Ganga is poised on top of a makara (hybrid crocodile-elephant), her vehicle. ⊠ *Royal Palace complex, Durbar Marg, Patan.*

15 **Patan Museum.** Entered from Mani Keshab Narayan Chowk, this museum specializes in bronze statues and religious objects, and has nearly 200 items. Some of the art dates back to the 11th century. Most of the statues are of Buddha, Vishnu, and Devi, representing both the Hindu and Buddhist iconographies. ⊠ *Royal Palace complex, Durbar Marg, Patan,* ☎ *01/521492.* ⊠ *120 Rs.* ⊘ *Wed.–Mon. 10:30–4.*

OFF THE
BEATEN PATH

Mahaguthi Workshop. Specializing in women's handicrafts, this workshop supports destitute women who otherwise have no commercial outlet or means of support. The sweaters, cards, and paper goods are of excellent quality and are priced competitively with those sold by Thamel salesmen. Their main product is *dhaki,* an intricately handwoven material. You can get strips of it for shawls or tablecloths; it is also used for making men's caps. Over the past decade, more than 20,000 women (mostly Limbu and Rai women of the Kosi hill area) have been employed weaving this material. They work outdoors on wooden and bamboo treadle looms, and they usually know about 100 different geometric designs. ⊠ *Durbar Marg, Patan,* ☎ *01/534091. MC, V.* ⊘ *Sun.–Fri. 10–5:30.*

19 **Sundari Chowk.** It means "magnificent courtyard." This 1620s courtyard is the southernmost square of the Royal Palace complex and site of the Tusha Hiti royal bath. The ground-floor rooms surrounding the courtyard were formerly stables, storehouses, and the barracks of the guards. The upper floors were the living quarters of the royal family. ⊠ *Royal Palace complex, Durbar Marg, Patan.*

② **Taleju Bell.** King Vishnu Malla erected the bell in 1736, so people who wanted a hearing before the king could ring the bell to call him. Soon afterward, the kings in Bhaktapur and Kathmandu copied the idea. ⊠ *Durbar Marg, Patan.*

⑰ **Taleju Temple.** You can see the tip of this temple from Mul Chowk. It is dedicated to Taleju, the personal deity of many of the Malla kings. It was built in 1640 by Siddhinarsingh Malla, then rebuilt after the 1934 earthquake. ⊠ *Royal Palace complex, Durbar Marg, Patan.*

⑳ **Tusha Hiti.** This royal bath in Sundari Chowk is an exquisite creation, with a gold waterspout depicting Narayan (Vishnu) and his consort, Lakshmi, astride Garuda. It is a sacrilege to put your feet on the *naga* (snake/serpent) encircling the tank or to step into the basin. A stone Garuda faces the bath. ⊠ *Royal Palace complex, Durbar Marg, Patan.*

⑥ **Vishnu Temple.** Built in 1590, this temple is dedicated to Narsingha, Vishnu's man-lion incarnation, hence the **Narshinga statue** to its left. ⊠ *Durbar Marg, Patan.*

⑩ **Vishwanath Temple.** Constructed in 1627, this temple has two stone elephants guarding the front entrance and erotic figures on the roof struts. In the back, you will see Shiva's vehicle, Nandi the bull, resting patiently. Many vendors selling masks, statues, and copper goods set up shop along this temple. ⊠ *Durbar Marg, Patan.*

A Good Walk

This walk takes you to the alleys north and south of Durbar Square. Start at the north side of the square, at Bhimsen Temple. Turn left on the road next to this temple and right at the next wide lane. When you come to a passageway guarded by lions, turn left, and walk toward a gate with an image of Buddha. This is **Hiranya Varna Mahavihar (Golden Temple).** From the Golden Temple, walk about four city blocks north toward the river (away from Durbar Square) to see the **Khumbeshwar Temple.** When you head back to Durbar Square from this temple, instead of retracing your steps, turn right (if your back is to the temple complex), then right again at the next lane, onto a lane that leads past more stupas and temples.

When you reach Durbar Square, walk to the southern end and start the tour of the lanes south of the square. Go straight on the busy alley after the square. Walk past copper and brass salesmen for about a block, until you reach the sign pointing down a lane to the right (west) to **Bishwakarma Temple.** Next, on the right side, you will see the **Baha Bahi.** Two blocks farther south, on your left, is the **Minanath Temple.** On your right, down an alley (there are clearly marked signposts pointing the way) is the **Rato (red) Macchendranath.** Now backtrack to the **Baha Bahi.** Turn right at the water pump, and walk three city blocks (follow the signs again), then make a left and another quick left, into the alley leading to the **Mahaboudha Temple.**

Sights to See

Baha Bahi. This wooden-and-brick temple was founded in 1427 and later became a school. From 1990 to 1995, the Nippon Institute of Technology worked with the Nepali government and local artisans to restore the building. Now, locals congregate here again to pray, play cards, and socialize. Two stone lions guard the entrance, usually with two blond dogs curled up beneath the lions' bellies. ⊠ *Patan, south of Durbar Square.*

Bishwakarma Temple. This brick temple is dedicated to artisans and blacksmiths, which may explain the hammered metalwork of brass and copper on its facade. ⊠ *Patan, just south of Durbar Square.*

Hiranya Varna Mahavihar (Golden Temple). This three-story golden pagoda is dedicated to Avalokitesvara and was built in the 14th century, with periodic later additions. It is one of Patan's most handsome structures. You must remove your shoes before you step into the courtyard to examine the small shrine with ornate silver doors and a gilded roof. Inside, you can see numerous statues and chaityas. Look for the little Buddhas peering over the edge of the shrine roof, and listen for the pigeons cooing their own mantra. ⊠ *Patan, just north of Durbar Square.* ▤ *25 Rs.* ☉ *Daily 9–5.*

Khumbeshwar Temple. The bottom two tiers of this five-story, pagoda-style Shiva temple topped in gold date back to the 14th century, making it one of the oldest temples in the country. The top three tiers were added in the 17th century. The temple is covered with carvings associated with Shiva.

Inside the courtyard is a gold Nandi on a brick pedestal. Two lions guard the inner sanctum with its multiheaded image of Shiva dressed in orange and covered in sandalwood paste. Around the complex are other shrines with statues of Vishnu, Surya (the Sun God), the elephant Ganesh, and the goddess Baglamukhi (goddess of poisons), who protects devotees from black magic. The nearby grassy courtyard is a grazing ground for Nandi, as well as for the goats, chickens, and ducks that wander around. Unfortunately, sometimes the stench of urine pervades these pastoral grounds. ⊠ *Patan, just north of Durbar Square.*

Mahaboudha Temple. This tall, pyramid-shape, Indian-influenced temple, built of red brick and terra cotta, was constructed in 1585. It is a replica of the temple in Bodhigaya, India, where Buddha attained his enlightenment. The structure was extensively damaged by the 1934 earthquake and subsequently rebuilt. Unfortunately there were no blueprints, so when the replica of the replica was put together, the artisans ended up with leftover bricks. These "extras" were used in constructing the small chaitya behind the tower. Each brick has a tiny image of the Buddha in his meditation pose or of important scenes in his life. All the oil lamps are dedicated to Maya Devi (Buddha's mother.)

The temple dominates the small courtyard, which is often smoky with incense and filled with the chirping of the birds who congregate around the temple. Unfortunately, the birds often have to compete with Nepal pop tunes blaring from neighboring shops. Despite the jarring accompaniment, the temple is awe inspiring and well worth a visit. ⊠ *Patan, south of Durbar Square.*

Minanath Temple. This gold-roofed temple holds an image of Avalokitesvara, whom Buddhists consider a brother of Macchendranath. The small bronze image of Minanath, which is adorned with clothes, is taken out during the annual procession in his honor. ⊠ *Patan, south of Durbar Square.*

Rato (red) Macchendranath. Macchendranath is another manifestation of Shiva. Constructed in 1408, this temple is a place of worship for both Hindus and Buddhists. During the festival of Red Macchendranath Jatra, the dark-red wood image of Macchendranath, whom many call the guardian of Patan, is taken out of the temple and paraded through the city on a huge chariot. Notice the pigeon feathers inadvertently glued to the temple by the butter-lamp drippings. The pastoral grounds here are rather relaxing, and often you will find shepherds lounging while their charges munch on the grass. ⊠ *Patan, south of Durbar Square.*

Lodging

$$$ 🔁 **Hotel Himalaya.** The white lobby with gilded touches is brilliantly bright. The light color scheme is carried through in the bedrooms, although the hallways are dark. The bedrooms have modern furniture and all the typical international hotel amenities, including fresh flowers and complimentary fruit. Ask for rooms on the upper floors where the views of Patan and Kathmandu are excellent. Set far back off the road, on a hill within walking distance of Patan's old city, it is a quiet hotel. There's a complimentary shuttle into the city. ⊠ *Box 2141, Lalitpur, Kathmandu,* ☏ *01/523900,* ℻ *01/523909, E-mail: himalaya@lalitpur.mos.com.np. 100 rooms, 3 deluxe suites, 3 business suites. 2 restaurants, bar, room service, pool, beauty salon, tennis court, badminton, meeting rooms. AE, DC, MC, V.*

$$ 🔁 **Hotel Greenwich Village.** This redbrick building with a terra-cotta tile roof has an expansive wooden reception desk. Out back, there is an inviting pool set in a nicely manicured garden area. You can have a drink in the nearby redbrick courtyard with wooden pillars that are beautifully carved pieces of art. The rooms also have exquisitely carved closet doors and mirror frames. The bathrooms and the carpets in the bedrooms are clean, but a bit worn. ⊠ *Box 837, Kupundole Height, Lalitpur, Kathmandu,* ☏ *01/521780,* ℻ *01/526683, E-mail: hotel@greenwich.wlink.com.np. 38 rooms. Restaurant, bar, room service, pool, business services, meeting room. AE, MC, V.*

$$ 🔁 **Summit Hotel.** This guest house evokes images of a Raj-era hunting lodge. You can lounge in the junglelike garden sitting area around ★ the pool, or stare at the Himalayas from your balcony built of intricately carved traditional woodwork and tile. The rooms are cozy and comfortable, with madras-covered bamboo chairs, marble baths, and terra-cotta and tile ornaments throughout. Ask for a second-floor room for optimum viewing. There are no TVs in the rooms, but there's a TV and VCR in the lounge. ⊠ *Box 1406, Kupundole Height, Patan,* ☏ *01/521810,* ℻ *01/523737, E-mail: summit@wlink.com.np. 75 rooms, 4 one-bedroom apartments, 2 suites. Restaurant, bar, pool, beauty salon, library, meeting rooms, travel services. AE, MC, V.*

Shopping

Patan is one of the best places to buy handicrafts, especially metalwork. There are literally hundreds of shops, so you can wander and price-check. One way to gauge the quality of statues (metalwork or wooden) is to look at the hands and feet and evaluate how fine the details are on each digit. Expect to pay around 5,000 Rs. for a small statue and 12,000 Rs. or more for larger ones.

For exquisite woodwork, stop by the **Woodcarving Studio** (⊠ Box 2633, Patan, ☏ 01/538528 or 538827, E-mail: asianart@mos.com.np), where Lee Birch, an American artist, has spent more than 15 years developing a wood-carving atelier in Patan. Lee personally seasons all of the groups' wood, which ranges from rosewood to haldu. You can purchase traditional works, like a lattice panel carved with monkeys playing with mangoes, following a Newar design from the Pujari Math temple pillar. Or you can ask for more traditional Western looks, like art deco-style boxes. Lee sells mirrors, boxes, frames, pillars, and other woodwork. The studio is open Sunday–Friday 9–5. On Sunday from noon to 5, Lee holds an open house and gives talks about the tradition of wood carving. If you call ahead on other mornings, she'll arrange a tour for you. A visit here is certainly as much a cultural experience as a tempting shopping spree. The Woodcarving Studio is near the Tibetan

Refugee Camp. Just before you reach the camp, turn right at the fork
in the road with the big tree in the middle. Immediately after (only 30
meters), turn right. You will see the studio on front of you.

Bhaktapur (Bhadgaon)

14 km (8½ mi) east of Kathmandu.

Raja Ananda Malla supposedly created Bhaktapur around AD 889. Some
sources say he designed his kingdom in the shape of Shiva's conch shell,
others claim it was Shiva's drum. Today the original shape is impossible to detect. It seems more like a town of squares connected by a
vein of a road that runs through them all. Unfortunately, many of the
structures in Old Bhaktapur were destroyed in the 1934 earthquake
that wreaked havoc on Nepal. Still, Bhaktapur's beauty and ancient
character remain intact. To help maintain it, you will pay a hefty fee
of 300 Rs. to enter.

*Numbers in the text correspond to numbers in the margin and on the
Bhaktapur map.*

A Good Walk

A large gate flanked by statues of Bhairava and Hanuman leads to Durbar Square. To your left, behind two ornate stone lions, are 17th-cen-
tury statues of **Bhairav** and the goddess **Ugrachandi** ①, a manifestation
of Durga. To your right, as you face Durga, you see another pair of
stone lions that guard the entrance to the **Bhaktapur Art Gallery** ②,
formerly the Royal Palace, which extends nearly the length of Durbar
Square.

The main entrance to the former palace is through the **Golden Gate** ③,
actually copper and gold, which has in the center an image of the goddess Taleju, with three heads and numerous arms. Walk through the
Golden Gate to the entrance of **Taleju Chowk** ④. You can't go inside
the courtyard, because it is closed to non-Hindus, but it is here that
the **Taleju Temple** is located.

Return to Durbar Square and look for two large bells. The smaller of
the two is the Bell of the Barking Dogs. Its high-pitched ring triggers
crooning from canines, which is unusual during the daytime. Normally
Kathmandu Valley dogs only bark *throughout* the night. The larger
bell is the Taleju Bell, which was erected in the 18th century. Hemmed
in by the bells is the Vatsala Temple, dedicated to Shiva and constructed in 1737. Behind the Vatsala Temple is the oldest temple in Bhaktapur, the two-story **Pashupatinath Temple** ⑤.

Head down a short street behind the Pashupatinath Temple to Taumadhi Tole (Taumadhi Square). This is a good place to stop for a drink
of tea or coffee, in one of the many restaurants with window seating
(☞ Dining and Lodging, *below*). The square is dominated by the
tallest temple in Nepal, the **Nyatapola** ⑥. North of the Nyatapola
Temple is the large **Bhairabanath Temple** ⑦.

From Taumadhi Square you have two options. If you head southwest
you will reach Potter's Square, where you can watch the potters mix
the clay, spin, shape, dry, and paint it. If you head north from Taumadhi Square, back to the edge of Durbar Square, then turn right (so
you move in a northeastern direction) you will reach Dattatreya Square
(Tachapal Tole). There are buildings here with intricately carved windows. The Peacock Windows, carved in 1492, which grace the **Pujari
Math** ⑧, are considered among the finest examples of Newari wood
carving. Pujari Math stands beside the three-story **Dattaytraya Temple** ⑨. On the opposite side of Pujari Math is the **Brass and Bronze**

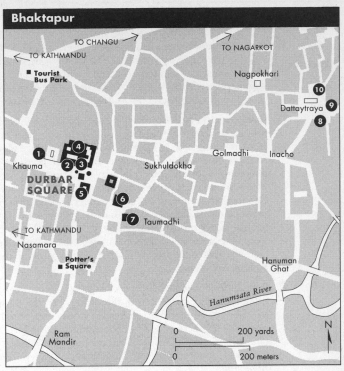

Museum ⑩, which houses a collection of Nepalese brass and bronze work dating from the 18th century.

Sights to See

❼ Bhairabanath Temple. Dedicated to Bhairav, this temple is a place of worship for Hindus and Buddhists. Constructed in stages from 1617 to 1718, and renovated after the 1934 earthquake, it is often the scene of sacrifices. Do not be surprised if you see animal heads and inflated intestines hanging from its beams. ⊠ *Durbar Square, Bhaktapur.*

❷ Bhaktapur Art Gallery. Known as the Durbar Hall, or Palace of 55 Windows, the former Royal Palace that now houses the gallery was constructed in 1427 and renovated in the 17th century. Each balcony has carved windows that are increasingly more ornate at each ascending level. The wood carvings are considered some of the best in Nepal. The museum has a lovely collection of scroll paintings, as well as bronze, brass, stone, and wooden images spanning from the 13th to the 19th centuries. Most pieces depict Hindu and Buddhist tantric deities. ⊠ *Durbar Square, Bhaktapur,* ☏ *01/610004.* ☑ *20 Rs.* ☉ *Wed.–Mon. 10–5 (3 on Fri.).*

❿ Brass and Bronze Museum. Housed in another exquisitely carved building, this museum is a good place to see household brass and bronze items. However, if you are looking to see a large collection of religious statues, you won't find them here. ⊠ *Durbar Square, Bhaktapur,* ☏ *01/610448.* ☑ *5 Rs.* ☉ *Wed.–Mon. 10:15–4:45.*

❾ Dattaytraya Temple. A legend asserts that the wood for this three-story temple came from the trunk of a single tree. Built in the first half of the 15th century, it is one of the oldest temples in the valley. As is typical of Nepal, it is important to Hindus and Buddhists alike: Dattatraya is an incarnation of Vishnu, according to Vaishnavas. However Shaivas say he is Shiva's guru, and Buddhists call him a bodhisattva.

The statues standing out front are the Bhaktapur wrestlers. ☒ *Durbar Square, Bhaktapur.*

❸ Golden Gate. The gate was constructed in 1745 by King Ranjit Malla who put the image of wrestlers along the bottom edge. Facing the gate is a bronze statue of King Bhupatindra Malla, seated, with his hands together in a gesture of devotion to the goddess Taleju whose image is on the center of the gate. ☒ *Durbar Square, Bhaktapur.*

❻ Nyatapola. Built during the reign of King Bhupatindra Malla in 1702, this is one of the finest examples of Nepal's pagoda-style temples and is the tallest temple in the Kathmandu Valley. Five platforms lead up to the temple with its five-tier roof. On each platform stands a set of guardians, with each pair supposedly 10 times stronger than the pair below. At the bottom are a pair of wrestlers, Jaya and Pata, who were 10 times stronger than ordinary men. The deity enshrined inside, the tantric goddess Siddhi Lakshmi, is the strongest of all. Since the temple was never officially inaugurated, its doors have never opened to the public, although priests are allowed inside. Some days, a flag flies from the golden tip; one wonders how they got it up there. ☒ *Durbar Square, Bhaktapur.*

❺ Pashupatinath Temple. The struts on this two-roofed pagoda depict forms of Shiva and characters from the sacred text, the Ramayana. Inside, look for the large, black, four-sided stone linga of Shiva, which is a replica of the sacred linga of Pahupatinath. Some historians claim the temple was constructed in 1492, others say in 1682. It is a replica of the Pashupatinath Temple in the Kathmandu Valley. ☒ *Durbar Square, Bhaktapur.*

❽ Pujari Math. This 15th-century building, constructed by the Malla King Yaksha Malla, has intricate woodwork that was restored with German assistance in the early 1970s. Appropriately enough, it is now home to the **National Woodworking Museum,** where you can see a small collection of wooden statues and struts from old temples. You can also get an up-close look at the intricate carvings of the Peacock Window. ☒ *Durbar Square, Bhaktapur,* ☎ *01/610005.* 🎟 *20 Rs.* ☉ *Wed.–Mon. 10–5.*

❹ Taleju Chowk. Non-Hindus are not allowed to enter this sacrosanct courtyard, but you can peek in to see the Taleju Temple, with its rich carvings, and the smaller Kumari Chowk, in the far right-hand corner. They are said to be the most beautiful structures in Bhaktapur. During Dassain Festivities, the army sacrifices 108 water buffalo—each one killed with one strike of the knife. The blood is given to the goddess; the meat is distributed to government employees. ☒ *Durbar Square, Bhaktapur.*

❶ Ugrachandi and Bhairav statues. Surrounded by female attendants, the goddess Ugrachandi is shown killing the buffalo-headed demon, Mahishasur. Legend claims that King Bhupatindra Malla ordered the construction of these statues and was so delighted by the craftsmanship that he did not want any rivals: so he had the sculptor's hands chopped off. Note the garlands of human heads that both these deities wear. ☒ *Durbar Square, Bhaktapur.*

Dining

Dining in Bhaktapur is the typical trekkers' fare you may have come to recognize: basic Continental, Nepali, Indian, and Chinese fare that isn't gourmet but will fill you up. There are dozens of small cafés, all boasting that the vegetables are cooked and cleaned in boiled or iodinized water. After a a full day of sightseeing this is a comforting fact. Bhaktapur's famed for sweet milk curds, which you can try at any of the listed restaurants. There are no upscale hotels here. Most people looking for more comfortable accommodations either return to Kathmandu or head up to Nagarkot (10 km/6 mi east of Bhaktapur) to stay the night.

$$ ✕ **Café de' Temple Town.** On the right, just after you give your entrance ticket to the guard, this restaurant commands an excellent view of Durbar Square. The fixed lunch of Indian food includes two chapatis (unleavened, pitalike bread), basmati rice, chicken masala that is not too spicy, papadam (fried bread), butter-fried daal, pickles, and, of course, curd. The music is gentle, and the service is friendly. ✉ *Durbar Square, Bhaktapur,* ☎ *01/612357. AE, MC, V.*

$ ✕ **Café Nyatapola.** Next to Nyatapola temple, Kathmandu Valley's tallest temple, this crowded café is on the second floor of a pagoda-shape building that once served as a temple and makes for excellent viewing of the square. You can order anything from spring vegetable curry to hamburgers and french fries, although most people simply prefer to stop here to drink and people-watch. ✉ *Taumadhi Tole, Bhaktapur,* ☎ *01/610346. No credit cards.*

$ ✕ **Sunny Restaurant.** Not for tall people, this restaurant is in a traditional Nepali home, with low ceilings and local artwork. The bamboo chairs, dung floor (actually cleaner than most floors, since it has to be specially treated regularly), and linen-draped ceilings create a lovely setting. And if you do bang your head on the ceiling, you can climb the stairs and go out to the balcony. Their banana fritters with custard, mixed fruit pancakes, and *lassis* (milk-curd shakes) are all delicious. ✉ *Taumadhi Square 11, Bhaktapur,* ☎ *01/614094. No credit cards.*

Dakshin Kali

18 km (11 mi) south of Kathmandu.

The only time to visit this bloodbath of a temple is Tuesday or Saturday morning, well before noon, preferably around 9 AM. Dedicated to Kali, the goddess of destruction, this is where Hindus come to slaughter male animals as offerings to the deity. The eerie setting, in the woods on the southern side of the valley, at the confluence of two rivers, makes the events all the more ominous to first-time viewers.

The temple was built 300 years ago by a Malla king whose people were dying from a cholera epidemic. In a dream, Kali told him to build a temple for her in Dakshin, south of his kingdom, and then to sacrifice 108 buffalo. The king obeyed Kali's command, and the epidemic ended.

Follow the lane from the hillside parking area, past stalls selling Nepali fast food, including *khuwa* (sweet milk-and-cheese curd served on a large leaf); vendors pushing handicrafts and garlands; and, no doubt, at least one praying Shivite sadhu in an orange *dhoti* (a cloth garment worn like a sarong and drawn up between the legs), his face smeared with ash. Go under an arch, and take the steps leading down to a bridge that crosses over a stream. From here, you see Hindus queued up for the temple, plus numerous others bathing, picnicking, and washing their animals by the stream. If you have ever been to a Hindu movie and witnessed locals push to get in, you will be surprised at the sight of the lines at Dakshin Kali. The people are very quiet and subdued, as thousands reverently wait in a relatively hushed silence for their turn.

The temple is designed as a female tantric triangle, point aimed at the ground. Lion figures, vehicles of the goddess, guard the temple. A Bhairov idol stands under the canopy. On the side wall is a Ganesh idol. On the left side of the main temple entrance is the idol Dakshin Kali, with eight arms, lifting her body onto Shiva, who lies motionless.

The priest, nearly hidden, sits inside the inner sanctum and sprinkles holy water on each animal as it is presented to him. The barefoot temple butcher, with his trousers rolled up and covered in blood, grabs the squawking animals, usually roosters, walks over to the images of Kali and Shiva on the side wall, and very efficiently lops off their heads. Blood drenches the statue red. The butcher hands the headless creature to its owner and sometimes dabs a speck of its blood onto his own forehead, sanctifying himself. Look up at the surrounding pigeons who usually hang about the area; invariably there is at least one white one that has turned pinkish-red from the squirting blood.

Non-Hindus are allowed to stand back to the side and observe. Usually there are a few who push forward with their cameras, trying to take the bloodthirstiest, goriest shot. Try to remember this is a religious event, not a carnival.

In the midst of the ruckus and huge crowds, holy men sit under a covered pavilion reading aloud from holy scriptures. On the staircase back up to the exit, beggars line the path. Some street children from Kathmandu commute the 18 km (11 mi) to this site twice a week for the alms—proof that begging is a full-time job for many children.

Lodging

$ ⊞ **Dakshinkali Club Resort.** Just up the road, 4 km (2½ mi) from the temple (and the last kilometer is on a rough-and-tumble road), this much-advertised hotel is situated in a horseshoe-shape area of forested hills. The gardens are well tended, and the air is much fresher than in the city, but there isn't much to do here. The rooms are basic, with twin beds and Formica furniture. Bathrooms have showers but not tubs. ⊠ *Box 10872, Kathmandu,* ☎ *01/482001,* ℻ *01/482008, E-mail: cmsnepal@cms.wlink.com.np. 10 rooms. Pool, meeting room. No credit cards.*

Pharping

19 km (12 mi) south of Kathmandu.

On the way back to Kathmandu, consider stopping in at **Pharping Vajra Yogini,** a tantric temple dedicated to the angry female aspect of Buddhahood. Inside the temple you will find two dancing Vajra Yogini images holding skullcups and knives.

Beyond the temple, up a path through the hills, you will find **Gorakhnath cave.** Buddhists believe that Padmasambhava, the Bodhisattva who is said to have introduced Buddhism to Tibet, meditated here. They say the handprint and footprint in the cave were left by Padmasambhava, although Hindus say they are the imprints of Gorakhnath, a famous Hindu believer. For a few rupees, you can light butter lamps here. The caves are a major pilgrimage site for Tibetan Buddhists, many of whom have prostrated (kneeled and prayed, inching forward on their hands and knees) all the way to the caves from Tibet. The hillside, seemingly gift-wrapped in a maze of prayer flags, is a beautiful place to wander through; you will find stones that were carried by people who walked or prostrated here from Tibet.

Changu Narayan

18 km (11 mi) east of Kathmandu; 4 km (2½ mi) north of Bhaktapur.

Changu Narayan contains some of the best and oldest architecture in all of Nepal. Yet, very few people visit this site. You can stand in the courtyard and be the only visitor. The only hindrance to dreaming you have traveled back in time 300 years is the incongruous sound of Hits 100 FM radio blaring from nearby vendors' radios.

Finally, a travel companion that doesn't snore on the plane or eat all your peanuts.

123 456 7891 2345
J.D. SMITH

When traveling, your MCI WorldCom Card is the best way to keep in touch. Our operators speak your language, so they'll be able to connect you back home—no matter where your travels take you. Plus, your MCI WorldCom Card is easy to use, and even earns you frequent flyer miles every time you use it. When you add in our great rates, you get something even more valuable: peace-of-mind. So go ahead. Travel the world. MCI WorldCom just brought it a whole lot closer.

You can even sign up today at www.mci.com/worldphone or ask your operator to make a collect call to 1-410-314-2938.

EASY TO CALL WORLDWIDE

1 Just dial the WorldPhone access number of the country you're calling from.
2 Dial or give the operator your MCI WorldCom Card number.
3 Dial or give the number you're calling.

China	
Available from most major cities	108-12
For a Mandarin-speaking Operator	108-17
Hong Kong	**800-96-1121**
Japan ◆	
To call using JT	0044-11-121
To call using KDD	00539-121▶
To call using IDC	0066-55-121
South Africa	**0800-99-0011**

For your complete WorldPhone calling guide, dial the WorldPhone access number for the country you're in and ask the operator for Customer Service. In the U.S. call 1-800-431-5402.

◆ Public phones may require deposit of coin or phone card for dial tone.
▶ Regulation does not permit intra-Japan calls.

EARN FREQUENT FLYER MILES

AmericanAirlines
AAdvantage®

Continental Airlines
OnePass®

▲ Delta Air Lines
SkyMiles®

✈ MILEAGE PLUS.
United Airlines

U·S AIRWAYS
DIVIDEND MILES

MCI WORLDCOM

The first thing you need overseas is the one thing you forget to pack.

FOREIGN CURRENCY DELIVERED OVERNIGHT

Chase Currency To Go® delivers foreign currency to your home by the next business day*

It's easy—before you travel, call 1-888-CHASE84 for delivery of any of 75 currencies

Delivery is free with orders of $500 or more

Competitive rates— without exchange fees

You don't have to be a Chase customer—you can pay by Visa® or MasterCard®

 CHASE

THE RIGHT RELATIONSHIP IS EVERYTHING.®

1•888•CHASE84
www.chase.com

*Orders must be placed before 5 PM ET. $10 delivery fee for orders under $500.
©1999 The Chase Manhattan Corporation. All rights reserved. The Chase Manhattan Bank. Member FDIC.

Historians believe the original temple was constructed in the 3rd or 4th century and restored in 1708, after a fire. According to legend, once when Garuda was fighting with a snake-god who prevented his son from worshiping Vishnu, Vishnu intervened to restore peace. To prove his friendship, the snake wrapped himself around Garuda's neck. The three deities then flew off to this hill, where a statue of the trio remains.

Walk up the long staircase from the parking lot, and you will pass goats, chickens, and children skipping rope *up* the steps. Along the way, vendors selling wooden masks and statues, the lotus-shape water well with dragon-head spigots, and local women weaving on hand looms, are all excellent excuses to stop and catch your breath.

In the courtyard, elephant statues with orange eyeliner flank the entrance to the two-story temple. Oil lamps and bells hang from the lower tiled roof. Statues of birds are perched on each corner. Roof struts are carved with colorfully painted deities, animals, and erotic images. The finely wrought portal has a gilded overhead torana depicting Vishnu with his consorts. His symbols—conch shell, lotus, disc, and mace—appear repeatedly. A 5th- or 6th-century statue of Garuda kneels out front. Notice the stone pillar to the side of the temple with an inscription that dates to the 4th century. This is the earliest example of writing in Nepal. To the left of the temple stands the black statue commemorating the legendary flight, an image duplicated on Nepal's 10 Rs. note. Finally, notice the sculpture of Vishnu in all his incarnations, said to be one of the finest examples of 6th-century art in the subcontinent.

Dhulikhel

34 km (21 mi) east of Kathmandu.

Dhulikhel is a hill resort in the foothills of Panchkhal Valley, with excellent views of the northeastern Himalayas, including 12 peaks over 20,000 ft. Waking to these mountains, or even the verdant rice paddies and emerald forests beneath the peaks, with the marshmallow clouds in between, is an unforgettable experience. You can stay here and commute the hour to sites in Kathmandu, or simply spend a night for the splendid view.

Many people visit to warm their hearts and legs up for longer walks, as there are excellent day hikes from Dhulikhel. You can walk to **Namobuddha** (seven hours round-trip) or **Panauti** (five hours round-trip). Your hotelier will be able to provide maps, directions, and guides. Bring casual sportswear and comfortable walking shoes. In summer, light cotton clothes are sufficient, while a sweater for the daytime and coat for nights are recommended during the winter months.

Namobuddha is about 8 km (5 mi) due south of Dhulikhel. The trek takes you through countryside and a number of small villages where you can ask directions if you get lost. Locals will know where you are headed before you even open your mouth to ask, "Which way to . . .?" In Namobuddha, there is an undated, although probably 200- or 300-year-old stupa. Nearby are several huts selling tea and Nepalese snacks, but the most interesting site is on the hill above the stupa.

The climb up the trail from the stupa takes about five minutes. At the top of the hill, there are several more stupas, a retreat center for Buddhist monks, and an ancient carved stone depicting the legend of Namobuddha. According to the legend, many years ago, there was a king named Maharatha. He and his three sons were out hunting, when the youngest prince, Mahasatva, came across a dying tigress, with cubs sucking on her dry teats, starving to death. The prince was so saddened by the sight he took a sharp piece of bamboo and cut his own flesh to feed the starving tigress and her cubs. Dying during this act of compassion, he then achieved nirvana, or enlightenment, in heaven. His father placed his son's remains in a chaitya built at the site to commemorate Mahasatva's compassion. It soon became a pilgrimage site for Buddhists all over the world.

The historic city of Panauti is situated at the confluence of two rivers, the Rosi and the Punyamati. It is about 8 km (5 mi) southwest of Dhulikhel. There is a Shiva temple here with wood carvings on the roof struts that are considered masterpieces.

According to legend, Vedic was a sage who had a very beautiful wife named Ahilya. The god Indra transformed himself into the shape of Vedic when the sage was away, so he could seduce Ahilya. When Vedic returned home and discovered what had happened, he cursed Indra, turning him into a hermaphrodite. Indra spent many years repenting for his sins and became a devotee of Lord Shiva. After a long time, Shiva took pity, and when Indra took a bath in the two rivers, he became normal once more. To this day, the rivers are a sacred place for ritual baths.

Dining and Lodging

Do not expect televisions in the rooms, air-conditioning, or free transportation to the lodge, but unless otherwise noted, these hotels have rooms with attached bathrooms with tubs, restaurants, bars, room service, and currency exchange. Phone numbers and addresses, unless otherwise noted, are for booking offices in Kathmandu.

$$ ✕🏠 **Dhulikhel Lodge Resort.** This terra-cotta-color brick resort, set back from the main road, is multileveled, terraced into the hill to provide optimum viewing from its restaurant, bar, lounge, and rooms. The fragrant, flower-pot-lined pathways are an intricate maze from one viewing point to another. Many people choose to come here for the restaurant and bar, where a round brick fireplace with a copper flu lends a cozy, ski-resort atmosphere. For a nice dinner, try the deep-fried pork served with baked apples, grilled tomatoes, fried eggs, and buttered vegetables; or have the filet mignon marinated in herbs and cooked in a cream sauce, served with parsley potatoes and buttered vegetables. The coffee here is real. The rooms are plain and simple, with twin beds and showers only, although the best are the eight rooms with balconies that have stunning views of the V-shape valley and mountaintops. While the pathway around the rooms is wearing, the staff is helpful: if you are staying for more than a week, they will put a television, telephone, and minibar in your room. ✉ *Box 6020, Kamaladi, Kathmandu,* ☎ *01/247663, 011/6114 in Dhulikhel,* 🆇 *01/222926. 24 rooms. Restaurant, bar, room service, travel services. AE, MC, V.*

$$ ✕🏠 **Dhulikhel Mountain Resort.** Founded in 1981, this resort has steep steps leading to redbrick, thatch-roof buildings. The paths, which cut a lovely route through the forested hillside, are lined with banana trees, eucalyptus, and bamboo. The spacious rooms have a basic decor with a few nice touches, like fresh-cut flowers on the night tables and coffeemakers in each room. There are no TVs in the rooms, but you can watch in the lounge. The professional staff have earned their high reputation: repeat visitors are the norm here. Eating momos at their linen-set tables outside is a particularly indulgent treat. ✉ *Box 3203, Lazimpat, Kathmandu,* ☎ *01/420774, 011/61466 in Dhulikhel,* 🆇 *01/420778. 43 rooms. Restaurant, laundry service, travel services. AE, MC, V.*

$$ ✕🏠 **Himalayan Horizon Hotel Sun-N-Snow.** This hotel has two redbrick buildings with traditional Nepali wooden windows. The rooms are quite different in each building. The newest one, a four-story build-

ing finished in 1994, holds 16 deluxe rooms. They are large, each with a queen bed and a single bed, a grandiose ballroom-style chandelier, and gold-trimmed cornicing. A step down from the bedroom is a sitting area, with plastic chairs facing the balcony overlooking the mountains. The hallways in this building are already in need of a paint job; but everything else is sparkling clean. The standard rooms are in the traditional Newari building built in 1983. Here the rooms are more basic, but the ambience is more authentic. Narrow, steep stairways lead to rooms with wooden cross-beamed ceilings, which are typical of the traditional style. Both buildings have rooms with mountain views, international dial telephones, and bathrooms with showers. ⊠ *Box 1583, Kathmandu,* ☎ *01/225092, 011/61260 in Dhulikhel,* ☏ *01/ 225092, 011/61476 in Dhulikhel, E-mail: bagmati@dmn.wlink.com.np. 28 rooms. Restaurant, bar, laundry service. AE, MC, V.*

$$ ✕☷ **Himalayan Shangri-La.** This hotel built in 1997 is not connected with the Shangri-La hotels in Kathmandu and Pokhara, but it is one of Dhulikhel's upscale resort areas. It is a long, steep hike up to the hotel reservations desk, because, once again, the hotel is built into the hillside. It is set amid the forest, so you wake up to the sound of chirping birds. You can choose between two types of housing. Near the reception area, there are Nepali-style redbrick buildings with intricately carved wooden window sills. These have window benches and fancy window frames, but the rest of the furniture is basic. The newer rooms are in the mountain block. Here white buildings with thatched roofs house smaller rooms with bigger bathrooms. The plus of these buildings is better views, as they are higher up on the hillside. With either option, expect simple beds and fresh-cut flowers in your room. Because the rooms are spread across the hillside, there's no room service. The staff is very helpful and friendly; ask to use their binoculars while sitting on the back patio of the restaurant. ⊠ *Box 10886, Kathmandu,* ☎ *01/427837, 011/61613 in Dhulikhel,* ☏ *01/423939, E-mail: himalayan@hsr.wlink.com.np. 36 rooms. Restaurant, bar, meeting room. AE, MC, V.*

$$ ✕☷ **Mirabel Resort Hotels.** This jewel in the hillside literally sparkles.
★ Every time you turn around the friendly staff is polishing, scrubbing, and gardening. The best rooms are the double rooms in the separate blocks. They have individual terraces with fancifully carved, traditional Nepali-style balustrades. All of the rooms are tastefully decorated, with terra-cotta floors, Tibetan-style throw rugs, well-crafted blond wood furniture, and nicely tiled bathrooms. Each room has either paintings or photographs of local people, architecture, and landscaping; all have a view of the mountains. There are also televisions in the rooms. The two restaurants and the conference room have block prints of traditional Nepali architecture on their walls, huge plants, plus massive glass windows overlooking the mountains (forget doing any work in the conference room if it is a clear day). The rooftop bar and view terrace has an excellent telescope for checking out the ranges or bird-watching. ⊠ *Durbar Marg, Kathmandu,* ☎ *01/248056, 011/619725 in Dhulikhel,* ☏ *01/226642, E-mail: sre@vishnu.ccsl.com.np. 20 rooms. 2 restaurants, minibars, baby-sitting, laundry service, meeting room, travel services, car rental. AE, MC, V.*

Nagarkot

32 km (20 mi) east of Kathmandu.

You could go to this hill resort in the afternoon, spend a few hours at sunset, and return for dinner in the capital, but it is better to spend the night and wake up to the morning sunrise over the Himal. Many people plan to stay here after they have been sightseeing at Bhaktapur and Changu Narayan.

The views here stretch from Dhaulagiri in the west, all the way past Everest, to Kanchenjunga in the east. Beneath the pure white mountaintops there is usually a mist or clouds hanging low in the verdant valley before you, making for picturesque views without the hard work of trekking. But if you want to walk, there are plenty of short hikes in the area. If you are really game you can spend about six hours walking back (downhill) to Kathmandu—locals will point the way—but you simply can just walk toward the smog.

All of the lodges have porches where you can stargaze at a sky that lights up like New York City's Times Square. Nagarkot is windy year-round. A windbreaker, cap, lip cream, sunglasses, and sunscreen are advisable. As Club Himalaya advises, avoid loose-flying skirts and saris, unless you want to imitate Marilyn Monroe.

Dining and Lodging

Accommodations here are basic, so don't expect televisions or air-conditioning. Phone numbers and addresses, unless otherwise noted, are for booking offices in Kathmandu.

$$ ✕▤ **Club Himalaya.** A Nepalese–Hong Kong joint venture, this red-brick hotel is nestled in the hilltops in the valley. The hotel is strewn with artistic touches like dragon-headed stone water spouts. The rooms have large beds, televisions, comfortable blond-wood furniture, huge balconies, and even telephones in the bathroom. All also overlook the mountain range. You can arrange package deals with car or helicopter transport. Mountain-bike rental and pony treks are also available here. ✉ *Box 2769, Kathmandu or Windy Hills, Nagarkot,* ☏ *01/ 413632, 01/290883 in Nagarkot,* ℻ *01/290868 in Nagarkot. 42 rooms. Restaurant, bar, indoor pool, sauna, exercise room, mountain bikes, library, business services, meeting rooms. AE, MC, V.*

$$ ✕▤ **Niva Niwa Lodge.** This small Nepalese-Japanese joint venture lodge looks like a redbrick medieval Scottish castle. Although it primarily caters to Japanese tourists, you will find Newari dishes on the restaurant's dinner menu and a choice of regular or low tables. There are nine basic bedrooms, with thin mattresses on simple twin beds. The comforters are nice and thick, and the bathrooms are spacious. The rooms and their large balconies overlook the mountains. ✉ *Box 178 Kathmandu, or Naldum, Nagarkot,* ☏ *01/255490, 01/290797 in Nagarkot,* ℻ *01/255490. 9 rooms. Restaurant, bar. MC, V.*

$ ✕▤ **Hotel Chautari Keyman.** This hotel on a bluff has a spacious restaurant and patio overlooking the mountains. Although the hallways in the main hotel have worn carpets in places, the garden paths to the cottages are flowering walkways. The rooms have basic Formica furniture and shower-only bathrooms, but they compensate with big balconies. Opt for one of the six cottages for a more private experience. Management will set up tables and chairs on your back porch and serve your meals there. They will also put a television or telephone in your room, so you never have to set foot out of your little compound with a view. ✉ *Box 3011, Kamaldi, Kathmandu,* ☏ *01/419798, 01/ 290875 in Nagarkot,* ℻ *01/225136. 17 rooms, 6 cottages. Restaurant, bar. AE, MC, V.*

$ ✕▤ **Peaceful Cottage.** This small, inexpensive hotel (under $30) has rooms of varying standards, some with shared bath. Not surprisingly, the rooms with private baths are also the rooms with the best views. If you can book them, it is well worth the stay. The bedrooms are paneled, decorated with terra-cotta artwork, and have twin beds with big comforters. The windowed dining hall and balcony patio have panoramic mountain views. ✉ *Box 37, Bhaktapur,* ☏ *01/290877,* ℻ *01/290827. 12 rooms, 4 with bath. Restaurant, bar. No credit cards.*

Around Kathmandu Valley A to Z

Arriving and Departing
See Kathmandu A to Z, *above.*

Getting Around
BY HIRED CAR WITH DRIVER
See Kathmandu A to Z, *above.*

BY TAXI
If you are going to **Patan** from central Kathmandu, expect to pay 200 Rs.–300 Rs. To get to **Boudhanath, Pashupatinath,** or **Swayambhunath,** you should not have to pay more than 100 Rs. by day, 150 Rs. by night. It should cost about 600 Rs. to go to **Dakshin Kali,** and no more than another 100 Rs. if you want to include time at **Pharping.** If you are just going to **Bhaktapur** or **Changu Narayan,** expect to pay 400 Rs.–600 Rs.; make sure you hire the taxi for the day: it can be very difficult to flag one down in the area after 3 PM.

To get to **Nagarkot** and **Dhulikhel** from the airport it will cost about 800 Rs. If you call ahead, your hotel will send a car to pick you up for about this cost. If you are going to these sites from the city (and not from the more expensive airport locale), and just want to be dropped off, you will pay about 400 Rs.–600 Rs. If you want to spend a day touring **Bhaktapur** and **Changu Narayan** and then go to either of the hill stations, expect to pay 1,200 Rs.–1,600 Rs. for the day. You will have to pay more to have the taxi stay overnight (don't worry, hotels usually put the driver up for the night) or pick you up the next day. It is best to get your hotelier to do the negotiating for you; he may know a local taxi driver who will be cheaper. There are clearly marked billboards on the roads showing the direction to the various resorts. Your taxi driver or hired-car driver will probably know the way; if not, locals will be able to point the way.

Contacts and Resources
CURRENCY EXCHANGE
All of the accommodations provide currency exchange.

Note that in Bhaktapur you need 300 Rs. to enter the square, and all of the money exchangers are within the square—so make sure you arrive with enough money to get in. Once you are inside, **Nyatapola Money Exchange** (⊠ Café Nyatapola, Taumadhi Tole, Bhaktapur, ☎ 01/610346) is open daily 8–7. Just before you give your ticket to the second officer at the main gate of Bhaktapur, on the right-hand side, down the alley, is **Layaku Money Exchange Counter** (☎ no phone), which is open daily 7:30–6. In **Boudhanath,** you can use the **Mandala Money Changer** (☎ 01/484720); it's immediately to your left when you enter the stupa gate and is open weekdays 8–7, Saturdays 8–noon. In Nagarkot, the **Himalayan Bank Limited** (☎ no phone), on the main road connecting all of the hotels, is open Sunday–Friday 10–3. It handles cash advances on Visa cards, as well as foreign exchange.

All of the exchange counters listed are authorized by the Nepal Rastra Bank. The "official" hours are listed; however, if the exchangers run out of money (which happens), they will close early.

EMERGENCIES
For a medical emergency, if you can, head back to Kathmandu. If you are in Patan, contact the **Patan Hospital** (⊠ Lagan Khel, Patan, ☎ 01/522278), which has a 24-hour medical emergency room. To reach the hospital, head due south from Durbar Square to the Lagankhel area. The hospital is south of the road that the Netherlands Consulate is on; taxi drivers will know the way.

In Boudhanath the friendly guys at **Judgement Eyes (P) Ltd.,** down the street from the Double Dorjee Restaurant, handle mail, international telephone, fax and E-mail service (☎ 01/484264).

POKHARA

200 km (124 mi) west of Kathmandu.

Until the mid-1900s, Pokhara bustled only in the winter, when Tibetans from the north arrived with their mule trains to barter salt and raw yak wool for grain. In 1959, after the Chinese seized Tibet, the route was closed. In the late 1950s, however, malaria was finally eradicated from the region, so more people settled here. Then, in the 1970s, roads to Kathmandu were constructed, connecting the city to the rest of the world. That is when the hippies arrived, then more and more climbers and trekkers, and now, even families with toddlers make the trip. Pokhara has since become the second-biggest city in the country, with a population of 95,000.

The advent of tourism sped up the arrival of electricity, an airport, and improved social services, but it also increased the cost of necessities for local villagers. There was and is a certain haphazardness to the development of Pokhara. The airport, bazaars, and hotel areas are all spread apart. Sure, there are new roads, but the routes around Lakeside are still rough-and-tumble dirt streets. There is no rush to make everything perfectly fancy.

There is a hedonistic quality to the Lakeside district in Pokhara; the drug-pushing scene is even more blatant here than in Kathmandu, but it seems to be due to a laid-back, this-is-where-you-go-after-you've-trekked atmosphere that permits everything and anything. While it doesn't prohibit bringing kids to the region, keeping an eye on your teens after dark would be advisable.

Still, Pokhara continues to attract more and more visitors each year. The 8,000-meter walls of the Himal line the horizon in the north, while Phewa Tal, the 3 km-long (2-mi-long) emerald lake, is the jewel of Pokhara's resort district. It is not difficult to take a picture-perfect post-card photo in this city, with rhododendron in the foreground, a lake in the center, and snow-tipped peaks set against a pale blue sky in the background.

There are plenty of short walks in the surrounding Pokhara region that you can hike all year long. There are currently 21 flights a day from Kathmandu, carrying travelers and climbers, as well as Kathmandu residents who are moving to Pokhara. If you have been to Kathmandu before and are heading to Annapurna, consider immediately transferring from the international to the domestic terminals at Tribhuvan International airport and avoiding the pollution of Kathmandu altogether. If you have never been to Nepal before, do not miss Pokhara; now is the time to see the city, before it expands beyond recognition.

Exploring Pokhara

If you are hiring a bike, know that the 5-km (3-mi) stretch of Pokhara is hillier than it appears.

Most visitors stay in the **Lakeside** (Baidam) and **Damside** (Pardi) areas, which are about 1 km (½ mi) apart on the eastern and southeastern tip of **Phewa Tal** (aka Fewa Tal or Fewa Lake). This is where you will find dozens of restaurants serving middling-quality trekker food. The greatest selling point is that the food is diverse and not just daal baht, which Westerners tend to get bored with, quickly.

The airport is about 1 km (½ mi) east of Damside, where there are also several more upscale hotels. North of the airport is the bus station, near Prithvi Highway. The center of town is on the road at the bridge, Mahendra Pul, about 1½ km (¾ mi) north of the bus station. It is dusty and busy. Farthest north is the old, bustling, bazaar area.

Devi's Fall is southwest of Damside, as is the **Tashi Ling Tibetan Village.**

WHEN TO GO

The fall and winter are slightly milder in Pokhara than in misty Kathmandu. However, when monsoon season arrives here in the summer, it arrives with a vengeance (and lots of leeches); it's a good time not to be in Pokhara.

Lakeside and Damside

Lakeside is the tourist ghetto of Pokhara, where the primary occupations seem to be lounging and eating. Still, Phewa Lake is the second-largest lake in the country (Rara Lake, in western Nepal is larger) and a wonderful place to canoe, paddle boat, or simply sit on the shore. You can boat to **Varahi Temple,** dedicated to Varahi or Vishnu (☞ Boating, *below*). On Saturday morning, look for devotees crossing the lake with male animals and fowl for sacrifice to the deity.

At dusk, Lakeside is a good place to visit to watch the sunset and have a drink, while the mountains glow in a pink-orange halo. You can sit at any of the Lakeside bars and cafés, or take the rope-pulley ferry to the **Fishtail Lodge** on Phewa Lake Island, where you get the best views of the mountains. From left to right, the mountains start with Mt. Dhaulagiri (26,787 ft); next, the bumpy peak in the foreground is Annapurna South (23,737 ft). A little beyond that, in the background, lies Annapurna I (26,538 ft). The imposing peak, seen in the central foreground, is Machhapuchhare (22,950 ft), which literally means fishtail. Machhapuchhare does not look much like a fishtail from Pokhara, but if you trek in the Annapurna region, you will see that it twists and turns like a diving fish. The Nepalese government will not permit climbers to conquer this mountain, preserving at least one of their national treasures as truly sacred. Slightly east and beyond Machhapuchhare, is Annapurna III (24,780 ft), which almost looks like the back of a camel. Next is Annapurna IV (24,682 ft), and then Annapurna II (26,033 ft). On the right, you will see Lamjung Himal (22,914 ft), and finally Manaslu (26,781 ft) and Himalchuli (24,737 ft).

In Lakeside you can also catch up on movies at various movie-restaurant sites. Or you can simply wander the dirt road, people-watching, or better still, sit on a bench under a banyan or pipal tree and watch everyone else wander. Sit under the mountain's shadows and read one of the most amazing expedition tales, *Annapurna*, by Maurice Herzog. He was the first to climb an 8,000-meter peak.

The mountain views from rooftops in the Damside are excellent; plus this area has an atmosphere that's quieter and a bit more sedate than that of Lakeside. While you cannot walk across **Pardi Dam,** there is a footbridge crossing the Pardi River that leads to **Devi's Fall.**

A Good Tour

If you are fit (very fit), you can rent a bike; otherwise hire a taxi driver for the day, or a travel agent, such as **Pokhara Sight Seeing Tours & Travels** (☞ Pokhara A to Z, *below*). While Pokhara is not noted for its temples like Kathmandu, there are still a few places to visit. You can begin touring Pokhara at **Binde Basini Temple** in the north-central part of town, about 4 km (2½ mi) from Lakeside. There are good mountain views from this temple. Then, heading south, visit the **Bhimsen Temple**, and the surrounding old bazaar area. Next, stop by the **Pokhara Museum**, southeast of the Bhimsen temple, or visit the **Natural History Museum**, northeast of the temple. Afterwards, go to the Mahendra Pul (*"pul"* means bridge), so you can see the **Seti River Gorge**. After monsoon season, the river swells and can be an awesome sight; although in the spring it is often not much more than a trickle. That will bring you to the newer bazaar area, which is garbage strewn and busy, much like Kathmandu, but can be worth the visit for the perspective it provides on the modern Nepali lifestyle. Heading southwest to the Siddhartha Highway, about 2 km (1 mi) outside of Pokhara, you can visit **Devi's Falls**, also called Devin's Falls. Across the street are caves called the **Gupteswar Gupha**.

TIMING

The time required depends on how long you linger in the bazaar area, whether or not you opt to go to the museums, and of course, whether or not you bike or take a taxi. Most people who bike spend a half day wandering the area. The museums won't take more than 45 minutes each, and visiting the market can take as long. The temples are 10- to 15-minute photo opportunity stops. Devi's Falls can take an hour to wander around. Go anytime during the day; although if you are biking, the morning may be best for the cooler air.

Sights to See

Bhimsen Temple. This double-roof temple on the main road has erotic carvings on the roof struts. The surrounding bazaar area is the traditional bartering section of town. ⊠ *Pokhara.*

Binde Basini Temple. Dedicated to Durga (Parvati), the image of the goddess is actually a saligram, a black ammonite fossil of marine animals. It dates back to the Jurassic period, over 100 million years ago. Ammonites are found in the Himalaya region, and many Tibetan traders will try to sell them to you trailside, although you might just find one yourself. Considering Nepal is now landlocked, the marine element is proof that it once was under sea. On Saturday and Tuesday mornings local Hindu devotees flock to this temple and offer sacrifices on a mound here. ⊠ *Pokhara.*

Devi's Falls (Devin's Falls). Locally it's known as *Patale Chhango* (Hell's Falls). Phewa Lake flows into Pardi Khola, but at Devi's Falls it suddenly drops down into a hole. The falls flow after the monsoon, but in the spring it is little more than a dripping drain. According to one tale, a tourist named David fell into the hole, dragging his girlfriend along with him, disappearing forever. There are usually souvenir-selling Tibetans from the nearby Tashi Ling settlement on hand. ⊠ *Siddhartha Hwy., 2 km (1 mi) southwest of Pokhara.*

Gupteswar Gupha. This is a sacred cave that is almost 3 km (2 mi) in length. It is revered by Hindus because it contains a phallic symbol of Lord Shiva that has been preserved in the condition it was in when it was discovered. Inside are big, hall-size rooms and five lakes. The cave is not for the claustrophobic: there are some passages where you have to crawl on all fours. Photography is prohibited. ⊠ *Siddhartha Hwy., 2 km (1 mi) southwest of Pokhara.*

Natural History Museum. Managed by the Annapurna Conservation Area Project (ACAP), the museum displays precious and semiprecious stones, volcanic rock, and stuffed models of wildlife. The biggest draw is the butterfly collection. ⊠ *Prithvi Narayan Campus, east of the old bazaar,* ☎ *061/21102.* ☞ *Free.* ☉ *Sun.–Fri. 9–1 and 2–5.*

Pokhara Museum. Exhibits focus on the lifestyles and history of ethnic groups such as the Gurung, Thakalis, and Tharu. Jewelry, musical instruments, clothing, and costumes are on display. There is also a display highlighting the remains of an 8,000-year-old Mustang settlement. ✉ *Just off Pode Pole, between the airport and Mahendra Pul,* ☎ *061/20413.* ☜ *5 Rs.* ☉ *Wed.–Sun. 10–5.*

NEED A BREAK?	The **Hot Sandwich & Cheese Corner Shop** in Lakeside, across the road from the Old Blues Pub, is an excellent place to pick up a box lunch. Open 24 hours a day, this tiny deli heats the baguette bread before building you a Dagwood-size, take-away ham, egg, salami, cheese, or vegetarian sandwich that costs about a dollar.

Seti River Gorge. It's sometimes called the milky way river, because the limestone in the soil makes the water run milky-color. At full strength it can be breathtaking as it roars through the center of town in this incredibly narrow gorge. This boisterous river runs completely underground in some places. Although it is only about 2 meters wide, it is more than 65½ ft deep. If it is running strong under the **Mahendra Pul,** ask your driver to take you to the far side of the airport, where you will get a less polluted view of the forceful rush that created this deep gorge. ✉ *Pokhara.*

Dining

Most of the restaurants in Pokhara have similar menus of Continental, Indian, and Nepali food. Do not be afraid to try the down-market restaurants in Lakeside; the food is cheap but of good quality. The expensive hotels have upscale restaurants on par with those in Kathmandu, so if you want higher-quality service and food, visit the restaurants in the $$$$ hotels.

$$$$ ✕ **Koto's.** If you liked the Koto's Japanese restaurants in Kathmandu, try the one in Pokhara. The menu is slightly different, with more pork, chicken, and noodles and less fish. Try the chicken barbecued on bamboo skewers. There is also a wide selection of tofu and soybean meals. Inside the Bluebird compound, with a view of the pool, the setting is modern and relaxing. ✉ *Bluebird Hotel, Pokhara,* ☎ *061/25480. MC, V. Closed 3–6 PM.*

$$$$ ✕ **The Spice Route.** Try any of the meat dishes here. The beef is some
★ of the highest quality in town, especially the well-seasoned pepper steak. Sometimes the menu also includes a tasty stew, full of generous chunks of boar meat. The vegetable chow mein should keep vegetarians happy; it isn't too oily, and the plate is full of fresh peppers, onions, and cauliflower. The ambience is Asian, but the food is geared towards Western travelers. Despite the restaurant's name, the seasoning is not too spicy, but extra hot peppers are served on the side, if you want to add a little zest. ✉ *Box 333, in the Shangri-La Village hotel, Pokhara,* ☎ *061/22122. Reservations essential. AE, DC, MC, V. No lunch.*

$$$ ✕ **Caravanserai.** This restaurant in the Shangri-La Village is worth a trip anytime (literally, since it's open 24 hours a day). It's an excellent place for a high-piled chicken, egg, and salad club sandwich or a vegetarian sandwich of crunchy vegetables, both with chips on the side. The apple pie à la mode, served with chocolate syrup on the plate, is sinfully good. The poolside setting is casual, but the service is not: expect doting waiters to linger about you ready to light your cigarette or refill your water glass. ✉ *Box 333, in the Shangri-La Village hotel, Pokhara,* ☎ *061/22122. AE, DC, MC, V.*

$$$ ✕ **Mike's Restaurant.** This is another sister of a Kathmandu restau-
★ rant. Mike Frame has moved out to Pokhara, so now there are two

places to get his eggs Benedict. He says they are better in Pokhara; that may take several taste tests to determine. If you have dined at Mike's Breakfast in Kathmandu, you won't be surprised that his restaurant in Pokhara is an excellent place for Continental and Mexican food. The burritos ooze cheese and sour cream, the vegetables are often from Mike's organic garden, and the coffee is real. Seating is right on the edge of the lake. Coupled with Mike's garden, it is one of the most relaxing locations in Lakeside. ⊠ *Lakeside, Baidam, Pokhara,* ☎ *061/ 20151. No credit cards.*

$$ ✕ **Once Upon a Time.** This Lakeside restaurant offers seating at low tables or on bamboo, burgundy-cushioned furniture. It is crowded at night, during movie showings (movies are shown on big screen TVs in the restaurant), and at happy hour. The grilled steak with cheese on top is as good as you will get in the trekker restaurants on the Lakeside strip. The spinach-mushroom burger is a jaw-stretcher, but vegans should know it is prepared with cheese. The potato chips are nice-size chunks of potatoes, and the sautéed vegetables are cooked just enough, so all the vitamins have not been zapped out of them. ⊠ *Baidam, Lakeside,* ☎ *061/22240. AE, MC, V.*

Lodging

Pokhara has everything from one-room "inns" added to family homes to upscale, international-standard accommodations. Although there are dozens of establishments right in the midst of Lakeside, be warned that the area is unpleasantly noisy until about 11 PM. For this reason, the listed hotels are in the neighborhoods just a few minutes' stroll away from the bazaarlike shop-restaurant-and-bar area of Lakeside. Nearly every hotel in Pokhara has a stunning garden. Good rates are available in December and January, when most people think it is too cold to trek. While high-altitude trekking at this time can be risky, there are plenty of lower-altitude treks in the Pokhara area.

$$$$ 🏨 **Bluebird Hotel Pokhara.** Newer and nicer than its sister, the Bluestar Hotel in Kathmandu, this hotel has an expansive lobby with a waterfall flowing from its staircase, spacious atriums, and sprawling hallways. The bedrooms are not designed on quite as expansive a scale as the common areas, but they are still standard-size rooms. They have a modern feel, softened by traditional touches, such as the intricately carved headboards and fanciful woodwork. The mountainside rooms are the best, because they may have views of the Himalayas. In a city of blooming gardens, it is odd that the flowers in the rooms and on the coffee tables in the lobby are plastic. ⊠ *Box 983, Tripureswor, Kathmandu,* ☎ *061/ 25480,* 𝙵𝙰𝚇 *061/26260, E-mail: hotel@bluestar.mos.com.np. 80 rooms, 4 suites. 2 restaurants, bar, coffee shop, room service, pool, laundry service, business services, meeting rooms, airport shuttle. AE, MC, V.*

$$$$ 🏨 **Fulbari Resort-Pokhara.** This luxury hotel brings Durbar Square to
★   your hotel room. After a bumpy drive down a back road, along the edge of a stunning lichen-covered gorge, to the plateau above the Seti and Fusre rivers, you arrive in an expansive garden with ponds and sculptures that leads up to the gleaming marble steps of the hotel. Explore the lobby and halls for hidden courtyards, temple-style windows, and a dragon-spout fountain. The bedrooms all have balconies overlooking the gardens, parquet floors, masterfully carved furniture, and handmade paper-covered doors on the television cabinets. Construction is under way on a new health club and shopping arcade. All the rooms have smoke detectors and sprinkler systems, private balconies, minibars, electronic safes, and hair dryers. ⊠ *Box 334, Pokhara,* ☎ *061/23451,* 𝙵𝙰𝚇 *061/28482, E-mail: resv@fulbari.com.np. 100 rooms, 14 suites. 3 restaurants, bar, in-room safes, minibars, room service, pool,*

outdoor hot tub, 9-hole golf course, 2 floodlit clay tennis courts, laundry service, meeting rooms, airport shuttle, helipad. AE, MC, V.

$$$$ ⊡ **Shangri-La Village Pokhara.** Although it is difficult to imagine, this
★ luxury resort is even more beautiful than its Kathmandu sister. The rooms
have slate floors, Tibetan rugs, local pottery, and intricately carved furniture. Other lovely touches include Tibetan-style, cloud-shape bathroom mirrors, mask-faced clothes hooks, and fresh flowers. Private balconies overlook the expansive garden, koi-stocked fishpond, and waterfall pool that reflects the snow-tipped Himalayas. The staff is exceptionally friendly and helpful. ✉ *Box 333, Pokhara,* ☎ *061/22122,*
FAX *061/21995, E-mail: hosangp@village.mos.com.np. 65 rooms. 2 restaurants, bar, minibars, room service, pool, hot tub, sauna, steam room, health club, baby-sitting, laundry service, business services, meeting rooms, airport shuttle. AE, DC, MC, V.*

$$$ ⊡ **Hotel Fewa Prince.** This redbrick hotel is set amid the farming fields, but it's within 10 minutes of both the center of town and the airport. The huge rooms have basic furnishings but mountain views; the best are the four with the big double beds (the rest have twins). The plain, rough carpet on the lobby steps is fraying, but the staff is friendly and helpful. Environmentalists might appreciate that the water is solar heated. ✉ *Kundhar-14, Pokhara,* ☎ *061/24701,* FAX *061/ 24881. 31 rooms, 4 suites. Restaurant, bar, room service, laundry service, business services, meeting rooms, airport shuttle. AE, MC, V.*

$$ ⊡ **Fish Tail Lodge.** Getting there is half the fun at this hotel on Phewa Lake Island. You cross the short distance from the Lakeside shore to the island resort on a wooden raft floating on 50-gallon tanks. A guide pulls the raft, which is roped to both shores, across to the flower-garden-filled island, which has excellent views of the lake, the mountain, and the junglelike woods behind the lodge. Circular brick buildings house rooms with terra-cotta floors and comfortable window seats. The tasteful white and tan furnishings make the place feel less like a hotel and more like home. Only the deluxe rooms have bathtubs, and room service only brings drinks. Be careful on the walkways: the wide distances between the rocks make it easy to trip or stub your toe. For years this was the only luxury hotel in Pokhara, and its long list of repeat visitors is a testament to its good service. ✉ *Box 10, Pokhara,* ☎ *061/20071,* FAX *061/20072, E-mail: fishtail@lodge.mos.com.np. 48 rooms, 5 deluxe doubles. Restaurant, bar, laundry service, business services, airport shuttle. AE, MC, V.*

$ ⊡ **Hotel Fewa.** Run by Mike Frame of Mike's Breakfast fame, this hotel
★ bears his trademark of gentle, classical music drifting over a flowering garden. Built in 1972, it has always had the advantage of its locale—down a village path to the lake's edge, in a quiet grove, a stroll away from the buzz of Lakeside. When Mike took over in 1997, he began renovating the two-story hotel, adding spacious tiled bathrooms (no bathtubs) and a wide veranda for inside and outside dining. Futons are set up on platforms with Japanese-style dinner tables that can serve as mini-night tables. The rooms on the second floor have the best views. Mike is also renovating nearby cottages. The interiors have terra-cotta-color mud-and-clay walls and ground-floor fireplaces. The sleeping areas are above, in lofts reached by ladder, and have futons set underneath windows that overlook the lake. There are no televisions or telephones in the rooms. At press time, 10 rooms were ready. ✉ *Lakeside, Baidam, Pokhara,* ☎ *061/20151, E-mail: mike@fewa.mos.com.np. 10 rooms. Restaurant, bar. No credit cards.*

$ ⊡ **Hotel Stupa.** This grey-stone hotel, with two ministupas at its gate, gives new meaning to "a room with a view." The typical Western-style hotel rooms have huge panoramic windows that are nearly floor-to-ceiling and overlook the Himalayas. You can also take in the sights from the rooms' balconies and from the patio seating on the hotel roof. The furniture in the rooms is bamboo with soft cushions, and Tibetan rugs on the carpeted floor create a homey feel. The hotel is within strolling distance from the shops, bars, and restaurants of Lakeside, but far enough away to escape the noise. ✉ *Box 322, Lakeside, Pokhara,* ☎ *061/22608,* ℻ *061/28909. 18 rooms. Restaurant, bar, room service, massage, laundry service, meeting rooms, airport shuttle. AE, MC, V.*

$ 🏨 **Lake Palace.** Set in the quiet area of Lakeside, close enough for a view of the lake but a short walk from the restaurants and shops, this hotel is instantly recognizable by the miniature Tibetan stupa on its rooftop. You enter through stunning hand-carved doors with depictions of elements of Nepali, Hindu, and Tibetan culture. The rooms are basic, although the beds have nicely carved head- and footboards. Be careful going to the bathroom at night: you have to step up to the attached room. Enjoy your breakfast on your room's balcony overlooking the Himalayas. ✉ *Box 248, Lakeside, Pokhara,* ☎ *061/21027,* ℻ *061/21027, E-mail: paradise@pacific.wlink.com.np. 24 rooms. Restaurant, bar, business services, meeting rooms. AE, MC, V.*

$ 🏨 **Silver Oaks.** This quiet Lakeside hotel is actually in the home of its owners, a young couple who are both former Yak & Yeti employees. They run their home like a first-class hotel, complete with stationery, logo-imprinted herbal soap, mineral water, and fresh fruit in each room, but you will pay a fraction of what you would expect for these amenities. It is the little touches throughout that make this hotel: the family heirloom carpets decorating the walls along the marble staircase, the rice-paper artwork in the hallways, the brass statues throughout. For a relaxing evening, kick back in the rooftop bar and lounge and watch television (there are no TVs in the rooms). It is a good place to while away the hours reading, drinking, or just staring at the mountaintops. The best rooms are those with double beds (some rooms have twins), which are also the only rooms with tubs and balconies. All of the food in the hotel is fresh and prepared to order. The daal baht is excellent. ✉ *Schoolpatan, Lakeside, Pokhara,* ☎ *061/24247,* ℻ *061/26642, E-mail: silver@oaks.mos.com.np. 18 rooms. Restaurant, bar, baby-sitting, business services. AE, MC, V.*

Nightlife and the Arts

Most people who come down from the mountains just want to enjoy a hot shower and cold beer in Pokhara. Not surprisingly, bars abound in both the Lakeside and Damside areas; those on the waterfront are obviously the prettiest. The rest of the city closes down at about 10:30, so it is important to walk home with at least one other person at your side. While crime against travelers has not been an issue in Pokhara, it is a growing city, and precautions never hurt.

Performing Arts Venues

To see an hour-long Nepalese cultural dance show, go to the **Fish Tail Lodge** (☞ Lodging, *above*). The show is performed daily at 6:30, and admission is 150 Rs. per person.

Nightlife

A lovely spot for cocktails is the garden area on the lakefront at **Boomerang Restaurant** (✉ Lakeside, Pokhara, ☎ 061/22978). **Club Amsterdam** (✉ Lakeside, Pokhara, ☎ 061/22978) is another Lakeside open-air pub, with pool tables and typical bar food, plus a splattering of Indian snacks, like *pakodas* (vegetables fried in an egg batter). There is also a back garden area overlooking the lake and mountains. The **Monsoon** (✉ Lakeside, Pokhara, ☎ 061/27221) is a backpackers' favorite. For pizza, beer, and pool in a smoky bar, albeit with a thatched roof, visit **Moondance Restaurant & Pub** (⊠ Lakeside, Pokhara, ☎ no phone). Be aware that of all these spots, only the Boomerang accepts credit cards.

Outdoor Activities and Sports

Boating

You can hire a boat in the boat ramp area in Lakeside, down the road from the Moondance Restaurant & Pub (☞ Nightlife, *above*). One hour of rowing yourself costs 130 Rs.; to hire a local resident to row for you costs 170 Rs. per hour. A whole-day boat rental costs 350 Rs. Note that if you take a boat out for a half hour, you will still be charged for one hour. Unfortunately, you don't get to choose your boat.

Fishing

A rod with bait costs 250 Rs. a day. Ask the employees at **Mike's Restaurant** (⊠ Lakeside, Baidam, Pokhara, ☎ 061/20151) for more information; they're knowledgeable and offer good rental prices. Phewa Lake is stocked with fish as varied as the grass carp from China, common carp from Israel, and mezor carp from India, all of which can be anywhere from about 2 pounds to 154 pounds. Plus, there are plenty of local fish, including Bam Bitta, Rewa, Pagetta, and Bhudyna.

Golfing

The **Himalayan Golf Course** (☎ 061/27204), about 8 km (5 mi) from the center of Pokhara, is a 9-hole course that runs along the riverbank, which creates a natural hazard. Greens fee, including a caddy, is $20 for 9 holes, $30 if you play the course twice for an 18-hole game. Golf club hire is $10 for 9 holes, $15 for 18 holes. Taxi drivers know the way.

Paragliding

You can take a tandem flight from Sarangkot, the viewpoint above Lakeside, with **Sunrise Paragliding** (⊠ Box 125, Lakeside, Pokhara, ☎ 061/ 21174, E-mail: adahill@aol.com). The season runs from late October to early February. No experience is necessary. The flights last approximately 30 minutes, sometimes longer, depending on the weather. The cost is $30. Sunrise also runs a three-day introductory course to paragliding and a three-day intermediate course, each at $200. Reservations should be made a day in advance at the Sunrise Trekking office opposite the Monsoon restaurant in Lakeside; MasterCard and Visa are accepted.

Yoga

There are daily Hatha yoga workshops, as well as yoga and meditation retreats at **Sadhana Yoga** (⊠ Raging River Runner, Lakeside, Pokhara, ☎ 061/26839, ℻ 061/23246). Take a taxi or bike 2½ km (1½ mi) from Lakeside toward Sedi Bagar, which is past the Buddhist Meditation Centre if you are traveling west along Phewa Lake. Then follow the signs to Pame. Courses range from $10 for a day to $170 for a 21-day retreat (including room and three vegetarian meals a day). Days are filled with scheduled activities from 6 AM to 8 PM.

Shopping

There is not much to buy in Pokhara that you cannot buy in Kathmandu. To boot, the prices in Pokhara are 5%–10% higher than in Kathmandu. If you have a day or two in the capital, you might as well do your shopping there. However, if you have forgotten anything—from soap to anoraks—you can buy it in Pokhara. Stores open around 9 AM and close around 10 PM. Some stores are closed on Saturday.

Pokhara A to Z

Arriving and Departing

BY BUS

In 1997 **Greenline** (⊠ Box 3904, ☎ 01/253885 or 061/27271, ⊙ daily 7 AM–5 PM) started offering daily, air-conditioned service between Kathmandu and Pokhara. Buses depart from both locations at 7 AM, arriving at the other location at 1:30 or 2 PM. The fare is 600 Rs. (less than $10). In Kathmandu, Greenline is at Keshar Mahal on Tridevi Marg (near the taxi stands at the entrance of Thamel). In Pokhara, they're in Lakeside, opposite the Fishtail Lodge entrance.

BY HIRED CAR

For about $75–$100 you can hire a car from one of the Kathmandu travel agents for a one-night, two-day trip to Pokhara. The drive to Pokhara will take about 4½ hours.

BY PLANE

The Pokhara **airport** (☎ 061/21617) is at the southern end of Pokhara, about 1 km (½ mi) east of Damside. There are an average of 21 flights flights a day between Pokhara and Kathmandu. The trip takes 30 minutes. For the best view of the mountains, sit on the right side while flying from Kathmandu, and on the left while flying to Kathmandu. To reconfirm your flights, call: **Buddha Air** (☎ 061/21429), **Cosmic Air** (☎ 061/21846), **Gorkha Airlines** (☎ 061/25971), **Lumbini Airways** (☎ 061/27233), **Necon Air** (☎ 061/23120), **RNAC** (☎ 061/226574), **Yeti Airways** (☎ 061/30016).

Between the Airport and City: Taxis are available just outside the airport terminal. The fare between the airport and the city is 100 Rs.–150 Rs.

Getting Around

BY BICYCLE

Mountain bikes can be rented for about $1 a day, for a tour around the hilly city. Try **Himalayan Mountain Bikes** (⊠ Box 12673, Kathmandu, ☎ 061/21423); their Pokhara office is across from the boat ramp in Lakeside.

BY HIRED CAR

Touring the Pokhara valley by hired car costs about 800 Rs. a day. Ask your hotelier or travel agent.

BY TAXI

Although taxis here recently acquired meters, drivers will likely tell you theirs is already broken (don't be fooled). Aside from metered trips, taxis also ply fixed routes for set rates of 50 Rs.–200 Rs. an hour, depending on where you are going and how bad the roads are that have to be traveled. The driver will have an official rate card for sites in town. Often the fare is charged on a per-person basis, check with the driver before you get into the taxi.

Contacts and Resources

CURRENCY EXCHANGE

You can change money at your hotel or at any of the numerous money exchange stands in the Lakeside and Damside areas, including: **Ambassador Money Exchange** (⊠ Box 168, Lakeside, ☎ 061/22611, ⊙ daily 7:30–7:30) and **Mary Exchange Counter** (⊠ Lakeside, ☎ 061/26014, ⊙ daily 7:30–7:30). You may get a better rate at these small shops than in your hotel.

EMERGENCIES

Fire brigade (☎ 061/20222), **police** (☎ 061/20055).

Contact your hotel for a doctor on call. The **Manipal Hospital** (☎ 061/ 24811), near the Phulbari telecommunication center, is open 24 hours for emergencies; it also has an extensive pharmacy.

ENGLISH-LANGUAGE BOOKSTORES

There are at least a dozen secondhand book shops in the Lakeside district where you can trade in books that you read on the journey to Pokhara. Two worth checking out: **Fishtail Book Shop** (✉ Lakeside, ☎ 061/21368, ☉ daily 8–7) and **Perfect Book Shop** (✉ Lakeside, ☎ 061/22727, ☉ daily 8–7).

POST OFFICE AND E-MAIL

Most of the hotels and many of the bookstores will post your mail. If you really want to do it yourself, the **post office** (☎ 061/20032) is near Mahendrapul. It's open Sunday–Friday 10–4. E-mail users have a plethora of choices in the Lakeside area; the agreed-upon rate that shops charge is 9 Rs. per minute for Internet use.

GUIDED TOURS

☞ Guided Tours *in* Kathmandu A to Z, *above.*

PERSONAL GUIDES

Pokhara Sight Seeing Tours & Travels (✉ Box 49, Pokhara 17, ☎ 061/ 25352). Visit the Bindi Basini Temple, the Seti River Gorge, Devi's Falls, and Phewa Lake without the hassle of having to arrange transportation yourself. The narrated tours are conducted in a minivan; the cost is 200 Rs.

SPECIAL-INTEREST TOURS

See Kathmandu A to Z, *above,* for more information.

Equator Expeditions (✉ Lakeside, across from Nirula's Restaurant, ☎ 061/20688, E-mail: equatornepal.com).

Exodus Outdoor Enthusiast (✉ Lakeside, next to the Maya Pub, ☎ 061/ 25856).

Himalayan Encounters (✉ Hallan Chowk, Lakeside, ☎ 061/22682, FAX 061-21022).

Ker & Downey, Nepal (✉ Box 3863, Maharajgunj, Kathmandu; ✉ 13201 Northwest Freeway, Suite 800, Houston, TX, 77040-6098, ☎ 01/416751 or 800/324–9081 in the U.S.) runs a 10-day, luxuriously pampered trek and river rafting trip. You stay at the Shangri-La Village in Pokhara the first night, then you make short treks for six days, staying overnight at the company's own lush private lodges. Then, for a break, you spend another night at the Shangri-La, followed by two days rafting, staying overnight at the company's deluxe camping setup. The cost of all accommodations, meals, guides, ground transportation, permits, and even the loan of some camping gear are included in the price of $1,260 per person (single supplement of $400). A second, 14-day trip adds a visit to Temple Tiger in the Royal Chitwan National Park to the agenda, as well as accommodation for three nights in the Yak & Yeti Hotel in Kathmandu. The cost includes the same things as the previous trip, plus all domestic air transfers. It is $2,575 per person (single supplement of $660).

Ultimate Descents (✉ Hotel Snowland, Lakeside, ☎ 061/23240).

VISA EXTENSIONS

Visa extension applications, for up to 120 days may be submitted to the **Pokhara Immigration Office** (✉ Lakeside, ☎ 061/21167), which is between the airport and Lakeside. Applications are accepted Sunday–Thursday 10–1:30, and Friday 10–noon. You can pick up your passport Sunday–Thursday 3–5, or Friday 2–3.

A **Tourist Information Center** (☎ 061/20028) is located across the street from the airport. It's open Sunday–Friday 10–4, but information there is limited, at best. The **Annapurna Conservation Area Project** (✉ Lakeside, ☎ 061/21102) maintains a small office in Lakeside where you can get the latest information about the Annapurna region and conservation and development activities in the area.

POKHARA VALLEY

Most people come to Pokhara to make the 10-day-to-3-week treks in the Annapurna region, but there are also many interesting short day treks around Pokhara to hilltops with views of Machhapuchhare and the Annapurnas. For information on longer treks, read the Trekking and River Rafting sections, *below.* For shorter walks in the region, consider **Sarangkot**, a hill (5,223 ft) in the northwestern part of the valley, facing Pokhara and rising above Phewa Lake, or **Kahun Danda** (4,971 ft) to the northeast of Pokhara. Both places are popular at sunrise or sunset. Or you can wander the bat caves of **Mahendra Gufa**. If peace and quiet is what you are after, visit **Rupa** and **Begnas Lakes**.

Finally, while not quite in the valley, but on the way back to Kathmandu, you might be able to visit **Gorkha**, a historically important village.

Sarangkot

4 km (2½ mi) north of Lakeside in Pokhara.

Up until the 18th century, a number of Baise-Chauibise kings ruled this region from the hilltop. Weeds and grass have overrun the fortress. However, the best part of Sarangkot is the view of the city of Pokhara, dotted around Phewa Lake, with the mountains in the backdrop. If you go at sunrise or sunset, you can watch the sun sneak over the Himalayas. To the north, you can see the Seti River and to the south Phewa Lake. There is a view tower at the top of Sarnagkot hill.

It takes about three hours to walk up, taking the trail that leaves the paved road at **Binde Basini Temple**. From Bhairab Tole or square, walk northwest through the cultivated fields to reach the foot of Gyarjati Hill. From there, take the village trail west through forest and shrubs, until you pass through Gyarjati village. Here, you will see women weaving on hand looms. Continue walking (you will pass teahouses) until you reach the village of Silangabot. The incline gets a bit steeper from here until you reach the top of Sarangkot.

You can backtrack, or walk down a stone staircase that leads to Phewa Lake (it is way too steep to walk up this route, plus there are no mountain views on the way up). The pleasant downhill walk takes about two hours, wandering through terraced rice paddies and a forest, and past houses, to the Lakeside area where there are boatmen waiting to paddle you across to the Lakeside district.

If you go by tour, plan on a 45-minute drive from Pokhara, followed by an hour trek to the viewpoint. If you hike, as described above, the trip will take about three hours.

Kahan Danda

About 5 km (3 mi) northeast of Lakeside in Pokhara.

This viewpoint with a tower on top of the ridge (5,118 ft) is about a 1½-hour walk northeast of Pokhara. You are at a slightly lower altitude here than at Sarangkot, and the view is not quite as exquisite. However, it is not as popular a site and therefore is more quiet. Start at Mahendra Pul, and walk east to the southern base of Kahun Danda. Continue up the trail to the settlement of Phulbari and on to the tower, which is visible most of the way.

Mahendra Gupha

10 km (6 mi) north of Lakeside in Pokhara.

These limestone caves are also known as *Chamero Odhaar* (Bat Cave) or the House of Bats. They're about a two-hour walk north of Pokhara. You might want to bring your own flashlight to see the winged residents, and wear clothes you don't mind getting dirty, because you could end up crawling about (if you are game). Hire a guide to show you around; it will help support the local economy and enhance your experience. (Expect to pay 15 Rs. for a guide and 40 Rs. for a flashlight.) The guides are locals who congregate at the mouth of the cave.

After you walk into the cave, which is about 150 ft long, look up. Unfortunately, most of the stalactites have been stolen by sticky-fingered visitors, but you can still see a few and hear the eerie sound of water dripping from them. As you move farther into the cave, you will see and hear the bats hanging around. Your guide may reach out and pluck a bat from the ceiling and thrust it at you to hold, so he can take your camera and photograph you and your surprised bat. If you don't want the guide to do this, tell him before you go into the cave.

You can crawl out of a small hole in the back of the cave (pretend you're Indiana Jones), or you can retrace your steps to the entrance.

To reach the caves, from the bazaar area in the northern part of Pokhara, walk to the village of Batulechaur, and from there head up to the caves. It is a relentless uphill walk, and much easier to take a taxi, for 300 Rs.–400 Rs. Go during the day.

Gorkha

146 km (90½ mi) west of Kathmnadu, and 18 km (11 mi) north of the Kathmandu-Pokhara (Prithvi) Hwy.

King Prithvi Narayan Shah, who unified the Kingdom of Nepal during the 18th century, was born in the township of Gorkha. His story is truly remarkable: Born prince of a principality, he died king of a nation. He utilized diplomacy—and his brutal forces—to unify the country. And so it came that his fighters were named Gorkhas, a title that would live on for centuries, when the British recruited Nepali and Indian soldiers and labeled them all "Gurkhas."

The relatively obscure village is set along a ridge, with the **Gorkha Durbar** perched a thousand feet above. Set on the top of the fortified hill above the township, the square is about an hour walk uphill, through terraced walkways and lush forest areas. Start at the bus station and walk north. When you reach the temples to Vishnu, Krishna, and Ganesh, turn right and continue until you come to **Tallo Square**. There is a Rana-style redbrick and woodwork building that served as the kingdom's administrative headquarters. Walk east from here (about half an hour), until you see the steps going up to Gorkha Durbar. Every time the road forks, go left, until you reach the ridge where Gorkha Durbar is perched; you are rewarded with a spectacular view of Manaslu and Himalchuli peaks.

You are not allowed to wear leather or take photographs within the Gorkha Durbar complex. The **Kalika Mandir** shrine is off-limits to Westerners (or anyone other than priests and the King of Nepal), as is the palace. However, the latticed windows are beautiful, and there are numerous shrines and the usual beheadings of male animals in the square.

Since spring 1999, when Gorkha was first placed off-limits to foreigners due to the Maoist insurgency presence surrounding the elections, the town has been alternately open and closed to visitors. Before you go, check with your embassy for the current status.

Manakamana Devi

120 km (74 mi) west of Kathmandu; 90 km (56 mi) east of Pokhara; and 12 km (7 mi) south of Gorkha.

People believe that if you make a pilgrimage to Manakamana Devi your wishes will be fulfilled. The four story, pagoda-style brick-and-wood temple with two roofs looks much like the ones in Kathmandu, but it is set on a ridge overlooking the river valleys of the Trisuli to the south and Marsyangdi to the west. On a clear day, you can also see the snow-capped Manasulu-Himalchuli and Annapurnas, so at the very least, your wish to see beauty is likely to be fulfilled.

In the past, people hiked here from Gorkha, up the long, arduous ridge (4,270 ft), but now, thanks to Nepal's first-ever cable car service, the trip is considerably easier. The cable cars cover the 2.8-km (1.7-mi) stretch from the Prithvi Highway to the temple in less then two minutes. There are 31 cable cars that hold six passengers each. The cars run Sunday–Thursday 8–5, and Friday–Saturday 8–7; the ride costs $10.

Lodging

$$ ⚏ **River Side Springs Resort.** Set above the sand beach of the Trisuli River, this resort is an excellent place to get away from it all. Go river rafting, take a pony ride, or lounge in their luxurious, massive, sparkling, turquoise pool, which has its own jungle island in the middle, and is just yards away from the river. The resort is just 4 km (2½ mi) away from the cable cars, and staying there is a nice way to break up your trip to and from Kathmandu or Pokhara. You can also make this your headquarters for a trip to Royal Chitwan National Park (☞ *below*), which is a 40-minute drive away. The timber-roof cabins are basic, with low twin beds and simple furnishings; but the grounds are beautifully landscaped, and there's plenty to do—from the ponies to the mountain bikes to the beach—and plenty of room to do absolutely nothing. ⊠ *Box 4384, Kathmandu,* ☎ *01/241408,* ℻ *01/232163, E-mail: nangint@ccsl.com.np. 22 cabins, 4 with kitchenette. Restaurant, air-conditioning, pool, volleyball, beach, camping, fishing, bicycles, meeting room. AE, MC, V.*

Pokhara Valley A to Z

Getting Around
BY BICYCLE
Himalayan Mountain Bikes (⊠ Box 12673, Kathmandu, ☎ 061/21423), which is across from the boat hire on Phewa Lake in Pokhara, offers bike tours for $25–$55 a day that take you to Begnas Lake or Sarangkot. You can also book in Kathmandu (☞ *Kathmandu A to Z, above*).

BY HIRED CAR
For an overall tour of the valley, the average cost is about 800 Rs. To go to **Sarangkot** expect to pay about 700 Rs.; to go to **Begna Lake,**

about 500 Rs.; to **Rupa Lake** about 1,000 Rs. The trip to Rupa Lake is more expensive, because the road is quite bad, and you will need a four-wheel-drive vehicle to get there. People rarely go to Rupa, so you will have to bargain long and hard to get a rate. It will cost about 3,000 Rs. to make the 2½- to 3-hour trip to **Gorkha** and **Manakamana Devi,** whether you go from Pokhara or Kathmandu.

BY TAXI

Once you leave the immediate surroundings of Pokhara, expect to pay about 300 Rs. per hour of touring, depending on where you go. A taxi will charge about 400 Rs. for a round-trip to **Mahendra Gupha,** and will charge similar prices for a hired car for trips to **Sarangkot** and **Begna Lake.** Most taxis won't even try to get to **Rupa Lake.** It is best to visit **Gorkha** and **Manakamana Devi** en route to or from Pokhara, since a taxi to these places will cost just as much as a hired car.

Contacts and Resources

CURRENCY EXCHANGE

You can change money at your hotel or at any of the numerous money exchange stands in Lakeside and Damside areas (☞ Pokhara A to Z, *above*).

EMERGENCIES

Fire brigade (✉ Pokhara, ☎ 061/20222). **Police** (✉ Pokhara, ☎ 061/20055; ✉ Gorkha, ☎ 055/20199).

Contact your hotel for a **doctor** on call. The **Manipal Hospital** (☎ 061/24811), near the Phulbari telecommunication center, is open 24 hours for emergencies; it also has an extensive pharmacy.

PERSONAL GUIDES

Pokhara Sight Seeing Tours & Travels (✉ Box 49, Pokhara, ☎ 061/25352) has guides who, at sunrise or sunset, will bring you up to Sarangkot, the hill station north of the city. The trip costs 175 Rs. per person. A visit to the Mahendra Caves is part of the "around Pokhara" tour, which costs 200 Rs.

THE TERAI

A trip south to the Terai takes you from the mountains to the heat of the Indo-Gangetic plains, where there are groves of bamboo and banana trees jutting out above rice paddies. Naked children chase one another on the red-color earth, only to stop and frantically wave hello whenever foreigners pass. The otherwise slow-paced Terai is home to the Tharu, former nomads who migrated from the Thar desert in India during the 12th century to escape forced conversion to the Muslim religion. The women came first, accompanied by male servants who worked as helpmates and later became the women's lovers.

Their dark complexions make the Tharu easy to recognize. Many of the men wear wraparound cloth skirts—an ancient garb that contrasts with the modern black umbrellas that shield their exposed bodies from the sun. The women usually wear white saris and heavy silver ornaments on their ankles, wrists, and necks; gold adorns their ears and noses. Women also tattoo their legs. In the past, these markings kept away Muslims, offended by the practice. Now the tattoos are primarily an artistic embellishment. Around their neck or wrist, many Tharu wear a white thread as a symbol of purity and a black one to ward off evil spirits.

These nomadic people withstood malaria epidemics for generations, until Americans doused the region with DDT in the 1950s and eradicated malaria from the Terai. Then other groups of people moved into the region, including poachers who nearly killed off the rhino and tiger populations. Fortunately, since the area became a wildlife preserve in 1962, the animal population has rebounded.

In the Terai, you can visit the **Royal Chitwan National Park,** southwest of Kathmandu, and the **Royal Bardia Wildlife Reserve,** in the extreme west of Nepal. **Lumbini,** the birthplace of Buddha, is southwest of Chitwan. Earmarked to become a big visitor site, it still has minimal, yet good, lodging options. **Janakpur,** southwest of Chitwan, still has not developed good accommodations, but it is a historically important Hindu town.

Royal Chitwan National Park

165 km (102 mi) southwest of Kathmandu; 204 km (126 mi) southeast of Pokhara.

Chitwan is derived from *Chitravan,* meaning "heart of the jungle" or "leopard forest" in Nepali. The 932 sq km (360 sq mi) of protected forest and plains is noted for its resident 43 species of animals and more than 450 species of birds. The park was once the private playground and hunting preserve of Nepal's Rana prime ministers and British royalty on vacation. In 1962, King Mahendra turned the area into a wildlife sanctuary, forcibly removing 22,000 people from the area. Only 22 tigers and 100 rhinoceros had survived the hunters' guns. Eleven years later, in 1973, a part of Chitwan was designated a national park. In 1976, even more land was protected. Today, Chitwan is listed as a UNESCO World Heritage Site. Now, it is estimated that there are about 100 tigers and more than 400 rhinoceros in the park, although poachers are occasionally still caught.

The relationship between the animals and the people here is, as always, a difficult balance. Local residents do have problems with rhinos trampling through the rice paddies; and deer, monkeys, and wild pigs do their fair share of crop poaching. While it is rare, tigers and crocodiles have, on occasion, attacked humans. However, the region also provides opportunities for people. In February each year, villagers are allowed into the park to harvest the grass, which is then turned into roof thatching and a cash crop. Tourism has also provided a cash influx to the region. Locals are building more and more low-budget lodges, restaurants, and shops just outside the park that appeal to backpacking travelers. The bigger resorts, as you will see from the addresses, are owned by Kathmandu-based companies. However, even these companies employ local residents to work as guides. The local residents are a particularly friendly group of Nepalis who seem genuinely amused by the oddities of foreigners, with their funny clothing, camera-toting mania, and fascination with dangerous animals.

The hilly areas of the park are forested with *sal* (hardwood) trees. A fifth of the park is made up of the flood plains of the Narayani, Rapti, and Reu rivers. These plains are covered by dense elephant grass, interspersed with forests of silk cotton (*kapok*), acacia, and sisal trees. The elephant grass is not the sort you send your son out to mow on Saturday mornings: it grows higher than an elephant's back. Lurking between the blades are the endangered Asian one-horned rhinoceros, as well as the elusive and rare Royal Bengal tiger. Expect to see numerous rhinos, but don't hold your breath waiting to sight a tiger. The male peacocks that abound have a rainbow array of rich, colorful, long tails, far fuller than those of the birds you see in zoos. There are also four species of deer, plus leopards, sloth bears, wild boars, rhesus monkeys, common langurs, wild dogs, and white stocking gaurs (wild cattle). The swampy areas and numerous oxbow lakes of Chitwan provide a home for the deadly marsh crocodiles. In a stretch of the Narayani River, one of the world's four species of freshwater dolphins romps through the water. Bird-watchers can expect to see woodpeckers, hornbills, Bengal florican, and redheaded trogons. But even if you can't name the birds, their chirps and calls provide a constant musical background to your visit.

The Mahendra Highway (the east–west highway) runs through the region, connecting the park by road to Kathmandu. There is an airport in Bharatpur, just outside of the park. Several river rafting trips also travel to the park from the Kathmandu area (☞ River Rafting, *below*).

Great Itineraries

IF YOU HAVE 1 DAY

You will see the most if you take a jeep-ride safari, since the jeep can get you farther into the jungle more quickly than an elephant ride. However, try to squeeze in an **elephant-ride safari** as well. After all, how often do you get to ride an elephant in search of rhinos? On the elephant safaris, you sit in inverted-table-like chairs, often four to an elephant, plus the guide. All you need to do is reach out to pet the big beast. At the end of the tour, you can tip your guide (100 Rs., or so) by giving the money to the elephant's handy trunk.

IF YOU HAVE 2 TO 3 DAYS

Consider taking an elephant-ride safari, a jeep-ride safari, a canoe trip, and a trip to the elephant breeding camp. While many agencies and guides may push a jungle walk, don't do it. Although there are no exact figures, each year people are hurt or killed by rhinos and tigers during the annual elephant-grass-cutting harvest; and both guides and tourists have been maimed and killed on jungle safari walks. In the spring of 1999, a tiger killed a local who was sleeping with his hut door open. If pushed, most of the guides will say the walks are dangerous, but they do them to provide income for their families. Guides tell trekkers to climb a tree if they encounter a rhino. Unfortunately, many of the sisal trees are limbless at a low level, or too thin to climb. Many who have done the jungle walk say that every rustle of the grass made their hearts pound.

When to Go

Most people visit between mid-September and the end of June. However, in September and October, the leeches can still be a post-monsoon annoyance. The best time to go is February or March, because it is temperate. Plus, in late February the locals cut the elephant grass, making viewing easier. Book well in advance if you plan to visit during these months. Forget the summer months, when it is way too hot, wet, and buggy.

What to Bring

Bring binoculars, flashlight, insect repellent, swimwear, sun hat, sunglasses, and sunblock. Wear comfortable shoes and casual clothes that blend in with the natural surroundings; avoid brights, especially red, yellow, and white—these colors have been known to upset the rhinos. During the winter months, November through February, sweaters and jackets are necessary in the mornings and evenings.

Sights to See

ELEPHANT-RIDE SAFARI

The elephants circle rhinos, deer, and sloth bear once they are sighted. Amazingly, even a mama rhino with her baby will let a people-toting elephant stand right next to her. Take your ride in the morning, when the animals are more active and visible.

There are two types of elephant-ride services: One- to two-hour, government-run elephant rides for 600 Rs., and two- to three-hour privately owned elephant rides that cost about 525 Rs. (or are included in a package deal). Take a private trip, as long as it goes into the park and isn't just in the surrounding area. Not only are they cheaper, but usually they only put two people and a guide on each elephant; the government elephants carry four people and a guide. However, take into consideration how long you want to sit on the hard seats. Even with only two people, the seats get uncomfortable as they sway back and forth with each mammoth step, and the private trip is longer. If you take the privately owned trip, ask to feed, or if you like, help bathe the elephant afterward. It is a wet but memorable experience. If you opt for the government trip, know that two riders face forward, and two face the rear. Try to sit in the front, facing forward, otherwise you will be craning your neck back and forth and watching elephant dumpings.

JEEP-RIDE SAFARI

This is the best way to see the most wildlife.

Look at the treads on the tires before you go. You should feel confident that the jeep is well maintained and can get out of a rhino-charging situation (while elephants know how close to get to the rhinos without angering them, the jeep drivers aren't always so careful). Look for comfortable seats, preferably the type that allow you to stand up and hold a railing, so you can relieve your butt from the rough ride. Many places only offer jeep safaris from mid-November through June; after that, the monsoons make it difficult to get through the mud and cross rivers.

CANOE RIDE

Many lodges will only take you canoeing if you visit between October and mid-March; afterward the rivers are too high and dangerous. From the canoe, you can see crocodiles, birds, and even rhinos on the riverbanks. You can paddle about for anywhere from an hour to a half day.

ELEPHANT BREEDING CENTER

Take bananas with you to feed the elephants. Look for the elephant who bows when you say, "Namaste," the typical Nepali greeting. The breeding center feeds and looks after about 40 elephants. Elephants are not native to the Chitwan Jungle but were gifts from the Indian government or were purchased from keepers in India. Now, the Chitwan elephants are breeding to create their own community. Full-time caretakers look after the babies and the grown elephants, who usually work as guide elephants in the park. You may feed an elephant at the Breeding Center and ride him the next day on a safari. The elephants eat at least 500 pounds of food a day, including elephant sandwiches made of grass wrapped and packed with grain. If you want to visit the Breeding Center, ask your hotelier. Guides usually make this a normal stopping point, but ask to be sure. Admission to the center is free.

Dining and Lodging

If you book your trip at one of the resorts in the park, or one of the upscale lodgings just outside of the park, you will be transported directly to these lush locales, where you will be pampered.

Many travelers will tell you about the numerous budget hotels in the Sauraha area on the northern bank of the Rapti River, 6 km (4 mi) south of Tadi Bazaar, where buses and taxis drop you off to a throng of touts waiting to take you to "their" hotels. Sauraha is a jungle version of Thamel, complete with loud pubs and restaurants. Although budget travelers will try to convince you that they got a great deal in Sauraha, you might get nickeled and dimed, and you will invariably get frustrated in the area. By the time you pay for your room, for all of the trips (park entrance fee, elephant ride, canoeing, etc.), and for your food (which, by the way, will be nothing memorable), you'll probably find you've spent almost as much as you would have for one of the hassle-free, all-inclusive packages described below.

The downside of some of the all-inclusive deals is that the resorts can be run like boot camp. Some schedule wake-up at 5:30 AM, elephant rides at 6, breakfast at 8, canoeing at 9, and so on. Keep in mind though that you do not have to do it all, and *you* are paying *them*. If you want to do it all, but at your own pace, consider spending three nights in one of the resorts. This makes the stay far more relaxed.

If you are staying inside the park, you will be eating at your resort. There are restaurants serving basic trekker food in Sauraha.

Dining

$$ ✗ **Al Fresco Café & Pub.** This open-air restaurant serves Indian, Nepali, Italian, and Continental food, but go for the Indian dishes. The full Tandoori chicken is a meal and a half, fit for a hungry jungle trekker after a day of searching for tigers. The grilled vegetables are done al dente, and a favorite among vegetarian diners. The kitchen is open daily 7 AM to 9 PM, but you can linger later if you like. ⊠ *Sauraha, on the main street,* ☏ *056/21792 for the nearby Bharatpur office. MC, V.*

$ ✗ **Hungry Eye Restaurant and Bar.** Serving food in Sauraha for 12 years, this is one of the longest-standing restaurants in the tourist ghetto outside the park. The caught-that-day grilled catfish with chips and vegetables can be a treat, and many trekkers relish the beef steak as a break from the usual rice and lentils. ⊠ *Sauraha, on the main corner,* ☏ *056/ 29361. No credit cards.*

$ ✗ **KC's Restaurant & Bar.** This fragrant, flower-laden, rooftop restaurant is a backpacker's hangout, crowded at night with people buzzing about their adventures. The staff is exceptionally friendly and helpful, and cocktails are served up with a plateful of chips, popcorn, or french fries. The garlic-tomato macaroni is a plentiful, filling dish. The Swiss breakfast is good any time of day, complete with a hash-brown patty covered with Swiss cheese, two eggs any style, toast, several thick slices of bacon, and grilled tomato. ⊠ *Sauraha, on the main street,* ☏ *no phone. No credit cards.*

Lodging

Unless otherwise noted, rates include full board for one night, park entrance fees, elephant safari, nature walks, bird-watching, and canoeing. All lodges have bars, but drinks are not included in the rates. Exceptions are noted. Prices are per person in a standard double room, tent, or cottage, excluding taxes, service charges, and bar bills. Children under 10 usually get a discount of up to 50%. Rates are, as usual in Nepal, negotiable. Most resorts sell two-night package deals. If you are arranging transportation through these resorts, make sure the quoted rates are round-trip. If you are flying, find out if they charge extra to pick you up at the airport; the hidden charges can add up.

None of the lodges inside the park have electricity, although power in the dining halls is created by generator or solar power. The attached baths have showers. Resorts hope to have telephones within the park soon.

OUTSIDE THE PARK

$$ ✗▥ **Safari Adventure Lodge.** This resort has spacious, comfortable rooms in lovely thatch-roof huts with elephant grass–lined walls. Beautifully landscaped grounds lead to the main building, which was renovated in 1999. The new rooms here include lofts for living areas and have bathrooms with bathtubs, offering the rare treat of a long soak after a day on safari. The main dining hall has a central fireplace for

the cool winter nights. The Kathmandu booking office is on Durbar Marg in Saiyu **Travel Pvt. Ltd.** offices. Rates here also include a village visit, a Land Rover jungle drive, and a native folk dance performance. ⊠ *Box 3017, Durbar Marg, Kathmandu,* ☎ *01/221707,* ℻ *01/226430, E-mail: saujai@mos.com.np. 24 rooms. AE, MC, V.*

$$ ✕⌂ **Tiger Tops Tharu Village.** This resort is just outside of the park. The accommodations are in the traditional "longhouses" of the native Tharu people. They are decorated with local artifacts and traditional paintings done by unmarried Tharu women. Rooms have one queen-size bed and a single bed, solar-powered fans, and attached bathroom with solar-heated shower. The booking office in Kathmandu is behind the Royal Palace. Rates here do not include a $20 park entrance fee. ⊠ *Box 242, Kathmandu,* ☎ *01/411225,* ℻ *01/414075, E-mail: info@tigermountain.com. 11 rooms with bath. Pool, tennis, badminton, horseback riding. AE, MC, V.*

INSIDE THE PARK

$$$$ ✕⌂ **Temple Tiger.** These elevated lodges with thatched roofs actually have marble sinks. They have handsome bed frames, wooden chairs, and coffee tables inside, plus a hammock, umbrella, and private balcony outside. In the square dining hall, you will find a sunken fireplace in the center, warming the room. At the western end of the park, and built with conservation in mind, Temple Tiger truly puts you in the midst of the jungle. The booking office in Kathmandu is in Kamaladi, around the corner from the Hotel Sherpa, across the street from the Royal Singi Hotel. Rates here don't include a $14 park entrance fee. ⊠ *Box 3968, Kamaladi, Kathmandu,* ☎ *01/263480,* ℻ *01/220178. 32 rooms. AE, MC, V.*

$$$$ ✕⌂ **Tiger Tops.** There are two Tiger Top lodges in the park. The **Jungle Lodge** is the original. Built on stilts, the double rooms in this tree-top hotel have solar-powered reading lamps and ceiling fans, and solar-heated showers in the attached bathrooms. The **Tented Camp** is 3 km (2 mi) east of the lodge, on a bluff overlooking the valley. The safari tents here are furnished with twin beds and have attached bathrooms. The Jungle Lodge is open September–June; the Tented Camp is open October–April. The booking office in Kathmandu is behind the Royal Palace. A $20 park entrance fee and a $10 camping fee for staying in the Tented Camp are not included in the rates. ⊠ *Box 242, Kathmandu,* ☎ *01/411225,* ℻ *01/414075, E-mail: info@tigermountain.com. 28 rooms in lodge, 12 twin-bed safari tents; all with bath. AE, MC, V.*

$$$ ✕⌂ **Machan Wildlife Resort.** The timber-framed bungalows with private baths were planned around trees in the eastern end of the park. A stream flowing between them was widened, making a natural swimming pool in the jungle. While it is billed as the spirit of Mowgli in the world of Kipling, the beds are still just basic twin frames. Still, the A-frame lodges are tastefully designed, with murals painted by members of the Mithila ethnic group, art murals, lofts, and porches to relax on after your day out spying wildlife. Tents are the basic safari variety and will comfortably fit two people. The naturalists here are well informed and will guide you into the forest of the Churia hills, where you might glimpse wild elephants. Bring a swimsuit for the pool, not the crocodile-laden river. The booking office in Kathmandu is on Durbar Marg. ⊠ *Box 3140, Kathmandu,* ☎ *01/225001,* ℻ *01/240681, E-mail: wildlife@machan.mos.com.np. 36 rooms, 10 two-person tents. AE, MC, V.*

$$ ✕⌂ **Chitwan Jungle Lodge.** On the eastern end of the park, the simple mud huts have thatched roofs and private baths. The twin beds are covered with thick quilts, and there are flowers on the nightstands. At dinner, while eating off porcelain plates, you might forget you are in the jungle, until reminded by the chirping and animal sounds in the background. If you stay a third night, guides will take you by Land Rover into the heart of the park, for a good chance at spotting the rarer species. The booking office in Kathmandu is on Durbar Marg. ⊠ *Box 1281, Kathmandu,* ☎ *01/228458,* ℻ *01/228349, E-mail: wildlife@resort.wlink.com.np. 36 rooms. MC, V.*

$$ ✕⚅ **Gaida Wildlife Camp.** You can stay in the lodge or the jungle camp. The lodge is set along the Dungri River, not far from Sauraha. It's actually a collection of thatched-roof bungalows built in a semicircle around a central dining hall. The bungalow rooms have spacious balconies and attached baths with solar-powered hot water. The jungle camp is 85 km (53 mi) south of the lodge, in the foothills of the Churia range. The camp is open from October through May. There are 12 twin-bed tents with clothes shelves, closet racks, and attached baths. Or you can opt for the tents without attached baths and brave the walk to the common toilets at night. The booking office in Kathmandu is in a second-floor office on Durbar Marg. ⊠ *Box 2056, Kathmandu,* ☎ *01/220940,* ℻ *01/227292, E-mail: gaida@mos.com.np. The National Park entrance fee is an additional $15 and if you stay in the Jungle Camp the camping fee is an extra $7. 30 rooms in the lodge and 30 tents. MC, V.*

$$ ✕⚅ **Island Jungle Resort.** You can stay in either a lodge or tented camp at this resort favored by large groups of package tourists. In the northwest section of the park, on Bandarjhola island, it is surrounded by the Naranyani River. The lodges are simple jungle huts, with twin beds and attached baths. The tented camp has safari tents designed to accommodate two camp beds. Separate bathrooms with modern toilet facilities and showers are near the tents. Continental and Nepali dinner is served at a large, local-style round hut. The booking office in Kathmandu is on Durbar Marg. A $20 park entrance fee and a $5 camping fee (if you stay in the tented camp) are not included in the rates. ⊠ *Box 2154, Kathmandu,* ☎ *01/220162,* ℻ *01/225615, E-mail: island@mos.com.np. 43 rooms in the lodge, 20 two-person tents. No credit cards.*

Lumbini

136 km (84 mi) west of Chitwan; 284 km (176 mi) southwest of Kathmandu.

Siddhartha Gautama who would later become Buddha, the Enlightened One, is believed to have been born in Lumbini around 563 BC. You can hire a car from Chitwan (2½-hour drive), or you can fly from Kathmandu to Bhairawa (45 minutes), which is 35 km (22 mi) west of Lumbini. No matter how you travel, it is likely to be an exhausting trip.

Legend has it that Siddhartha was born in Lumbini while his mother, Maya Devi, was walking to her parents' house in Dewadaha. After resting in a shady grove, Maya Devi bathed in the nearby pool, and then her labor began. A pipal tree lowered its branches for her to hold.

In 249 BC, the great Indian Emperor, Ashoka, came to Lumbini and erected a stone column to commemorate the birth of Buddha. Years later, in the 7th century, when the Chinese traveler Hiuen Tsang visited, he reported that there were dilapidated sites of numerous monasteries and stupas here, which were also built to commemorate the holy site. In 1885, a German archaeologist discovered an inscribed pillar honoring Lumbini as the birth site of Siddhartha. The discovery triggered other archaeological excavations, and since then, Lumbini has become one of the holiest pilgrimage sites for Buddhists.

Other than the pillar erected by Ashoka, a temple, and several rubble-filled archaeological sites at the Sacred Garden, there is not much to see. Still, it is a very quiet and peaceful place. Hopefully, that will not change as Lumbini develops. Representatives from Buddhist countries around the world are building or plan to build temples in Lumbini that are representative of the Buddhist temples of their native lands.

It is not just Buddhists who revere this site; Hindus worship Maya Devi as Rupa Devi, goddess of abundance and fertility, and they consider Buddha the ninth incarnation of Vishnu. Today, the Lumbini area is a predominantly Hindu and Muslim region.

A Good Drive

Hire a car from your hotel to take you to the garden. If you want to see the surrounding temples, your driver may hire a rickshaw for you, because the roads are too poor for a car. Don't worry, your driver will wait for you. Expect to take an hour or two wandering around the other temples.

The central site is the **Sacred Garden,** which is no bigger than a football field. Here, you will see the **stone pillar** erected by Indian Emperor Ashoka in 249 BC to commemorate his pilgrimage to the birthplace. The surrounding area is covered with redbrick foundation mounds, ruins of the ancient stupas and monasteries that the Chinese traveler Hiuen Tsang noted on his visit in the 7th century. To the right of the pillar is the **Maya Devi Temple,** which houses a marble bas-relief depicting the nativity and a worn-down (from numerous prayer ceremonies) 14th-century stone carving of the nativity. To the left of the birth site is the **Puskarni pond,** where Queen Maya Devi took a bath before giving birth to prince Siddhartha and is said to have washed him after he was born.

Before leaving the complex, stop in at the garden and temple of the **Dharma Swami Maharaha Buddha Vihara,** a Tibetan monastery with a golden-color statue of Buddha. The rock garden, waterfall, roses, and flowering trees are stunning.

You will then have to take a rickshaw or walk to get to the nearby gold-and-white Lokamani Cula Pagoda, also known as the **Myanmar Temple.** It is one of the temples built here by representatives of countries with large Buddhist communities as part of the global initiative to promote Lumbini. Next to it is the International Gautami Nuns Temple, which looks like the stupa in Swayambhunath, in the Kathmandu Valley. From here, take your rickshaw back to the **China Temple,** which was built by the Chinese. It is a series of pagodas, prayer rooms, and meditation cells. There is a huge statue of the Buddha housed in the main pagoda at the **Zhong Hua Buddhist Monastery.** Across the road is the **Dae Sung Suk Ga Sa Korean Temple,** which at press time was still under construction.

Check with the **Lumbini Development Trust** (⊠ next to Sacred Garden compound, ☎ 071/80194) to see if any of the other temples planned for the area have been completed. Groups from Japan, Sri Lanka, Vietnam, and Thailand all want to erect temples and monasteries in the area.

Dining and Lodging

$ ✕🏠 **Lumbini Hokke Hotel.** This hotel is within a rickshaw drive from the Sacred Garden where Buddha was born. Consider staying in the Japanese-style rooms, with thick, soft futons on the bamboo-mat-covered floor and rice-paper partitions. The tubs here are small, deep, chair-shape, Japanese baths. All of the furnishings are imported from Japan. The Western-style rooms are basic, but spacious, with standard bathtubs. All rooms are air-conditioned and have a phone. The restaurant serves Japanese, Continental, Indian, and Nepali dishes. ✉ *Box 10, Lumbini Sacred Garden, Rupandehi,* ☎ *071/80236,* 𝕱𝕬𝕏 *071/80126. 27 rooms. Restaurant, bar, minibars, Japanese baths. AE, MC, V.*

Side Trip From Lumbini

Tilaurakot is an important, if rather sparse, archaeological site about 26 km (16 mi) west of Lumbini. The road to Tilaurakot, a bumpy mix of rocks and dust, is best traveled in a four-wheel-drive vehicle. Tilaurakot is the remains of the ancient palace of King Suddodhan, where the Buddha spent his formative years as Shakya Prince Siddhartha. Visitors will see redbrick foundations that are well shaded by huge trees. At first glance, it does not look like much, but archaeologists have found 13 successive layers of human habitations, dating back to the 8th century BC. If you go, visit the **Kapilavastu Museum**. Kapilavastu was the name of the ancient Shakya capital that was situated here, and the finds of the recent archaeological digs are stored in this museum. You will see shards of 8th- and 7th-century BC grey pottery and parts of figurines, stones, beads, and pendants. Copper coins from the 1st and 2nd centuries AD, the Kushana period, are also interesting to inspect. Perhaps the eeriest sites are the intact redware storage pots from the 1st and 2nd centuries AD; they look just like the storage pots you see for sale in the surrounding villages today. A driver will take you to this backroad site with no telephone. You may have to wake up or track down the guard, since visitors are infrequent. ▦ *5 Rs.* ◷ *Wed.–Mon. 10–5 (Fri. closes at 3). Closed Tues.*

Royal Bardia River Valley

380 km (236 mi) west of Pokhara, Kathmandu, Chitwan.

This 968-sq-km (600-sq-mi) park is in the sparsely populated far west of the Terai Region. Its grasslands and savannah are home to a rich and varied animal population, from wild elephants and great one-horned rhinoceros to swamp deer. This is where you have the greatest chance of seeing a wild Royal Bengal tiger. Plus, there are more than 300 bird species you can try to spy. Bardia is remote and still relatively free of tourism.

In 1969, the area was set aside as a Royal Hunting Reserve, and in 1976 it was declared the Karnali Wildlife Reserve, named for the Karnali River that threads through it, with an area of 368 sq km (143 sq mi). In 1982, more area was included, and it was renamed the Royal Bardia River Valley.

The park is surrounded by Tharu villages, so a visit can also be an interesting cultural experience. Unfortunately, because you have to fly, then drive, to get there, and due to tense political troubles in western Nepal, very few people go to this park. Only go with a guide, and inquire about the political situation before visiting. If you have access to the Internet, read the *Kathmandu Post* on-line before planning a trip here. While journalistic freedom could change, at press time the newspaper was reporting fairly evenhandedly the troubles going on in western Nepal. That said, no harm to foreign travelers has occurred. Furthermore, because so few people actually go to the park, you are more likely to experience pristine, Terai nature here than anywhere else.

When to Go

September, October, March, and April are the most temperate months and the best time to visit. From November through February, the days are pleasant, but the mornings and evenings can be cold enough for sweaters and warm jackets. In late April, the thunderstorms start; and

from May through August you can expect extremely hot and humid
days combined with monsoons.

Dining and Lodging

$$$$ ✕⊞ **Tiger Tops Karnali Lodge & Tented Camp.** Tiger Tops runs a jun-
gle-style lodge on the edge of the park and a tented camp within the
park, 15 km (9 mi) north of the lodge, on the banks of the Karnali River.
A stay here could include an early morning elephant safari, then a full-
day raft trip from the tented camp to the southern boundary of the
park. To get back to your tent, you would take a jungle jeep ride. You
can also arrange river rafting trips on the Bheri or Karnali rivers in conjunction with a stay here. The lodge is open all year; the tented camp
is open from October through mid-April. The campgrounds overlook
the Karnali River. There are safari tents with twin beds and attached
bathrooms with solar-powered showers. Permanent structures of bamboo and thatched roofing provide an extra shelter over the safari tents.
The lodge is built from local materials, such as thatching and bamboo,
and has comfortable, double beds with thick covers. The Kathmandu
booking office is a spacious compound behind the Royal Palace. A $20
park entrance fee and a $10 camping fee for those staying in the tented
camp are not included in the rates. ⊠ *Box 242, Kathmandu,* ☎ *01/
411225,* ℻ *01/414075, E-mail: info@tigermountain.com. 12 double
lodge rooms with bath, 12 twin-bed tents with bath. AE, MC, V.*

Janakpur

*165 km (102 mi) east of Birganj; 22 km (13½ mi) north of the Indian
border.*

A stop at this Hindu city, the ancient kingdom of Maithila according
to Hindu mythology, is like visiting India, but a smaller and cleaner
version. The trouble with visiting this beautiful and serene Terai town
is there are no tourist accommodations. You have to fly in and be met
by a driver, and then either fly back to Kathmandu (there aren't always flights available) or drive to the Royal Chitwan National Park
(at least four hours west on the Mahendra Highway) the same day.

Janakpur is described in the Hindu epic "Ramayana," which recounts
the adventures of Rama, Sita, Hanuman, and the demon king Rawana.
Reading or reciting this important tale is considered meritorious; and
visiting this city, which plays such a prominent role in the story, is said
to bring blessings.

The epic tells how the Maithila King Janak found a baby in a furrow
in a field. He took care of the little girl, and she grew up to a beautiful woman, Princess Sita (also known as Janaki). Ram, the god Vishnu
in mortal form, is believed to have wed Sita in Janakpur. Sita personified the perfect wife: beautiful, modest, and faithful. Ram personified
the perfect husband: virtuous and able to take care of his wife.

While there are no buildings more than a century old in this mythic city
of palm trees, ancient religion plays a strong role here. There are dozens
of sacred ponds (instead of river ghats), where ritual bathing occurs.
According to lore, Janak built the ponds for the gods, who (of course)
each wanted their own bath to wipe away the dust from the Himal.

Consider visiting **Janaki Mandir,** a huge, white, Mughal-inspired,
domed temple to Sita. It is said to be built on the site of the furrow
where King Janak found Sita and was built in 1911 by a local princess.
There is a statue of Sita with Rama and his three half-brothers, Lak-
shman, Bharat, and Satrughna. The viewing times of for the statue, when
the curtain is drawn back, change frequently, so check at the tourist

office to be sure you get a look. At press time, the statue was shown before 8 AM and around 4 PM. North of the temple is the **Ram Sita Bibaha Mandir,** a Nepali pagoda-style temple. This temple is located at the site where Sita and Ram were supposedly married. There is a life-size statue of the couple depicting the event; entry fee is 5 Rs. To the east of this temple there are two ponds, **Dhanush Sagar** and **Gangay Sagar,** where, as at Pashupatinath in the Kathmandu Valley, or Varanasi in India, you can see Hindus taking ritual baths.

The city of Janakpur is wonderfully devoid of cars, so you can tour on foot or by rickshaw. Keep an eye out for the paintings on the buildings. For 3,000 years, Hindu mothers have been passing down to their daughters the tradition of painting ritual motifs. They are an important part of festivals and the cycles of life, from marriage rituals to fertility prayers. Some women of the ancient Maithila region also reproduce these bright mandala-like images on paper, creating what is known as Maithili art.

Take a rickshaw (about 20 Rs.) to the **Janakpur Women's Development Center** (☎ 041/21080, ☉ Sun.–Thurs. 10–5, until 4 on Fri.), which is 3 km (2 mi) south of Janakpur. The Hindu women of the area, often uneducated and trained to be subservient, have turned their artistic skills into commercial skills. The co-op helps sell their Maithili paper art (as well as ceramics and paintings), but also teaches reading and writing and business skills. Some women have started their own businesses since getting training from the program.

The Terai A to Z

Arriving and Departing

BY BUS

Janakpur: You can take an overcrowded **public bus** (✉ Gongabu Bus Park, Ring Rd., on north side of Kathmandu, ☎ no phone) to Janakpur. It takes 9–10 hours to get there from Kathmandu. Book through your travel agent (really); the one-way fare is 207 Rs.

Royal Chitwan National Park: Greenline has offices in Kathmandu (✉ Box 3904, Kaiser Mahal, on Tridevi Marg, near taxi stands at entrance to Thamel, ☎ 01/253885), Pokhara (✉ Baidam, Lakeside, opposite Fishtail Lodge entrance, ☎ 061/27271), and Chitwan (✉ Sauraha Chowk, in Tandi Bazaar, and at ✉ Al Fresco Café & Pub, on the main strip of Sauraha, ☎ 056/60126 or 056/21792). It offers daily, air-conditioned service, departing Kathmandu or Pokhara at 7 AM and arriving in Chitwan at 12:30, and departing Chitwan at 9:30 AM, and arriving in Pokhara or Kathmandu at 2. The one-way fare is 480 Rs. Travel agents may charge a commission to book Greenline for you.

BY CAR

Janakpur and Lumbini: Expect to pay about $130 for a one-day tour (round-trip) to Lumbini or Janakpur from Kathmandu. From Pokhara to Lumbini it is $150, and to Janakpur $200–$250. Try to book an air-conditioned, four-wheel-drive vehicle, if you plan a side trip to Tilaurakot from Lumbini; for the rest of the region the roads are fairly good. Car hire (ask your travel agent) will be considerably cheaper (about $50) if you visit Lumbini as part of a package trip to Royal Chitwan National Park.

Royal Chitwan National Park: Travel agencies may charge $50–$75 to hire a car and driver for a one-night, two-day trip from Kathmandu or Pokhara. The trip from either city will take about 4½ hours. The agency may charge more for additional touring after you reach Chitwan. Book at least one day in advance.

In Janakpur, Lumbini, and Nepalgunj (near Royal Bardia National Park), getting around once you reach the airport is difficult. For example, a local bus services the Lumbini airport, but it could take you an hour to cover the 22 km (13½ mi) to Lumbini. If you are flying to these locales, have your travel agent arrange for a hired car to meet you at the airport.

Janakpur: Janakpur Airport (☎ 021/24641) is really little more than an airstrip 2 km (1 mi) south of the city, and there isn't always service there. The flight to Janakpur from Kathmandu takes 45 minutes. Check with your travel agent to see which airlines are flying there; schedules change frequently. You can also fly to **Biratnagar Airport** (☎ 021/24641), west of Janakpur, and drive to the city, but the drive is roughly 200 km (125 mi).

Lumbini: Gautam Buddha Airport (☎ 071/21885) is at Bhairawa, an industrial town 22 km (13½ mi) east of Lumbini. It is a 45-minute flight from Kathmandu; there are no flights from Pokhara. To reconfirm your flight, call: **Buddha Air** (☎ 071/21893) or **Necon Air** (☎ 071/21244).

Royal Bardia River Valley: To reach the park, fly for 90 minutes from Kathmandu to **Nepalgunj Airport** (☎ 081/21586), then make the two-hour drive to the park or a three-hour drive to a river put-in point. To reconfirm your flight, call: **Buddha Air** (☎ 081/20745), **Necon Air** (☎ 081/20307), **Nepal Airways** (☎ 081/20119), or **RNAC** (☎ 081/20102).

Royal Chitwan National Park: It's about a half-hour flight from Kathmandu to **Bharatpur Airport** (☎ no phone), which is just outside the national park. There are daily flights to and from Kathmandu, but flights to and from Pokhara operate only during the fall, which is the peak tourist season. To reduce the hassle of touts trying to take you to "their place," arrange to be met at the airport by the staff from your resort. To reconfirm your flight, call: **Cosmic Air** (☎ 056/24218), **Gorkha Airlines** (☎ 056/21093), **Lumbini** ☎ 056/23858), or **RNAC** (☎ 056/20326).

Royal Bardia River Valley: Fly to Nepalgunj, then drive about three hours to a put-in someplace along the Bheri River. Contact the **Tiger Tops Karnali Lodge** (✉ Box 242, Kathmandu, ☎ 01/411225) or a travel agent.

Royal Chitwan National Park: A travel agent can book you a rafting trip down the Trisuli River to Chitwan. It will take any length of time, depending on the rapids and where you put in, but you get to see flora, fauna, and local village life on the banks as you drift past.

Getting Around

In Janakpur and Lumbini, auto or bike rickshaw is the best, and sometimes only, transportation option, if you are finding your own way around the temples in these two sacred towns. Bargain long and hard; you should not ever have to pay more than 100 Rs. It will be easier to bargain if you learn your Nepali numbers, although most drivers will know enough English to bargain with you.

In Chitwan and Bardia, your lodge will arrange jeep transportation for you. In Janakpur or Lumbini, if you arrive by hired car, the cost of touring will be included in the price of getting there. If you get to Janakpur or Lumbini by flying, make sure your travel agent books a hired car to meet you; expect to pay an additional $100 for this service.

Contacts and Resources

CURRENCY EXCHANGE

When visiting the Terai, it's best to change money before leaving Pokhara or Kathmandu, since there are no exchange agencies in most areas. In Royal Chitwan National Park, most of the upscale resorts here have currency-exchange facilities for their guests. Also in Royal Chitwan, you can change money at **Sauraha Money Changer** (☎ 056/60445), open daily 7–7, or **Chitwan Money Exchanger** (☎ no phone), open daily 6–8. Both are on the main road of Sauraha and have prominent signs out front; they are authorized by the Nepal Rastra Bank.

EMERGENCIES

Fire brigade: Bhairawa (Lumbini area; ☎ 071/20215), Janakpur (☎ 041/20011), Nepalgunj (Bardia area; ☎ 081/20111). **Police:** Bhairawa (Lumbini area; ☎ 071/20199), Bharatpur (Chitwan area; ☎ 056/20155), Janakpur (☎ 041/20099).

Hoteliers that we list will help you evacuate to Pokhara or Kathmandu if you are seriously ill; otherwise, do not expect much in the way of Western **medical care** in the region. In Lumbini, the **Lumbini Hokke Hotel** (☞ Dining and Lodging, *above*) has a doctor on call. The **Lumbini Dharmodaya Committee** (✉ Secret Garden compound, next to Nepal Buddha Temple, ☎ no phone) provides free first aid during the day.

When visiting Royal Chitwan National Park, medical care is available at the **Raj Medical Hall** (✉ Sauraha, next to KC's Restaurant and Bar, ☎ no phone). It is staffed by a physician's assistant from 6 AM to 7 PM daily. It is also the location of the only pharmacy in Sauraha. Tourists are charged a minimal amount for the assistance, and the money is used to subsidize free medical care for locals.

TRAVEL AGENCIES

Trips to the Terai are best organized through the agencies in Kathmandu (☞ Kathmandu A to Z, *above*).

VISITOR INFORMATION

Janakpur: The **tourist office** (✉ Station Rd., east of Bhanu Chowk, Janakpur, ☎ 041/20755) has brochures about the city. It's open Sunday–Thursday 10–4 and Friday 10–3.

Lumbini: The **Lumbini Department Trust** (✉ next to Secret Garden compound, ☎ 071/80194) has an information desk. It does not keep regular hours, so calling is your best bet.

TREKKING

Trekking is an extremely rewarding experience in Nepal. The surroundings are beautiful—from the subtropical banana trees and rice plantations, to the alpine forests with jade rivers and snow-tipped rhododendron flowers, to the desolate and dry Tibetan plateau, to the blue ice of the Khumbu region. You will encounter nose ring–wearing locals and singing children. You might be pushed out of the way by a mule caravan walking an ancient trade route. You'll wonder how in the world the yaks graze on such steep hills. To wake to the sight of a 26,240-ft mountain at your doorstep, or to turn a bend on a hillside and suddenly see a monster of a mountain, is a Himalayan experience you will never forget.

To perpetuate this beauty, try to make your trip as eco-friendly as possible. The heating, feeding, and cleaning of hikers is annihilating Nepal's trees. You can help stop the destruction in a few simple ways: Resign yourself to several days without showering, and when you do bathe, try to use solar-heated water. When ordering food in restaurants, try to do so at the same time as the locals (who usually eat between 10 and 11 AM and at dusk) and the other trekkers, so energy is not wasted by constant cooking. Treat stream or river water with iodine, rather than boiling it; and do not buy bottled water. There are Sagarmatha-size piles of empty plastic bottles throughout the Himalayas, because Nepal has not yet started to recycle plastic.

Teahouses vs. Camping

Trekking teahouses, so called because they began as places for weary travelers to get a hot cup of tea, are all about the same: a small wooden room with a bunk, a quilt, a thin pillow, and maybe a candle, all at the going price of $1–$2 a night. You cannot book a teahouse room in advance. There are usually no phones, no addresses, and certainly no faxes—although, in some places, like Jomsom, there are satellite dishes. The houses work on a first-come, first-served basis, which means in the busier areas, like Annapurna and Everest, you may end up racing from village to village to make sure you get a room. Although you are never guaranteed a private room, space will always be found for everyone; which means you have to be prepared to share a space with strangers. In really busy times, you may end up sleeping on dining room tables, rolling over to find someone else sleeping on the nearby bench. Dining room tables have their advantages though, they usually don't have bedbugs. If you opt to trek by teahouses in the busy areas, try to go against the grain of other hikers: sleep at the teahouse where they eat lunch and vice versa. After a day of walking, you will understand the ebb and flow of the teahouse trekkers, and you can adjust your trip to counter the norm.

If you camp, you get far more privacy, a guaranteed level of quality (in both the food and the bedding), and a better chance to talk to the local guides, porters, and cooks. Camping can actually be luxurious in its own way—with a team of people setting up the tents and a cup of tea, cocoa, or coffee handed to you, through the tent flaps, each morning. Some of the best cakes you may ever taste will be baked by camping cooks (maybe they taste so good because of the sheer insanity of their presence here!). Disadvantages of camping can include slow porters who deliver your gear to the camp hours after you've arrived, and the more regimented schedule mandated by traveling with an entire camp of people. Although such scheduling means you can't whiz ahead of everyone else, leaving them in a dust of powdered snow, it also makes sure you don't push your endurance limits and jeopardize your health.

Guides and Porters

Whether you choose to camp or stay in teahouses, make sure you hire a guide. It is the safest way to travel, and it supports the economy. Even for more straightforward treks, on which you are unlikely to lose your way, you should hire a guide for protection. More and more often, hikers traveling alone (particularly women) complain of constant come-ons by locals offering "help." Furthermore, on the higher-altitude walks you need an experienced partner to make sure you don't get hit by altitude sickness, which can kill if you do not heed the warnings of nausea and headaches, and descend. Often, it is those who are most fit, and most inclined to ignore discomfort, who end up seriously ill because they disregard the symptoms. A guide makes it his business to watch for these signs. It may sound indulgent at sea level, but having someone look out for you when you are above the clouds is a priceless, lifesaving, sensible decision.

You should also consider hiring a porter. In the Everest region, it is not difficult to hire Sherpanis, women porters, which helps these Nepali women become more financially independent. After you have been walking for more than two hours, even a 10-pound pack can feel like a ton. You should always be sure your porter has warm clothes, shoes, and sunglasses, especially if you are crossing a pass. You may be surprised by the number of barefoot porters; this can be a difficult issue. Many people give porters clothes only to find they've bartered them away. If you know you're going to be enduring harsh weather, you can wait until the time arrives, then insist that the porter wear the clothing. It is often best to talk to your guide about this sticky situation. Although it may seem odd to be responsible for your porter's wardrobe, they often can't afford to equip themselves adequately, and in the past, porters have become seriously ill, or have even frozen to death.

Trekking Routes

The following are thumbnail descriptions of some of Nepal's major treks. Each agency has its own preferred route for each trek. Treks are also being gradually shortened, as starting points move farther into the wilderness, out past the end of the area's improving roads. There are dozens of variations on each trek. This is wonderful, because it means you can do the same trek again and again, each time varying it slightly.

The number of days listed for each hike below is a ballpark figure. It depends on how fit you are, the conditions of the trail, and the weather. You may also want to stop and spend a few days in a particular village because it is beautiful, or you need a break, so it is difficult to guesstimate exactly how long you will spend on each hike. The following routes take you from one village to the next. You can use these descriptions to match up against maps of the treks (that you can purchase in Kathmandu or Pokhara at local bookstores) to get a general picture of the distance covered in each trek.

Mt. Everest Region

History
Everest, known to Nepalis as **Sagarmatha** ("Brow of the Ocean"), and by Sherpas as **Chomolungma** ("Mother Goddess of the Earth"), is an experience. Many people opt to fly past it, getting up close and personal from the comfort of an airplane seat, but the spirit of Everest is found in feeling her ever-changing moods. One moment the mountain is sparkling clear, the next, wind is whipping over her summit, causing a blizzardlike haze around her peak.

In 1849, when the region was surveyed from the Indian plains, Everest was simply noted as "Peak XV." After studies showed Peak XV was the tallest in the world, it was renamed after Sir George Everest who had led the Survey of India from 1823 to 1843. Climbing parties began attempting to reach the summit in the early 20th century, "because it is there," as **George Mallory** so flippantly put it. At the time, Nepal was closed to foreigners, so all attempts were made from the difficult Tibet side of the mountain. Today, climbers scour the mountain peak looking for the Kodak camera that may or may not prove that Mallory and Andrew Irvine were the first to reach the summit, during their 1925 expedition, then perished on the descent.

There were several more summit attempts in the 1930s, but then World War II and the Chinese invasion of Tibet suspended climbing activities. Innovations during the war were used to create more sophisticated equipment, and a new era of climbing began. **Maurice Herzog's** French expedition climbed **Annapurna** in 1950, leading the way to the opening Nepal to tourists and climbers in 1951, and the race to the top of the world was truly on. Herzog had scaled a 26,240-ft mountain, proving it was possible to soar this high (read his book, *Annapurna,* to find out at what price). On May 29, 1953, a British team lead by John Hunt finally put New Zealander **Edmund Hillary** and Sherpa **Tenzing Norgay** on Everest's summit; and they lived to tell the tale.

There have been numerous Everest climbs since, from big expeditions to solo attempts. In 1975, Junko Tabei of Japan was the first woman to ascend Everest. She climbed the southeast ridge. Using the same approach, in 1978, **Reinhold Messner** and **Peter Habler** conquered the mountain without oxygen. This led to smaller parties attempting the challenge, without the need for porters to carry oxygen tanks. Two years later, Messner set a new record as the first solo climber to summit. Since then, people have walked, climbed, hiked, and biked their way to the summit, even bringing satellite phones, faxes, and stereo systems.

There have also been tragedies. You can learn about the heartrending 1996 disaster, in which 12 climbers perished, by seeing the IMAX movie, *Everest,* or reading Jon Krakauer's *Into Thin Air.* Everest is indisputably a mountain of dreams and nightmares. Since 1953, when Hillary and Norgay set foot on top of the world (neither has ever said who reached the summit first), there have been 147 deaths on the mountain. For every five climbers who reach the summit, one dies trying.

Although Everest is the highest mountain in the world, it ranks second to Annapurna as a popular trekking ground, in part because Annapurna is easier to get to and can be broken down into smaller treks. Everest can be divided into two areas: the lower, populous countryside known as the Solu, and the icy Khumbu, which abuts the Tibetan border and is in the Sagarmatha National Park. Walking up and down the deep canyons and steep ridges is very hard going in the Solu region, made worse by the fact that there are not many mountain views. And when you reach the stunning scenery of the Khumbu region, you have to cope with acclimatization to altitudes of 13,120 to 16,400 ft.

To get to these regions you can either fly from Kathmandu or go by road. Both have their distinct disadvantages: Flights are often fully booked by trekking groups or canceled due to bad weather; and the 13-hour road trip is long, tedious, and uncomfortable, causing even adults to whine, "Are we there yet?" In this region, it is best to book through an organized trekking agency who will arrange a flight to Lukla and a camping trip.

The Everest Trek

Lukla, the starting point of an Everest trek, is about 240 km (149 mi) east of Kathmandu.

15-DAY LOOP

Every agency has its own favorite route, its own stopping ground, and its own schedule, but the basic 15-day round-trip walk starts with an eye-opening 35-minute flight to Lukla (9,184 ft) from Kathmandu in a Twin Otter airplane.

The hike follows the Dudh Kosi River from Lukla to **Namche Bazaar** (11,283 ft). You can rent high-altitude equipment here (for equally high prices), if you do not want to lug it along with you. It's better to rent the equipment in Kathmandu, through your travel agency. (You might also want to stock up on chocolate bars in Kathmandu, where they are cheaper.) Namche Bazaar has always been an important trading post for goods being ferried by yak caravans across the border from Tibet, although these days it seems the entire village is involved in the tourism industry.

From Namche Bazaar, the trail veers northeast, in a steep climb through the juniper forests to **Thyangboche,** where the oft-photographed monastery once stood. It burned down in 1989 and has since been rebuilt. During the full moon of November or December, you can still see Sherpa dance performances here.

Next, you can either go to **Dingboche** (14,300 ft) or **Pheriche** (13,907 ft) to acclimatize for the ascent along the Khumbu glacier. Either way, you have entered the domain of high altitude. On the way to Pheriche, you pass **Pangboche** (12,660 ft), home to the region's oldest monastery, which you may want to check out. In Pheriche, the **Himalayan Rescue Association** holds talks on mountain conditions and AMS (acute mountain sickness) every afternoon during the trekking season (there are signposts announcing the times). It is well worth the visit, and probably more useful on the way up than on the way down. While acclimatizing here, you might consider a round-trip hike to Dingboche, to get used to higher altitudes. When acclimatizing, it is always better to go higher, then drop back down and sleep lower.

Next, you walk on the moraine of the Khumbu glacier to **Lobuje** (16,199 ft) or **Gorakshep** (16,924 ft), both places where you would probably rather be camping than staying in the really cold dormitory lodgings that are available.

Finally, it is up to the black rock—**Kala Patter** (18,187 ft)—where you are rewarded with panoramic views of Mt. Everest (29,021 ft), Lhotse (27,932 ft), and Nupse (25,784 ft). Try to get there before noon, before the clouds roll in.

You can then walk to **Everest Base Camp,** where you may get a chance to talk to anxious mountain climbers heading up or down the great wall. You can return via Pheriche or Dingboche, then backtrack through Thyangboche and Namche to Lukla, where you can fly back to Kathmandu.

Some travel agencies will do shorter eight-day walks to Dingboche. But as long as you are up this high, if you are healthy and can afford the time, you may as well push on.

20-DAY KHUMBU LOOP

This extended, high-altitude, camping-only trek goes up the **Dudh Kosi** from **Lukla** to **Namche,** but then heads west to Thame, where you can visit a monastery built on a ledge high above the valley. From Thame you partially retrace your steps to Namche, then climb the ridge to tranquil Khumjung. Then you ascend the Gokyo Valley to **Machermo,** where you should spend two days acclimatizing before you push on to **Gokyo Lake** (15,580 ft). The lake is a good place to rest before crossing the 17,777-ft **Cho La** ("La" means mountain pass) into the Khumbu Valley, where you join the expedition route to the **Everest Base Camp.** From **Gorkashep** (16,924 ft), you can climb up to **Kala Patter** (18,187 ft) for breathtaking panoramic views of Everest and the surrounding high peaks. You return via the 15-day route to Dingboche, Thyangboche, Namche, and Lukla.

Annapurna Region

Dumre, the starting point for the Annapurna circuit, is 137 km (85 mi) west of Kathmandu, 70 km (43 mi) east of Pokhara.

The Annapurna region is the busiest but most geographically and culturally diverse of Nepal's popular trekking areas. You trek through tropical areas to reach alpine flora and fauna. Along the way, you encounter people ranging from the Thakalis, who used to control the salt trade route between Nepal and Tibet and now run the trekking lodges in the region, to the Tibetans, who live higher up, nearer their homeland.

The region is bounded in the east by the Marsyangdi River and in the west by the Kali Gandaki River. This river slices the deepest gorge in the world, with the water flowing at an elevation of less than 7,216 ft, between the 26,240-ft giants, Annapurna I and Dhalagiri. Within the 64 km (40 mi) between the two rivers are 12 mountains higher than 22,965 ft.

The Treks

This is a heavily trafficked trek. Be prepared for queues during the high season. At the same, do not hike alone. There were several violent attacks against solo trekkers between Chhomrong and Ghorapani in late 1996.

The ease of access means you can spend a few days here: some trekkers fly to Jomsom from Pokhara (30 minutes), walk a few days in the immediate vicinity, then fly back. At press time, there were no direct flights from Kathmandu to Jomsom. However, weather permitting, you can make the trip, via a connecting flight in Pokhara, in a day or two. You could easily spend a month in the region, walking the circuit and then the Annapurna Sanctuary.

Jomsom is quickly turning into a Disneyland version of a ski resort. There are sunroofs and satellite dishes in this town of Tibetan traders. It is essential to get your trekking pass stamped in Jomsom, because it will be checked farther down the trail.

JOMSOM TREK

Nicknamed the apple-pie trek for the teahouses in the apple-grove district that serve apples in everything—from momos to pies—this is a versatile trek. You can walk up to **Muktinoth** from Pokhara, and then return on the same trail (about 14 days). Or you can fly into **Jomsom,** walk up to Muktinoth, then walk back down to **Birenthanti** (3,493 ft; 7–10 days), which is the nearest village to Pokhara. You would then take a taxi from Birenthanti to Pokhara (about 100 Rs.). You can also take a detour from the trail to go into the Annapurna Sanctuary.

The following is the walk from Jomsom down, which is the way you would walk if you were walking the full circuit.

From Jomsom, you walk up to Muktinoth. This 2,000-year-old sacred grove is revered by Buddhists and Hindus who flock here. According to Hindus, Brahma lit a fire upon the water, thus reconciling the two elements. The temple here enshrines the flaming water, actually lit by a natural gas seepage. For a small donation, you can see the flames, hidden behind a curtain. The Hindus call the temple **Jawala Mai Temple,** and have it dedicated to Vishnu. Buddhists call the temple **Salemebar Dolamebar Gompa** and claim that the footprints embedded in a rock north of the shrine belong to Guru Padmasambhava who introduced Buddhism to Tibet. You will see pilgrims along the Jomsom trail, headed here. The Hindu women invariably wear auspicious red saris; sadhus in orange garb may also dot the trail.

Next, you head back down to Jomsom, and from there, down to **Marpha** (8,741 ft), **Tukuche** (8,495 ft), or **Kalopani** (8,396 ft). This part of the walk can take from one to three days, depending on your pace. Where you stay will depend on your guide, the wind, and the crowds. If you are trekking by teahouses, it is fairly easy to gauge where the big crowds are going and alter your walk to avoid them. The winds howl between Tukuche and Jomsom, and it can be hard going if you are headed south in the afternoon. No matter where you stay, there are marvelous apple groves here.

The next string of towns along your walk, which can be covered in one to four days (again, it's up to you) includes **Ghasa** (6,560 ft), **Dana** (4,592 ft), and **Tatopani** (3,870 ft). Dana is where Herzog got lost, and while you are here, it is easy to get lost in daydreams about his expedition. However, it is Tatopani that draws the crowds. "Tato" means hot, "pani" means water, and together they signify hot springs. There are municipal hot springs, as well as several springs along the banks of the river. Here the apples are joined by oranges growing from trees that hang over the trail.

The next one or two days of walking take you along the rhododendron-lined trail to Ghorapani (7,462 ft). Spend the night here, so you can wake early and climb Poon Hill for the splendid views of Dhaulagiri, Tukche, Nilgiri, Annapurna I, Annapurna South, Hiunchuli, and Glacier Dome. Then you can walk to Annapurna Base Camp, or continue south along the Kali Gandaki, which is emerald colored in parts, then runs dark blue in Birethanti. Finally, you can head back to Pokhara and Kathmandu.

You cannot walk this trail without encountering packhorse and packmule caravans. The lead beast wears a colorful headband with bells to alert you that he is bearing down. Get out of the way or you will be pushed out of the way. Similarly, do not blaze past water buffalo; respect those horns.

17–20-DAY ANNAPURNA CIRCUIT TREK

Road conditions permitting, you can take a four-wheel-drive vehicle to **Besisahar**, where you will begin the walk. Your trekking guide will gauge how fast and how far you walk each day, but you will follow the Marsyangdi River, through rice paddies and banana groves, into oak and pine forests, up **Chame** (8,807 ft), where you have views of Annapurna II. Eventually, usually seven to eight days into your hike, you emerge in the high desertlike, yet cold, country at **Manang** (11,798 ft). This is a good place to rest. Be warned, the handicraft traders in this area are brilliant negotiators; they may also work as yak herders but they are not country bumpkins.

From Manang, you head up to **Ledar** (13,940 ft) and on to **Phedi** (14,497 ft). Phedi literally means "foot of the hill," and it is the final stop before pushing over Thorung La. If you are suffering from altitude sickness, descend to Ledar, at the least, Manang if you can make it. It is remarkable, but despite an onslaught of warnings, people die here every year. Phedi also suffers from a shortage of beds during the high season. If the Thorung La pass gets closed by snow, which happens from year to year, there can be a backup of hundreds of trekkers in Phedi waiting to cross. Before proceeding to Phedi, ask locals what the conditions are like; word travels fast on the trails.

Crossing **Thorung La** is a steady four- to five-hour uphill trod to 17,764 ft, where there are numerous chortens, or small stupas, and prayer flags and a magnificent view of the clouds and peaks beneath you. It is followed by a downhill, two- to four-hour stroll to **Muktinoth** (12,188 ft). Tricks for handling the uphill walk include pacing your breathing to your steps and listening to your favorite tapes on a Walkman (it helps, really).

From Muktinoth, you pick up the Jomsom trail (☞ *above*). The number of days this trek takes depends on the number of rest days you take and whether or not you get stuck at Thorung La. A rest at Manang is mandatory to acclimatize. Another rest day in Muktinoth makes sense; you can ease your muscles and heart after the slog over Thorung La, plus the nearby Hindu and Buddhist monasteries are worth visiting. A day spent in the hot springs of Tatopani on the Jomsom trail is akin to a thousand minimasseurs working your calf muscles.

10–15 DAY ANNAPURNA BASE CAMP TREK

Sometimes nicknamed the ABC trek (Annapurna Base Camp) or the Sanctuary Trek, this can be the most rewarding walk from a mountain-viewing standpoint. Done alone, it takes about 10–15 days, or you can add it on to the Jomsom Trek or Annapurna Circuit.

Always check in Pokhara, and again in Ghandruk or Ghorapani, to find out what the conditions are like in the Sanctuary. It can get as heavily snowed in as Thorung La, and it is prone to avalanches.

If you are walking the Jomsom trail, the trailhead for the ABC trek is at Ghorapani, plainly marked by a huge sign at the center of the town that points the way east. If you are starting in Pokhara, you can take the road to Phedi, then cross the bridge and walk up to **Dhampus** (5,182 ft), and from there on to Ghandruk. From Ghorapani or Ghandruk you walk to **Chhomrong** (6,396 ft). From there, you push up the trail through some leech-laden areas and bamboo forests, then through rhododendron-filled and alpine sections. It takes another three days to reach Machhapuchhare Base Camp (MBC), which of course, is not really a base camp, considering you are not permitted to climb the mountain. There are spartan teahouses here, or you can camp, but do stay the night, because the views are incredible in the morning (but slowly covered by clouds as the day wears on). From the base camp, it is about a two- to three-hour hike to Annapurna Base Camp, where unbelievably, the views are even more thrilling than at MBC.

Dhorpatan Hunting Reserve

You start by walking or driving from Pokhara to **Beni,** which is west of the Kali Gandaki. It then takes about four days to hike from Beni to the Dhorpatan Valley, where you can explore the **Dhorpatan Hunting Reserve.**

The reserve extends over 1,325 sq km (516 sq mi), on the southern flanks of Mt. Dhaulagiri. The altitude varies from 9,840 ft to 22,960 ft, and the higher elevations remain snowcapped throughout the year.

With a license to hunt, you can seek out the coveted blue sheep that hide in the fir, pine, and birch forests. Other indigenous animals that can be hunted include Himalayan black bear, barking deer, wild boar, and the elusive leopard. However, the musk deer, wolf, red panda, and cheer pheasant, are all endangered and off-limits to hunters.

Plan on camping, and bring your own medical supplies; there is no hospital in the region. For more information, contact the **Department of National Parks and Wildlife Conservation** (✉ Babar Mahal, Box 860, Kathmandu, ☎ 02/20912 for Dhorpatan Reserve Headquarters).

Trekking North of Kathmandu

The region is roughly 75 km (47 mi) north of Kathmandu.

Lower altitudes and fewer people are advantages to the treks close to Kathmandu. Treks here are also good if you are short on time. What they lack is the world's tallest mountain or the sheer abundance of peaks in Annapurna. Still, there are splendid views here.

Huge glaciers sprawl down mountain slopes, spread across high valley floors, and dip into the sacred Goasinkund Lakes. The people who inhabit the region are Tamangs and Sherpas, although they are only distantly related to the Solu-Khumbu Sherpas. Their handsome villages and gompas add a peaceful touch to the formidable landscape.

In 1976, to save the beauty of the Langtang Valley and Gosainkund, Nepal turned the area into its second-largest national park, the Lantang National Park, a protected area for the endangered musk deer, Himalayan thoar (wild goat), red panda, and snow leopard.

Helambu Trek

This trail is an hour's drive from Kathmandu. Although it does not have the same views as Annapurna or Everest, it also is not as dangerously high; the maximum altitude is 9,184 ft. The trek can take from two to six days and is a teahouse trek.

You start the trek at **Sundrajil** (4,592 ft), where you must pay a 250 Rs. entrance fee to the Seopuri Water Resources & Wildlife Conservation Project. Then you walk through a populous area to the police checkpost at **Pati Bhanjyang** (5,805 ft). From there, the trail roller coasters up and down hills, with good Himalayan views on the upswings. The yo-yo-like terrain continues until you reach the entrance to the Langtang National Park, which has a 650 Rs. permit fee (you can get the permit in Kathmandu). You follow a rhododendron-lined ridge, where there are views of the Langtang and Gosainkund peaks. You can stop here or, on the same day, you can take the arduous hike due north up to the large, medieval-looking Sherpa village of **Tarke Gyang** (8,997 ft), where you encounter shrewd traders. The alpine-forested region around Tarke Gyang is full of rhododendron. You might want to spend the night in Tarke Gyang before descending to the west where the trail enters the region of rice paddy fields in the more tropical village area of **Kiul** (4,198 ft). It will only take you one day to walk from Kiul back to Pati Bhanjyang, completing the circuit. The trail follows a river, descending slightly, then crosses the river on a suspension bridge. A short distance beyond the bridge, the trail joins the road to Pati Bhanjyang.

Langtang Trek

The slightly higher elevations of this trek (maximum altitude 12,464 ft) give you better views than you get on the Helambu trek.

You start with a seven-hour drive from Kathmandu to **Syabrubesi** (4,657 ft). From there, you walk northwest, through rhododendron, toward **Kyanjin Gompa** (11,411 ft). This part of the trip, including the drive, takes about two days—every agency has its own stopping point—but once you get to **Kyanjin**, you get a picture-perfect view of Langtang Lirung (23,771 ft). Kyanjun has dozens of trekker inns, but there is still plenty of space away from the development for camping. You can spend a day or a week here. You will see yak herders scrambling up and down unbelievably steep paths as if it were no more taxing than a walk on the beach. You can take one of these paths up to the **Langshisha Glacier** (13,395 ft), or you can spend a full day hiking up the valley, where the views of Langtang Lirung are stunning. Back in Kyanjin, stop by the cheese factory that was built with Swiss assistance; good luck not eating all of the nak (a nak is a female yak) cheese you buy before you get back to Kathmandu. The route back to Kathmandu can be varied slightly, but essentially you must backtrack.

Weather permitting, you can cross the 16,747-ft **Ganja La** and go into Helambu. You need a guide for this traverse: for two days there is no water; for four there are no settlements. The pass is invariably blocked by snow from December through March, and it can get snowed in as early as October.

Trekking A to Z

Arriving and Departing

BY BUS

Mountain climbers joke they would rather scale Everest than take the local bus to Jiri to start the trek to Everest. If you must take the bus instead of flying, you can have your travel agent book the 10- to 13-hour local bus trip for you (143 Rs.). However, then you have to walk from Jiri to the Everest trekking region, which can take up to eight days.

BY HIRED CAR

If you are going by hired car, it means you have booked a trek through a travel agency. The cost of the hired car will be included in the package, along with the cost of the guide and porter.

BY PLANE

To Everest: It is a 35-minute, $83 flight to the Lukla airport from Kathmandu. To reconfirm your return flight to Kathmandu, call **Gorkha Airlines** (☎ 038/21144 in Lukla, 01/435121 in Kathmandu) or **Lumbini Airways** (☎ 038/21142 in Lukla, 01/483381 in Kathmandu). Leave at least two days between your return flight to Kathmandu and your international flights, because Lukla flights are often overbooked or canceled due to bad weather.

To Jomsom: There are eight daily flights from the **Pokhara airport** ☎ 061/21617) to Jomsom. To reconfirm, call **Yeti Airways** (☎ 061/30016). Flights cost about $55 and take 20 minutes.

BY TAXI

The starting points for Annapurna treks keep changing as the road keeps inching its way farther into the hike. Expect to pay anywhere from 400 Rs. to 2,000 Rs. to take a taxi to any of the Annapurna starting points. It costs about 2,000 Rs. to take a taxi from Pokhara to Beni, which is where you head out to the Dhorpatan Hunting Reserve; it is a three-hour drive, and the last bit is quite rough. Expect to pay 100 Rs.–300 Rs. for a taxi to the Helumbu and Langtang starts.

Climbing and Trekking Permits

All of the popular trekking regions are within national parks. Everest treks are in **Sagarmatha** National Park, Annapurna area treks put you in the **Annapurna Conservation Area,** and when you go to Helambu or Langtang, you enter **Langtang National Park.** Park fees start at 650 Rs. per person, and you can get the ticket at the park entrance. Check with your travel agent for the latest rules.

The permit for **Everest** is $50,000 per group of climbers. But there are 18 smaller "trekking peaks," which are more accessible both physically and financially. Permits for these mountains cost between $1,000 and $3,000, for up to 10-member teams. Every mountain expedition must be represented by a local trekking agency in Nepal.

Trekking Peaks:

1. Mera Peak	21,825 ft
2. Chulu Peak	21,596 ft
3. Singu Chuli (fluted peak)	21,323 ft
4. Hiunhuli	21,126 ft
5. Chulu West	21,054 ft

6. Kusum Kangaru	20,884 ft
7. Parchemuche	20,293 ft
8. Imja Tse (Island peak)	20,280 ft
9. Lonuche	20,070 ft
10. Pisang	19,978 ft
11. Kwangde (Kawande)	19,716 ft
12. Ramdung	19,434 ft
13. Pador Peak	19,339 ft
14. Khongma Tse (Mehra)	19,185 ft
15. Kangja Chuli	19,168 ft
16. Pokalde	19,044 ft
17. Tharpu Chuli (Tent Peak)	18,575 ft
18. Mardi Himal	18,325 ft

Trekking permits for those areas that require it (Dolpa and Kanchenjunga) can be obtained in Kathmandu (☞ Kathmandu A to Z, *above*). All permit fees are payable in Nepalese currency (even though prices are fixed at American dollar rates) and require two passport-size photographs.

If you want to go to **Mustang** and **Upper Dolpa,** the charge is $700 for the first 10 days, then $70 per day for each day afterward. You will also have to travel to these areas with a guide, because individual trekking permits are not issued.

Remember that you must also have a valid visa for Nepal.

Contacts and Resources

CURRENCY EXCHANGE
Change money in Pokhara or Kathmandu before leaving on a trek. You will not be able to use credit cards in the mountains. Carry small denominations of rupees; you cannot pay for tea with a 500 Rs. note.

EMERGENCIES
The **Himalayan Rescue Association** maintains a medical clinic in Manang, before Thorung La on the Annapurna Circuit. In 1999 there were two full-time, volunteer, Western doctors here during the trekking season. The association also has a clinic in Pheriche, for Everest treks. At press time, this clinic had three Western doctors on duty. Signs for both clinics are clearly posted on the trails. For more information about the clinics, as well as background information on altitude sickness, check out the Himalayan Rescue Association web page at http://www.nepalonline.net/hra/. You can also E-mail them at HRA@aidpost.mos.com.np.

HEALTH AND SAFETY
Acute Mountain Sickness (AMS) can be a danger if you ascend too quickly to high altitudes without allowing your body time to acclimatize. After ascending 3,000 meters, adjust your schedule so that you are not sleeping in an area any more than 300–400 meters higher than the one you slept in the previous night. If you fail to allow time for acclimatization, you may develop symptoms of AMS, including nausea, headaches, and dizziness. The AMS may be mild enough to go away with a day's rest, but if ignored, it can lead to death. All that is required to ensure a safe trek is a basic awareness of AMS and a willingness to rest or descend if symptoms worsen. Avoid alcohol, sleeping pills, and narcotic pain medicines unless absolutely essential.

See Tour Operators, *in* Kathmandu A to Z *and* Nepal A to Z, *above.* Also, *see* Trekking and River Rafting Companies *in* Kathmandu A to Z, *above.*

When to Go
In the fall, the sky is usually sparkling and clear. In the spring, the rhododendrons bloom. The winter is obviously cold, but trekking below 3,000 meters is fine. The leech-sucking summer is laden with the pitfalls of landslides.

For Everest, the season consists of two fairly short periods: early October to mid-November and late March to late April. Because the window of opportunity is so small, the number of people flocking to Lukla airport during these times is great. Book well in advance.

NEPAL A TO Z

Arriving and Departing

By Bus
You can take a bus from India to Nepal. You can go from Sunauli, India, into Bhairawa, south of Pokhara; from the Raxaul Bazaar, India, across the Birganj border, south of Kathmandu; or you can cross the Karkabhitta border, entering the far east of Nepal. The public bus tickets cost around $10, but many travelers buy tickets at stations only to find that they must buy new ones when they reach the border. (There is little you can do if you are told to buy a new ticket or get off.) The bus ride is an overnight, overcrowded, often terrible experience. Poorly padded seats, with no legroom, are the norm. This is not a recommended means of travel, but if you decide to risk it, you'll have to book the trip through an Indian travel agency.

By Plane
AIRPORTS
The major gateway to Nepal is Kathmandu's **Tribhuvan International Airport** (☎ 01/471933).

CARRIERS
Royal Nepal Airlines Corporation (RNAC) flies nonstop to Kathmandu from Frankfurt, **Austrian Airlines** flies nonstop from Vienna, and **Transavia** flies nonstop from Amsterdam. All other major airlines flying from Europe, North America, Australia, and New Zealand use connecting flights from Bangkok, Singapore, or Delhi. To see the mountains as you fly into Kathmandu, request a window seat on the right side of the plane, if you are arriving from the east. If you are flying from the west, request a window seat on the left side. Flights in the fall, and to a lesser degree in the spring, fill up early; book well in advance. Expect to spend at least a full day in transit, including layover, taxi, and check-in time.

The main airlines serving Nepal are: **Aeroflot Russian Airlines** (☎ 01/227399), **Air France** (☎ 01/223339), **Austrian Airlines** (☎ 01/241470), **British Airways** (☎ 01/222266), **China Southwest Airlines** (☎ 01/419770), **Delta Air Lines** (☎ 01/220759), **Gulf Air** (☎ 01/430456), **Indian Airlines** (☎ 01/410906), **Japan Airlines** (JAL) (☎ 01/222838), **Lufthansa** (☎ 01/223052), **Necon Air** (☎ 01/480565), **Northwest Airlines** (☎ 01/410089), **Qatar Airways** (☎ 01/256579), **Royal Nepal Airlines Corp.** (RNAC) (☎ 01/220757), **Singapore Airlines** (☎ 01/220759), **Thai Airways** (☎ 01/224387), **Transavia Airlines** (☎ 01/247215).

Nearly all flights to Nepal include stopovers, so the length of time you spend in the air depends on where you stop. For example, it could take from 11 to 14 hours to travel from London to Kathmandu, depending on whether you stop in Delhi or Frankfurt and then Dubai. Similarly, it can take 11 to 14 hours to reach Nepal from Sydney, depending on whether you stop in Bombay or Bangkok. From the United States, it also depends on your point of departure, and of course, where in Asia you stop off. On average, the trip from the United States or Canada takes about 19 hours.

Getting Around

By Bus

The best company to use for trips between Pokhara, Chitwan, and Kathmandu is **Greenline Tours** (✉ Box 3904, Kaiser Mahal, Kathmandu, on Tridevi Marg near the taxi stands at the entrance of Thamel, ☎ 01/253885; ✉ Baidam, Lakeside, Pokhara, opposite the Fishtail Lodge entrance, ☎ 061/27271; ✉ Sauraha Chowk, Tandi Bazaar, Chitwan, ☎ 056/60126; or ✉ Al Fresco Café & Pub, Sauraha, on the main strip, ☎ 056/21792). The seats are comfortable, with plenty of legroom, and complimentary breakfast is served at a rest stop. Unlike other "tourist" buses, Greenline does not stop and pick up locals along the way. Trips between Kathmandu and Pokhara are seven hours. It takes 5½ hours to go from Kathmandu or Pokhara to Chitwan. Book reservations at least one day in advance.

By Car

Getting around Nepal by car means hiring a car *and* a driver. It's the only kind of car rental available here, and you wouldn't want to drive yourself anywhere, even if you could. In the Kathmandu Valley, accidents are frequent, and jams are the norm. Once you leave the Kathmandu Valley, the roads are not as jam-packed, but they are still dangerous. The two-lane highways are dominated by "Tatas," garishly painted Indian trucks and buses. These big vehicles overtake one another on bends, even though they can't see oncoming traffic. You are much safer in a chauffeured car. At least the local drivers are accustomed to the roads.

EMERGENCY ASSISTANCE

There is no national roadside automobile service in Nepal.

RENTAL AGENCIES

You can hire a car and driver in Kathmandu for about $60 a day. You can get anything from a compact car to a Land Rover. You can also hire a Mercedes with a driver. A compact car is usually fine, but if you're going to a remote area, a four-wheel-drive vehicle is recommended. All car-and-driver hires are handled by travel agencies or hoteliers.

ROAD CONDITIONS

The conditions of the roads varies from year to year and season to season. The Kathmandu–Pokhara and Kathmandu–Chitwan routes have significantly improved in the past few years and are totally paved now. However, landslides are a persistent problem in Nepal and they can wipe out new work any day.

Farther afield, many of the routes are still rock and gravel. Even in parts of Kathmandu and Pokhara, there are entire sections of town where the roads are unpaved or marred with manhole-size potholes.

Regardless of the pavement conditions, the roads are dangerous in Nepal. Children, dogs, cows, and chicken mindlessly wander into the middle of the road, with little or no warning. Oncoming vehicles don't always stay on their side of the road. Bicyclists don't wear helmets and never signal.

By Plane

Air travel in Nepal is an experience. The domestic airlines have been improving their on-time rates, but delays and cancellations are still frequent, especially on the Kathmandu–Lukla route, which is plagued by bad weather and overbooked flights. Do not plan on returning from the Everest region on one day and making an international connection the next day.

Most domestic flights take less than one hour and are on small (often prop) planes that make a lot of noise. On many flights, particularly from Pokhara to Jomsom and Kathmandu to Lukla, you get excellent mountain views.

The Kathmandu domestic airport is Tribhuvan International Airport. The Pokhara airport is in the southern part of the city, about 1 km (½ mi) east of Damside There are 21 flights a day between the two cities.

Other airports in the country have at least one flight a week to Kathmandu. The Bharatpur airport services the Royal Chitwan National Park, and is 20 minutes to an hour away from the various park lodges. The Nepalgunj airport, servicing the Royal Bardia National Park, is a two-hour drive away from the park. The Gautam Buddha Airport is in Bhairawa, an industrial town 22 km (13½ mi) east of Lumbini. You can also fly to Janakpur's airstrip, 2 km (1 mi) south of the city, but service here is unpredictable.

Lukla's and Jomsom's airports are in the mountains. Lukla has connecting flights with Kathmandu while Jomsom has connecting flights with Pokhara.

Contacts and Resources

Customs and Duties

ON ARRIVAL

You can bring into Nepal, free of duty, 200 cigarettes or 50 cigars, a 1.15 liter bottle of distilled liquor, and 15 rolls of film. You can bring binoculars, a movie or video camera, a still camera, a laptop computer, and a portable music system, but only on the condition that you take them back with you when you leave.

ON DEPARTURE

When you leave Kathmandu, you are required to pay an airport tax of 600 Rs., if you are flying to a country that is part of the South Asian Association for Regional Co-operation (SAARC): Bangladesh, Bhutan, India, Maldives, Pakistan, or Sri Lanka. The tax is 1,000 Rs. for all other international destinations. The domestic airport tax is 100 Rs.

It is illegal to export objects more than 100 years old. If you buy something that looks old, you need to get a certificate from the **Department of Archaeology** (☎ 01/250687, ⊘ Sun.–Fri. 10–4) at Ramshah Path, near Signha Durbar. This certificate will prove to airport security that the item is allowed to leave the country. Handicraft dealers and travel agents should be able to assist you in this process.

Dining

Most Nepalis eat with their fingers, using their right hand only. The left hand is unclean as it is the hand of choice in bathrooms. In hotels and restaurants cutlery is available.

Most Nepalis eat the same meal twice a day: lentils, rice, and mixed vegetables known as **daal baht tarkari**, or simply daal baht. It is served with a chutney, **acchaar**, that adds a spicy zing to the meal, and sometimes with buffalo meat.

MEALTIMES

Nepalis eat their first serving of daal baht at 10 AM and their second meal at 6 or 7 PM.

PRECAUTIONS

Do not drink the tap water. Do not even brush your teeth with it. Do not eat any fruits or vegetables that you cannot peel, unless you are confident they were washed with purified water.

The milk is unpasteurized, so drink it with caution.

Etiquette

Ask before taking a photograph of a person or holy object. If you are photographing beggars or holy men, you should give them an offering of a few rupees. Some people believe you steal their soul by photographing them; others believe foreigners make a fortune reselling photos of the poor.

Begging is a problem in the country. Some parents take their children out of school, dress them in rags, and encourage them to beg from foreigners. As difficult as it is to say no, do not encourage this practice of begging, which only reinforces a cyclical nature of poverty and dependence upon Western generosity. Instead, give to reputable aid agencies in the country.

Do not eat off of a Nepalese person's plate or drink from a Nepali's bottle or glass. This is considered impure by the Nepalese. Do not point with your feet or sit in a place that requires others to climb over you (for example in a doorway or throughway).

Nepalis and Indians tend to shake their heads in a half-yes, half-no fashion, when they mean, "yes." It can be confusing at times, so always double-check the meaning of the gesture.

While public displays of affection between men and women are more and more commonplace among the young, movie-watching crowd, they are still frowned upon by the vast majority of the public. Be discreet. It is perfectly acceptable for people in Nepal of the same gender to hug and touch so do not be surprised by such familiarity.

Health and Safety

CRIME

Beware of pickpockets In Kathmandu and Pokhara. It is worth the money to take a taxi and avoid local buses and the six-seater tempos, where the thieves are particularly expert.

HEALTH

Before you go, check with the Centers for Disease Control and your physician about the latest recommended vaccinations. Some vaccinations require a series of shots so be sure to see your doctor well in advance of your trip.

The poor water conditions make illnesses such as typhoid a possibility. Myriad stomach ailments are likely if you drink the local water. Boil it, buy it bottled, or treat it with iodine before drinking it or eating any food washed in it.

Acute Mountain Sickness (AMS), often known as altitude sickness, is an illness you can get from ascending too rapidly to elevations above

3000 meters (9,840 ft). Even if you have gone higher in the past without getting sick, this doesn't preclude you from getting sick in the future.

The initial symptoms of AMS are:

- Nausea, vomiting
- Loss of appetite
- Insomnia/sleeplessness
- Persistent headache
- Dizziness, light-headedness, confusion
- Disorientation
- Weakness, fatigue, lassitude, heavy legs
- Slight swelling of hands and face
- Breathlessness and breathing irregularity
- Reduced urine output

You should take these symptoms very seriously. If you get them, descend immediately. Acclimatization by ascending no more than 300 to 500 meters per day above 3,000 meters is the best way to prevent AMS.

Language

Nepali, written in the Devanagiri script, is the national language. It is also the *lingua franca* for Nepal's diverse communities. More than 70 different languages and dialects are spoken in the Kingdom. However, only six (Nepali, Maithili, Bhoijpuri, Tharu, Tamang, and Nepalbhasa) are spoken by more than a half-million people.

English and Hindi are widely understood in Kathmandu and Pokhara. Most restaurant workers and store owners will know some English, and taxi drivers will know a few basic words.

Lodging

The quality of lodging in Nepal ranges from upscale, international-standard hotels in Kathmandu to teahouses that provide no more than a simple bed. Pokhara is also developing a high-standard hotel system. However, when you go to the jungle and the mountains expect camping conditions.

Mail

Lines at the post office in Kathmandu are extremely long. Most hotels, however, will sell you stamps and mail your letters. Unfortunately, mail is extremely unpredictable in Nepal. Letters can take as little as two weeks to arrive in Kathmandu or reach their destination in the West, or they can take months. Packages from home often don't arrive in Nepal, and if you are sending something back, expect half of the contents to disappear along the way. To improve your chances of getting postcards out of Nepal, you might want to use an envelope. You need to buy glue to seal the envelopes sold here.

POSTAL RATES

The cost of an airmail letter (weighing 20 grams) is 20 Rs. for the United States and Canada, 18 Rs. for the United Kingdom and Europe. Aerograms cost 17 Rs. for the United States and Canada and 12 Rs. for the United Kingdom and Europe. Air mail postcards cost 15 Rs. for the United States and Canada and 10 Rs. for the United Kingdom and Europe.

RECEIVING MAIL

You can receive mail via the Poste Restante. The Poste Restante office in Kathmandu is near the Dharahara Tower in lower Kantipath; it's open Sunday–Thursday 10–4 and Friday 10–3.

Money and Expenses

CURRENCY

Nepalese currency is the rupee (abbreviated Rs.), which is divided into 100 paisa. Banknotes come in denominations of 1, 2, 5, 10, 20, 25, 50, 100, 500, and 1,000 rupees. There are 1-, 2-, and 5-rupee coins, but they are rarely used. Paisa rates are rounded up to the nearest rupee.

The approximate exchange rate from the Nepal Rastra Bank at press time was 67 Rs. to the U.S. dollar, 72 Rs. to the Euro, 108 Rs. to the British pound, 42 Rs. to the Australian dollar, and 44 Rs. to the Canadian dollar.

EXCHANGING MONEY

You can bring any amount of hard currency, including travelers checks, into Nepal, but you must fill out a currency declaration form when you arrive.

Convert your currency at authorized Foreign Exchange Counters. A passport is legally required (but not always requested). You can reconvert to U.S. dollars any Nepalese Rupee balance remaining with you at the time of your departure at the **Himalaya Money Exchange** counter at the Tribhuvan International Airport. However, you must produce foreign exchange encashment receipts equivalent to what you are reconverting.

FORMS OF PAYMENT

Carry small denominations. Few taxi or rickshaw drivers will make change. When you go on a trek or river rafting, change enough money for the entire venture before you leave Kathmandu or Pokhara.

You will only be able to use your credit cards in Kathmandu and Pokhara, in the Western-style hotels, travel agencies, and shops. They will accept American Express, Diners Club, MasterCard, and Visa.

Many establishments prefer cash and may give a discount if you pay in U.S. dollars or Nepali rupees instead of using a credit card.

Indian rupees are widely accepted, but the bills must be in perfect condition, with no torn edges. However, 500–Indian rupee notes are rarely accepted; they are apparently easily counterfeited. The Euro, British pound, and other dollar currencies are best exchanged at foreign currency desks rather than in shops.

TAXES

State-run and joint-venture restaurants and major hotels often charge a 2% Tourism Service Fee and 10% Value Added Tax.

WHAT IT WILL COST

Backpacker hotels can cost as little as $2 a night; although you get what you pay for in Nepal. On average, expect to pay $50 a night for a basic, nice room; $100–$200 a night for the upscale hotels.

After your room cost, prices drop significantly. A cup of tea or coffee or a can of soda will cost less than $1; a bottle of water costs about 15 Rs., or about 25¢. Beer costs anywhere from $1.50 to $2 for a large bottle of Tuborg, San Miguel, or Karlsberg. Kingfisher beer is usually a few rupees more. You will be hard-pressed to spend more than $10 per person for dinner. Taxis cost an average of $1 to $2 per local trip.

National Holidays

Nepal cannot get enough of holidays and festivals. They even celebrate New Year's day four times: January 1 on the Gregarian calendar, the mid-February Tibetan Losar New Year, the April 13 or 14 Nepali New Year, and the mid-November Newari New Year.

The Nepalese calendar begins in the middle of April and is on a lunar cycle. The following national holidays are from the Nepalese Calendar, which runs from April to March on the Gregorian calendar. These will give you a rough idea when each national holiday falls, annually. However, check with your travel agency to get the exact date before planning your trip.

New Year's Day (April); Buddha Jayanti (April); Law Day, a court holiday (May); Bhanu Jayanti (July); Rakshya Bandhan (August); Gai Jatra, a Kathmandu Valley holiday (August); Krishna Astami (September); Sapta Rishi Panchami (September); Indra Jatra (September); Dassain (October); Tihar (November); Human Rights Day (December); His Majesty's Birthday (December); Prithvi Jayanti (January); Saheed Deewas (January); Democracy Day (February); Education Day (February); Shivarati (March); Nari Diwas (March); Holi day (March); Ghode Jatra (April); Ram Nawami (April); Chaitra Dashain (April).

Many of these above-mentioned national holidays are festivals. To learn more about them, *see* Smart Travel Tips A to Z.

Opening and Closing Times

During Nepal's countless festivals, government offices and banks close. Government offices and many stores are closed on Saturday.

Government offices are open Sunday–Thursday 10–5 and Friday 10–3. Most banks are open Sunday–Thursday 10–3 and Friday 10–noon.

Passports and Visas

All travelers, except for Indian nationals, need a visa to enter Nepal. You can get a visa for 60 days from any Royal Nepalese Embassy or Consulate. You can also get a visa at the airport upon arrival, but expect a long line. Make sure you have a passport photo and a valid passport. If you get your visa at the airport pick up the application form at the side counters before you get in line. (You can fill out the form while you wait.) A 60-day, single-entry visa costs $30; a 60-day, double-entry visa costs $55; a 60-day, triple-entry costs $70; and a 60-day, multiple entry visa costs $90.

If you have already visited Nepal within 150 days of the same calendar year, you must pay $50 for a 30-day visa. (Only 30-day visas are issued if you have visited Nepal within that time.) After your first 60- or 30-day visa, it then costs $50 for an extension, which will be given for up to 30 days. You must pay $50 whether you wish to stay one or 30 more days. A second 30-day extension costs another $50. You can stay a maximum of 5 months in a calendar year. Children under 10 do not have to pay any visa fees, but the visa form, with requisite photo, must be filled out.

Taxis

Metered taxis are common in Kathmandu and increasingly more common in Pokhara. By day, metered taxis start at 7 Rs. and then charge 2 Rs. for every 200 meters. At night, the rate starts at 9 Rs. and then charge 4 Rs. for every 200 meters. For sightseeing, it is best to negotiate a fixed price. Ask your hotelier or local travel agent what a good price should be for your destination.

Taxis are available at hotels and at taxi stands in shopping areas and can be flagged down from the street. To wave an empty cab down, extend your arm at chest-level and wiggle your fingers, palm down. Don't whistle or yell.

Telephones

LOCAL CALLS

You can make local calls from your hotel, from an ISD/STD (International Subscriber Dialing/Subscriber Trunk Dialing) store, or from any grocery shop. They usually cost 2 Rs. to 5 Rs. a minute if you use a local shop and as much as 10 Rs. a minute if you call from your hotel. To dial a Kathmandu number, while in Kathmandu, drop the 01. If you are calling from outside the region, add it.

COUNTRY & AREA CODES

The country code for Nepal is 977. City codes are: Banepa (Dhulikhel region) 011; Bharatpur (Royal Chitwan National Park area), 056; Bhairawa (Lumbini) 071; Gorkha, 064; Janakpur 041; Kathmandu, 01; Nepalgunj (Royal Bardia National Park area), 081; Pokhara, 061. When dialing a number from abroad, drop the initial 0 from the local area code.

LONG-DISTANCE AND INTERNATIONAL CALLS

Most hotels and communications shops are connected to the International Subscriber Dialing (ISD) system, which eliminates the need to use an operator. With ISD you just dial 00, followed by the country code, the area code, and the number. There is no surcharge for using the ISD system, but most hotels will add their own surcharge, which can be extremely high. Check before you use the hotel facility. To avoid the surcharge, make your calls at ISD/STD offices. Even then, the price will be around $2–$3 per minute to most countries. It's a good idea to time the call yourself, as well. If you're on the phone for 3:01, you'll be charged for 4:00. Local shops will charge 10–20 Rs. for a long-distance call within the country.

Tipping

At the larger, more upscale establishments a 10% tip is the norm. The cheaper places and taxi drivers do not expect to be tipped, although leaving small change behind is appreciated.

Transportation around Nepal

You can get around Nepal by either flying or taking hired cars and taxis. Most domestic flights and long-distance car rentals cost less than $100. Flights are subject to the weather and overbooking, so be prepared for delays.

In some instances, you can river-raft much of the way from one destination to another. For shorter hauls, you can take auto and bicycle rickshaws and three-wheel motorized vehicles called Tempos. Some people choose to bike short distances.

Travel Agencies

Green Hill (⊠ Box 5072, Lazimpat, ☎ 01/428326, ℻ 01/419985, E-mail: ghill@wlink.com.np) has an office to the right of the driveway to the Kathmandu Guest House, if you are facing the entrance. They arrange sightseeing trips in the Kathmandu Valley ($25–$35), trekking ($20–$30 per person, per day), and full-service camping trips ($40–$60 per person, per day). This efficient agency also specializes in trips to Tibet and Bhutan.

Himalayan Journeys (⊠ Box 989, Kantipath, ☎ 01/226138, ℻ 01/227068, E-mail: hjtrek@mos.com.np) is in Kantipath near the Mandela Book Point, three-quarters of the way up the street on the left side, if your back is to the Royal Palace. This 21-year-old agency will charge from $545 to $640 for two people on a six-day trip (transportation and luxury accommodation included) touring Kathmandu City, Patan, Swayambhunath, Bhaktapur, and Pokhara. If you are interested in a 15-day, fully supported tented trek in the Everest region, expect to pay about $1,042. The staff is outgoing and environmentally friendly (no firewood used, etc.).

Natraj Tours & Travels (⊠ Box 495, Kamaladi, ☎ 01/222906, for Kathmandu Guest House compound office 01/417083, ꜰᴀx 01/227372, E-mail: natraj@vishnu.ccsl.com.np) was established in 1967 in Kamaladi but also has an office in the Kathmandu Guest House compound. In addition to tours around the Kathmandu Valley and Pokhara, and trips to the national parks in the Terai, **Natraj Trekking** also guides treks throughout the region. You will pay about $65 for one or two people taking a six-day, full-service, tented, trekking trip. The price drops to $50 a person on trips 21 days or longer; land transportation is in public buses.

Saiyu Travel Pvt. Ltd. (⊠ Box 3017, Durbar Marg, Kathmandu, ☎ 01/221707, ꜰᴀx 01/226430, E-mail: saujai@mos.com.np) is a 17-year-old, full-service travel agency that will arrange tours around the city, book flights, and make hotel reservations. It also has a trekking agency, **Jai Himal Trekking Pvt. Ltd.**, with expert, friendly guides who bake a delightful apple pie over an open flame. Many have worked for the company for more than a decade, a noteworthy point in ever-changing Nepal. Expect to pay about $60 a day for a full-service, tented, trekking trip and $40 a day for a teahouse trip. The company also owns **Safari Adventure Lodge,** a luxurious resort just outside of Royal Chitwan National Park. A two-night stay there, including all meals, transportation, and wildlife activities, is a relative bargain at $175 per person.

(☞ Kathmandu A to Z for special-interest tour operators.)

Visitor Information
The **Nepal Tourism Board** (⊠ Bhrikuti Mandap, ☎ 01/256909, ꜰᴀx 01/256910, E-mail: ntb@mos.com.np).

Vocabulary and Useful Details
NEPALESE CALENDAR
The Nepalese calendar begins on April 13 or 14. It is 57 years ahead of the Gregorian calendar.

Baisakh	April/May
Jestha	May/June
Ashadh	June/July
Shrawan	July/August
Bhadra	August/September
Aswin	September/October
Kartik	October/November
Mangsir	November/December
Poush	December/January
Magh	January/February
Falbun	February/March
Chaitra	March/April

The Newari calendar is also a lunar calendar, divided into twelve months, each dedicated to a god. The months are then broken down into two halves: the two weeks after the full moon are "badi" and usually not auspicious, the two weeks before a full moon are "sudi" and considered more auspicious times. The Newari New Year is in November.

DAYS OF THE WEEK:

Sombaar	Monday
Magalbaar	Tuesday
Budhbaar	Wednesday
Bihibaar	Thursday
Sukrabaar	Friday
Sanibaar	Saturday
Aitbaar	Sunday

NUMBERS:

ek	1
dui	2
teen	3
char	4
panch	5
chha	6
sat	7
aht	8
nau	9
das	10
bees	20
tees	30
chalis	40
panchas	50
sathi	60
satri	70
assi	80
nabbe	90
saya	100
ek hajar	1,000

FOOD AND DRINK

syaau	apple
keraa	banana
bir, chang	beer
chapati, puri	flat bread
gaajar	carrots
cauli	cauliflower
phul	eggs
maasu	meat
dudh	milk
peeyaj	onions
baht	cooked rice
daal baht	lentils and rice
masalaa	mixed spices
aloo	potatoes
noon	salt
chini	sugar
chiyaa	tea
pani	water
dahi	yogurt
dosa	fried, crepe-style pancake
tato pani	hot water

BASIC WORDS

namaste	hello/goodbye
namaskaar	hello/goodbye, more polite
dhanyabaat	thank you
bujhe	I understand
bujhdina	I don't understand

bujhdinu bhayo?	Do you understand?
Mero ghar amerikaa ho/iglaid	I am from America/ England.
pati	husband
patni	wife
dhaai	elder brother (older man)
bhai	younger brother (younger man)
didi	elder sister (older woman)
bahini	younger sister (younger woman)
ama	mother
amala	grandmother
Nepal man parchha	I like Nepal.
Malai madat dinu hunchha?	Can you help me?
Tapaaiko photo khichnu?	May I take your photo?
Kolaagi kati paisa laagchha..	How can I get to...?
Jaana kati parchha?	How much does it cost?

When to Go

The best time to visit is fall, when the mountain views are excellent and the Dassain and Tihar festivals take place.

Late January or February is usually when Losar, the Tibetan New Year, rings in. This is a good time to see Tibetan cultural events. If you head out to the Terai at this time, you will also get good animal viewing, since the grass is cut in February. However, mountain views are often clouded in these months.

The summer is not a good time to visit: too much rain and too many leeches. Conversely, the winter can be too cold.

CLIMATE

From September until the beginning of December, the weather is warm and the air is clear. From December to mid-February, high-altitude inns and trekking routes sometimes get snowed in. In the Kathmandu Valley and in the Lake District of Pokhara, it remains cool during the day and rarely snows. Mornings can be damp and misty in Kathmandu. It is not too hot in the Terai, and there aren't too many visitors, so it's a good time to check out the national parks in peace. Spring usually arrives around the last week of February, and the whole country is temperate. Once the monsoon arrives (usually around May or June), daily clouds obscure the mountain views and heavy rains cause landslides that block the roads.

What follows are average daily maximum and minimum temperatures for three locations in Nepal.

KATHMANDU

Jan.	66F	19C	May	86F	30C	Sept.	81F	27C
	36	2		60	16		66	19
Feb.	68F	20C	June	86F	30C	Oct.	73F	23C
	39	4		52	11		39	4
Mar.	77F	25C	July	86F	30C	Nov.	73F	23C
	25	8		70	21		39	4
Apr.	86F	30C	Aug.	84F	29C	Dec.	68F	20C
	52	11		68	20		36	2

POKHARA

Jan.	68F	20C	May	86F	30C	Sept.	84F	29C
	46	8		66	19		68	20
Feb.	70F	21C	June	86F	30C	Oct.	81F	27C
	46	8		68	20		64	18
Mar.	81F	27C	July	86F	30C	Nov.	73F	23C
	52	11		70	21		52	11
Apr.	86F	30C	Aug.	86F	30C	Dec.	68F	20C
	60	16		70	21		46	8

CHITWAN

Jan.	75F	24C	May	95F	35C	Sept.	90F	32C
	44	7		68	20		72	22
Feb.	79F	26C	June	95F	35C	Oct.	88F	31C
	46	8		73	23		64	18
Mar.	91F	33C	July	91F	33C	Nov.	84F	29C
	54	12		75	24		54	12
Apr.	95F	35C	Aug.	91F	33C	Dec.	75F	24C
	64	18		75	24		46	8

3   TIBET

Whether it's the altitude or the cultural purity of Buddhist Tibet, every traveler feels a little light-headed in this country perched on the roof of the world. So long isolated from the West, the Tibetan peoples reached the 20th century with a unique, sophisticated medieval culture that, despite the shock waves of the Chinese Cultural Revolution, still prevails. Monasteries, weathered by the Chinese storms, fill the countryside; prostrating pilgrims and twirling prayer wheels challenge the severe landscape; and the great Buddhist institutions display outstanding works of Tibetan art.

TIBET LIES ON A VAST PLATEAU as large as Western Europe, sandwiched between two Himalayan ridges whose peaks reach 8 km (5 mi) high. The plateau is the source for all the major rivers in South and East Asia: the Indus, Sutlej, and Brahmaputra from the far western highlands; the Mekong, Salween, Yangzi, Yalong, Gyrong, Yellow, Minjiang, and Jialing from the eastern region. Under the People's Republic of China the western half of the plateau has been designated the Tibet Autonomous Region, comprising the traditional Tibetan provinces of Ü (capital, Lhasa), Tsang (capital, Zhigatse), and Ngari (sometimes called Western Tibet). The remainder has been swallowed up by the Chinese provinces of Sichuan and Qinghai.

By Nigel Fisher and Lily Tung, with Michael Koeppel

Until 1707, when Jesuit missionaries established themselves in Lhasa, the West had no serious contact with Tibet. Before then the Roof of the World, as this Himalayan nation is poetically called, was isolated. Long, long ago, so one story goes, an ogress, Sinmo, and a monkey, Avalokiteshvara, were the only living creatures on the Tibetan plateau. In her loneliness, Sinmo lured the meditating monkey into her cave, where their combined efforts produced six offspring. These were to become the ancestors of the country's six main tribes.

Tibet did not become a nation until the 7th century, when a chieftain, Songsten Gampo, consolidated his rule by subjugating the ancient kingdom of Zhangzhung in the west. Songsten became the first true king of the unified Tibetan Empire, making Rasa (later renamed Lhasa) the capital.

For two centuries, the Tibetan Empire prospered, establishing advantageous treaties with its neighbors. Trade and knowledge were exchanged. The teachings of Buddha were brought to Tibet and received with enthusiasm by the ruling class. Elements of the shamanistic Bön faith, which the Tibetans had previously embraced, were incorporated into Buddhism. Riven by political and religious differences, the empire broke up in the 9th century. The influence of Buddhism diminished, and Tibet subsided into isolation for the next four centuries. When the Mongols swept through Central Asia in the 13th century, Buddhism had a rebirth in Tibet, as it did all over east Asia, and it became the country's official religion.

Tibet emerged again as an autonomous nation state in the 15th century when the monk Tsongkhapa rose as both a spiritual and a political leader. He established a new Buddhist doctrine, which emphasized moral and philosophical rigors rather than mysticism, and, in 1409, he renovated and enlarged the Jokhang temple and brought the Great Prayer Festival to Lhasa. He also founded three great monasteries: Ganden, Drepung, and Sera. This building frenzy was supported by the widening acceptance of Tsongkhapa's doctrine, which later was embodied in the Gelugpa order, or order of the Virtuous Ones.

Though political power lay in the hands of the kings of Tsang, a Tibetan tribe who ruled out of Zhigatse, the country's second-largest city, the spiritual power now rested with the head lama of the Gelugpa order. This leader was (and still is) chosen from among newborn infants on the death of the previous head lama in the belief that the latter's spirit had entered the newborn. Eventually the division between the spiritual lamas and the temporal kings of Tsang became untenable. The Mongols sided with the lamas, defeating the king of Tsang and paving the way for Dalai Lama V (1617–82) to become both spiritual and temporal head of state. Lhasa was once again securely positioned as the nation's capital and a theocracy was established.

As the next Dalai Lama, Dalai Lama VI, was ineffectual, the declining influence of the Mongols gave the Manchu Qing dynasty (1644–1912) its opportunity. Chinese troops moved into Lhasa, and the Chinese emperor Kang Xi declared Tibet a protectorate. Chinese control, sometimes manifest, sometimes latent, lasted until 1912.

In 1904 the British sent an expeditionary force into Tibet to combat the Chinese influence and guard against possible Russian encroachment, which could threaten British interests in India. At the fall of the Manchu dynasty in 1912, Tibet, with British support, gladly expelled all Chinese and declared the country's total independence. The withdrawal of the British from India in 1947 made Tibet again vulnerable, and in 1950, 30,000 veteran troops of the new People's Republic of China attacked a defending force of 4,000 ill-equipped soldiers. The result was slaughter on a gigantic scale, culminating in the death of 1.2 million Tibetans and the destruction of virtually every historic structure. Tibet became a vassal state of China.

In 1959, to quell a massive popular uprising in Lhasa, the Chinese ruthlessly shelled Norbulingka Palace and the crowds surrounding it, as well as the Potala (palace of the Dalai Lamas) and the Sera Monastery. When a crowd of 10,000 sought sanctuary in the Jokhang, the Chinese bombarded that, too, and after three days of gunfire in the capital, some 10,000 to 15,000 Tibetan corpses littered the streets. Dalai Lama XIV (the present Dalai Lama), three days before the massacre, had sought asylum in India, where he later set up a government-in-exile in Dharamsala. China then formally incorporated Tibet into the People's Republic, began a process of dissolving the monasteries and stripping Tibetans of their culture, and in 1965 renamed the country the Xizang Zizhiqu (Tibet Autonomous Region; TAR).

In 1966 the Chinese Cultural Revolution reached Tibet. Virtually every sacred and cultural monument was damaged if not destroyed outright. Monks and Tibetan loyalists were jailed and tortured or simply killed. Not until the death of Mao did the havoc abate, and by then some 6,250 monasteries and convents had been destroyed or severely damaged, thousands of Tibetans tortured and killed, and another 100,000 put in labor camps. The rest of the world virtually turned a blind eye. Eventually, in 1980, Deng Xiaoping's era of tolerance began. Some religious institutions have been restored and religious practices are now permitted. Massive numbers of Han Chinese, encouraged with incentives, are moving into Tibet, changing the face of this country, particularly in Lhasa, where probably half the population is Chinese. In some provinces the percentage is even higher.

Demonstrations still take place, and the call for Tibetan freedom is still heard. In 1988, 1989, and 1993, a series of bloody uprisings inspired by the monks challenged Chinese rule. Martial law was temporarily instituted. Discontent with the Chinese "invasion" continues, and the possibility of more demonstrations is always present. But, at the slightest hint of public protest, the Chinese make a few more Tibetans disappear and deny foreigners permission to enter the TAR. Tibet may not seem to the casual observer to be a police state, but it is.

Not all of Tibet is open to foreigners. Certain "closed" regions may be visited with a special permit, sometimes granted on request from the Public Security Bureau in Lhasa. Travel may be suspended without notice, which you'll only discover on being denied an entry permit or by finding that the flights to Lhasa are "fully booked." This is likely to occur at politically sensitive times such as the Tibetan New Year, the anniversary of the 1959 uprising on March 10, the anniversary of the 1989 demonstration in June, and International Human Rights Day in December.

On the Roof of the World, people live at altitudes that average between 3,500 and 5,000 m (11,500 and 16,400 ft). At the higher elevations vegetation is sparse. Wild grasses in the mountain wilderness are covered by a blanket of snow in winter. Narrow gorges make passes between sky-scraping peaks, where the larger-than-life clouds literally look 15,000 ft closer to the touch of the earthbound dweller. A few valleys are open to cultivation, and freshwater lakes perfectly mirror the color of the sky through the rarified air. Tibet may lack the magic that Western sensibilities so often exaggerate, and it can even be an excruciatingly frustrating place to travel; but ignore, if you can, the Chinese intrusion, the ugly modern buildings, and the open-pit mines around the towns, and you'll nonetheless journey along the top of the world knocking at the doors of the deities' heavens.

Pleasures and Pastimes

Architecture

Monasteries, some small, some vast, usually follow a similar layout: Entrance is through a portico. Murals depict the Four Guardian Kings (four directions of the compass), who display their prowess in martial arts. The Wheel of Rebirth is also represented. Often there are the two gatekeepers, Vajarapani on the east side and Hayagriya on the west side. The murals on the inner wall of the portals portray protector deities of the town or of that particular monastery. Through the portico is the central hall, whose size is determined by the number of columns. The rows of seats are for lamas attending ritual ceremonies—the elevated seats are for the head lamas. Clockwise around the hall you usually find a series of murals telling the story of the Lord Buddha's life or that of other critical historical figures. Facing the entrance and at the back of the elevated seats are the rows of sacred images and scriptures. In major temples, there is usually an inner sanctum: the treasure-house where the most revered images are kept. Also within the monastery complex are *klangtsens* (residential units) with their own chapels and assembly halls. In the larger monasteries the complex will have *tratsangs* (colleges), where various aspects of Buddhist precepts are taught.

The most common sight in Tibet is the Buddhist stupa, called a *chorten*. A chorten is built both as an act of merit and to serve as a reliquary for the ashes of a religious leader. The Potala has the most celebrated ones, which contain the ashes of past Dalai Lamas. Everything about the chorten has religious significance. In its totality, it embodies the Buddhist concept of true reality, in which the bonds of temporal and physical needs are dissolved. The chorten has a square base, a rounded dome, an oblong slab, a tiered triangular spire, and a small ornament. These five elements represent fire, earth, water, air, and space. Motifs tell the principal events in the life of Buddha.

On the domestic front, private houses have flat roofs and slightly inward-leaning walls built of brick. More picturesque are the homes of the nomads who follow their flocks of sheep and herds of yak on the mountain slopes. These yak-hair tents are large enough for a whole family to sleep, eat, and cook in. A hole in the roof over the fire pit in the tent's center acts as a chimney, but because there's no exhaust fan, the smell of yak butter permeates the whole tent.

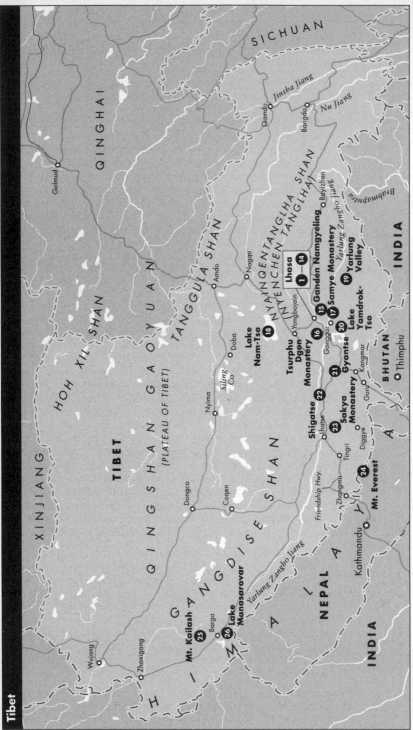

Art

With a history of 13 centuries of Buddhist influence, Tibet is an extraordinary repository of religious art, especially illuminations, murals, and *thangkhas* (painted cloth scrolls or banners). Sculpted images of deities and historic figures are mostly in metal, clay, or stucco, although a few are made of wood or stone. Despite destruction by the Chinese and the persecution of artists since 1950, an abundance of Tibet's art treasure still remains. In the new era of tolerance, Tibetans are relearning their art and are actively restoring the masterpieces of their past.

Buddhism and all of its art forms arrived in Tibet from India at a time when Buddhism was on the wane there, and soon Nepalese art began to influence the Tibetan style. Chinese influence came much later, in the 16th century, and was limited principally to the development of the landscape background in portraits of historic figures.

Tibetan art in general, and images in particular, are not meant to serve as accurate representations or portraits, but rather to express states of the mind and to assist in reaching higher levels of consciousness. Art is intended to represent purity of spirit and to nurture meditation—most images are to guide the meditator in his communication with a particular deity, with the goal of assimilating the deity's attributes and taking the next spiritual step on the path. Deities and historic figures have been sculpted or painted by artists from the 7th century onward in various postures expressing myriad spiritual attributes. In the 1,000 rooms of the Potala alone there are more than 200,000 images.

Dining

Tibetan cooking is simple. The staple is *tsampa* (roasted barley flour) washed down by bowls of *soja* (butter tea). You are likely to eat tsampa more than once only if starvation is imminent. A more enjoyable dish is *momo*, a steamed or fried dumpling filled with meat or vegetables, often served with *then-thuk* (noodles). Other common dishes include *lasha* (lamb with radish), *gyuma* (black pudding), *thu* (cheesecake), and *dresi* (sweet rice). If you are invited to a Tibetan banquet, you'll have these and more—18 dishes in all.

With the explosion of tourism in Tibet over the past few years, the quality and variety of food available in the region has improved greatly. In Lhasa, Tibetan and Chinese fare is supplemented by a competitive market of Western restaurants offering fast food, Italian, Nepalese, Indian, and other standard Continental cuisine offerings. Outside of Lhasa, the variety of food available may not come close to rivaling the capital city. But rest assured, unless you are in a small village or in an area not commonly visited by tourists, you should be able to find a satisfying meal and more often than not, a familiar one. Fussy eaters should order a picnic from their Lhasa hotel before going off for trips into the countryside.

Beer and soft drinks are available nearly everywhere. The local drink is *chang* (a fortified barley ale). Local water is not potable; it must be boiled or treated with iodine before it passes your lips. In Lhasa and in other towns, however, bottled water is plentiful.

CATEGORY	COST*
$$$$	over $27
$$$	$21–$27
$$	$8–$21
$	under $8

Prices are per person for a three-course meal, excluding drinks, taxes, and tip.

Festivals

The most colorful times to visit Lhasa are during festivals, when pilgrims come into town and banners fly, adding to the gaiety. Festivals occur according to the Tibetan lunar calendar, and so the dates vary every year. The following times, therefore, are approximate. **Losar,** the Tibetan New Year Festival (February or March), is Tibet's most colorful celebration, with performances of Tibetan drama. During **Mönum** (the Great Prayer Festival; February) the image of Maitreya is paraded from the Jokhang around Barkhor. At the **Lantern Festival** (the Day of Offerings; February) huge sculptures made of yak butter are placed on the Barkhor pilgrimage route. **Buddha's Enlightenment Day** (May/June) draws many pilgrims, and there are outdoor opera performances. **Drepung Zöton** (Yogurt Festival; August) takes place at the monastery, with the hanging of a monumental thangkha and dances by the monks. **Zöton** (August—two days after Drepung Zöton) is known as the Popular Yogurt Festival; it starts at the Drepung Monastery and moves to Norbulingka, where operas and dances are held). **Labab Düchen** (October/November) commemorates the deities' coming to earth and attracts numbers of pilgrims. **Paldren Lhamo** (November) honors the protective deity of Jokhang, whose image is paraded around the Barkhor.

Lodging

With Tibet's continued popularity as a tourist destination, the quality of service and variety of accommodation available has slowly improved in an effort to meet the standards demanded by the Western traveler. Throughout Lhasa and at several of the more important tourist sites, new hotel projects are either under way or planned for the future. While there may be no five-star luxury hotels in Tibet, Lhasa does have several large hotels that are more than adequately comfortable.

Most of Lhasa's hotels, be they large or small, offer rooms of varying quality and price. Ask and you may be shown rooms ranging from a depressing 20-person dormitory to a deluxe room with private bath, balcony, and minibar. Outside Lhasa in the major towns there are bland Chinese hotels, about half of which have hot running water. You may prefer to seek a Tibetan guest house, many of which are quite clean, where the hospitality is warm and welcoming. However, be forewarned that the shared bathing facilities in these guest houses are primitive: some toilets are no more than a cement or wood slab with a hole in it, placed over a pit.

CATEGORY	COST*
$$$$	over $102
$$$	$78–$102
$$	$54–$78
$	under $54

Prices are for a standard double room with bath at peak season, excluding tax and service charges.

Photography

Place Tibet's unique art, architecture, dress, and culture against the backdrop of the majestic Himalayas, studded with 6,000 monasteries, and you have a photographer's heaven. However, taking photos within the monasteries and temples is usually forbidden, unless you pay a fixed photography fee per room (*not* per sight). This can get expensive. The highest fee may be at the Potala, where the price to take a picture in front of Dalai Lama V's chorten was about $20. Print, slide, black-and-white, and APS format films are all available in Lhasa; but prices are a bit higher than those charged in China's larger cities, and the variety of film speeds is somewhat limited. Check the expiration dates on the film boxes and make sure the packaging hasn't been opened.

When it comes to buying film, you are always better off paying a little more at an established store than buying from a street vendor. Do not photograph Tibetans without their permission—it's considered rude and an affront to their culture.

Shopping

The bazaars are fun and Tibetans love to bargain. They respect you for doing so, too. The best buys are traditional jewelry, metalwork, carpets, woodwork, and textiles. Appliquéd thangkhas make superb gifts. Antiques, according to government regulations, require a permit to export.

Exploring Tibet

Lhasa lies in Central Tibet, in the province of Ü, in the fertile Kyi-chu Valley, which extends north to its glacial origins in the Nyenchen Tanglha range. This region is the most heavily populated within the Tibetan Autonomous Region (TAR). South of Lhasa and Ü are the Lower Brahmaputra valleys that pass into Assam (India) and Bhutan.

Western Tibet is the region of the Upper Brahmaputra Valley, whose main city is Shigatse. Through the central part of southern Tibet, you can make the land trip from Nepal, crossing the border at Kodari/Zhangmu and traveling up to Tsongdu and Zhigatse en route to Lhasa. The southern county of Dingri is traditionally known as the highland region of Tibet and is bordered on the south by the high Himalayan range that includes Mt. Everest and the popular trekking routes around Everest Base Camp. The traditional province of Tsang lies within central-western and southern Tibet.

Far Western Tibet, or Ngari, one of the least populated parts of the country, has only recently been open to foreigners and includes Tibet's holiest mountain, Kailash. Eastern Tibet, some 1,200 km (750 mi) east of Lhasa, is characterized by rugged mountains with steep rocky slopes often topped with glaciers and broken by deep gorges. Less than half of this region is in the TAR. Northern Tibet, Jangtang, is a vast lakeland wilderness with elevations ranging from 14,760 ft to 16,400 ft; it's rarely visited by outsiders.

Great Itineraries

Travel in Tibet is primarily limited to Lhasa and the provinces of Ü and Tsang, with some hard-core travelers heading out to Western Tibet, or Ngari. Most visitors use Lhasa as a hub, or jumping-off point, to other destinations and break up their ventures into the hinterland with rests in the capital city.

Numbers in the text correspond to numbers in the margin and on the Tibet and Lhasa maps.

IF YOU HAVE 3 DAYS

Take it easy on your first day in Lhasa, adjusting to the altitude. Keep your sightseeing to the heart of the old city, around **Barkhor Square.** Off the square is **Jokhang Temple,** the most sacred temple in Lhasa. If you are up to it, you can also visit the **Temple of Meru Nyingba** (adjoining the east wall of Jokhang) and the **Ani Tshamkung Nunnery** southeast of Jokhang on Waling Lam. In the morning of the second day go up to the **Potala.** Spend the afternoon exploring the religious cave paintings and carvings on the hill of Chagpo Ri, being sure to visit **Chogyel Zimuki.** On the third day, go out to **Drepung Monastery,** and then make the pilgrimage along the Drepung Lingkor. Return to Lhasa for an afternoon at the **Norbulingka Palace,** the summer palace of the Dalai Lamas. At the end of the day, you can do some final shopping around the Barkhor or to the less visited but charming area comprising the **Ramoche Monastery** and the small **Tsekung** chapel adjacent to it. On one evening, have a traditional Tibetan feast while enjoying a performance by Tibetan singers.

IF YOU HAVE 10–14 DAYS

Enter Tibet by land from Kathmandu, Nepal, and take two or three days to reach Lhasa, traveling through the towns of **Gyantse** and **Shigatse** and seeing **Lake Yamdrok-Tso.** Give yourself three or four days visiting the sights in the capital city (☞ 3-day itinerary, *above*). During this time, arrange to go on a tour or two, climbing into the Himalayas on the Nepalese border, hiking around **Lake Nam-Tso,** discovering the attractions of the gorges, or visiting off-the-beaten track monasteries like **Ganden, Samye,** and **Tsurphu.**

If you arrive in Lhasa by plane from China or Nepal, spend your first three days in Lhasa. Take a day trip to **Ganden Monastery** or **Tsurphu.** Visit **Gyantse** and **Shigatse,** and then take a two-to-three-day tour to **Lake Nam-Tso** or **Samye Monastery.**

IF YOU HAVE 15–20 DAYS

Fly into Lhasa from China, and spend a few days there, seeing the sights and getting adjusted to the altitude. During the first few days, check out Lhasa itself (☞ 3-day itinerary, *above*). On days 4 and 5, take day trips to **Ganden Monastery** and **Tsurphu.** Take a two-day/one-night tour to **Lake Nam-tso.** Spend two to three days at **Samye Monastery** or in **Yarlung Valley.** Get on a five- or six-day four-wheel-drive tour headed into Tsang, and visit **Mt. Everest Base Camp** and **Rongbuk Monastery,** passing through the towns of **Shigatse** and **Gyantse,** and stopping at **Sakya Monastery** and **Lake Yamdrok-Tso.**

IF YOU HAVE 1 MONTH TO 5 WEEKS

Visit the above places and, if you want to rough it a bit, take a tour to Western Tibet's **Mt. Kailash** and **Lake Manasarovar.** This can be an extension of your tour to the province of Tsang, but generally the trip to Western Tibet from Lhasa will take you from 16 to 20 days.

Great Treks

Not all of Tibet is accessible by road, which makes trekking all the more thrilling. The scenery is staggering and the discoveries enthralling. In many places you feel as if you are the first person to tread on the land. The best months for clambering over the Roof of the World are April through June and September through November, although the summer rainy season often is not that wet. Self-sufficiency is important, since once you leave Lhasa, not much is available. On the other hand, the high altitude respects those who pack light. Trekking equipment can be rented or purchased in Lhasa. The selection, quality, and price may not equal what is available in Kathmandu or your hometown outfitter, but it will suffice (☞ Shopping *in* Lhasa, *below*). Since trails in Tibet are not well marked, you will most likely have to travel with a guide. The trek routes in this chapter are only generally described, so if you choose not to go with a guide, be sure to do your research—try to obtain topographical maps in your home country, and take a look at trekking guidebooks. Many routes have become well trod, but with the vast number of mountains in Tibet, new trails will always continue to be blazed. The following are brief descriptions of some of the most popular treks in Tibet.

GANDEN MONASTERY TO SAMYE MONASTERY

This four-day trek begins and ends at two of Ü's most impressive monasteries. With its hikes through verdant mountains and flower-covered meadows, above valley streams, past herds of yak and sheep, and over two passes, it has become one of the most popular treks in Tibet. Trekkers can not only enjoy the scenery and pieces of Tibetan history found along the way, but also make friends with the herders and villagers who live and work in the area. After four days of hard work, your reward is a peaceful stay at Samye, by the shore of the Bhamaputra River.

MT. EVEREST

Some people are satisfied by seeing it; some by reaching its peak; and still others by trekking near its presence. The north side of Mt. Everest is barren and severe, but well-acclimatized and experienced trekkers still brave the environment on foot. There are two popular three- to four-day treks in the area, to and from the Friendship Highway—one from Shegar to Everest Base Camp and then another from Everest to the town of Tingri. The first is less remote than the other, partially following the dirt road jeeps use to get to the mountain, while the other is reserved for trekkers who accept complete self-sufficiency. Both offer majestic views of Everest and the rest of its Himalayan family.

MT. KAILASH KORA

For Buddhists, Hindus, and followers of Bön, Mt. Kailash is the most sacred mountain in Asia, and its kora the most holy. Shrouded in myth and magic, Mt. Kailash is believed to lie at the center of the universe, where the gods reside. Pilgrims from India and Tibet flock to Mt. Kailash to complete its kora, several times if possible, to erase their sins. If you decide to undertake the long, arduous journey to Western Tibet, one of the most remote places on earth, you, too, can complete the kora around Mt. Kailash. Along the three-day journey you'll find important religious and ritualistic sites, as well as incredible landscapes—plains, rivers, glaciers, and the majestic mountains of Nepal, Tibet, and India.

THE HOLY LAKES

Three of Tibet's holy lakes are visited by travelers for their otherworldly beauty and godly shades of blue. Just south of Mt. Kailash is the holiest of all, which, like Mt. Kailash, attracts pilgrims to its important kora. North of Lhasa lies the highest lake in the world and the second-largest saltwater lake in China—the breathtaking Lake Nam-Tso. To the southwest of Lhasa, Lake Yamdrok-Tso curls its snakelike tentacles around the surrounding mountains. Although most travelers explore the lakes through day hikes, some die-hard trekkers spend several days circumambulating the lakes along with the zealous pilgrims completing their koras. Due to marshes and other challenging terrain, unclear trails, trek lengths, and mercurial temperatures around some of these lakes, it's almost necessary to go with a guide.

OTHER TREKS

Although Nepal is really the trekker's paradise in the Himalayas, there are a good number of treks in Tibet, and new ones are constantly being found. The hearty trekker could find that the options in Tibet are ever-expanding. For instance, for an alpine trek around lands frequented by Tibetan nomad herders, try the trek between Tsurphu Dgon Monastery and Yangpachen. One easier trek is the one from Shalu to Nartung in Tsang near Shigatse.

When to Tour Tibet

Tibet is a land of extremes. In winter temperatures can sink to −23°C (−9°F), but in summer the thin mountain air permits the sun to penetrate, to heat the days to 30°C (86°F). The best touring weather occurs from mid-April through June, but with pleasant weather comes hordes of tourists. Summer can bring heavy rain that often closes roads to popular tourist destinations, including Everest Base Camp. If you can't visit in the spring, the period from September through mid-November is another good option. Wintertime is frightfully cold, but at least the climate is dry and the skies perpetually blue. Cold weather also means fewer tourists, which can make for a more rewarding experience. Travel is also less restricted in winter, because the police monitoring the checkpoints are more concerned with keeping warm than turning back curious tourists.

LHASA

Lhasa, the small city on the Roof of the World, may have lost some of its reputed magic and mysticism to the sterile modernity of Communist China, but it still remains the beating heart of Tibet. The most important pilgrimage destination for Tibetan Buddhist devotees, Lhasa holds the culture's treasures—Jokhang Temple and the surrounding Barkhor—the most holy and active temple and circumambulation route on the plateau.

With a population of a little over 160,000, Lhasa is remarkably small, considering its long history. Its major sights, both historically and architecturally, fall into three eras: first, the 7th- to 9th-century building boom, which produced the first Potala Palace on Mt. Marpori (AD 637) and the Buddhist-influenced Jokhang temple (641); second, the 15th century, when Tsongkhapa renovated and enlarged the Jokhang temple (1409) and founded the three great monasteries of Ganden, Drepung, and Sera (1419); and third, when Lhasa again became the capital and Dalai Lama V (1617–82) rebuilt (and expanded) the Potala on the foundations of the original. Over the next three centuries the lamas constructed the great Gelugpa monasteries and palaces, of which the Norbulingka Palace is the most notable.

The city today, 50 years after the Chinese invasion, still contains a generous amount of Tibetan architecture, art, and culture, but primarily on one side of town. Lhasa is basically divided into an eastern old Tibetan section and a western Chinese section. Its main road also has east–west delineations, with the notorious Chinese-erected Golden Yaks statue more or less marking the line of division. The dusty but colorful eastern end—Beijing Dong Lu in Chinese or Dekyi Shar Lam in Tibetan—runs past Potala Palace and some of the more popular low-end accommodations, north of Jokhang. Meanwhile, in the west end, Beijing Xi Lu, or Dekyi Nub Lam, runs through sterile, bathroom-tiled buildings, including the Lhasa Fandian and other higher-end hotels. The Tibetan/Chinese "coexistence" can get somewhat confusing, even down to the basic fact that all of Lhasa's streets have both Chinese and Tibetan names.

This juxtaposition has defined Lhasa at the millennium, with a jarring dichotomy between China's brutal push towards modernity and Tibet's oppressed yet unstifled spirituality and traditionalism. Let yourself get carried along in the Barkhor's cycle of movement, however, with its deep colors, medieval pathways, vivid people, religious scents, and whirlwind of life, and you will see that the Tibetan enclave still embodies the earthbound otherworldliness and old-world charm that has brought travelers to Tibet for centuries.

Exploring Lhasa

A Good Tour (or Two)

The high altitude of Lhasa will tax your stamina on your first day (maybe even your second and third . . .), so take it easy. Go down to the **Barkhor** ① for lunch, then spend the afternoon in the **Jokhang** ② tem-

In case you want to be welcomed there.

We're here to see that you're always welcomed at establishments everywhere. That's why millions of people carry the American Express® Card – for peace of mind, confidence, and security, around the world or just around the corner.

do more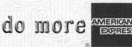

Cards

To apply, call 1 800 THE-CARD
or visit www.americanexpress.com

In case you're running low.

We're here to help with more than 190,000 Express Cash locations around the world. In order to enroll, just call American Express at 1 800 CASH-NOW before you start your vacation.

Express Cash

And in case you'd rather be safe than sorry.

We're here with American Express® Travelers Cheques. They're the safe way to carry money on your vacation, because if they're ever lost or stolen you can get a refund, practically anywhere or anytime. To find the nearest place to buy Travelers Cheques, call 1 800 495-1153. Another way we help you do more.

do more AMERICAN EXPRESS

Travelers Cheques

ple. If there is time, you can visit the **Ani Tshamkung** ③ nunnery, just south of the Jokhang, and the temple of **Meru Nyingba** ④ (adjoining the east wall of the Jokhang). Nearby is the **Gyel Lhakhang** ⑤, Lhasa's mosque. Or, if you've had enough of sacred matters, wander the streets of Barkhor checking out the smells and sounds. North of Dekyi Shar Lam are the 15th-century **Ramoche** ⑥ and **Tsekhang** ⑦ temples.

The **Potala Palace** ⑧, which beckons you to visit from the moment you arrive in Lhasa, should be your first stop on the second day. It will take the full morning to cover both the White and Red palaces. Spend the afternoon exploring the religious cave paintings and carvings on Chakpo-Ri, being sure to visit **Chogyel Zimuki** ⑨.

On the third day, go out to the **Drepung** ⑩. Give yourself at least an hour and a half to inspect the monastery, then make the Drepung Lingkor, the 90-minute pilgrimage walk around the monastery. The next stop is the **Nechung** ⑪ monastery, just southeast of Drepung. Finish by returning to old Lhasa to shop around the Barkhor.

For the fourth day, go out to **Sera Thekchenling** ⑫ northeast of Lhasa. Return to spend an afternoon at the **Norbulingka** ⑬ complex and the **Tibetan Museum** ⑭, if it has opened to visitors. The completion of the new $12 million museum complex, which is supposed to include exhibitions on Tibet's history and natural resources, has been behind schedule, but is slated to take place in late 2000.

If you have more than four days in Tibet, you can head out of town, to other sights in Ü and Tsang provinces. Close by are the enormous **Ganden Monastery,** 40 km (25 mi) from Lhasa, and **Tsurphu,** 70 km (43 mi) from Lhasa. If you're really adventurous and have a lot of time, head out to Western Tibet for a two- to three-week road trip.

Sights to See

③ **Ani Tshamkung.** The main temple at this nunnery was built in the early 14th century; a second story was added in the early 20th century. Before the Chinese invasion of Tibet, the nuns were responsible for lighting the butter lamps in the Jokhang. Considerable damage occurred during the Cultural Revolution, but the nunnery was restored in 1984 and now has more than 80 nuns in residence. The chief pilgrimage site is the Tsamkung (meditation hollow) where Songsten Gampo concentrated his spiritual focus on preventing the flood of the Kyi-chu River. ✉ *Waling Lam, southeast of Jokhang, look for a front entrance painted yellow.* ▨ *Y10 (additional Y10 for each photo).* ☉ *Daily 8–6.*

① **Barkhor.** This plaza around the Jokhang temple, the spiritual and commercial hub of old Lhasa, is now the only part of the city that has not been overrun by the migrating Chinese. Properly speaking, the Barkhor is only the intermediary circumambulation surrounding the Jokhang, but the name is commonly used to refer to the heart of Lhasa. Off the Barkhor walkway are marketplaces and more temples. Join the myriad prayer-wheel-turning pilgrims making the Barkhor circuit and you will step back into the "Forbidden City," passing monks sitting before their alms bowls, chanting mantras. The circuit is crammed with stalls where vendors sell trinkets, carpets, hats, prayer shawls, and just about anything you might not know that you want. The streets running north off the Barkhor walkway to Dekyi Shar Lam are shopping streets (☞ Shopping, *below*).

Along the north wall of the Jokhang is the **Nangtseshak,** a two-story former prison that had more than its share of notoriety in the past.

South of the Barkhor plaza are several notable buildings, many of them former residences of important advisors to Dalai Lama XIV.

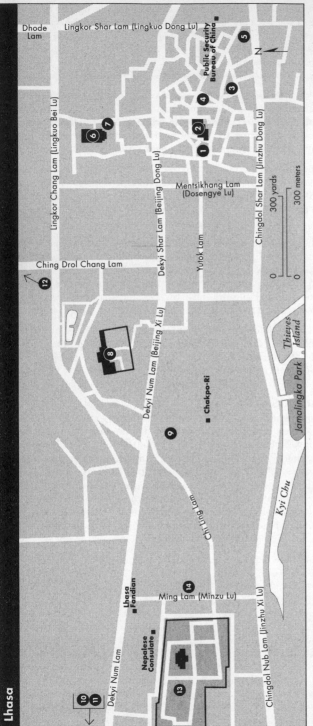

Lhasa

Dhode Lam

Lingkor Shar Lam (Lingkuo Dong Lu)

Public Security Bureau of China

Lingkor Chang Lam (Lingkuo Bei Lu)

Mentsikhang Lam (Dosengye Lu)

Dekyi Shar Lam (Beijing Dong Lu)

Yutok Lam

Chingdol Shar Lam (Jinzhu Dong Lu)

300 yards

300 meters

Ching Drol Chang Lam

Dekyi Num Lam (Beijing Xi Lu)

Chakpo-Ri

Thieves Island

Jamalingka Park

Kyi Chu

Chi Ling Lam

Lhasa Fandian

Ming Lam (Minzu Lu)

Nepalese Consulate

Dekyi Num Lam

Chingdol Nub Lam (Jinzhu Xi Lu)

Ani Tshamkung, **3**
Barkhor, **1**
Chogyel Zimuki, **9**
Drepung, **10**
Gyel Lhakhang, **5**
Jokhang, **2**
Meru Nyingba, **4**
Nechung, **11**

Norbulingka, **13**
Potala Palace, **8**
Ramoche Temple, **6**
Sera
Thekchenling, **12**
Tibetan Museum, **14**
Tsekhang, **7**

⑨ Chogyel Zimuki. In caves scattered over Chakpo-Ri, a hill opposite and to the southwest of the Potala, are as many as 5,000 religious rock carvings and paintings. How old they are is uncertain, but arguably some were made in Songsten Gampo's time—the 7th century. The best and most interesting are at Chogyel Zimuki, sometimes called Dragla Lugug, a grotto-style temple in which the inner sanctum is a cave. Beyond the temple's gate is a monastic building from which you can mount the steps of the two-story grotto chapel. On the right, on the second floor, is the entrance into the spherical cave, which has a central rock column. Inside, three of the walls and the column bear 71 sculptures carved into the sheer granite. They are thought to be the work of Nepalese artists in the 7th through 9th centuries. ⊠ *Follow Mirik Lam south from Lhasa Fandian (former Holiday Inn) to dirt road along base of Chakpo-Ri facing Marpo Ri, hill on which Potala stands, to Chogyel Zimuki.* 🎫 *Free.* ☉ *Daily sunrise–sunset.*

⑩ Drepung. The largest of the Gelugpa monasteries was the residence for lesser lamas. Founded in 1416, it was enlarged in the 16th century by the Dalai Lama II to become the effective center of political power in Tibet before the Potala was completed. By the era of the Dalai Lama V (1617–82) it had become the largest monastic institution in the world, with 10,000 residents. During the Cultural Revolution it suffered only minimally; the most important chapels were left intact. Now about 500 monks live here.

The Drepung complex comprises the Tshomchen, the four main *tratsangs*—institutions for teaching, often translated as colleges—and the Ganden Potrang, from which Tibet was ruled before the Potala existed. Each of these has its own *klangstens* (residential units). The layout of each is a courtyard, a large hall, and inner chapels. Each klangsten is arranged on a slope, with the courtyard at the lowest level. The monastery's most important building is the Tshomchen. The roof of its vast assembly hall (the **Dukhang**) is supported by 183 columns. The hall is 164 ft by 118 ft, with the central portion of the ceiling raised for an atrium effect. Banners add to the ceremonial pomp. On this, the ground floor, are several chapels. More chapels populate the second and third floors as well as the roof. Visit them all. Look especially for the two-story **Düsum Sangye Lhakhang** (Buddhas of Three Ages Chapel) at the rear of the Dukhang on the ground floor. Here in the large illuminated room each of the three Buddhas of past, present, and future is guarded by two bodhisattvas. Other statues adorn the room; along the western side are images of the four spiritual sons of the Buddha. Smaller statues represent past kings and their consorts.

To set out on a pilgrimage around the monastery, the **Drepung Lingkor,** leave from the upper left corner of the parking lot. The walk takes about 90 minutes. The path winds west of the perimeter wall and uphill in the direction of Gephel Ritrö, then descends in the direction of Nechung. You can also walk 3½ hours up to the **retreat of Gephel Ritrö.** The retreat (now restored) was founded in the 14th century where the monks tended their yak herds. Reaching the summit, **Gephel Ütse,** takes another 2½ hours of strenuous climbing. ⊠ *Off Dekyi Num Lam, 7 km (4 mi) west of Lhasa center; take bus that passes Lhasa Fandian (former Holiday Inn), get off at base of Gephel Ri, and walk 1 km (½ mi) north; or hire a car or minibus taxi from town.* 🎫 *Y30.* ☉ *Daily 9:30–5; some chapels close noon–2.*

⑤ Gyel Lhakhang. In perhaps the most Buddhist of cities, Gyel Lhakhang is a bit of an anomaly. It is Lhasa's largest mosque, for the approximately 2,000 Muslim residents in the city. It was built in 1716 for the immigrants who arrived in the 17th century from Kashmir and Ladakh.

To spot it, look for a green-painted minaret and an entrance behind a congregation of fruit and vegetable stands. ⊠ *Linghor Lho Lam (near East Linghor Lam).* ⊙ *Daily 8–5, except during prayers Fri.* AM.

★ ❷ **Jokhang.** Believed to be the country's first significant Buddhist-inspired temple, this is the most sacred building not only in Lhasa but in all of Tibet. Day and night, Tibetans pay homage and, during the pilgrimage season, long queues of devotees shuffle toward the inner sanctum, where they touch their foreheads on the sacred image of Jowo Sakyamuni (Buddha).

Built probably in 647, during Songtsen Gampo's reign, Jokhang stands in the heart of the old town. The site was selected as the geomantic center of Tibet by Queen Wengcheng, a princess from China brought to Songtsen Gampo as his second wife. Her site selection, in the middle of Othang Lake, posed an elementary problem that was eventually solved by thousands of goats carrying loads of earth to fill the lake. Perhaps unfairly after so much goatly effort, the original name of the city, Rasa (Place of the Goats), was changed to Lhasa (Place of the Deity). But the building of the temple was further delayed. Queen Wengcheng also divined that before the completion of the temple a threatening demon ogress needed to be pacified. This required the construction of 12 outlying temples geomantically sited so as to be positioned on the body of the "supine ogress." Through divination, temples were built on her thighs, knees, and so on, to pin her down; this, conveniently, formed three successive rings of four around the location of Jokhang.

Songtsen's first wife, Princess Bhrikuti from Nepal, financed the building of Jokhang. (She had already undertaken the building of the Potala when she arrived in Lhasa in 632 and remained active even after Songsten took Princess Wengcheng as his second wife.) In honor of her, and in recognition of Tibet's strong reliance on Nepal, Jokhang's main gate was designed to face west, towards Nepal. Among the few bits of the 7th-century construction that remain are the door frames of the four inner chapels, dedicated to Mahakarunika, Amitabha, Sakyamuni, and Maitreya.

Over the centuries, several renovations have enlarged the Jokhang to keep it the premier temple of Tibet. It came close to losing this position when, in the 1950s, the Chinese Army shelled it and the Red Guards of the Cultural Revolution ransacked it. At one time during this period of sacrilege, parts of it were used as a guest house and as a pigsty. About a third of the damage has since been repaired.

The Inner Jokhang consists of three stories and forms a square enclosing the inner hall, Kyilkhor Thil. Encircling the Inner Jokhang is the inner circumambulation, known as the Nangkhor. The Outer Jokhang, sometimes referred to as the western extension and constructed in 1409, contains the lesser chapels, storerooms, kitchens, and residential units. The whole complex is circled by the Barkhor walkway, fringed by the old city of Lhasa.

Start your visit in the Barkhor (☞ *above*), a wide plaza in front of the Outer Jokhang. Look for the two willows of recent vintage flanking the stump of a willow tree planted by Queen Wengcheng. A wall now gives the tree some protection. Enter the temple through the portico supported by six fluted columns. At the small threshold courtyard, pilgrims prostrate themselves and, over the course of centuries, have worn the flagstones smooth. The side murals of the portico depict the Four Guardian Kings and the Four Harmonious Brethren. Within the main courtyard is the assembly hall that Tsongkhapa had constructed for the Great Prayer Festival in 1409—which, incidentally, greatly enhanced Lhasa's claims as the spiritual capital of Tibet. Along the outer walls are 19th-century murals, and in the inner hall are murals dating from 1648. On the north side is the residence of the Dalai Lamas.

Before entering the Inner Jokhang, you should walk the Nangkhor (Inner Circumambulation), as you should all circumambulations, in a clockwise direction. It's lined with prayer wheels (to be turned in a clockwise direction) and murals on the east side, which is also known for its series of Buddhist images. On the north side are several chapels of minor consequence. Outside the wall on the south side is the debating courtyard, renovated in 1986, which contains the platform where thrones for Tsongkhapa and other dignitaries were set up for the Great Prayer Festival. Enter by the **Zhung-go** (Main Gate), which has finely carved door frames from the early Tibetan period. Left of the door is a painting of the Future Buddha; on the right a painting of the Past Buddha. A footprint of the Dalai Lama XIII is enshrined in a small niche. Continue on through to the large Entrance Hall, whose inner chapels have murals depicting the wrathful deities responsible for protecting the temple and the city of Lhasa. Straight ahead is the inner sanctum, the three-story **Kyilkhor Thil**, some of whose many columns probably date from the 7th century, particularly those with short bases and round shafts.

The chapels on the ground floor of the Kyilkhor Thil are the most interesting. In the West Wing be sure to see the **Je Rimpoche Dakpa Namgye Lhakhang**, a chapel whose central image is Tsongkhapa flanked by his eight pure retainers. In the North Wing, in the chapel **Mahakarunika Lhakhang**, whose entrance has a heavy metal chain curtain, is an image of the deity Mahakarunika. The chapel also contained Buddha relics from Bodha Gaya, but some of the sacred treasure was smuggled out during the Cultural Revolution, and some was destroyed. The most revered chapel of the inner hall is **Jowo Sakyamuni Lhakhang**, in the middle of the East Wing, opposite the entrance. Here is the 5-ft image of Jowo Rimpoche, representing the Buddha at the age of 12. It was brought to Tibet by Queen Wengcheng and somehow has survived, despite an exciting history of being plastered up, buried in sand, and lasting through the Cultural Revolution. ⊠ *Barkhor.* 🚋 *Y25.* ☉ *Daily 9:30–12:30, 3–6.*

❹ **Meru Nyingba.** The original temple, built soon after the Jokhang, is where the Tibetan alphabet was finalized by the scholar Tonmi Sambhota. Within this 20th-century reconstruction are murals portraying many of the forms taken by Pehar, the chief guardian of the Gelugpa Buddhist sect. ⊠ *Eastern wall of Jokhang off northern arc of Barkhor.* ☉ *Daily sunrise–sunset.*

⓫ **Nechung.** This monastery is dedicated to Pehar, a deity that protects Tibet. From its construction in the 12th century, the temple has been home to important oracles whose advice on political appointments and future events has been sought regularly. The Lhasa government made no major decisions without first consulting the oracle; even today, the current oracle resides in Dharamsala as an advisor to the Dalai Lama and his Tibetan government-in-exile. Except for the gilded roofs and their embellishments, the Nechung buildings largely survived the Cultural Revolution. The three-story temple building at the north end of the courtyard is approached by steps flanked by lions. The murals on the portico depict Pehar and his retinue. In the assembly hall murals show the *Deities of the Eight Transmitted Precepts,* and in the Jordungkhang chapel on the western side, you'll find more images of Pehar. Also in this chapel is the tree trunk where, as a dove, Pehar landed after making his successful escape from imprisonment in a casket thrown into the Kyi-chu River. There are two other chapels on the ground floor, two on the second floor, and a single chapel on the third floor. You can also visit the residence of the Nechung Oracle, located behind the main building. ⊠ *Dekyi Num Lam, 8 km/5 mi west of Lhasa center, 1 km/½ mi southeast of Drepung Monastery.* ▧ *Y20.* ⊙ *Daily 9–noon, 2–4:30.*

⑬ **Norbulingka.** The Dalai Lama VII, a frail man, chose to build a palace on this particular site because of its medicinal spring. In 1755, not content just to have a summer home for himself, the Dalai Lama enlarged the palace with the construction of the **Kelzang Podrang,** to the southeast, a three-story palace whose ground floor is dominated by his throne, and had his whole government move down to the palace from the Potala. The next Dalai Lama expanded the property, adding a debating courtyard, the **Tsokyil Podrang** in the center, to mark the site of the medicinal spring, the Lukhang Lho pavilion, and the Druzing Podrang to serve as a library and retreat. The gardens were landscaped by Dalai Lama XIII (1876–1933), who later (1930) oversaw the construction of a new complex, **Chensel Lingka Podrang** to the northwest, containing three small palaces. The last addition was **Takten Migyur Podrang** in the north, an ornate two-story building notable for Buddha images on the ground floor and the impressive European-style reception room on the floor above, by Dalai Lama XIV in 1954–56, three years before he fled to India. In fact, it was from here that the Dalai Lama, disguised as a soldier, made his escape on March 17, 1959, three days before the Chinese massacred the Tibetans and fired artillery shells into every Norbulingka building. Only when the Chinese searched through the corpses did they recognize that the Dalai Lama had escaped.

The work done to repair the damage in the aftermath of the March 1959 uprising is not of high caliber. The palace's 80 acres are divided into three areas: the opera grounds (where Tibetan operatic performances are held during the Yogurt Festival), government buildings, and the palaces. The palaces are in four complexes and are visited by pilgrims in the following sequence: Kelzang Podrang to the southeast, Takten Migyur Podrang to the north, Tsokyil Podrang in the center, and Chensel Lingka Podrang to the northwest. ⊠ *Mirk Lam.* ▧ *Y25.* ⊙ *Daily 9–12:30, 3:30–5:30. Closed Thurs.*

★ ⑧ **Potala Palace.** Virtually nothing remains of the original 11-story Potala Palace built in 637 by King Songtsen. What you see today is a 17th-century replacement. The Dalai Lama V, anxious to reestablish the importance of Lhasa as the Tibetan capital, employed 7,000 workers and 1,500 artisans to resurrect the Potala Palace on the 7th-century foundation, using the original palace as its prototype. After eight years, the White Palace was completed in 1653. The Red Palace, the central upper part, was not completed until 1694, 12 years after the Dalai Lama's death, but his death was kept a secret by the regent Desi Sangye Gyatso in order not to interrupt the construction. The Potala has been enlarged since then, mostly in the 18th century, with continual renovations, including stabilizing and strengthening the structural walls in 1991. The vast Potala, once the spiritual and political headquarters of Tibet's theocracy, is now a museum.

The Potala was the world's tallest building before the advent of 20th-century skyscrapers. Towering above the city from the slopes of Mt. Marpori, the structure is 387 ft high; its 1,000 rooms house some 200,000 images. The outer section, the White Palace, was the seat of government and the winter residence of the Dalai Lama until 1951. The inner section, the Red Palace, contains the temples and the reliquary tombs of the Dalai Lamas. The Eastern Gatehouse is the main entrance used by pilgrims, who climb up from Zhol Square below. Other visitors usually reach the Potala at the rear drive-in entrance on the north side so as to avoid the steep climb. By coming in from the north and entering directly into the White Palace, you miss the ancillary buildings, including two printing presses dating from the 17th century.

Between the White and Red palaces is a yellow building that houses the Thangkha Rooms, in which are kept huge thangkas. Once used in the celebration of the Yogurt Festival, they are no longer displayed, although one was unfurled in 1994. In the White Palace you can pass through the spartan quarters of the Dalai Lama. On either side of the palace are the former secular apartments and offices of the government. The Red Palace, looming up from the White Palace, is the spiritual part of the Potala. Murals chronicle Buddhist folklore and ancient Tibetan life. Within the four stories that make up the functional part of the Red Palace are dozens of small chapels, where often a human skull and thigh bone are the only decoration. Interspersed among the chapels are eight golden chorten containing the embalmed remains of Dalai Lama V and Dalai Lamas VII–XIII.

Underneath the 13-story, 1,000-room fortress are the dungeons. Past justice was rough—as it still tends to be today, though under different masters—and refusal to pay taxes, displaying anger, or insulting a monk meant torture and jail. The worst place to be sent was the Cave of Scorpions, where prisoners became target practice for the stinging tails. ✉ *Zhol.* 🎫 *Y40.* ⊙ *Mon., Wed., Fri. 8:30–noon; Tues., Thurs., Sat., Sun. 9:30–noon; hrs extend until 3:30* PM *if there is a sufficient number of visitors.*

❻ **Ramoche Temple.** On the northern side of Dekyi Shar Lam, this temple was founded by Queen Wengcheng at the same time as the Jokhang. The temple's present three-story structure dates from the 15th century. Despite restorations in the 1980s, it lost much of its former glory after the Chinese used it to house the Communist Labor Training Committee during the Cultural Revolution.

Ramoche was to be the home of the most revered statue of Jowo Rimpoche. A threat of a Chinese invasion in the 7th century induced Queen Wengcheng to hide the image in a secret chamber in the Jokhang. Some 50 years later it was rediscovered and placed within the main chapel of Jokhang. As a substitute, Jokhang reciprocated with a statue of Jowo Mikyo Dorje, which had been brought from Nepal and represented Buddha as an eight-year-old. It was decapitated during the Cultural Revolution and its torso "lost" in Beijing, but both head and body were later found, put back together, and placed in a small chapel at the back of Ramoche's Tsangkhang (Inner Sanctum). ✉ *Ramoche Lam, off Dekyi Shar Lam, north of Tromzikhang Market.* 🎫 *Y20.* ⊙ *Daily 8:30–5:30.*

⓬ **Sera Thekchenling.** This important Gelug monastery, founded in 1419 on 24 acres, contains numerous chapels, with splendid murals and icons. Originally it was a hermitage for Tsongkhapa and his top students. Within a couple of hundred years, the community numbered 5,000 to 6,000 monks. The complex comprises the *tsokchen* (great assembly hall), three tratsangs, and 30 klangstens.

On the clockwise pilgrimage route, start at the two buildings that will take most of your visit. **Sera Me Tratsang** (founded in 1419), which promotes elementary studies, has a dukhang rebuilt in 1761 with murals depicting Buddha's life. Among its numerous chapels, the most interesting are the five along the dukhang's north wall: the Ta-og Lhakhang is hard to forget as it's a little macabre, with skeletons and skulls adorning its exterior. The three-story college for tantric studies,

Ngagpa Tratsang, is the complex's oldest surviving structure (1419), where the dukhang is supported by 42 short and four tall columns. Here you find statues of famous lamas and murals depicting paradise.

Continue to **Sera Je Tratsang** (the largest of the three colleges, with four stories), where you can take time out in the shaded courtyard, once the site for philosophical debates; today pilgrims come here to offer scarves and talismans. Other sites on the pilgrimage route are **Hamdong Khangtsang** (a principal residential unit), the **Tsokchen** (covering 6,560 square ft, with 89 tall columns and 36 short columns), and Tsongkhapa's **hermitage** on Mt. Phurbuchok, which has a two-story chapel. ⊠ *5 km (3 mi) north of Lhasa at base of Mt. Phurbuchok.* 🏯 *Y30.* ⊙ *Daily 9:30–4.*

⓮ **Tibetan Museum.** At press time, the spanking-new museum was not yet open but was slated to debut in late 2000. It looks great from the outside, and the inside will supposedly house Tibetan history, art, and culture—from whose point of view is the question. ⊠ *On Ming Lam, across from Norbulingka.*

❼ **Tsekhang.** If you really want old-world charm that is less popular with foreign tourists, come to this quaint, tiny temple that has one row of prayer wheels, a small chapel with three large golden Buddhas—Maitreya, Amitayus, and Sakyamuni—and a short but very crowded kora (circumambulation route undertaken by Buddhist devotees and pilgrims). Be warned, the tide of pilgrims will pull you along in its concentrated, quick rotations. Walk fast! Next door is a small assembly hall. Outside the chapel is a charming minicourtyard where the very friendly pilgrims gather, converse, and spin their prayer wheels. ⊠ *Xiaojianshe Lu, Damen, No. 29 (adjacent to Ramoche; if you're facing Ramoche, it is to your left).*

Dining

In an attempt to satisfy the tourist appetite, Lhasa has become inundated with Western-style cafés and restaurants to the point where it is now more difficult to find a traditional Tibetan meal than an order of cheeseburger and fries. The Barkhor area is swarming with reasonably priced restaurants offering extensive Western and Asian menus. In West Lhasa, the options are more limited, so you may want to stick to your hotel. Many of the larger hotels offer a full meal plan (breakfast, lunch, and dinner). Although these plans can save money, they do discourage you from trying local restaurants and various ethnic fare.

$$$$ ✕ **Lhasa Fandian.** With five restaurants to choose from, you are sure to find a meal in the Lhasa Fandian to satisfy your appetite. At its Himalayan Restaurant you can try Tibetan cooking that will include momo and *thukpa* (noodle soup, usually with meat and vegetables), as well as Nepalese dishes. Chinese cuisine is served in its Sichuan restaurant and, would you believe it, Western meals are served in the Hard Yak Café. If you're just hankering for a sundae, you can get that here, too. ⊠ *1 Minzu Lam,* ☎ *0891/683–2221,* 📠 *0891/683–5796. AE, DC, MC, V.*

$$ ✕ **Crazy Yak.** This restaurant offers well-prepared Tibetan and Chinese food that is reasonably priced. The interior uses Tibetan artifacts for atmosphere, made all the more pleasant by Tibetan operatic and folk dance performances nightly at 7:30. ⊠ *107 Dekyi Shar Lam, near Yak Hotel,* ☎ *0891/633–1999,* 📠 *0891/632–9316 Reservations essential. No credit cards.*

$$ ✕ **Kirey Mad Yak Restaurant.** The Mad Yak entices patrons with rooftop dining inside a Tibetan tent (more like a canopy than a Western enclosed tent) and folk dance performances downstairs in the main dining room. Order from an extensive menu or better yet, get together a group and try the banquet meal. As dancers entertain, your taste buds will be treated to such traditional items such as sautéed yak lung, cheese momos, fried snow peas, and cold yak tongue. The dishes are much tastier than they sound. ✉ *105 Dekyi Shar Lam,* ☎ *0891/632–3987. Call ahead to arrange banquet meal. No credit cards.*

$$ ✗ **Snowlands Restaurant.** This cozy, colorful café with carpeted floors, small tables, and cramped booths, is a good choice for those looking to unwind after a long day of sightseeing. Although a bit more expensive than its competitors, the kitchen does turn out consistently tasty food and delicious bakery goods, including cinnamon rolls, apple pie, and croissants. Combining the chicken sizzler and an order of garlic naan bread makes for a hearty meal. ✉ *4 Mentsikhang Lam,* ☎ *0891/632–3687. No credit cards.*

$$ ✗ **Yeti Café.** Curious about how Tibetan food is prepared? Then stop off at the Yeti, where you will find an English menu that indicates whether a dish is fried, steamed, braised, or boiled. The front dining area is crammed with couches covered by Tibetan rugs, and the rear of the restaurant offers plenty of private rooms for more intimate dining. The Shoguonomo, an appetizer of mashed potatoes filled with meat and deep fried, is recommended for those not adverse to oil and calories. ✉ *206-10 Dekyi Nub Lam, north of Lhasa Fandian,* ☎ *0891/633–0856. No credit cards.*

$ ✗ **Barkhor Café.** The Barkhor's covered outdoor patio is an ideal place to have a bite to eat while enjoying the views of the adjacent square and surrounding mountains. Chinese, Tibetan, and all of the usual backpacker favorites are available from their extensive menu. The large indoor seating area also houses several computers providing Internet access at Y40 per hour. The veggie burger is highly recommended. ✉ *Southwest corner of Barkhor Square, up a spiral staircase.* ☎ *No phone. No credit cards.*

$ ✗ **Makye Ame.** Finding yourself tired and hungry during a walk around the Barkhor circuit? Then stop off at Makye Ame—one of the most pleasant and relaxing restaurants in Lhasa. A decorative menu that feels more like an artsy scrapbook offers a flavorful assortment of dishes that includes ginger carrot soup, spinach tofu raviolis, and a great yak burger. In the main room, the intricately carved wooden bar proudly displays a wide assortment of wines and spirits, while upstairs the rooftop patio has both Internet service and an amazing view of the pilgrims walking down below. For those just looking for an energy boost, the brownie will not disappoint. ✉ *Southeast corner of Barkhor Circuit,* ☎ *0891/632–4455. No credit cards.*

Lodging

$$$–$$$$ 🏨 **Lhasa Fandian.** With a $9 million renovation, the Lhasa Fandian (former Holiday Inn) has solidified its position as one of the premier hotels in Lhasa. Bright, modern rooms come equipped with cable television, IDD phone, comfortable sitting chairs, minibar, and even piped-in oxygen (to ease the stress of the altitude) in all but the most economical of rooms. The Hilsa health and recreation center has an indoor swimming pool and bowling alley. For evening entertainment, you can check out the karaoke bar. The hotel lacks Tibetan charm, but it does have a well-trained staff, offer a full range of services, and cater to the demands of the package tour traveler. ✉ *1 Minzu Lam, Lhasa 850001,* ☎ *0891/683–2221,* ℻ *0891/683–5796. 468 rooms, 12 suites. 5 restaurants, bar, minibars, room service, pool, beauty salon, laundry service, meeting rooms, business services. AE, DC, MC, V.*

$$ 🏨 **Grand Hotel.** A former government guest house that was converted into a hotel in 1998, the Grand is a large hotel complex with several buildings offering a wide variety of accommodation. The higher-priced rooms are nicely decorated with floral wallpaper, brightly colored bedspreads, and even Italian-made whirlpool bathtubs. On the other end of the spectrum, the economy rooms are a bit dark and dingy. Popular with Asian tourists, the Grand is attempting to capture a portion of the ever-expanding Western market. ✉ *196 Beijing Zhonglu, Lhasa 850001,* ☎ *0891/682–6096,* FAX *0891/683–2195. 380 rooms, 20 suites. 6 restaurants, beauty salon, laundry service, business services, travel services. No credit cards.*

$$ 🏨 **Himalaya Hotel.** With the 1999 addition of a new nine-story building, the Himalaya Hotel provides accommodation ranging from luxury suites to budget triples. Although the original part of the hotel is quite basic, the new building's entrance is lavishly appointed with four grand columns, a marble floor, and a central chandelier, where it welcomes guests through its sliding glass doors. The new rooms are some of the finest to be found in Lhasa: they're luxurious, with fluffy carpet, Western-style bathrooms, and televisions. Some have great views of the Potala. The location is near the Kyi River and a 10-minute walk from the Barkhor. ✉ *6 Linghor Donglu, Lhasa 850001,* ☎ *0891/ 632–1111,* FAX *0891/633–2675. 116 rooms, 16 suites. 3 restaurants, massage, sauna, laundry service, meeting rooms, business services, travel services. AE, MC, V.*

$$ 🏨 **Kechu Hotel.** A small, charming hotel in the heart of the Tibetan Quarter, the Kechu veers away from the modern sterility of the other hotels in its class. Hallways with ornate ceilings and old black-and-white Tibetan photographs lead to rooms with traditional door frames, hardwood floors, dark-wood furniture, and thangkhas on the walls. On the main floor is a small restaurant that offers buffet meals of Indian, Chinese, Western, and Tibetan cuisine. The lobby has a small sitting area, book exchange, and a well-stocked art shop near the front entrance. ✉ *148 Dekyi Shar Lam, Lhasa 850001,* ☎ *0891/633–8824,* FAX *0891/632–0234. 17 rooms, 4 suites. Restaurant. No credit cards.*

$$ 🏨 **Tibet Hotel.** Down a notch from the Lhasa Fandian (☞ *above*) in price and farther from town, the Tibet Hotel has a well-worn lobby but renovated rooms decorated in Italian-country fabric and Italian-style fixtures. The floor-to-ceiling windows add brightness to clean, well-apportioned rooms. On the lobby level is a high atrium sitting area with a Chinese rock fountain and a tile mural of an egret. A small discotheque is the evening entertainment. ✉ *221 Dekyi Nub Lam, Lhasa 850001,* ☎ *0891/683–6887,* FAX *0891/683–6887. 93 rooms, 4 suites. 4 restaurants, beauty salon, dance club, laundry service, business services, travel services. DC, MC, V.*

$ 🏨 **Banak Shol.** A popular Tibetan-Quarter choice with the backpacker crowd, the bright, monasterylike Banak Shol is built around a long, narrow central courtyard with several large trees reaching higher than the hotel's three stories. The rooms are basic but clean, and the all-Tibetan staff is incredibly friendly and helpful. Originally established by a farmer's cooperative to house visiting farmers on market days, the hotel is dedicated to providing a relaxed atmosphere for the weary traveler at reasonable prices. The ground-floor restaurant with its outdoor seating is always a popular meeting spot to relax over a meal, a beer, and conversation. The Banak Shol also has one computer available for Internet access (guests pay per minute) and a storage room where you can leave your belongings before going on long treks. ✉ *43 Dekyi Shar Lam, Lhasa 850001,* ☎ *0891/632–3829,* FAX *0891/633–8040. 30 private rooms, 2 suites, dormitories. Restaurant, laundry service, meeting room, travel services. No credit cards.*

$ 🏨 **Pentoc Guesthouse.** Located a block north of Barkhor Square, the Pentoc is a clean and comfortable option for the budget-minded traveler. All rooms have colorful Tibetan-style bedcovers, dark-blue curtains, and either a love seat or chair. Rooms on the street side are larger, but beware of the traffic noise below. While there aren't any rooms with attached bath, the communal toilets and showers are kept immaculately clean. Videos are shown nightly at 8 PM in the lounge. ⊠ *Tibetan Hospital Rd. #5, Lhasa 850001,* ☎ 𝙁𝘼𝙓 *0891/633–0700. 24 rooms. Business services. No credit cards.*

$ 🏨 **Snowlands.** Enter the inner courtyard of the Snowlands and you will soon forget the hustle and bustle of Lhasa's busy streets. This quiet hotel has comfortable rooms with walls painted in Tibetan designs, along with televisions and telephones. Try to get a room with its own bath, since the communal bathrooms are very basic (although reasonably clean). A good-natured staff is always eager to please. ⊠ *4 Mentsikhang Lam, Lhasa 850001,* ☎ *0891/632–3687,* 𝙁𝘼𝙓 *0891/632–7145. 18 rooms, 2 suites, dormitory. Restaurant, bicycles, laundry service, travel services. No credit cards.*

$ 🏨 **Yak Hotel.** The Yak is the first choice for travelers on a tight budget who want to be in the Barkhor area. It offers a range of accommodations from beautiful doubles complete with bathrooms, telephones, air-conditioning, and TVs, in its newly renovated building, to immaculate, six- to 10-bed dorms with shared bathroom facilities. Inspect the rooms before accepting, as they vary widely, from rather depressing to light, fresh, and comfortable. The Yak has a great roof area to lounge around on. ⊠ *100 Delyi Shar Lam, Lhasa 850001,* ☎ *0891/ 632–3496. 28 doubles, dormitories. No credit cards.*

Nightlife and the Arts

Tibetan operas are performed at the **TAR Kyormolung Operatic Company** and the **Lhasa City Academy of Performing Arts.** Traditional Tibetan music and dance is presented by performers donning traditional costumes at the **Himalayan (in the Lhasa Fandian), Crazy Yak,** and **Kirey Mad Yak** restaurants (☞ Dining, *above*). The **Lhasa Song and Dance Ensemble** (⊠ on the east side Lingkor Dong Lu, just south of Lingkor Bei Lu) also plans performances for private groups from time to time.

Shopping

Arts and Crafts

Handicrafts, religious artifacts, paintings, and carpets are available all around the Barkhor circuit. The **Thangkha Mandala Gallery & Workshop** (⊠ Barkhor Circuit, South Side, Door 32) has an especially excellent collection of traditional Tibetan paintings—the best in town. Here, you can also watch artists working on their thangkhas in the front room.

The **Friendship Store** (⊠ Yutok Lam), **Tibet Da Peng National Arts Craft** (⊠ outside entrance to Norbulingka, *in* Sights, *above,* ☎ 0891/681–8066), and the **Potala Palace Art Gallery** (⊠ outside entrance to Potala Palace *in* Sights, *above,* ☎ 0891/633–4854) also have traditional artifacts.

The quaint **Lhasa Kitchen** (⊠ 180 Beijing Dong Lu) has a small arts-and-crafts window out front that sells handmade Tibetan paper products, including picture frames, hanging lanterns, and postcards. The shop also sells silver jewelry, including miniature prayer-wheel pendants, and door hangings—all great gifts at incredibly reasonable prices.

For Tibetan cloth tents and wall hangings try **Cuo Mei Lin Tent Factory** (⊠ off Dekyi Shar Lam, down alley east of Yak Hotel, ☎ 0891/632–7904). **Lhasa Carpet Factory** (⊠ 17 Jin Zhu Donglu [Chingdol Lu], ☎ 0891/632–3447) provides informational tours on carpet making and sells its wares on the premises.

Markets

The **Tromsikkhang** (⊠ alley northeast from Barkhor) market is worth popping into, if only to look at all the yak butter you'll ever want to see or smell. In the **traditional market** extending all around the Jokhang and the Barkhor, you will find such Tibetan handicrafts as textiles and carpets, as well as religious artifacts and paintings. Bargain hard.

Outdoor Equipment

North Col Mountaineering Shop (⊠ West side of Potala Square, ☎ 0891/633–1111) has the best collection of outdoor equipment.

Lhasa A to Z

See Tibet A to Z for more important information about Lhasa.

Arriving and Departing

See Tibet A to Z, *below.*

Getting Around

BY BICYCLE

Bicycle rickshaws are also available for short trips and normally cost between Y2 and Y5. You can bargain a little (by sign language) with the driver.

Pedaling your own bike is also a good way to see the city and some of the sights bordering Lhasa, such as Drepung Monastery. You can rent reliable bicycles for a few yuan an hour at the Snowlands Hotel (☞ Lodging, *above*).

BY BUS

Minibuses ply a fixed route, with fares of Y2 or less. Most buses go up and down Beijing Lu.

ON FOOT

Part of Lhasa, especially the old Tibetan quarter in the eastern part of town, are best explored by foot. The town is fairly small, and walking offers some of the most interesting experiences and sights of the city.

BY TAXI

Lhasa is congested with numerous taxis, which are the easiest way to get around, and cheap, too. A set fare of Y10 will get you anywhere within the city's limits. To order a taxi call 0891/683–4105 or arrange through your hotel.

Currency Exchange

See Tibet A to Z, *below.*

Guided Tours and Travel Agencies

See Tibet A to Z, *below.*

Internet Service

You can access E-mail and the Web at the Banak Shol, Makye Ame restaurant, and the Barkhor Café (☞ Dining *and* Lodging, *above*). There is also a small Internet shop across the street from the Banak Shol. These places use Netscape and Microsoft Outlook and charge you by the minute online. Be forewarned: although access is fairly reliable, connections in Tibet are notoriously slow. Be prepared to be patient.

Post Office

The **post office** is located on Beijing Dong Lu or Dekyi Shar Lam, at the intersection just east of Potala. Although it's a bit disorganized, there is also a poste restante at this main branch. (⊠ Lhasa GPO, 64 Beijing Dong Lu, Lhasa, ⊗ Mon.–Sat. 9–8, Sun. 10–6).

Ü PROVINCE

Ü, the most central of Tibetan provinces, surrounds and includes Lhasa. The province of Tsang is also considered central, and both Ü and Tsang make up the most historically and politically important region of Tibet. However, it is the more eastern Ü that is the birthplace of Tibetan culture. The first Tibetan kings unified Tibet in the 6th and 7th centuries from the Yarlung Valley, home to what is supposedly the oldest building in the country. Although political control of the plateau fell into the hands of the kings of Tsang a few centuries later, Ü and Lhasa again held the seat of power when Dalai Lama V became both spiritual and temporal head of state in the 17th century. Full of verdant valleys, impressive and important monasteries, vast grasslands, and a spectacular lake ringed by majestic mountains, Ü is more than just a historical journey.

A Good Strategy

Both **Ganden Namgyeling** ⑮ and **Tsurphu Dgon Monastery** ⑯ can be visited on day trips out of Lhasa. If you only have the option of seeing one monastery outside of the capital, Ganden is probably a better (and easier) choice. The magnificent **Samye Monastery** ⑰ requires a stay of at least one night away from Lhasa, perhaps two, but is definitely worth the effort and time. **Lake Nam-tso** ⑱ is also worth a trip, if your schedule can bear an overnight stay. Fewer tourists end up in **Yarlung Valley** ⑲, which requires at least a two- to three-day excursion.

Most of Ü's sights are most easily seen as a series of short trips beginning and ending in Lhasa. However, it is possible to take a four-wheel-drive tour to **Yarlung Valley,** with a stop at **Samye** on the way, or to **Nam-tso** with a stop at **Tsurphu.** Some adventurous visitors also do one of Tibet's most popular treks, from **Ganden** to **Samye.**

Ganden Namgyeling

★ ⑮   *45 km (28 mi) southeast of Lhasa.*

Established by Tsongkhapa, the founder of the Gelugpa sect, in 1409, this enormous monastery became the foremost center of the sect. Unlike other monasteries, where abbots were often selected on the basis of heredity, this one was supervised by an abbot chosen on the basis of his worthiness who served a term of seven years.

Of the six great Gelugpa monasteries, **Ganden** was the most seriously desecrated and damaged by Chinese using artillery and dynamite during the Cultural Revolution. Since the early 1980s, Tibetans have put tremendous effort into rebuilding the complex. Some 300 monks are now in residence; the Ganden community once numbered around 3,000 monks. Pilgrims come daily from Lhasa (buses leave the Jokhang at 6 AM) to pay homage to the sacred sites and relics.

The monastery comprises eight major buildings on either side of the dirt road. The most impressive structure is the **Serdhung Lhakhang** (Gold Tomb of Tsongkhapa) in the heart of the complex, easily recognized by the recently built white chorten before the red building. On the second floor is the chapel of **Yangchen Khang,** with the new golden chorten of Tsongkhapa. The original (1629), made of silver, later gilded, was the most sacred object in the land. In 1959 the Chinese destroyed it, although brave monks saved some of the holy relics of Tsongkhapa, which are now in the new gold-covered chorten. Above the **Assembly Hall**, you may be lucky enough to find monks arguing and gesticulating wildly—they're debating.

If necessary, cut short your visit to the buildings of the complex to make the **Ganden Linghor**, a splendid pilgrimage walk that takes about an hour to complete. Start at the prayer flags, and pass the shrines on the way to the spot where Tsongkhapa meditated and decided upon the locations of the six great Gelugpa monasteries. Go on to the rock known as the Gauge of Sin, where you may want to test yourself by squeezing through the narrow cleft. It is believed that the pilgrim who becomes stuck is too full of sin. Primitive guest house accommodations (no showers, squat toilets, dorm rooms) are available for those wishing to stay the night at the monastery. ⊠ *36 km (22 mi) southeast on main Tibet–Sichuan Hwy., then right onto winding road 9 km (5½ mi)* ☎ *Y15.* ☉ *Daily sunrise–sunset.*

Dining and Lodging

Most visitors to Ganden don't overnight here, since it is possible to see the monastery in one day and return to Lhasa.

$ ✕⌂ **Ganden Namgyeling Guesthouse.** This bare-bones structure just below the monastery has rural Tibetan housing for a dollar or two a night. You will probably want to avoid staying here by returning to Lhasa after you tour the monastery. However, if you're on your way to a trek to Samye, you'll probably spend your first night here. Downstairs is a simple earth-floor restaurant that serves oily stir-fried potatoes and packaged noodles, as well as yak butter tea. There is also a small store that's located up the hill, towards the monastery, that sells cookies, packaged noodles, and other simple necessities. ⊠ *Below the Ganden monastery, down the road of Ganden.*

Outdoor Activities and Sports

TREKKING FROM GANDEN TO SAMYE

The four-day trek from Ganden to Samye, with its hikes through verdant mountains and flower-covered meadows, above valley streams, past herds of yak and sheep, and over two passes, has become one of the most popular treks in Tibet. Trekkers cannot only enjoy the scenery and pieces of Tibetan history found along the way, but also make friends with the herders and villagers who live and work in the area.

The trek starts at Ganden Monastery towards Shug-la Pass, passing through the villages of Hepu and Yama Do on day one. Day two is spent getting to the pass and then Tsotup Chu Valley, spotted with local herders. Day three brings the trekker over the second pass, Chitu-la, past three lakes, and to more campgrounds also used by herders. The village of Changtang is reached on day four, followed by Yamalung Hermitage—a sight where Guru Rimpoche meditated—the villages of Nyango, Wango, and Sangpu, and finally, the north side of Samye.

It's always best to go with a guide, as the trails can be hard to follow. If you hang out at Ganden Monastery, you may be approached by a few Tibetans touting their guide services. For Y500 per person they will provide gear and food, offer you two yaks per person to carry your equipment and bags, and lead the way. However, the quality of the camping equipment could be questionable. A safer option is to make arrangements for a guide with the travel agencies in Lhasa (☞ Travel Agencies *in* Tibet A to Z, *below*).

Whatever you decide to do, be sure to acclimatize for at least a few days in Lhasa and then a day or two at Ganden. The two prayer-flagged passes that are crossed during this difficult trek are above 15,000 ft. ⊠ *The trek follows a route from Ganden directly south to Samye. It's best to go with a guide.*

Tsurphu Dgon Monastery

16 *70 km (43 mi) northwest of Lhasa.*

A green valley covered with yellow blankets of flowers, a babbling brook that chases a dirt road through the mountains—this is the road to Tsurphu, where the daily public blessing of Tibet's Karmapa, the head of the Kargyupa order, traditionally takes place. Now that the Karmapa is in India, much of Tsurphu Dgon's appeal has faded, but it's still a beautiful spot where you can observe the religious community's daily rituals.

Founded in 1187 by Tibet's first Karmapa, Dusum Khyenpa, Tsurphu is the main monastery of the Kargyupa order's Karmapa sect. Dusum Khyenpa was historically responsible for the Tibetan practice of *trulku,* the belief that a Buddhist lama can, before his death, choose his reincarnation. Although the Karmapa allied with the Tsang kings and thus lost their political power when Dalai Lama V defeated the Tsang, Tsurphu has remained a spiritual center.

During the latter half of the 20th century—and into the 21st—Tsurphu and the Karmapa sect have been a center of contention. During the protests of 1959, the 16th Karmapa fled to Sikkim. After his death in 1981, the 17th Karmapa was announced in 1992, amid much controversy, which began as a conflict between the regents responsible for finding the reincarnation. Many Tibetans question the legitimacy of the present Karmapa, who was installed at Tsurphu in 1992 and who fled to India in 1999, and there is actually another boy in New Delhi who many believe is the rightful heir and true reincarnation. The official Karmapa is backed by the Dalai Lama as well as the Chinese government, who enthroned him and discredited the New Delhi boy's claim to the throne. The Karmapa's flight to India was thus a slap in the face to the Chinese. This conflict holds special weight in light of the fact that the Karmapa is traditionally the third-highest Tibetan lama, behind the Panchen Lama and the Dalai Lama. With the Panchen Lama under house arrest in Beijing and the Dalai Lama in exile, the 17th Karmapa was the only lama actually living in Tibet.

After the beautiful bumpy ride to Tsurphu, along the Tsurphu River, you can get out of your bus or Land Cruiser and walk through the monastery's front gate, into the main courtyard. Before 1 PM, visitors can venture into the dark **Assembly Hall** where the monks gather in the smoke of incense, mystically chanting to the deep beats of the gong. When he resided here, the Karmapa oversaw the meditation from his throne at the front of the hall. Most visitors offer small monetary donations or traditional Buddhist offerings, such as *kathaks* (white ceremonial scarves), which can be purchased in the courtyard.

If you walk west of the assembly hall, you'll find stairs leading to the monastery's **Protector Chapel.** You can't miss the row of rooms that make up the chapel, since it's lined outside by real stuffed yaks and goats hung from the rafters. If you keep moving clockwise around the grounds, to the area in back of the assembly hall, you'll find the **Lhakhang Chenmo,** a chapel that holds a very tall statue of Sakyamuni. Other buildings that you can wander into house the residences of the Karmapa and the Regent. Tsurphu also has a **kora,** a hard uphill walk of at least two hours that offers great views of the monastery and the valleys below. There's a restaurant right below the monastery, to the east, where you can get very basic noodles with yak meat. ✉ *Travel northwest on main Tibet–Sichuan Hwy., then left onto the road to Nakar and Tsurphu.* 🕾 *Y20.* ☉ *Daily sunrise–sunset.*

Samye Monastery

★ ⑰ *55 km southeast of Lhasa.*

There's little cause for wonder that Samye is the most popular sight in Ü province for travelers who have time to get farther out of Lhasa than Ganden. One part of the immense magic of Samye may be the river crossing that is required to get there. Another could be that the Samye Monastery is a life-size version of a Tibetan Buddhist mandala.

Whether you begin the journey to Samye by public bus or private Land Cruiser, you will finish it with a ride on the small motorboat that serves as a ferry. The one-hour trip is all part of the experience, as the boat-man steers through the Brahmaputra River and its sandy extensions.

Once on the other side of the river, Tibetans and travelers alike pay Y10 to jump on a truck that takes them up almost 10 km (6 mi) to the entrance gate of the monastery. Once within its gates, you'll discover the mandala, an architectural depiction of the Buddhist universe, with the center of the universe, Mount Meru, represented by a central tem-ple. The temples surrounding the center are situated in two concentric circles that represent the continents and the oceans that traditionally surround Mount Meru.

Samye is important not just because it is a life-size mandala, but be-cause it is Tibet's first monastery. It was built in the 8th century, at the time when Bön was the plateau's main religion. With Guru Rimpoche's exorcism of Tibet's demons at the neighboring hill of Hepo Ri (which metaphorically marked Buddhism's win over the Bön), Samye and its immediate environs became the setting for the beginning of Buddhism, which irrevocably changed the future of Tibet. Soon after its found-ing, the monastery ordained the country's first monks. Later it was also the site of an event called the Great Debate at Samye, in which Indian and Chinese Buddhist scholars argued over the central tenets of Tibetan Buddhism. The Indians won the debate. In its early days Samye was close to the Nyingmapa order of Tibetan Buddhism, that of Guru Rimpoche, but later the Sakyapa order took over.

The most important structure at Samye is the central temple, the Ütse. Built around a central pole that represents the center of the universe, the Ütse takes its place as the center of the monastery. Much of Samye, including the Ütse, was damaged during the Cultural Revolution, so you will find renovation under way, as it has been here for about 15 years. The Ütse incorporates the architectures of three cultures—Ti-betan, Chinese, and Indian. Start at the left of the central building's main door, where you will see a stele from the 8th century that announces, by royal authority, that Buddhism is the state religion of Tibet. The **Assembly Hall** is on the first floor of the Ütse, with Samye's most im-portant chapel at the back of the hall. The chapel, set behind three doors of Liberation (wishlessness, signlessness, and nothingness), holds a statue of Sakyamuni and ancient murals and mandalas. On the assembly hall's left side is a chapel that contains a statue of Avalokiteshvara, the Bodhisattva of Compassion and father of all Tibetan people; in this representation he has 1,000 arms. Be sure to climb all four floors of the Ütse. There are several chapels with impressive murals relating historical stories of Dalai Lama V, Guru Rimpoche, and the beginnings of the monastery, as well as the living quarters of the Dalai Lama.

Outside of Ütse are four chortens. The chortens are in turn circled by 12 **Ling Chapels,** which represent the continents and subcontinents. Today the chapels are gradually being renovated. The lings that housed the printing room and the translation center have already been rebuilt. The building that was Samye's first has also reopened, as has the ling where the Great Debate occurred.

Samye is also surrounded by some climbs and hikes that offer good views of the monastery. To the east is **Hepo Ri,** where history says Guru Rimpoche subdued Tibet's demons. The fairly short climb begins at the monastery's eastern gate. A climb that will take a whole day to complete is the one up to the **Chimpuk Hermitage.** Guru Rimpoche once meditated in these caves, and the occasional hermit still uses them for the same purpose. You can climb up the trail, which leads from the northeast end of Samye, in about five hours and then start back down again. Keep to the left when following the path. You'll find a monastery on the way up. You can try and hitch a ride with a truck going up the hill. Maybe then you'll have the energy to try the strenuous climb from Chimpuk to the top of the peak. ⊠ *Travel southwest from Lhasa on the Friendship Hwy., past Chushul. After Chushul, turn east on the road that follows the Brahmaputra River and continue until you reach the Samye ferry.* ☉ *Daily sunrise–sunset.*

Dining and Lodging

$ The three-floor **Samye Monastery Guesthouse** is to the east of Samye's central compound. All of the rooms—most are dorms—are cheap. The least expensive (about Y10 per bed) are the dingy ones on the bottom floor. As the floors get higher, the rooms get brighter and more comfortable, and there are even a few doubles. There's no restaurant, but basic food, including noodles, rice dishes, and Tibetan momos, can be found at **Snowlands,** which is just east of Samye, outside the monastery gate, and at the neighboring **Gompo's,** which is a better bet. The **Monastery Restaurant,** which is to the north of Samye's central compound, also has basic food.

Lake Nam-tso

★ ⑱ *190 km (118 mi) northwest of Lhasa.*

This lake is a sight to behold. At over 14,000 ft above sea level, sacred **Nam-tso** is the highest lake in the world; and the magnificent pool perfectly embodies its place near the heavens. Its waters beautifully mirror the color of the sky, deepening from a pure, clear turquoise during the day to a sapphire blue at dusk.

Reached by crossing the Largen-la Pass, this, the second-largest saltwater lake in China, rests on the green and brown plains of Tibet, amid the guarding peaks of the Nyenchen Tanglha Mountains. Here, where the influence of man and his machines is diminished to the drone of a jeep engine, the waves and placidity of Nam-tso revel in their holiness. It was in this wondrous region that Heinrich Harrer (on whose life the film and book *Seven Years in Tibet* was based) crossed the mountains into Lhasa with Peter Aufschnaiter.

Due to its awesome juxtaposition with mountains and plains, Namtso is visually inspiring at any time of the day. The natural changes in light can alone shift the shades of the magical colors of earth and water from pink, to brown, to purple.

Although just sitting lakeside is impressive enough, it is best to view the vastness of Nam-tso, whose sacred waters are known for their healing properties, by circumambulating the kora. The walk, which begins at the **Tashi Dor Monastery** and continues in a clockwise direction, can be completed within an hour, and gives you views of the prayer flags, stupas, surrounding mountains, and the lake, of course. At the end of the kora is a prayer wall made from thousands of *mani* rocks hand-carved with Buddhist mantras. Just past the wall, on the right side, you can climb up the hill for a great view of the sunset or sunrise.

The **Tashi Dor Monastery** also offers a tranquil place from which to view the lake and its backdrop of mountains. The monastery also has a cave chapel.

Before coming to Nam-tso, it's a good idea to acclimatize for a few days in Lhasa. ⊠ *Travel north on main Tibet–Sichuan Hwy., towards Yangpachen and then Damxung. Turn left onto the road to Namtso Qu.* ▨ *Monastery entrance gate Y15.*

Dining and Lodging

$ ✕▨ **Nam-tso Guesthouse.** There is only one very basic guest house at Nam-tso Lake, just adjacent to Tashi Dor Monastery. There are 10 dirt-floored rooms, each with three to four twin beds. A bed will cost you about Y5–Y10. At night, the howling wind can make the barely closed window and hooked-shut wooden door rattle, although some could find it interesting to experience Tibet's high-altitude nighttime nature. The guest house also has a small, bare-bones restaurant, where you can get warm around the central stove and eat noodles, fried rice, tsampa, and some simple dishes. The restaurant also has drinking water available. ⊠ *Adjacent to the Tashi Dor monastery. 10 rooms.*

Outdoor Activities and Sports

TREKKING

Although going to Nam-tso usually involves only the short walk of the kora, there are also possibilities for longer treks in the grasslands.

To get to Nam-tso, for example, you can hike from Damxung, the village that lies on the Tibet–Sichuan Highway. Once you arrive in Damxung by car, simply follow the road, over the pass, to the lake. It will take you about two days; you can camp along the route.

There is also a 10-day route to Nam-tso from Damxung, through another pass—the Kong-la. A guide is a good idea for this trek. You can take treks around the lake, but due to the terrain, weather, and difficulty of these treks, you will need to travel with a guide.

One big caveat for all trekkers near Nam-tso: This mercurial area is susceptible to extreme temperatures, so you and your equipment must be well prepared.

Yarlung Valley and Tsetang

⑲ *Tsetang lies 183 km (113 mi) southeast of Lhasa, with the Yarlung Valley spread out underneath it on its south side.*

The first Tibetan kings unified Tibet in the 6th and 7th centuries from the Yarlung Valley. The area is home to what is supposedly the oldest building in Tibet, **Yumbulagang.** Not many foreigners make it to Yarlung, as compared to other parts of Ü. Although the sights around the valley can be seen in one to two days, some travelers extend their trip to hike in the area.

The town of **Tsetang** is not very interesting itself, but it can be used as a point from which to explore the Yarlung Valley. Nearby is **Gangpo**

Ri, the mountain where the goddess Sinmo and the monkey Aval-okiteshvara conceived and bore the Tibetan race. You can reach the hill by going up the trail that is about 2 km (1 mi) south of the Tse-tang Hotel (☞ Lodging, *below*). The trail leads 3 km (1.8 mi) to the meditation cave, or **Monkey Cave,** from which Avalokiteshvara was lured by Sinmo. The round-trip walk from Tsetang will constitute a good day trip.

Out past **Tandruk Monastery**—one of the oldest monasteries in Tibet (about 6½ km/4 mi south of Tsetang Hotel on the main road)—is the historic **Yumbulugang.** This tiny, narrow building is perched atop a ta-pering ridge above the valley. From afar it looks like an abandoned castle straight out of King Arthur's Court. Although records are un-clear, the building was probably built in the 7th century for Tibet's great king Songtsen Gampo. Legend has it, however, that it was built much earlier for Tibet's first king, Nyentri Tsenpo, and that it was where the 28th Tibetan king received Tibet's first Buddhist scriptures from the sky in the 3rd century. Whatever its true origins, Yumbulugang is known as Tibet's oldest building, although much of what you see today was most recently rebuilt in the early 1980s. The fortresslike tow-ered structure is now a chapel dedicated to Tibet's early kings. The large tombs, or **burial mounds,** of these kings are in the **Chongye Valley,** south of Tsetang and Yarlung Valley.

Outdoor Activities

There are many hiking opportunities in Yarlung Valley, but be aware of the permit situation (☞ Permits *in* Ü A to Z, *below*).

Lodging

$–$$ 🏨 **Tsetang Hotel.** This typical mid-range Chinese hotel is comfortable enough. Double and triple rooms are available, all with air-condi-tioning, TV, telephone, and bathroom with tub and shower. There's a Cantonese restaurant here, but it's overpriced. You may want to try the other Chinese and Tibetan restaurants nearby on the main street. ✉ *Main north–south road, Tsetang,* ☎ *0891/782–1899,* 🅵🅰🆇 *0891/782–1688. Restaurant, business services. No credit cards.*

Ü Province A to Z

Getting Around

BY BUS

Ganden Namgyeling. Public buses leave for Ganden Namgyeling from the west side of Barkhor Square in Lhasa every morning at 6:30 AM. Just wait by the fountain, along with the pilgrims heading there. A big rattly bus will arrive, and there will be a mad rush trying to board it. Be careful of pickpockets. Once on the bus, you can buy a round-trip ticket for about Y20.

The ride on the crowded bus takes about 2½ hours. The same bus then leaves Ganden to return to Lhasa at around 2:30 PM; be sure to check with the bus driver as to the exact time of departure.

Tsurphu Monastery. Tsurphu can be reached by public minibuses, which leave from the west side of Barkhor Square whenever they're full, usually at around 7 or 7:30 AM. Mingle with the waiting pilgrims and fruit sellers, and ask around for the bus to Tsurphu. Someone will point the way. Don't listen to the driver if he tells you that he can't take you since you don't have a permit. A permit is not required for Tsurphu, so most likely he is trying to steer you in the direction of his buddy who has a Land Cruiser conveniently waiting nearby, and is will-ing to take you there for more money. The round-trip minibus ride costs less than Y20.

The ride there is beautiful, but bumpy. After 2½–3 hours, the bus lets you off just below the main gate of Tsurphu and waits to bring you back—usually between 2 and 3 PM.

Some travelers prefer to go to Tsurphu by private Land Cruiser, often as part of a tour to Nam-tso (☞ By Car, *below*). The public minibuses don't allow you much time to take a good look around, although most of Tsurphu's sights can be seen in the time allotted.

Samye Monastery. Buses from Lhasa to Samye leave from the west side of Barkhor Square at 7:30 AM. Ask around and you'll get directed to a crowded bus with *a lot* of luggage tied to the top of it. Buses to Tsetang, which stop in Samye on the way, also leave from this departure point, but about an hour later.

Passengers deboard the bus at the Samye ferry stop. The ferry across the Brahmaputra River costs Y10. Once on the other side, you can hop into the back of a truck with the other pilgrims going up to Samye for another Y10 (☞ Samye Monastery, *above*).

For the return trip, the trucks head down to the ferry from Samye at 8 AM and 2 PM. Cross back to the south side of the river once again, and then jump on a bus waiting to take you to Tsetang or Lhasa.

Yarlung Valley and Tsetang. Although many people choose to go to Samye first and then to the Yarlung Valley region, buses to Tsetang do leave from the west side of Barkhor Square at around 8:30 AM. Return buses to Lhasa, via Samye, leave Tsetang every hour between 9 AM and 2 PM.

Getting around Yarlung Valley by public transport is more of a challenge, compounded by the fact that you technically need a permit to travel within the area. Thus, most travelers explore this region on a guided tour or by hired jeep. However, to get from Tsetang to Yumbulagang, you can first walk an hour or two to Trandruk Monastery (it's about 6½ km/4.2 mi south of Tsetang Hotel on the main road) or hitch a ride with a tractor for a couple of yuan. From Trandruk to Yumbulagang, you'll probably have to walk the 6 km/4 mi (another 1–1½ hours) to Yumbulagang. Getting to the neighboring Chongye Valley is even more difficult, since it is much farther south of Tsetang. Most people see the sights there as a day trip from Tsetang, on a guided tour organized in Lhasa or Tsetang.

BY CAR

Jeep travel within Ü is most easily done by Land Cruiser, arranged in Lhasa. This is especially true when you are traveling with a group, since you can split the cost and avoid the uncomfortable and inconvenient bus system. It also allows you to control your own schedule. Most sights are seen individually, as one- or two-day trips from Lhasa. Alternatively you can see them collectively on a guided tour starting in Lhasa. For example, travel agencies in Lhasa offer Land Cruiser tours that take you to Lake Nam-tso with a stop at Tsurphu, or to Yarlung Valley and Tsetang with a stop at Samye.

Some examples of prices for tours, including car and driver, but not food and accommodation: day trip to Ganden, Y400; day trip to Tsurphu, Y400; two-day/one-night trip to Nam-tso, Y1,200; four-day/three-night trip to Samye, Tsetang, and Yarlung Valley, Y3,000.

See Getting Around by Car, Guided Tours, *and* Travel Agencies in Tibet A to Z, *below.*

In Tsetang, you can also hire a vehicle to get to the sights in the Yarlung Valley (☞ Guided Tours and Travel Agencies, *below*).

Contacts and Resources
CURRENCY EXCHANGE

It's best to change money in Lhasa, since none of the sights in Ü, with the exception of the Tsetang Hotel (☞ Lodging *in* Yarlung Valley and Tsetang, *above*), will have exchange counters.

GUIDED TOURS AND TRAVEL AGENCIES

Most guided tours and hired cars can only be arranged through agencies in Lhasa (☞ Travel Agencies *in* Tibet A to Z, *below*). The one exception is that if you manage to get to Tsetang without taking a tour from Lhasa, you can arrange for a hired car to get to sights in Yarlung Valley at Tsetang's **China International Travel Service (CITS)** (✉ Tsetang Hotel, Tsetang's main road, ☎ 0891/782–1899, ∬ 0891/782–1688).

PERMITS

There is no special permit required for Ganden, Tsurphu, Lake Namtso, or Tsetang. However, permits are required for travel to Samye and the Yarlung Valley region. For this reason, most travelers are forced to visit these areas via a tour from Lhasa.

It's possible to get a permit to go to Samye independently. The best way is to do this is to visit the Shigatse Public Security Bureau (PSB) Surprisingly, the workers at the office here are very friendly and will most likely give you a permit on the spot for Y50. Don't even try at the Lhasa PSB. They don't give permits to anyone but licensed travel agents. (Yes, it is, for all intents and purposes, a government-approved racket.)

TSANG PROVINCE

To the west of Lhasa and Ü is a dusty and brown land, rich in tradition and religion, home to a hearty, weathered, yet spiritual people. As Tibet becomes more rugged, heading west on the Friendship Highway, life and land grow more severe. The mountains scrape the heavens, a fractured lake lifts itself towards the sky, and towns the color of dust seem to rise spontaneously out of the earth. These holy places have all been named, of course—Mt. Everest, Lake Yamdrok-Tso, and the spiritual settlements of Shigatse and Gyantse.

Historically, Tsang, along with Ü, has played a significant role in Tibet's internal struggles for political and religious power. In the 10th century, Sakya held Tibet's political power. It later lost it to Ü. But in the mid-16th century, political power fell into the hands of the kings of Tsang, a Tibetan tribe who ruled out of Shigatse. The spiritual power, however, lay in the head lama of the Gelugpa order in Lhasa. Eventually the division between the spiritual lamas and the temporal kings of Tsang became untenable. With Mongol help, the lamas defeated the king of Tsang and paved the way for Dalai Lama V (1617–82) to become both spiritual and political head of state. Lhasa was once again the nation's capital; a theocracy was established. Although Shigatse lost its secular power, it did remain an important center of trade and kept its place as the second-largest city in Tibet and home to the second-highest lama in the land, the Panchen Lama.

A Good Route
From Lhasa, head out on the Friendship Highway towards the west. First you will come to **Lake Yamdrok-Tso** ⑳. The road then leads to the traditional Tibetan town of **Gyantse** ㉑ and the larger town of **Shigatse** ㉒. Moving along west, you will then come upon the short turnoff for **Sakya Monastery** ㉓. At the truck-stop town of **Lhatse**, the Friendship Highway separates from the road to Western Tibet and continues southwest towards the 70-km (43-mi) turnoff to **Mt. Everest** ㉔ and

the nearby town of **Tingri**. If you are on a round-trip tour from Lhasa
to Mt. Everest, you'll turn back here, backtracking from Everest to the
main highway. If you're headed all the way to Kathmandu, you'll
backtrack to the highway and then continue west to the border town
of Zhangmu, which hangs on the side of a mountain and gives the first
signs of the more verdant terrain of Nepal.

Just reverse the above tour if you are departing from Kathmandu for
Lhasa. The road to Western Tibet also passes through most of the listed
Tsang sights, east of the town of Lhatse. If you are going to Western
Tibet and would also like to see Mt. Everest, you'll have to veer a bit
off the Ngari road and then backtrack after you've seen the mountain.

Allow about five to seven days for a trip through Tsang, including Mt.
Everest.

Lake Yamdrok-Tso

㉟ *100 km (60 mi) southwest of Lhasa.*

Although the Friendship Highway can speed (in Tibetan terms) travelers between Lhasa and Kathmandu, there is still an old dirt road called
the Southern Route that leads to Gyantse from Lhasa, slowly winding
its way through mountain passes. Along the way prayer flags flutter,
and slow-cutting glaciers, like the massive Nojin Kangtsang, overhang
the narrow road. You pass dusty Tibetan towns and the occasional nomadic family with its wandering herd of yak. Also on this road, just
over Ganba-la Pass, lies a stunning, turquoise-blue ribbon that unravels
through the sloping brown mountainsides to form a spectacular spidery lake called **Yamdrok-Tso.**

Like Nam-tso and Lake Manasarovar, Yamdrok-Tso is one of Tibet's
three holy lakes. However, unlike massive Nam-tso, fragile Yamdrok-
Tso coils snugly around the hill of Tonang Sangwa Ri, stretching out
fat tentacles into the landscape. The lake's spindly arms have created
16 islands—most of which have large populations of birds; some of
which are inhabited by nomads.

Down by the lake, you can camp on a small sandy beach that turns
muddy at the shoreline, and stare out at the stars. At sunrise and sunset, the blues and greens grow dramatic, and purples and oranges
creep into the winding landscape. Just behind the beach is a simple restaurant with outdoor tables and couches shaded by a Tibetan tent. The
owner's children look at you wide-eyed, while their dog yelps at your
arrival. Besides you and the family, and the occasional interrupting truck
weaving down the road, no other person is in sight. Although now the
remote lake is incredibly quiet, rumor has it that a Chinese travel
agency will soon be offering yachting services.

Although you can ask your requisite tour guide to stop at Yamdrok-
Tso's middle-of-nowhere campground for the night, most travelers stay
at the lakeside town of **Nangatse**, a small, dusty Tibetan village. To
the east of Nagatse is **Samding Monastery** (*follow the road that heads
east out of of Nangatse;* ✉ *Y10*) where you can catch a great view of
the lake and surrounding hills and mountains. Unlike most Tibetan
monasteries, the head lama at Samding is a woman. You can ask your
driver and guide to take you there or walk about two hours from Nangatse. ✉ *Head out west from Lhasa, following the southern route of
the Friendship Hwy.*

Dining and Lodging

If you're not equipped to camp, you can stay in one of two simple Tibetan guest houses in Nangatse. Your guide will probably choose the

guest house, as well as a place for you to eat. There are a few typical bare-bones Chinese restaurants in Nangatse, as well as the lakeside family restaurant mentioned above, which is right on the highway, between Nangatse and Ganba-la Pass. If you have a sleeping bag, the family may also let you stay sheltered in their large Tibetan tent.

Gyantse

㉑ *260 km (161 mi) southwest of Lhasa.*

Probably the most pleasant Tibetan town outside of Lhasa, Gyantse still retains a rural, old-world charm. Although many towns along the Friendship Highway are merely drive-through stops, Gyantse is worth a longer stay. Most people come to Gyantse to see **Kumbum Temple,** but if you hang around the old part of town for a little while, you'll also experience elements of traditional Tibet, with rows of muddy houses standing beside trees that shade the dusty roads, and the occasional donkey obliviously resting on its feet, with his cart waiting behind him. Children run down the sidewalk, and cattle twitch their tails as they sit on the side of the street. Gyantse is one of the few towns in Tibet that has escaped the complete domination of Chinese influence.

Despite its quaintness, Gyantse is considered the third-largest town in Tibet, behind Lhasa and Shigatse. It lies on a major crossroads between these two towns, as well as Bhutan to the south, making it a significant trading center. In the 1300s and 1400s the town was a spiritual center, strongly influenced by the Sakyapa Order, which gave rise to the amazing Kumbum Temple, inside the **Palkor Choide Monastery,** and to **Gyantse Dzong.** It later lost much of its religious and political power but gained importance as a center for trade between Tibet, India, and Nepal.

Sights to See

Gyantse Dzong. South of Kumbum is Gyantse's fort, or the Gyantse Dzong. This 14th-century fort is mostly in ruins, but its great height offers spectacular views of the valley and town below (if the walk up doesn't kill you first). There is also a very Chinese **Museum of Anti-British Imperialism** up there, where you can see government propaganda at its best. ⊠ *The entrance is up a small alley off the main east–west road, Guangchang Lu, east of the central circular intersection of Guangchang Lu and Zhongshan Lu.* ▩ *Y20.* ☉ *Daily sunrise–sunset.*

★ **Kumbum Temple.** Within the entrance of **Palkor Choide Monastery** sits the electrifyingly colorful Kumbum Temple. Although you can view the interesting murals, thangkhas, and even a three-dimensional mandala in the chapels and assembly hall of the monastery, the real experience is in climbing the colorful tiers of Kumbum. This mystical building was erected upon the order of one of Gyantse's princes in the mid-15th century. Its white tiers built atop one another, laced with golds, reds, and blues, grow more and more narrow until culminating in a gold chorten with four pairs of mysterious, piercing blue eyes staring out in the cardinal directions.

You can follow the clockwise rotation up and around Kumbum's six floors. On each level are tiny dark alcove chapels full of richly painted murals and frescoes—10,000 in all. There are also eight tight, narrow, two-story chapels facing the cardinal directions that all house larger statues of Buddhas and Buddhist teachers and interpreters. Although many of the statues were damaged during the Cultural Revolution, the Chinese- and Nepalese-influenced murals are mostly original.

Once through the chapels, you can climb the final narrow stairs to the sixth floor. (If it's locked, the monks will open it for you, but you'll have to go all the way back downstairs to ask them to do so!) From the roof of Kumbum, you can stare out over the entire town of Gyantse. Except for the green lines of trees, all of Gyantse is the color of mud; the symmetrical houses seem to merge into the monochrome hillside, which then sweeps up into the dust-hued, castlelike fort. Behind you, the sight of Kumbum's four sets of eyes is especially intense here.

It all makes a great photo, but be warned—the monks charge a photography fee, and if you don't pay it, they'll make you leave your camera with them to ensure you don't sneak any snapshots. ⊠ *North end of Gyantse, on the main north–south road, Zhongshang Lu.* 🎫 *Y30.* ⊙ *9 AM–1 PM, 3–6 PM.*

Dining and Lodging

$ ✕ **Tashi Restaurant.** With colorful traditional Tibetan fabric on the ceiling, Tibetan tables, and long couches, the Tashi offers an attractive and relaxing setting, if only average food. The fried rice with chicken and the vegetable momos are both hearty choices. Paintings of the Kumbum and the Dzong decorate the walls. ⊠ *Intersection of Zhongshan Lu and Guangchang Lu, Gyantse,* 🕾 *no phone. No credit cards.*

$ ✕ **Zhuang Yuan Restaurant.** Four small tables, a guest comment book, and a menu full of photographs of foreign guests are all that adorn this basic restaurant. However, 11 years of experience are evident in the tasty kung pao chicken, sweet-and-sour pork, apple pancakes, and other dishes. No English is spoken, but there is an English menu. ⊠ *4 Yinxiang Lu, Gyantse,* 🕾 *0892/817–2526. No credit cards.*

$$ 🏨 **Gyantse Hotel.** Gyantse's main hotel has all the trappings of a typical three-star Chinese hotel, which means it's comfortable and somewhat geared for Western travelers. A large covered entrance leads to an even larger lobby with a glass-ceiling atrium sitting room. Down long hallways you'll find bright rooms with large windows, peach floral wallpaper, bathtubs, televisions, and IDD phones. ⊠ *8 Yinxiang Nanlu, Gyantse 857400,* 🕾 *0892/817–2222,* 🖷 *0892/817–2366. 122 rooms, 3 suites. 2 restaurants, bicycles, billiards, meeting room. No credit cards.*

$ 🏨 **Chanda Hotel.** The Chanda has a small reception area with grapevines hanging from the walls, and stairways with AstroTurf-like carpet. The rooms have a clashing mixture of patterns, soiled carpets, and drapes that are too long. On the bright side, at least there are televisions and phones. ⊠ *8 Weiguo Lu, Gyantse, 857400,* 🕾 *0892/817–2573. 91 rooms, 1 suite. Restaurant. No credit cards.*

Shigatse

㉒ *250 km (155 mi) southwest of Lhasa.*

Tibet's second-largest town may not be as charming as Gyantse, but it still gets a lot of visitors who come mostly to see Tashilunpo Monastery. Much of the influx may also have to do with the fact that Shigatse is connected to Lhasa by relatively smooth roads.

Located on the Nymchi River, Shigatse is traditionally the capital of Tsang and was the seat of the kings of Tsang when they held political power over Tibet in the mid-16th to mid-17th centuries. Although the Gelugpa Order in Lhasa overtook both religious and secular power during the reign of Dalai Lama V, Shigatse remained the home of the Panchen Lama, Tibet's second-highest lama, as well as a flourishing center of trade. Like Gyantse, it has always been an important stop on the road between Lhasa and India and Nepal.

Like Lhasa and Gyantse, Shigatse has Tibetan and Chinese sections. Although much of this grungy town is full of Chinese Communist bloc buildings, the Tibetan section, which lies between the old fort in the northern end of town and Tashilunpo in the west, has a more traditional feel. There's a lively market where travelers like to pick up prayer wheels, thangkhas, and other Tibetan crafts. The Chinese section runs up and down Jiefang Lu and the north–south street running parallel to it. It's full of sterile hotels, seedy girlie bars, and Chinese restaurants.

If you didn't get a chance to take care of all your traveling errands in Lhasa or Kathmandu, you can do so in Shigatse—changing money, sending letters, and getting permits. Shigatse has a Bank of China, a post office, and an unbelievably helpful PSB (☞ Contacts and Resources *in* Tsang A to Z, *below*).

To the north of Shigatse's main east–west road, the **Tashilunpo Monastery** sprawls on a hill, with glimmering buildings with rust-color walls and golden roofs. These are the burial chortens of the Panchen Lamas.

Although Tashilunpo is one of the most important monasteries of the Gelugpa Order, it is by no means the most popular amongst the Tibetans. One guide voiced the belief, which many Tibetans hold, that some of the monks at Tashilunpo are pawns of the Chinese government. Nonetheless, many visitors and pilgrims make a trip to Tashilunpo to see the burial chortens of the Panchen Lamas, as well as Tibet's largest standing monastery, the plateau's least damaged by the Cultural Revolution.

The monastery was founded in 1447 by Genden Drup, a follower of Tsongkhapa who was posthumously named the first Dalai Lama. The monastery only became important on the Tibetan plateau when Dalai Lama V proclaimed that the monastery's head abbot was the human incarnation of Amitabha. Thus, Tibet's second-highest lamas, the Panchen Lamas, were created. Ironically, rivalry between the two lines of lamas began brewing, with the Panchen Lama acting as head of Tsang and Lhasa's Dalai Lama as head of all of Tibet. In the 1920s, Dalai Lama XIII and Panchen Lama IX had a conflict over the monastery's self-rule, and the Panchen Lama fled to China in the hope of finding political backing. He died there. Although Panchen Lama X was groomed to be a puppet of the Chinese government, in 1959 he finally took up his people's fight against China, openly criticizing the government's policies towards Tibet. Eventually he was thrown into jail, where he stayed until 1978. After he died in 1986, China demanded a part in choosing his successor. The present Panchen Lama is under house arrest in Beijing, where the Chinese most likely hope to create another government puppet. If they succeed at doing so, it could affect the selection of the next Dalai Lama, since the Panchen Lama traditionally has a say in finding this reincarnation.

Tashilunpo encompasses a vast set of grounds, with several tombs, chapels, temples, colleges, and monastic residences, and of course an assembly hall. During your explorations, you could hear the atmospheric chanting of the monks in the assembly hall, or their animated debating in the courtyards.

On the main pathway, just north of the entrance, are the College of Philosophy and the Tantric College. Before you come to these buildings, there is a pathway on the left that leads northwest to the monastery's most spectacular building, the **Chapel of Maitreya** (the westernmost building on the grounds). Inside is a gold-plated statue of the Future Buddha, rising almost 30 m (100 ft). Although the statue is not very old by Tibetan standards (built in 1915), its creation required four years of labor by 1,000 men. To the east of the Chapel of Maitreya is the **Chapel of Victory,** and then the **Chorten of the 10th Panchen Lama,** which flanks the historic white **Panchen Lamas' Palace.** You can't walk into the palace, but you can view its state reception room, as well as several of its chapels, which are housed in separate buildings. On the far end is the **Chorten of the 4th Panchen Lama.** The other Panchen Lama tombs are located within the **Kelsang Temple,** which has a lively courtyard full of prayer-wheel-turning pilgrims and maroon-robed monks. Inside the temple is the dark, 15th-century, thangkha-lined **Assembly Hall,** which is fronted by the throne of the Panchen Lama. The Panchen Lamas' tombs in Kelsang Temple are those of Dalai Lama I and Panchen Lamas II, III, and V–IX. Tashilunpo's **kora** is an hour long, with some nice views of the buildings and surrounding town.

As at many monasteries in Tibet, you must pay extra charges to take photos. ⊠ *On Xiangchun Lu at the western end of town.* ☎ *Y30.* ☉ *Daily 9–noon, 4–6. No shorts allowed.*

Dining and Lodging

$ ✕ **Ten Zin Restaurant.** Two long tables with plastic tablecloths, walls covered with posters of food, and music coming out of a radio create the "ambience" at the Ten Zin. A wide assortment of Chinese and Western food including lassis, pancakes, and mixed fruit are available. Unfortunately, the food is ordinary at best. ⊠ *Across from the market stands in the old part of Shigatse,* ☎ *0892/882–2018. No credit cards.*

$ ✕ **Warmly Welcome to Our Restaurant, Foreign Guests!** This restaurant, with more of an invitation than a formal name, serves up big portions and has an English menu. A large selection of soups and Chinese dishes and a hearty breakfast can be found at this small, basic place. Don't be in a hurry after you order; the cook's husband often needs to go to the market to buy the produce. ⊠ *23 Xiangchun Lu, Shigatse,* ☎ *0892/882–5873. No credit cards.*

$$ 🏠 **Shangai Hotel.** Completed in 1999, this joint-venture hotel has an entrance of sliding glass doors that open to a bright lobby with brown leather couches. The clean, efficient rooms have balconies, minibars, sitting chairs, and textured wallpaper. ⊠ *45 Yinxiang Nan Lu, 857000,* ☎ *0892/882–4120. 16 rooms, 6 suites. Restaurant, meeting room. AE, MC, V.*

$$ 🏠 **Shigatse Hotel.** Popular with tour groups, the Shigatse is a full-service, three-star hotel with an English-speaking staff. The bottom floor features a high-ceiling lobby, shopping counters, and a large sitting area in the rear. Both Western- and Tibetan-style rooms are available, with plush red carpeting, refrigerators, heaters, sitting chairs, televisions, and IDD phones. A Finnish-made sauna is also located in the hotel. ⊠ *13 Jiefeng Lu, Shigatse 857000,* ☎ *0892/882–2550,* ℻ *0892/882–1900. 119 rooms, 4 suites. Restaurant, bar, beauty salon, massage, exercise room, business services, travel services. No credit cards.*

$ 🏠 **Gang-Gyen Fruit Orchard Hotel.** Frequented by pilgrims, monks, and tourists alike, the Gang-Gyen is a two-story hotel with long corridors and concrete walls. Carpeted rooms with big windows and comfortable beds look onto the fruit garden in the back of the hotel. The rooms on the second floor are far superior to the rooms down below. All rooms share a common bath. Fifty percent of the hotel's annual income goes to the monastery to support the lamas. ⊠ *12 Zhufeng Lu, Shigatse 857000,* ☎ *0892/882–2282. 17 rooms. Restaurant. No credit cards.*

$ 🏠 **Post Hotel.** Located on the bank of the Nymchi river, the Post has a lobby with a black-and-white-check floor and oversize leather couches. The rooms have wooden floors, televisions, and IDD phones. Small dormitories with four to six beds are also available. For entertainment, there are also KTV rooms—individual karaoke centers, each with a long couch, coffee table, karaoke TV, and hostess service. Note that

KTV in some cases has a notorious reputation, with hostesses providing more than simple party service. ✉ *12 Jiefeng Lu, Shigatse 857000,* ☎ *0892/882–2938,* 𝔽𝔸𝕏 *0892/882–1928. 35 rooms, 3 suites. Restaurant, meeting rooms, travel services. No credit cards.*

$ ☷ **Ten Zin Hotel.** Above the restaurant of the same name, the Tenzin Hotel has basic rooms and dorms arranged around a cramped (rooftop) courtyard. In keeping with the traditional Tibetan part of town in which it lies, Ten Zin's interiors are brightly painted, and its floors are covered with Tibetan rugs. The roof also provides good views of the Shigatse Dzong. ✉ *Across from the market stands in the old part of Shigatse, 857000,* ☎ *0892/882–2018. Restaurant. No credit cards.*

Shopping

Many a Tibetan souvenir—prayer wheels, prayer beads, and a few thangkhas—can be found in the open-air market in the old part of town. Don't expect real antiques, but do expect high prices. Bargain hard, but you'll probably get a better deal in Lhasa.

Sakya Monastery

★ ㉓ *20 km (12 mi) south of the Friendship Highway, between Lhatse and Yalung-La Pass.*

Another dusty, traditional Tsang town, Sakya is defined by its famous monastery—**Sakya Monastery.** A popular stop just off the Friendship Highway, many travelers come here to see the monastery on their way to Mt. Everest, Kathmandu, or Lhasa.

After passing through the many Tsang towns that match the hue of the earth, Sakya's gray houses striped with splashes of red and white are a pleasant surprise. Like the one-road, drive-through town of Lhatse that lies to the west, Sakya is a scruffy town where it's obvious that the residents have persevered a rough, weathered life. But unlike Lhatse, there is little Chinese influence here.

Sakya Monastery dates to the late 11th century, when it was built by a son of Tibet's Kon family, the family who founded the Sakyapa order. The order, with Sakya at its center, became important for its Buddhist scholasticism. It was here that Tibetan teachers started contributing to the study of Buddhism that was going on throughout Asia. Tibet's most famous scholar is still known today as Sakya Pandita, an abbot who was also responsible for allowing Mongolian involvement in Tibetan politics. With the help of Kublai Khan, his successor became secular leader of Tibet, the first lama in Tibetan history who also held a political seat. However, in the 1350s, Sakya lost political power to Ü.

The monastery is known to be dark and mystical, a place where you can witness the monks congregating on floor cushions and chanting sutras in unison to the beating drum in the incense-filled **Assembly Hall.** When you walk through the gate, you are in the monastery courtyard, which is spread around a central prayer pole. The bordering chapels house numerous Buddha statues and murals. The assembly hall is probably the most impressive building in the compound, with large holy pillars and huge statues of Buddhas, several of which hold the remains of former abbots, including Sakya Pandita. There are more tombs of abbots in the chortens of the northern chapel. You'll also notice a protecting wall surrounding the complex, with guard towers jutting above it. It offers good views of the monastery and town. ✉ *The 20-km (12-mi) side road to the town of Sakya is off the Friendship Hwy., east of Lhatse. It runs south toward Sakya; the monastery is on the west side of town.* ☉ *Daily 9–6; some buildings open only in the morning.*

Mt. Everest

★ ㉔ *70 km (43 mi) south of the Friendship Highway, west of Shegar.*

Many a dream was born here, and many a tragedy. **Mt. Everest**—the goddess of mountains, the highest on earth—is truly majestic in its intimidating 8,850-m-high (29,028-ft-high) presence, piercing open the clouds with the peak of its massive blue-gray-and-white face. That is, if you're lucky enough to see it. For most of the year Mt. Everest is shrouded in clouds and fog, and only the lucky traveler arrives at the **Base Camp** on a day when the entire mountain is in full view.

Still, there is an allure to being at the base of Everest, taking in the view from the **Rongbuk Monastery**, and yes, being able to tell your friends that you camped at the foot of the world's tallest mountain. If you're planning to go up the mountain in search of its peak, that's a different story altogether.

The Tibetans call Mt. Everest *Qomolangma,* or the Goddess Mother of the Universe. As you bounce your way from Shegar, over the brutal dirt road that winds its way through the isolated, monochrome severity of the mountain's north side, you will come upon a simply painted concrete sign reading "Qomolangma National Level Nature Preserve," marking the entrance to the 16,800-sq-mi (27,000-sq-km) Mt. Everest National Park.

Once the police gate lifts to let your Land Cruiser into this area, the barren, harsh landscape is uncompromising. Although the Nepalese, south side of Everest is lush and verdant, the north side looks almost like a rocky desert, with pockets of green only in and around small Tibetan villages.

The twisting and turning road seems endless, with its long climbs to the tops of passes covered with motley stone chortens and prayer flags snapping in the wind. You will probably have to stop for the night at a simple village guest house, where the villagers gather around and ponder at your presence.

The next day, at the top of the Pangla Pass, just over its ridge, appears a panorama of the daunting yet picturesque Himalayas—Everest, Cho Oyu, Lhotse, and Makalu—shining with snow in the distance, 100 km (60 mi) away. Finally, you'll come around a turn, and find yourself in a standoff with that singular great mountain.

The best views of Everest's Tibetan face are from the Rongbuk Monastery, which gives you a straight-ahead view of the massive goddess and the valley below. Rongbuk is the highest monastery in the world, at 4,575 m (15,000 ft). Founded in 1902, the small institution has a few monks and nuns in residence. There is also a basic guest house, shop, and restaurant.

Just ahead of Rongbuk—a 10-minute drive or two-hour walk—the **Base Camp**, at about 4,750 m (15,500 ft), appears. It's merely a flat surface that only whispers of the famous climbers who have anxiously taken brief residence there. You can take photos of yourself in front of the chorten surrounded by waving, colorful prayer flags and silent memorials to those who lost their lives climbing the mountain. Everest looms in the background, shrouded by streaming fog, with its presence felt but reality only imagined. Note that if you are visiting Everest with a hired Land Cruiser, your guide will arrange for your meals and accommodations. ⊠ *There is a 70-km (43-mi) turnoff to Mt. Everest off* *the Friendship Hwy., just west of Shegar.* ☎ *Y65 per person for a park permit, plus Y400 per vehicle. Permits are sold at the office in Shegar, just before entering the preserve.*

A Mt. Everest Trek

There's a popular trek that leads from Shegar to Everest (three to four days) and then back to the town of Tingri. You can hire a guide in Lhasa. If you choose to go alone, be sure to have a good trekking guide on hand. The southwest route starts at the Friendship Highway, towards Chay village. It then leads south to the Dzaka Valley through the Geula Pass, which provides majestic views of the same part of the Himalaya Range seen from the Pangla. After passing the Geula, you can head back towards the road leading to Everest, and follow it until arriving at Rongbuk and Everest Base Camp. The road passes through valleys, villages, ruins, and monasteries. Instead of veering off the main road to trek over the Geula Pass, you can also follow the road, which crosses Pangla Pass after heading out of Chay.

You'll be able to stay in the guest houses of some of the villages you pass through, but it's a good idea to prepare yourself with a tent, sleeping bag, and cooking equipment. You may be able to hire a guide and yaks to carry your bags in Chay, but bargain hard; negotiation is expected. If you get really tired, you can hitchhike the rest of the way to Everest, or back to Shegar.

After arriving at Base Camp (or higher, if you're an experienced trekker), you can head back to the Friendship Highway the way you came, or, for a little hard-core hiking, trek to **Tingri**—a small town on the Friendship Highway that enjoys gorgeous views of the looming Mt. Everest and Cho Oyu. This trek takes three to four days; it begins at Base Camp and departs from the main Everest road at the bridge over Dza Chu. This northwest departure means that you won't be passing through many villages and must be completely self-reliant. You climb over the Namla Pass, past scattered streams, and through valleys and the Tingri plains. There is a small track after Namla that you can follow to Tingri. The track goes by a ruined fort, Lungchang village (the one place you can find accommodations), Rachu village, and several shepherd camps.

HEALTH AND SAFETY

Many a visitor has arrived at Everest feeling the uncomfortable symptoms of altitude sickness. If not dealt with responsibly, these symptoms can get worse, sometimes leading to serious conditions or death. Be careful; there's no place to go for help up here.

If you are going to Everest from Kathmandu, it's especially likely you will undergo some altitude sickness, since the climb amounts to 2,380 m (7,800 ft). If you choose to trek from Tingri or Shegar to Everest—a 800–1,150-m (2,600–3,800-ft) climb—try to spend about a week acclimatizing in town before setting off. If you're coming from Lhasa, you've probably already acclimatized sufficiently in the capital, but you should still be vigilant of any changes in your health.

Most trekkers enjoy the Everest National Park from April through October. However, as with most of Tibet, it's important to bring warm clothes, since the winds can be incredibly strong and the weather unbearably cold. Trekking past Base Camp is only recommended for experienced hikers and mountaineers, and only ones who are well acclimatized.

Tsang A to Z

Arriving, Departing, and Getting Around

BY BUS

There is no public transportation available to or in Tsang that is open to foreigners without permits. The catch-22 is that the only way to get a permit is to take a guided tour, in which case you won't be taking public transportation.

BY CAR

As special permits are required to travel in Tsang and there is little public transportation even open to the Tibetans, most travelers go from Lhasa or Kathmandu into Tsang by hired jeep. Travelers can also get on a bus tour from Kathmandu to Lhasa, which stops at Tsang sights along the way (☞ Arriving and Departing *in* Tibet A to Z, *below*). In addition, jeep tours to Ngari take in Tsang sights along the way (☞ Ngari, *below*).

You can arrange a variety of Tsang tours in Lhasa or Kathmandu. In Lhasa, you can tailor-make your tour to pass through as many destinations in Tsang as you would like to visit, as a one-way trip to Kathmandu or a return trip back to Lhasa. Like all tours in Tibet, Land Cruisers headed through Tsang are usually shared by several people in order to cut down individual costs (☞ Guided Tours *and* Travel Agencies *in* Tibet A to Z, *below*). Five-day tours from Lhasa to Kathmandu and five-day Lhasa return trips, passing through several Tsang destinations, run Y5,000–Y7,000 per vehicle, not including food and lodging. If you arrange the tour, the guide will organize accommodations, but you'll still pay the hotel directly in most cases.

BY TAXI

The only town in Tsang that has taxis is Shigatse. As in Lhasa, you can take a ride to any destination in town for a flat fee of Y10. In Shigatse, there are also tractors that serve as "stop-and-jump-on" buses for Y1.

Contacts and Resources

CURRENCY EXCHANGE

Although it's easier to take care of money transactions in Lhasa (☞ Currency Exchange *in* Tibet A to Z, *below*), there is a **Bank of China** (✉ just south of the Shigatse Hotel on Jiefang Lu, ☉ weekdays 9–1, 4–7; weekends 10–4) in Shigatse. Although these banks don't handle credit card cash advances, they do change traveler's checks and cash.

GUIDED TOURS AND TRAVEL AGENCIES

Guided tours to Tsang can begin in Lhasa or Kathmandu. They can be arranged at Lhasa's several travel agencies (☞ Guided Tours *and* Travel Agencies *in* Tibet A to Z, *below*).

PERMITS

Permits are required to visit Tsang, and there are a couple of police checkpoints along the Friendship Highway. As with most permits in Tibet, these are not generally available to individuals at the PSBs. If you're lucky enough to get to Shigatse on a bus or minibus without a permit, there's a chance you could obtain permits for Mt. Everest, Sakya, Gyantse, and other Tsang locations at the very friendly **Shigatse PSB** (✉ Across the street and to the west of the "Warmly Welcome to Our Restaurant, Foreign Guests!" Restaurant, on Xiangchun Lu—the road that runs east–west in front of Tashilunpo. ☉ Weekdays 9–1 and 4–7; weekends 10–4.) Permits cost Y50 per person for an unlimited number of destinations.

Getting on a tour in Lhasa or Kathmandu is the only guaranteed way to get the permits you need, since the travel agency will arrange all your permits for you.

POST OFFICES

There is postal service in Shigatse at the **main post office** (✉ Zhufeng Lu, at the intersection one block west of Jiefang Lu). You can send mail here, as well as make international and domestic phone calls and send faxes.

NGARI

Western Tibet, that vast unknown, the least-visited part of Tibet, is home to two of Tibet's most magnificent sights. But it is perhaps getting there that is the real adventure. Few travelers end up in this faraway place, as the roads are rural (*very* rural), traveling is difficult, there are almost no creature comforts (in the Western sense), and the path there is long. A trip to Ngari could redefine the meaning of "roughing it."

However, those who do make it out to Western Tibet get the pleasure of exploring a truly Tibetan land, immersed in tradition and holiness, one that is of utmost historic and religious importance to both Tibetan Buddhists and Indian Hindus. This journey culminates in the sight of the magnificent Lake Manasarovar and the experience of the majestic Mt. Kailash kora. The two complementary natural wonders of mythological legend are said to represent a god and goddess living side by side.

Buddhists, Hindus, and Bön followers call this region one of the most sacred, because the Brahmaputra, Indus, Sutlej, and Ganges rivers all begin here.

A Good Route

Although Tibet can be visited during most of the spring and fall months, the ideal times to visit Ngari are more limited—May through June and mid-September to mid-October.

If you're coming from Lhasa, your tour will first pass through the province of Tsang on the Friendship Highway. You can plan the tour so that you can stop to see some of Tsang's sights, from east to west: **Lake Yamdrok-Tso,** Kumbum in **Gyantse,** Tashilhunpo in **Shigatse, Sakya Monastery,** and maybe even **Mt. Everest Base Camp.** Once you pass the truck-stop town of Lhatse, you will no longer enjoy the comforts of a paved road. The barren, brown Tibeten landscape becomes more severe and rugged. From here on, it's a ride of jolts and dust. Through valleys and villages, the road heads toward the towns of Raka and Saga. If you're coming from Nepal, you'll head out to Saga from Zhangmu, a border town where people from Tibet, China, Nepal, and India gather haphazardly. (For information on Tsang sights, *see* Tsang, *above*.)

There are two roads that head out to **Mt. Kailash** ㉕ and **Lake Manasarovar** ㉖ from Saga and Raka. Most tours use the southern road starting at Saga. This road passes through Zhongba and Paryang before arriving in Dhaqin, the stepping-off point to Mt. Kailash and Lake Manasarovar. This southern road is much shorter and in better condition than the northern route. The scenery is also more breathtaking, as you get views of the Himalayas, the dunes, and the Tibetan plains. (Beware the river crossings: trucks and jeeps have been known to get stuck in the sandy bottom or else slide on the icy surface.) The circuitous northern road that leads from Raka passes through the towns of Geyser, Tsochen, Gertse, Yanhu, Gekyi, and Ali, before turning southwest back down to Namru and Dhaqin.

After visiting these two main sights, and perhaps the Guge Kingdom ruins at Tsaparang and Toling and a few monasteries and hot springs along the way, most tours either head back to Lhasa or Zhangmu, again via the southern road.

Mt. Kailash

★ ㉕ *10 km (6 mi) north of Dhaqin.*

It could be that no other mountain in the world holds as much religious importance for so many as does Mt. Kailash. For the Buddhists and Hindus, Mt. Kailash is a magical mountain—the most sacred of all. In myths that cross Asia, there is a mountain called Meru that lies at the center of the universe. The gods live in its might, and four life-creating rivers flow from it. As Mt. Kailash sits with its four-directional faces and four rivers extending from it in each cardinal direction (the Brahmaputra, Indus, Sutlej, and Karnali or Ganges), it seems to be the earthly incarnation of Meru. Natural markings on the mountain even resemble a Buddhist swastika, which turns clockwise and is a symbol of good luck. The gods of Buddhism, Hinduism, and Bön have all lived on Mt. Kailash, and their followers come regularly to pay tribute.

The mountain that Tibetans call the "Jewel of the Snow" reaches over 6,700 m (21,975 ft). But it's not its summit that pilgrims come here to conquer. They come to complete the kora, Tibet's holiest, at its base. While tourists usually circumambulate Mt. Kailash in three days, pilgrims often do it in one, so that they can economize their time and complete several rounds. One kora erases all your life's sins, but to pilgrims, three is really the minimum, with 13 the more common goal. Others aim for a staggering 108. With 108 complete circumambulations, you not only erase all your sins, but are immediately promised nirvana once this lifetime is over. Some pilgrims even choose to prostrate themselves through the entire kora.

Considering the significance of the Mt. Kailash kora, you will see untold numbers of religious and ritualistic sites along this difficult 50-km (30-mi) trek. Amid views of plains, rivers, glaciers, and the majestic mountains of Nepal, Tibet, and India, you'll pass unending rows of prayer flags, lucky chortens, several prostration points, and monasteries.

Along the way are also places that are steeped in legend. The Sky Burial Site of the 84 Mahasiddhas was once used only for lamas and monks. Sky burials are traditional ceremonies in which the corpse is left in the open for vultures to consume; the belief is that the body is thus returned to the sky. Although there may be sky burials going on while you are at Mt. Kailash, don't venture into the area and disturb the proceedings. They're extremely private, and foreigners with cameras are not welcome. You'll also come to the Shiva-tsal, a rocky section of the landscape, where pilgrims play out a ritualistic death, so as to leave this life behind. What they really leave behind is a material memento of their visit, so that the rocks are left covered with items of clothing. At Bardo Trang, pilgrims test their sins on its stone: If you can pass through the narrow passageway, your level of sin is acceptable; if you get stuck, you fail the sin test and your kora may not be able to erase all your wrongdoings. Near the end of the circumambulation you'll come across Lake Gouri Kund, where Hindu pilgrims plunge into the icy waters to erase their sins.

If you want an even more intense religious experience, try coming to Kailash during the festival of Saga Dawa (☞ Festivals and Seasonal Events *in* Chapter 1), as the kora is particularly crowded with pilgrims.

Outdoor Activities and Sports
TREKKING

If you are doing the three-day kora (☞ Mt. Kailash, *above*), your tour agency will most likely be responsible for taking care of your dining and lodging. Be sure, however, that your accommodations are determined before you get there, and come, if you can, with a tent. If you have a reputable tour agency, you'll probably stay at one of the monastery guest houses along the way. However, there's always the possibility that a room won't be available—or that you'll prefer to pitch a tent on one of the grassy spots, instead. Good planning is also vital in terms of food, since dining options are limited; you'll find basic meals at the guest houses, and you can buy some things in Dhaqin and Ali. But again, it's wise to be prepared. You and your tour group will probably have to carry your own food and cooking gear. The weather is often cold and changeable this high up, so bring warm clothes and a sleeping bag. Basically, be prepared for a serious, challenging hike.

Lake Manasarovar

26 *30 km (18 mi) south of Dhaqin.*

The Hindus believe that to plunge into the freezing cold waters of Lake Manasarovar and walk around its circumference is to erase a whole lifetime of sins. Tibetans believe that they can negate their wrongdoings merely through walking.

To the Tibetans, this lake they call "Victorious" is the holiest in the land, believed to be where the gods washed Buddha's mother before she gave birth. According to the Hindus, Brahma created the lake for his sons to bathe in while they meditated on Mt. Kailash. Whether Indian pilgrim, Tibetan pilgrim, or Western traveler, one can see Lake Manasarovar's holy origins manifested in its breathtaking beauty: it's ringed by mountain peaks and filled with clear, bright-blue waters that look just a breath away from the sky. The lake was once surrounded by eight monasteries, which symbolized the eight points of the wheel of Dharma, but Red Guards destroyed most of them during the Cultural Revolution. Restoration is in the works.

Manasarovar is home to many other Buddhist mythological landmarks, as well. There's the Menmo Nanyi, a peak where the goddess of wisdom lives. The lake also represents the sun or lightness, while its smaller neighbor, Lake Rakshas Tal, is its complementary moon or darkness. According to Tibetans, it's a good omen when the waters of Manasarovar flow into the Rakshas Tal, and while the former's waters are healing, Rakshas Tal's are poisonous.

Most travelers explore the lake during day hikes from **Chiu Monastery**, which lies on the northwest corner of Manasarovar. The monastery overlooks the lake from a hilltop; the views from the roof are tremendous. There is also a cave at the monastery that is considered one of Guru Rimpoche's meditation sites.

Only a handful of zealous travelers undergo the four- to five-day kora around Lake Manasarovar, due to its challenging terrain. It basically goes along the circumference of the lake, diverging slightly at the northern shore to avert the marshes. Beginning at Chiu Monastery, the kora moves in a clockwise direction, of course. On the trek you will see mountain views, hot springs, mani stones, geysers, glaciers, caves, cliffs, ritual bathing sites, and several monasteries. Although your tour agency will have probably helped you plan your trek, it is vital that you be prepared for self-sufficiency—in both food and housing—as there are few places to stay in all of Ngari. Good camping and cooking gear is absolutely necessary.

Ngari A to Z

Arriving, Departing, and Getting Around

Once in Tibet, the only viable way to explore Ngari, besides under-taking a long and strenuous hitchhiking trip, is to arrange a guided tour out of Lhasa. Like all Land Cruiser tours in Tibet, those headed for Western Tibet are usually shared by several people to cut down in-dividual costs (☞ Guided Tours *in* Tibet A to Z, *below*). Most tours begin and end in the capital city and will take from 16 to 20 days total. There is also a possibility that you can get a tour that begins in Lhasa and takes you to faraway Kashgar in China's Xinjiang province, or to the border of Nepal. Tours to Ngari can also be arranged in Kathmandu. There is no public transportation available to or in Western Tibet.

Contacts and Resources

GUIDED TOURS AND TRAVEL AGENCIES

Guided tours to Ngari begin in Lhasa and can be arranged at Lhasa's several travel agencies (☞ Guided Tours *and* Travel Agencies *in* Tibet A to Z, *below*).

PERMITS

There are more permits required for foreigners traveling in Ngari than you can count. As with most permits in Tibet, these are not generally available to individuals. Joining a tour is the only way to get the per-mits you need, since the respective travel agency will obtain them for you.

TIBET A TO Z

Arriving and Departing

A visa valid for the People's Republic of China is required. The PRC embassy in Kathmandu will not issue these visas: you need to obtain one elsewhere—New Delhi, Bangkok, or your home country, for ex-ample. That's standard; beyond that, requirements for entry into Tibet are always in a state of flux. Access for groups (a minimum of four people) normally poses no problem, and the travel agent takes care of the details. Access for individuals is more difficult and sometimes im-possible.

Travel to Tibet is more often than not restricted, so you will probably be required to join a tour to be allowed into the region. At times the Chinese Government will only allow foreign travelers to enter Tibet via a flight from Kathmandu or the Chinese city of Chengdu, or by bus from Kathmandu or the Chinese city of Golmud.

Many travel agents in Chengdu will gladly arrange budget group tours for independent travelers. Three-day tours can be arranged quickly, and normally include round-trip airfare from Chengdu to Lhasa, all neces-sary travel permits (which may never be shown to you), three nights' accommodation, transportation to and from the airport, and a tour van/bus with guide for each day. After the tour ends, you can change your return date and stay in Tibet for as long as your visa will allow. However, officially your tour agent is responsible for your entire visit and may want you to leave as planned. Check your tour agent's policy before you depart for Lhasa. Tours can also be arranged that take you from Chengdu to Kathmandu with three days in Lhasa in between. If you are required to take a tour, be sure to find out (in writing) what hotel your travel agent uses and other tour details—such as what sights you'll see, how you will get around, or if room and board is included in the price. This is the best way to distinguish between travel agents in the competitive tour market. The only other difference between operators is the quality of their guides, which you may learn of by word of mouth, but most likely won't be sure of until you're on the tour.

There are plenty of tour companies that offer similar tours from Kathmandu. If you come from Kathmandu and you'd like to have the option to stay behind in Tibet when your tour is over, be sure to get your Chinese visa before you get to Nepal. The Chinese Embassy in Kathmandu almost never gives out individual visas, and Nepali tour agencies can only arrange group visas that will require you to leave Tibet when your tour group leaves.

Public Security Bureau (PSB) personnel seem to be everywhere in Tibet, sometimes in uniform and sometimes in civilian clothes with dark glasses, reading a newspaper upside down and watching you. The PSB monitor civil unrest, visa extensions, crime, and traffic. Beware of the charming Tibetan who may be a secret policeman happy to entrap you into giving him a photograph of the Dalai Lama (it's illegal to have his picture). PSB offices are in all towns and many of the smaller townships. However, visa extensions are possible only in Lhasa, Shigatse, Tsetang, Kermo, and Ziling. These offices can also issue Alien Registration Permits for the "closed" areas, which includes anyplace outside of Lhasa and its environs. If you plan to travel to these areas, get the special permit from the PSB Aliens Exit and Entry Division. However, be forewarned that sometimes the offices give the permits, and sometimes they don't. Most travelers seem to have their best luck obtaining permits from the Shigatse office. Of course, if you want to book a tour, your Lhasa travel agent will have no problem making all of the arrangements for you.

Whenever there is a whiff of unrest, individual travelers are prevented from entering Tibet. The Chinese government considers individual tourists harder to monitor and prevent from fraternizing with local Tibetans. Journalists, for example, are officially denied the right to go to Tibet.

By Airplane

The easiest direct route is from **Hong Kong,** with a change of plane in Chengdu. China Southwest Airlines has twice-weekly nonstop flights from **Kathmandu** (with fantastic views of the Himalayas, including Everest) to Lhasa, and twice-daily flights from Chengdu. Both cost about $200 one way. Other flights to Lhasa include the twice-weekly trips from Xining and Xian, and the weekly direct flight from Beijing. Individual travelers cannot buy their airline tickets before reaching Kathmandu or Chengdu. Sometimes, even then you will not be given a ticket, in which case, you can hook up with others and have a Kathmandu or Chengdu travel agent book you as a group.

You can change the date of your return ticket out of Lhasa free of charge (as long as it is not a discounted ticket) at the **CAAC/China Southwest Airlines Ticket Office** (⌧ 1 Niangre Rd., Lhasa, ☎ 0891/683–3446, ☉ 9–8:30). Note that this is the only airline that flies to Tibet.

By Road

FROM KATHMANDU

By road from Kathmandu, you can (usually) cross the border at Kodari. The Tibetan border guards have been known to grant individuals a permit at the border, though the norm is for groups to enter on a pre-arranged tour. The 900-km (560-mi) route from Kathmandu to

Lhasa takes two or more days to travel, traversing passes as high as 16,400 ft. Overnight stops are in Zhangmu and Shigatse. Minivans are available to shuttle you across the 8-km (5-mi) trip between the two border posts—Kodari in Nepal and Zhangmu in Tibet. The cost from Zhangmu to Lhasa is about $55 in a minibus. Hiring your own four-wheel-drive vehicle with driver and unlimited passengers costs about $160. Exiting Tibet from Lhasa to Kathmandu is easier. The police do not stop you; the Nepalese frontier is always open, and a Nepalese visa is granted at the border.

FROM CHINA

Entering Tibet from China by road is difficult. The way that is most likely to meet with success is to cross the frontier by bus from Golmud, a sprawling town in Qinghai, at the end of the railway line from Xining. The distance by bus is 1,115 km (691 mi) and the trip takes anywhere from 30 to 50 hours (cost: Y160); it can get very bleak and cold at night. Private buses also make the run, but there is more likelihood that police will turn individual Westerners back.

Getting Around

By Bus

Buses that travel outside of Lhasa's general environs are generally crowded, old, slow, and bumpy. Traveling by bus is not the most ideal mode of transportation but can save you quite a bit of money if you're in Tibet on a tight budget.

There are some public bus routes that travel to a few destinations, especially around Lhasa and between Tibet's largest towns and monasteries. However, most of them are technically off-limits to foreigners, since you can't get on a bus without a permit, and you can't get a permit unless you're on a guided tour. Some drivers will give you a break and let you on, but your fate is in the hands of the gods, so to speak. Better to stay on the buses open to foreigners, such as from Lhasa to Ganden, Samye, Tsetang, and Tsurphu. These regions can be explored without a special permit.

By Car

Foreigners are not permitted to drive in Tibet. All cars, mostly Toyota Land Cruisers, are hired with a driver. Rates depend on mileage, with a minimum daily charge if the mileage is low. Daily rates start at Y3 per km (½ mi) plus permits, but will vary from agent to agent. Try the travel agents listed below (☞ Travel Agencies, *below*), the Lhasa Fandian (☞ Dining *and* Lodging *in* Lhasa, *above*), and CITS. Rates are charged per car, not per person, so try to get a group together. Land Cruisers can fit up to six travelers if the tour doesn't require a guide, and five if a guide is present. However, for longer trips, it's more comfortable to limit the group to four or five passengers.

Contacts and Resources

Books

The **Xinhua Bookstore** (✉ 219 Bejing Xi Lu, ☎ 0891/681–3003) in Lhasa, sells mostly books in Chinese, but also has maps, dictionaries, and postcards.

Consulates

Nepalese Consulate (✉ 13 Norbulingka Lu, Lhasa, ☎ 0891/632–2881).

Currency Exchange

It's best to change all your money in Lhasa, since doing so can be difficult in the Tibetan countryside. All of the larger hotels in Lhasa offer foreign exchange service. The main branch of the **Bank of China** (✉ Dekyi Linghor Lam, Lhasa, ◷ weekdays 9–1 and 3:30–6:30, weekends 10:30–3) will exchange traveler's checks or cash into RMB, and also processes credit card cash advances. For a nominal fee you can even change traveler's checks into U.S. currency. A smaller branch office in the Barkhor area (✉ Dekyi Shar Lam [1 block west of Banak Shol hotel]) exchanges traveler's checks and U.S. cash. You can also change traveler's checks at the Bank of China branches in Zhigatse, Zhangmu, and Shiquanbe.

Customs and Duties

ON ARRIVAL

Chinese customs no longer care what you bring into Tibet, as long as it's not an oversize TV camera. There is no customs check at the Lhasa Airport.

ON DEPARTURE

When you leave Tibet, you'll have to pay an airport tax of Y90 (Y50 for domestic flights). Travelers arriving and leaving China are not required to go through customs. When departing, be sure to go through the green channel; don't get caught in the red. One caveat: if you are leaving the country with antiques, only items dated after 1797 can be legally exported.

Emergencies

The **Lhasa Fandian** (☞ Dining *and* Lodging *in* Lhasa, *above*) has a clinic with a doctor on call 24 hours a day. **People's Hospital** (✉ Linghor Lam, Lhasa, ☎ 0891/632–2200 or 632–4883) has some English-speaking doctors. There are also the **Tibetan Hospital** (✉ 14 Niangre Lu., ☎ 0891/632–3390), which has some Anglophone doctors and nurses, and the **No. 2 People's Hospital** (✉ 8 Jinzhu Dong Lu., ☎ 0891/633–2462.

Etiquette

Don't openly talk politics with Tibetans. It can put them on the spot, because although they may wish to explain their feelings about China's occupation, this can get them charged with treason and sentenced to a 20-year jail term.

Don't photograph Tibetans without first asking their permission.

When visiting monasteries, take off your hat when going inside temples or chapels. Although many travelers wear shorts or short skirts to monasteries these days, it's nicer to wear long pants or skirts, just as a sign of respect. Don't take photos unless you're willing to pay the corresponding photo fee.

Guided Tours

Beware of guides, especially of group tours, whose descriptions and explanations of things Tibetan reflect the Chinese party line. Try to find a Tibetan, not a Chinese, guide. Tours can be arranged either outside of Tibet or once you arrive in Lhasa. The adventure or "eco-travel" business has become an increasingly popular way to visit Tibet with dozens of companies advertising their tours in the back of travel and outdoor magazines. Typically the cost of an organized, weeklong tour based out of Lhasa is around $1,000, plus airfare.

Coming to Tibet during a restrictive period may call for some frustrating traveling, and you may be forced to take a tour to see many of the sights outside of Lhasa. If this happens, be prepared for some serious runaround. First, you'll have to spend time talking with several different tour companies and the PSB to uncover the "official" policy for independent travel outside of Lhasa. Next will be numerous trips to the varying travel agents around town to find out pricing, scheduling, and itinerary information.

Before booking a tour, be careful; many agencies are just out to make a buck. So many tourists have had bad experiences on their tours that the Tibet Tourism Bureau has its own complaints hot line (☞ Visitor Information, *below*). Make sure you meet your tour guide and get a test drive in the vehicle to be utilized. The better companies will also provide you with a written contract that includes an itinerary and a list of what is provided for your money. Often, accommodations and food are not included. Most tour companies will tailor a trip to meet your needs and your budget.

Land Cruisers can fit up to five passengers (four is more comfortable for long trips). Sharing the ride lowers the cost of a tour, since tours are paid for per car, not per person. If you are traveling alone, check the message boards at the hotels in the Barkhor area for notices left behind by fellow travelers looking for others to join their tours.

Health and Safety

Although going to Tibet can be an extraordinary journey, be sure to look at your trip realistically. Much of the ancient magic of the plateau has been lost in the modern push of Chinese domination. It can be a frustrating location—full of rules, regulations, and police checkpoints. The repression and lack of freedom in Tibet can be emotionally disturbing.

Meanwhile, the altitude sickness can take a physical toll; your companion for the first few days in Tibet may be an oxygen bag. At the 12,000-ft altitude, shortness of breath is a constant companion. You may have to pause when mounting steps, and you may experience some physical discomfort. Symptoms of Acute Mountain Sickness (AMS) include: headache, dizziness, nausea, and insomnia. Mild symptoms can usually be managed by taking aspirin and making sure to drink a lot of water. In fact, start drinking a lot of (bottled) water on the plane to Lhasa. Avoid cigarettes and alcohol, and don't overexert yourself. If you're planning to go on a trip that involves a great increase in altitude (such as to Mt. Everest, Ngari, or Lake Nam-tso), be sure to spend a few days in Lhasa to acclimatize before you depart. If you experience more than mild symptoms of AMS, descend to a lower altitude and seek the attention of a physician immediately. If you have high blood pressure, heart ailments, or respiratory problems, you may want to reconsider high-altitude routes.

Like anywhere else, with the change in food, you may run into the occasional bug. Diarrhea is not uncommon. Some people come to China and have stomachs as tough as steel. Some come and can't get out of bed for the first few days. Local water is not potable; it must be boiled or treated with iodine before it passes your lips. In Lhasa and in other towns, however, bottled water is plentiful.

Packing

It's important to bring both summer and winter clothes to Tibet. Lhasa can get hot in the day and then cold at night. If you're traveling outside of Lhasa, the weather at higher altitudes can start off nippy but sunny and then get excruciatingly cold. This is especially true in places like Mt. Everest and Lake Nam-tso. However, even sights close to Lhasa, such as Ganden, can be cold, windy, and rainy. It's a good idea to pack a pair of hiking boots or good walking shoes, khakis, a shell that protects from the wind and rain, a fleece or sweater, and some shorts. It's also smart to bring a sleeping bag, since guest houses outside of Lhasa can get a little hairy. If you're going on adventures farther from Lhasa and want to camp, it's a good idea to bring a tent; the ones available in Lhasa are adequate but not optimal (☞ Trekking *in* Pleasures and Pastimes, *and* Shopping *in* Lhasa, *both above*). Unfortunately, bringing a tent means you'll have to carry it around. Warm clothes, sleeping bag, and tent are essential for a trip to Ngari.

Passports and Visas

You'll need a passport, valid Chinese visa, and a special permit to enter Tibet. Permits are not handed out to individuals. You have to arrange your permit through a travel agent in Chengdu, Kathmandu, or your home country.

Police

The **Public Security Bureau (P.S.B.; Gongan Ju)** in Lhasa (✉ south side of Beijing Dong Lu, east of Lingkor Dong Lu, ☎ 0891/632–4528; ☺ weekdays 9:30–noon, 2:30–6) is the branch that deals primarily with foreigners. Although the bureau is responsible for handing out travel permits to tour agencies, on behalf of travelers, it will not give permits directly to foreign individuals. Permits are not required for Lhasa or the outlying counties of Lhasa that include Ganden Monastery, Tsurphu Monastery, and Nam-tso Lake.

Taxes

A 15 percent tax will be added to your room rate at higher-end hotels, such as the Lhasa Fandian.

Taxis

In Lhasa and Shigatse, you can wave down a taxi easily and travel anywhere within city limits for a flat fee of Y10.

Telephones and the Internet

In Lhasa, Shigatse, and Tsetang, you can make international direct-dial calls at major hotels and guest houses and at the telecommunications building and post office. IDD rates are quite expensive, and calls made at hotels will be more expensive than at the telecom building.

Outside of Shigatse, Tsetang, Gyantse, and Lhasa, telephone access is minimal. You can find DDD phones at some restaurants and guest houses. If you do find a phone, lines are good and rates extremely reasonable, making it easy to dial DDD within China and Tibet. Tibetan phone numbers are seven digits long.

COUNTRY & AREA CODES

The country code for China is 86. The area code in Lhasa is 0891, Shigatse and Gyantse 0892, and Tsetang 0893. When dialing a Tibetan number from abroad, drop the initial 0 from the local area code.

DIRECTORY & OPERATOR INFORMATION

Operators in Tibet don't speak English. You can try to call 114 for directory assistance, but you will have to know Tibetan or Chinese.

INTERNATIONAL CALLS

When making international calls from hotels and guest houses in Lhasa, Shigatse, or Tsetang, the receptionist will tell you how to dial the number. At smaller places, a meter will count off your minutes to tally up your charge. You'll have to pay cash. At larger hotels, you can follow the instructions placed by the phone in your room, and your charges will appear on your hotel bill. At the telecom building and post office, the receptionist will assign you a phone and then will charge you after you've completed your call. You'll pay cash here as well. You may have to leave a deposit at the counter before using your assigned phone. IDD calls are made by dialing 00 + country code + area code + number.

LOCAL CALLS

There are few public coin phones, but if you find one that works, they usually take one-yuan or mao coins for local calls. Most public phones are found in guest houses, hotels, businesses, and restaurants. Some places offer local calls for free. Other public phones are manned by an individual who will time your call and charge you a few mao after your local call is completed.

LONG-DISTANCE CALLS

You can make DDD calls by dialing 0 + area code + phone number. You can make DDD calls from the locations that offer IDD dialing, as well as other guest houses that have telephones.

THE INTERNET

You can do your E-mail and access the Web in Lhasa. *See* Lhasa A to Z, *above*.

Transportation around Tibet

Transportation is not easy in Tibet, given the bad roads. The best way to travel around is by hired jeep. Long-distance buses are crowded, slow and inconvenient.

In Shigatse and Lhasa, taxis are plentiful and cheap. There are also minibuses in Lhasa and tractors in Shigatse that run along the main streets. You can jump on these pretty easily. Cheap pedicab rides are also available in Lhasa.

Travel Agencies

Travel agencies in Hong Kong know the ropes and can handle efficiently group travel arrangements: **Mera Travels** (☎ 0852/391–6892, Hong Kong) is experienced in adventure travels for Tibet. **Tibet Tourist Corporation** (TTC) is part of the nationally run China International Travel Service (CITS; ✉ Dekyi Nub Lam, Lhasa, ☎ 0891/633–6626; branch: ✉ 208 Beijing Xi Lu, ☎ 0891/683–5046). **Tibet International Sports Travel** (TIST; ✉ Himalaya Hotel, Shar Linghor Lam, Lhasa, ☎ 0891/633–4082) is a fairly helpful and knowledgeable agency. **China Tibet Nature International Travel Service** (✉ 8 Tibetan Hospital Rd., Lhasa, ☎ 0891/633–8475) and **Tibet Ningchi International Travel Co.** (✉ Tibetan Hospital Rd., below Pentoc Guesthouse, Lhasa, ☎ 0891/634–1391) both specialize in budget tours.

Visitor Information

Lhasa Official Guide is a tourist publication with general information and listings published by the Foreign Affairs Office of the People's Government of Lhasa Municipality. This handy guide is available at the major hotels in Lhasa and sells for Y20. *Lhasa Tour Map* is sold at bookstores and hotel lobby shops for Y7. One side is a map of Lhasa and the other contains useful information on Lhasa's tourist attractions, Tibetan festivals, and emergency phone numbers.

Tibet Tourism Bureau (✉ 18 Yuanlin Lam, Lhasa, ☎ 0891/683–4315 information, 0891/683–4193 to register a complaint).

4 BHUTAN

The very name of the Himalayas evokes
majesty and grandeur. The nearly impossible
terrain and controlled tourism have daunted
the most intrepid of travelers. Until now, the
beauty of these mountains and the delightful
people who inhabit them have lain beneath
a veil of mystery. Bhutan itself has, until
recent years, been subject to a state of self-
imposed isolation, with changes coming
only with the present, enlightened
government.

By Wendy
Kassel

THERE IS A CERTAIN MAGIC ABOUT BHUTAN. When you visit this tiny kingdom, you become enthralled by its natural beauty, mystical religion, vibrant culture, and charming people. Nestled on the slopes of the eastern Himalayas, surrounded by China and India, Bhutan is no bigger than Switzerland and has a population of just 600,000. Bhutan is the only surviving Buddhist kingdom of the Himalayan region. One of the world's last unspoiled frontiers, Bhutan is truly an exceptional place.

The country of Bhutan indeed presents a modern paradox, a traditional society that is still richly intact and vital. While the basic conservatism of the Bhutanese has enabled them to preserve their past achievements, it has just begun to allow them to accept innovation.

Many historians believe the name Bhutan was derived from the Sanskrit name Bhotanta, which means the end of Tibet. Early British explorers called it Bhotan or Bootan. The Bhutanese refer to their country as Druk Yul, or the Land of the Thunder Dragon. Druk, meaning dragon, comes from the Drukpa school of Tibetan Buddhism. Much of Bhutan's early history remains a mystery, since many historic documents were lost in fires at the printing works and at Punakha Dzong in 1828 and 1832. In the mid-8th century, Padma Sambhava, who was later called Guru Rimpoche, made his legendary trip from Tibet over the mountains, flying on a tigress's back. Guru Rimpoche is acknowledged as the founder of the Tibetan Buddhism, now known as Nyingmapa.

Many of Bhutan's notorious ancestors were descendants of the Nyingmapa School. Pema Lingpa, the best-known Nyingmapa saint, died in his home region of Bumthang in 1521. Pema Lingpa was said to be the reincarnation of Guru Rimpoche and the philosopher Longchen Rabjampa. He founded monasteries at Kungzandra, Petsheling, and Tamshing, in the Bumthang Valley.

In 1616 the Gelugs seized control of Tibet's Ralung Monastery, the religious center of the Drukpa Kagyus, forcing the lamas and their powerful leader, Ngawang Namgyal, to seek refuge in Bhutan. Over the next 35 years, he unified Bhutan and built massive *dzongs* (fortresses) and monasteries. An astute military leader, Ngawang Namgyal repulsed invading troops from Tibet, assumed the title of *Shabdrung Rimpoche*—Supreme Religious Power—and proclaimed himself the temporal and spiritual ruler of Bhutan.

With the end of Ngawang Namgyal's rule in 1651, disparate factions fought for the title of Shabdrung Rimpoche. Though the 1865 Treaty of Sinchula ushered in an era of cooperation between the British and Bhutan, internal fighting led to a new civil war in 1869. In 1884, the British recognized Ugyen Wangchuck as the supreme power. In 1907, he became the first hereditary monarch of Bhutan, and three years later signed a new treaty with the British in which the Bhutanese agreed to British "guidance" in external affairs, and the British agreed to a hands-off policy inside the kingdom.

With Ugyen Wangchuck's death in 1926, his son Jigme Wangchuck ascended the throne. Jigme instituted numerous reforms—founding schools, repairing monasteries—and concluded a treaty with India, after it gained its independence in 1947. His son, Jigme Dorji Wangchuck, became king in 1952, and set up institutions to preserve the language and culture. Jigme Dorji Wangchuck abolished serfdom, built roads, instituted long-range economic planning, created a comprehensive education system, started the postal system, and brought in trained doctors. He established the National Assembly, called Tshogdu, thus creating a constitutional monarchy.

After Jigme Dorji's death in 1972, his son Jigme Singye Wangchuck ascended the Golden Throne. Two years later, the formal coronation took place. When His Majesty became king, he desired, as his father had before him, to open and modernize the country in a cautious manner. This was to be done by developing industry, agriculture, hydroelectricity, and other infrastructure, so that the standard of living could be improved. In addition, the king is committed to maintaining Bhutan's cultural identity. All new buildings, including private homes, must be made with traditional techniques, and in the late 1980s, a national dress code was established.

Until the early 1960s, Bhutan had its back turned to the world. The fabled Land of the Thunder Dragon—a country of Buddhists and dzongs, yaks, blue sheep, alpine valleys, and snowcapped peaks—was unknown to foreigners. Bhutan had remained a mystery, untouched by foreign influence. When the kingdom opened its doors to the world for the first time in history, development soon followed.

The southern regions are inhabited mainly by people of Nepalese descent, who immigrated here from the late 19th century until the early 1950s. They are full Bhutanese citizens and have kept their own national dress, language, and Hindu beliefs. Until the late 1980s, recognition was given to the Nepalese regarding their customs, language, festivals, tradition, and dress. However, in 1988, in order to preserve the kingdom's national identity, the government conducted a nationwide census aimed at identifying illegal immigrants who could not prove their residence prior to 1958. Numerous ethnic Nepalese lacked proper documentation, and a series of violent acts took place, followed by a mass exodus of Nepali speakers.

Shortly thereafter, citing the unrest caused by the census results, dissident leaders demanded political changes and more democracy, in order to guarantee respect for human rights in the treatment of Nepalese in Bhutan. Years later, at press time, Bhutan and Nepal still have not completely resolved the situation, and tens of thousands of Nepali speakers still remain in refugee camps in southeastern Nepal. However, discussions are taking place between the Royal Government of Bhutan and His Majesty's Government of Nepal regarding the issue of repatriating these Bhutanese refugees.

Pleasures and Pastimes

Dining

Bhutanese cuisine is simple, yet tantalizing. It combines a unique blend of spicy hot, Himalayan flavors, with a variety of meats, cheeses, and chilies. The wide use of cheeses really distinguishes the cuisine from that of other Asian countries. Unlike chilies grown in other countries, which are used mostly as a spice, those in Bhutan are treated as vegetables. Considered to be the national dish, *ema datsi* is made entirely of chilies and served in a creamy cheese sauce.

A delicacy in Bhutan is pork fat, served in large chunks. Hands down, it is the second most popular dish (after *ema datsi* of course). In addition to pork, preferred meats are yak, beef, and chicken. The Bhutanese particularly like their meats dried, and you will often see strips hanging from lines or in windows. Bhutanese dishes are traditionally served with a massive amount of either white rice or a special red variety grown locally. In fact, it is common for a Bhutanese to consume approximately one kilo (2.2 lb) of rice per day. The Bhutanese often employ natural

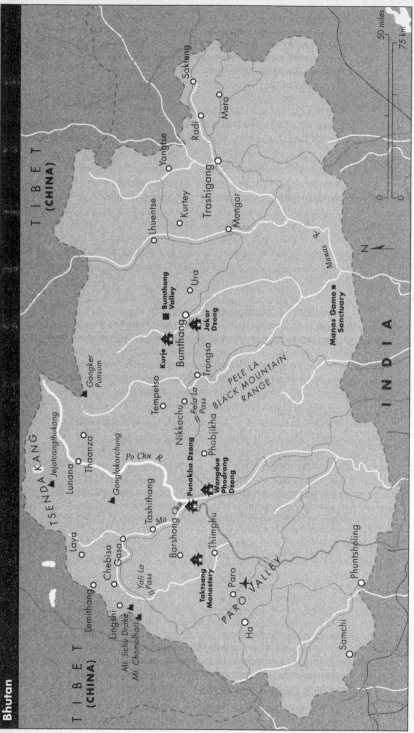

Bhutan

foods found in the forests in their cooking. A few of the more widely used products are chanterelle mushrooms, wild asparagus, fiddlehead ferns, bamboo, wild orchids, taro, and dried river weed.

Since a Westerner's palate is quite different from that of the Bhutanese, many hoteliers have had international culinary professionals train local chefs. When preparing food, there is an emphasis on safety and health standards. Most of the restaurants and hotels in Bhutan serve Indian, Chinese, and Continental foods. However, if you would like to taste Bhutanese food, your chef can prepare it tempered to your liking. During the peak season, most restaurants serve buffet style, and you will find delicious Continental food offered. One final note, except in Thimphu, most of the restaurants are located within hotels.

Here are a few more traditional food items that are found in Bhutan:

datsi—melted, soft fresh cheese
dheysee—saffron-seasoned sweet rice
eze—a salad comprised of chopped chilies, cilantro, soft cheese, onions, and tomatoes
gongdu churu tsoem—curry prepared with eggs and river weed
hontay—buckwheat dumplings filled with cheese and spinach or turnip
jangbuli—whole-wheat pasta served with curd and chives
khule—buckwheat pancake
mengey—rectangular rice cake with seeds from the Shar district
momo—flour dumplings filled with meat or cheese and cabbage
nosha pa—beef strips, cooked with radish or dried spinach
paccha tsoem—tender cane shoots, cooked with pork and chilies
phagshapa—pork fat, stewed with radishes or turnips and dried chilies
phinda bjeli namchu—soya bean noodles, stir-fried with mushrooms
puta—buckwheat noodles from Bumthang
shagi menge—cooked rice, kneaded and flattened into thin cakes, topped with black amaranth paste, eggs, and herbs
sha-ngazam—minced beef, fried in ginger sauce, garnished with spring onions
sha-ngazam tsoem—minced beef with peas in ginger-flavored gravy
suja—salted butter tea
tsip—beaten maize
zow—fried rice mixed with sugar and butter

CATEGORY	COST*
$$$$	over $10
$$$	$7–$10
$$	$4–$7
$	under $4

per person, excluding drinks and service

Dzongs

Bhutanese fortresses are known as dzongs and are easily one of the most bewitching aspects of the kingdom. Their classic lines, carefully sloped walls, and finely detailed woodwork make them one of the most exquisite architectural designs in Asia. These impressive, castlelike buildings were constructed in commanding locations, usually on hilltops overlooking an expansive river valley. Dzongs are located in each of the country's district headquarters, and house both the administrative offices of the district governments and the monks of the regional monastic communities.

The dzongs were built using ancient construction methods; no architectural plans were drawn, and no nails were used. All are built in a formal pattern, most with a central tower in a courtyard, surrounded by buildings that hold the monks' quarters and administrative offices.

The Wangdue Phodrang, Thimphu, and Punakha dzongs have two separate courtyards divided by a central tower. One courtyard is flanked by the administrative sector and the other by the monastic residences.

Foreign travelers are forbidden to enter the inner sanctuaries of many temples, monasteries, and dzongs. Exceptions are made during festival times, when you may enter the dzongs' courtyards to observe the religious dances. To enter the dzongs at any other time, you need written permission in advance from the Special Commission for Cultural Affairs. However, such permission is rarely granted and is only considered for practicing Buddhists. Make your request well in advance through your tour operator.

Festivals

Many travelers visit Bhutan to observe the religious festivals. These rare mask and sword dances are held annually and are performed in dzongs, courtyards, and temples throughout the country. They mark the busiest time of the year, when airplane tickets and hotel rooms are extremely hard to come by. There are many different types of festivals, each having its own spiritual meaning. The most commonly known are the *tsechus,* dances in honor of Guru Rimpoche, which take place September through December, and in March and June. The dances of the tsechu are performed by monks or lay villagers dressed in brightly colored costumes. The dzongs come to life with color, music, and dancing, creating a joyous atmosphere.

Shacham, Dance of the Four Stags. This dance reenacts Guru Rimpoche's triumph over the demonic God of the Wind, who created much havoc in the world. After his triumph, Guru Rimpoche rode the stag, which was the mount of the demon. Dancers wear knee-length skirts and masks of horned deer.

Shana, Black Hat Dance. The dancers wear large hats, felt boots, and brocade robes, without a mask. Accompanied by drums and the sound of the dancers' pounding feet, this dance tells the story of a Tibetan king who once lived in Bhutan and murdered an important lama. A Bhutanese monk killed the king with an arrow concealed in his robe, and thus destroyed the power of evil.

Tungam, Dance of the Terrifying Deities. Dancers wear beautiful brocade robes, boots, and horrific masks. The dance has a very symbolic meaning, and a ritual sacrifice is performed. Dancers representing the power of good encircle the evil demons and capture them in a box. Thus, they not only save the world from the evil spirits, but deliver it to salvation.

Pacham, Dance of the Heroes. The dancers are dressed in yellow skirts and golden crowns, without a mask. This dance explains how Pema Lingpa arrived at Zangto Pelri and saw Guru Rimpoche in a vision. It is performed to lead believers into the presence of Guru Rimpoche.

Lodging

Throughout Bhutan, hotels, guest houses, and lodges vary in style and quality. All are attractive, built in the traditional Bhutanese architecture. In Thimphu and Paro, interiors often continue the traditional motif, with both carving and painting. Since your visit to Bhutan must be booked through a licensed tour operator, you will be placed in a government-approved hotel. All hotels listed are government approved and are very clean and well maintained. Although many hotels do not have phones in their rooms, all hotels are equipped with telephones, fax machines, and international dialing. During the cooler months (Nov.–Feb.) most hotels provide extra blankets and heaters. The traditional heaters, or *bukhari,* are woodstoves that have rocks piled on top of them to retain the heat. Most hotels have private bathrooms that are reasonably modern, with hot water available at all times.

Many of the guest houses and lodges in Bhutan are family-run operations. This allows you to meet the proprietors and experience Bhutanese culture firsthand. The accommodations range from basic to plush. They usually provide friendly service, spotless (if basic) rooms, and a homey environment. If you are traveling to eastern Bhutan, facilities are more limited.

Many hotels and lodges in Bhutan have traditional hot stone baths. These tublike structures are usually wooden with a metal or wooden chute connected to them. Nearby, a fireplace heats large stones, which, when fully heated, are rolled down the chute into the tub to heat the water. It takes some time to heat the rocks, so let the hotel proprietor know in advance if you would like to take a bath. When the weather is cooler, a hot stone bath may be the perfect end to a great day.

The limited number of rooms in Bhutan can cause a shortage during the busy festival times in September, October, November, February, and March. During these periods, some tourists are relegated to tent accommodations. In the event that you are one of the many in this situation, your tour operator should notify you well in advance. The Bhutanese tour operators strive to ensure that the tents are comfortable and warm—some even provide electricity—and they'll often compensate for the inconvenience by providing extras, such as special food or dances.

CATEGORY	COST*
$$$$	over $45
$$$	$30 –$45
$$	$20 –$30
$	under $20

All prices are for a double room, excluding tax and service.

Outdoor Activities and Sports

ARCHERY

Bhutan's much-loved national sport, archery, is slowly catching on with visiting travelers. Even if you don't participate in the sport, you are bound to have a great time watching the inter-village competitions. The revelry begins the night before, when astrologers are hired to assist in the selection process and to help cast spells on the opponent. The rivalry between villages during tournaments is fiercely expressed. Although the tournaments are taken very seriously, the celebrations include lots of laughter, festive dining, and cheering. They are generally held around Losar (Bhutanese New Year) in February or March, but smaller competitions are held throughout the year. In addition, if you would like to participate, your tour operator can organize a tournament in which you can compete with other travelers and local marksmen.

BIRD-WATCHING

If you like to bird-watch, Bhutan is the place to visit. Thanks in part to its moist climate and wide altitudinal range, Bhutan supports over 700 bird species, including some of the most exotic and endemic species in the eastern Himalayas. In 1988, Bhutan was identified by renowned environmental scientist Norman Myers as one of 10 biodiversity hotspots in the world. These spots are designated for the great number of endemic species in their ecosystems, in an effort to draw attention to the threats posed to these species.

Approximately 70% of the country is forested, and unlike other Himalayan countries, most of Bhutan's original forest remains intact, and in its untouched condition. The Buddhist philosophy of respect for all living things has resulted in a healthy environment where wildlife flourishes. Ten species of birds that are in danger of extinction reside in Bhutan, including the rare black-necked crane, which traditionally winters in the valleys of Phobjika, Bomdeling, and Gyetsa. Due to an increased interest in bird-watching, many tour operators now run trips tailored for avian enthusiasts.

GOLF

The **Royal Thimphu Golf Club** (⊠ Chhophel Lam, Thimphu, ☎ 02/3–25429) was initiated in the mid-1970s, under the patronage of His Majesty the King, Jigme Singye Wangchuck. One of the highest golf courses in the world, this beautiful nine-hole circuit is located next to Tashichho Dzong. It offers a nice way to relax after a long day of sight-seeing. The course is open to the public; fees are $25 a day, with an additional Nu 500 to rent golf clubs. The Royal Government has added more land to the club, and a redesign of the course will take place in the near future. There is a large canteen on the premises that serves snacks and cold drinks.

MOUNTAIN BIKING

Adventure tourism has recently made its way to Bhutan. Bhutan is slowly developing the best off-road biking in the eastern end of the Himalayas. At press time, new off-road trails were being developed in the Phobjika Valley. The country's single-lane highway (its only highway), makes for one of the world's greatest cycling journeys, offering challenging climbs and mind-blowing descents. Since biking has only recently gained popularity in Bhutan, few operators are running special bike trips. One such operator who works in conjunction with the Tourism Authority of Bhutan is **Himalayan Mountain Bikes** (⊠ Thamel, Kathmandu, Nepal, ☎ 977/1–437437, FAX 977/1–419237, hmb@visitnepal.com).

RAFTING AND KAYAKING

Although the Himalayas have long drawn Western visitors interested in rafting and kayaking, these activities have only recently been offered in Bhutan. Now it is one of the most exclusive destinations for the sports. Paddling white water in Bhutan allows you to experience some of the most beautiful and undeveloped areas in the world.

There are three spectacular rivers—the Mo Chhu, the Puna Sang Chhu, and the Mangde Chhu—all located west of Thimphu, in the central region. The rivers are primarily class III and IV runs, with many rapids. Bhutan's diverse terrain starts from sea level in the south, rising to the soaring peaks of the Himalayas, creating abundant white-water challenges. The scenery is stunning: Rivers cut through lush, virgin forests, and wind along beautiful white sandy beaches and intricately sculpted rice terraces. Some runs offer world-class paddling, through canyons with sheer vertical walls of black bedrock, and around massive boulders the size of houses. A few such runs have been affectionately named Suicide Alley and Devil's Canyon.

Currently, there are only two companies running rafting trips in Bhutan: **Equator Expeditions Bhutan** (⊠ Thimphu, ☎ 02/3–22191, FAX 02/3–25678, equabhu@druknet.net.bt) and **Ultimate Descents International** (⊠ No. 3 Lodder La., Riwaka, New Zealand, ☎ 64/3543–2301, FAX 64/3432302, www.ultimatedescents.com). To ensure the utmost in safety measures, it is advised that only experienced rafters and kayakers take on the waters in Bhutan. Check with these two reputable companies to see which rivers they are running in the upcoming season. A continued interest in Bhutan's rivers will ultimately open up new territories and avenues for rafting in the western region of the country.

Exploring Bhutan

Bhutan's Tourism Policy

In 1991, the Royal Government of Bhutan privatized the tourism industry, which had previously been run completely by the government. Today the industry is thriving, with over 60 tour operators in business. All tourism in the country is conducted according to the principal of sustainability. In order to preserve the natural environment and the lifestyle of the Bhutanese people, and avoid upsetting the socioeconomic balance, the number of tourists permitted to visit Bhutan is limited.

The Royal Government of Bhutan insists that foreign travelers entering Bhutan visit via a packaged tour, with a pre-planned itinerary. If traveling in a group isn't your style, there are certain provisions for an independent traveler. You may gain a little more freedom traveling without a group, but your tour will still be planned in advance. You can work with your tour operator to establish guidelines for what you would like to see and do while visiting.

Tourists are not allowed to enter many sites in Bhutan, including national monuments and religious institutions. You will only view these destinations from the outside. Religious institutions are considered living institutions, sites for worship and religious ceremonies. Travelers, it is argued, disrupt these daily activities. All dzongs are closed to tourists, because they house the local administrative and religious center. Visitors are allowed to enter the courtyards of the Thimphu and Punakha dzongs when the Je Khenpo, Chief Abbot of Bhutan, and the monk body are not in residence. Thus, the Punakha Dzong is open to visitors in the summer, the Thimphu Dzong in the winter. All dzong courtyards are open to visitors during the tsechus, or festivals.

There are a vast number of rules governing tourism that all travelers must conform to in order to visit Bhutan. First, travelers to Bhutan must book through one of the registered tour operators. You can either work with a Bhutanese tour operator directly, or via your international agent. After you have chosen an itinerary and paid for your trip in its entirety, your tour operator will take appropriate steps to arrange a visa for you. The package rate is inclusive of accommodation, meals, guides, and transportation within Bhutan, as well as the tourist tariff.

The Tourism Authority of Bhutan imposes a tariff on all visitors. At press time, the tariff was $200 per person per day during peak season, and $165 per person per day during off-season. Individual travelers and groups of fewer than three people are subject to an additional surcharge of $30 per person per day for groups of two or $40 per day for solo travelers.

All travelers to Bhutan stay in government-approved hotels, guest houses, and lodges. During the busy festival seasons in the spring and fall, travelers are placed in hotels on a first-come, first-served basis. Regardless of your accommodation, or the type of tour you choose, the rates remain the same, so book early if you plan on traveling in high season.

Travel within the country is limited to foot or car. Your tour operator will arrange to have a knowledgeable guide and driver with you throughout your stay. Thus, transportation, including airport transfers, is not a concern for the traveler. Unless you are a personal guest of a Bhutanese national or an invited delegate, it is impossible to travel unaccompanied in Bhutan. Taxi service is only available in Thimphu. Depending on the size of the group, you will travel in a bus, minivan, or car. A four-wheel-drive vehicle is a necessity if you are traveling to central and eastern Bhutan during the winter (late Nov.–Feb.) or monsoon season (late June–early Sept.). Most of the utility vehicles used to transport guests are relatively new and comfortable.

Foreigners are only allowed to enter Bhutan via air into Paro, or by road into Phuentsholing, although they may exit by road through Samdrup Jongkar. Guwahati, the capital town of the northeastern Indian state of Assam, has a domestic airport located about three hours from the border at Samdrup Jongkar that offers daily flights to Calcutta and Delhi. There is one main road in Bhutan, which takes you through lush pastures, alongside sheer rock cliffs, down mountains, and over high passes. The road takes many twists and turns. At times, the views are spectacular, and the drive can be quite an adventure.

Great Itineraries

It is possible to tour Bhutan even under the most stringent time constraints. However, if you want to observe Bhutan's cultural heritage, exotic festivals, pristine environment, and historic sites, or you wish to trek in one of the greatest natural wonders, the Himalayas, a longer stay is recommended.

If you would like a short cultural tour that includes visits to the larger cities, a four-day visit will allow you to visit Paro and Thimphu, as well as the National Museum and many other historic sites. To really gain insight into this magical kingdom, eight days is the absolute minimum. During this time, you can take a short trek or travel to the central region, the lovely Bumthang Valley. In order to visit eastern Bhutan or take a trek into the Himalayas and other remote areas, you really need to stay two weeks.

As interest increases in this small Himalayan kingdom, the Tourism Authority of Bhutan and tour operators are constantly researching new ideas and creating different tours. Some new packages that are popping up include nature walks through the rhododendron forests, birdwatching tours, fly-fishing trips, textile tours, ballooning, mushroom hunting, and even fertility tours. If you have a special interest, mention it to your tour operator, or contact several different agencies, since they may offer different tours.

IF YOU HAVE 4 DAYS

Arrive in **Paro,** via air, and spend a day or two exploring this picturesque town. Drive through the valley to **Drukyel Dzong,** visit the **National Museum,** and see the 7th-century **Kyichu Lhakhang,** one of the oldest monasteries in Bhutan. A two-hour drive will take you to **Thimphu,** Bhutan's capital city. Visit the **Memorial Chorten,** the **National Painting School,** and **Tashichho Dzong,** the center of government and religion. Thimphu has a great selection of traditional Bhutanese arts, crafts, and textiles. Take time to browse through some of the many handicraft shops.

IF YOU HAVE 8 DAYS

Start your trip with two full days in **Thimphu,** then drive east over the **Dochula Pass,** towards the central region of Bhutan. Visit the **Tongsa Dzong,** and then move on to the beautiful **Bumthang Valley,** where you will see **Kurje Lhakhang, Jambey Lhakhang,** and the **Jakar Dzong.** If time permits, explore the many beautiful walks in the valley. En route back to Paro, spend an evening in **Punakha.**

IF YOU HAVE 2 WEEKS

Although 14 days won't permit you to cover all of Bhutan's highlights, it does offer a lot of flexibility and allows you to visit eastern Bhutan. Stop in the **Phobjika Valley,** home of the black-necked crane. Explore the valley and visit **Gangtey Monastery,** the only Nyingmapa monastery in Bhutan. The journey continues eastward from Bumthang, winding through more rugged terrain. Pass through **Ura** village, before climbing to Bhutan's highest motorable pass, **Thrumshingla Pass** (3,800 m/12,465 ft). Spend an afternoon visiting the **Tashigang Dzong** and **Chorten Kora.** This region is known for finely woven traditional fabrics. Stop in one of the many villages to observe the women busy weaving. Exit via **Samdrup Jongkhar.** You can also spend a few days trekking instead of continuing east from Bumthang. There are several short treks, both cultural and scenic, that take as little as three days and give you a more varied look at the country.

Great Treks

A journey on foot into one of the most remote corners on earth is a magical experience. You can't help but be moved by the beauty of the landscape—the breathtaking views, lofty mountains, and sparsely inhabited villages—and the kindness of the people you meet along the way. The terrain ranges from dense forests of subtropical jungles to alpine tundra. Trails are clean and unspoiled, and the mountains are filled with exotic species of plants and flowers. The forests brim with animals like takins, snow leopards, golden langurs, elephants, and tigers.

Unlike trekking in other parts of the Himalayas, here there are few villages and facilities, no lodges or hotels. To ensure the safety and comfort of trekkers, trained guides, cooks, and horsemen accompany groups throughout the journey. Pack animals—ponies and yaks for the higher elevations—carry the provisions, baggage, and equipment. Trekking programs in Bhutan promote and contribute to local cultures and ecosystems. Thus, the Tourism Authority of Bhutan requires all trekkers to travel in an organized group and be led by a licensed guide and crew.

Treks vary from two-night trips around the peaceful Bumthang Valley and the Druk Path, to the gut-busting three-week Snowman Trek, which covers 356 km (221 mi) and climbs three of Bhutan's highest passes. The most challenging treks are in the northwest, where the highest peaks of the Himalayas divide Tibet and Bhutan. There are several reputable agencies that can arrange a trek to fit your travel schedule, physical needs, and interests. These agencies are nationally run, and your treks will be set up in advance like all of your other travel in the kingdom.

Some of the northern routes cross passes as high as 5,500 m (18,040 ft) and require that trekkers be in good physical condition. The more challenging routes are not for those who suffer from altitude sickness, and proper acclimatization is a must. Altitude sickness, or Acute Mountain Sickness (AMS) can be very serious; start slowly, drink lots of water, and allow yourself time to acclimatize after each stage of your ascent. The Bhutanese guides are trained to look out for the symptoms of AMS and other ailments that can affect trekkers.

Each tour operator has his own preferred route for each trek. Thus, the time spent on treks varies slightly, as do start and finish points. The names of a trek also vary, so if you can't seem to find the one you want, explain the route to your tour operator—chances are it's offered. Because treks are prearranged, you are traveling on a rather strict itinerary. Most of the time, no changes will occur in your schedule, unless of course the weather plays a role. It's a good idea to find out what gear and equipment your tour/trek operator will provide and what you must bring. There is no place to buy gear once you're in Bhutan. Most operators provide necessary camping equipment, including mattress pads and kitchen utensils.

Below is a small sample of treks available in Bhutan. Slight variations in timing and route occur depending on your tour operator. The number of days mentioned accounts for trekking time only; it does not include sightseeing time. For a full list of treks, with complete itineraries, contact the Tourism Authority of Bhutan or your tour operator (☞ Bhutan A to Z).

DRUK PATH TREK (4–6 DAYS)

This five-day trek begins in either Paro or Thimphu and crosses the chain of mountains that separates the two valleys. The route is sparsely inhabited and filled with spectacular rhododendron forests that bloom in May. In late autumn and winter the views of the Himalayas are crystal clear.

Most operators begin the trip in Paro. First you take a drive to the northwest, up the winding mountain road past Drukgyel Dzong, to the trek start point. From here, the trail slowly ascends to Jele Dzong. If the weather is clear, there are gorgeous views of the snowcapped peaks of Jhomolhari and the Paro valley.

The walk gets more exciting as the trail takes you through rhododendron forests and yak pastures, on the way to to Jangchulakha (3,350 m/10,988 ft). As the path follows the contours of the ridge, you catch glimpses of the mountains and the valley. Most groups stay a night at a campsite near Lake Jimilangtso (3,800 m/12,464 ft), known for its giant trout. As you continue along the route, you'll see the unusual dwarf rhododendron trees that hover at knee's height in this region; and every so often you'll pass a yak herders' camp. A night will be spent at Simkota Lake (3,117 m/10,220 ft), which also brims with delicious trout. Toward the end of the trek, there are magnificent views of Mount Gangkar Puensum, the highest peak in Bhutan.

JHOMOLHARI TREK (8–10 DAYS)

Leaving from Drukgyel Dzong, northeast of Paro, you follow the Paro Chhu as it passes through small villages, gradually ascending through an agricultural valley to Shana (2,800 m/9,184 ft). It's a beautiful place to spend an evening, at campsites that are in a meadow surrounded by trees. The river valley slowly narrows from here, and the trail ascends and descends through pine, oak, maple, and spruce forests, crossing several small streams along the way. After crossing a small bridge, it's a short distance to the campsite at Soi Thangthangkha (3,630 m/11,906 ft).

As you continue, the valley widens. You are entering yak country, where the huge, wise-looking creatures graze along the hillsides. To proceed into higher elevations, pack horses are exchanged for yaks. From the campsite at Jangothang (4,152 m/13,612 ft), the views of Mount Jhomolhari are superb.

The trek continues through forests of pine and juniper, into alpine meadows. Gorgeous vistas open before you, and prayer flags flutter in the wind. While in this region, you may see rare bharal (blue sheep). The trail heads northeast to Lingshi village (3,800 m/12,464 ft) and the 600-year-old Lingshi Dzong. From Lingshi, trails through pristine forests lead to Thimphu.

LAYA/GASA TREK (14–16 DAYS)

If you have enough time, consider this trek, which goes beyond Lingshi into the remote Laya region of western Bhutan. This itinerary is the same as the Jhomolhari trek (☞ *above*), but from Lingshi you continue through Chebisa and Robluthang, across three passes—Gobu La (4,352 m/14,268 ft), Jari La (4,602 m/15,088 ft), and Singe La (4,902 m/16,072 ft)—and down into Laya, the second-highest settlement in the country (3,702 m/12,136 ft).

Laya, in the far northwest of the isolated Gasa district, consists for the most part of two monasteries and is rarely visited by outsiders. The people of Laya live seminomadic lives, and are known for their distinctive conical bamboo hats and their warm hospitality. The women of Laya wear their hair long and dress in robes made from the wool of goats, sheep, and yaks. Laya's views of Masagang (7,167 m/23,500 ft), looming high above the village, are stunning.

After Laya, the trek continues down to the Gasa Tshachu hot springs, a great place to relax and enjoy a soak. The trail winds through picturesque valleys, across wild rivers, and past waterfalls, before ending in the lowlands near Punakha.

BUMTHANG TREK (3 DAYS)

The valleys of Bumthang are the spiritual, historical, and geographical heartland of this Buddhist kingdom, and the best way to explore them is on foot. This trail follows the Chamkar Chhu, until it enters Ngang Yul (2,801 m/9,184 ft). Snowcapped mountains tower over you, and surrounding you are lush forests where flowers, fruit, and medicinal herbs grow in abundance.

The trail meanders through several small villages, climbing to Phephela La (3,354 m/10,997 ft), the highest point of the route. Then it slowly descends, following the banks of the Tang Chhu until arriving back at the main road.

SNOWMAN TREK (21–24 DAYS)

The Laya and Lunana Snowman trek is a very strenuous wilderness adventure, unmatched in the cultural experience it provides. It is considered one of the most difficult treks in the world, and its high passes and heavy snowfalls prevent many from completing the route. The seven passes, four of them well over 4,800 m (16,000 ft), cut through the highest and wildest corner of Bhutan.

The trek takes you up the Mo Chhu river to its source near Laya, at the foot of Gangchey Ta, which forms the border with Tibet. After Laya, the route continues east over a series of passes to the most inaccessible corner of the kingdom, Lunana. Here, the kingdom's highest peaks sit majestically, with emerald and turquoise lakes spread at their feet.

The trail drops down into the Lunana valley, which is sprinkled with little villages. The largest local populations are in Thega and Chezo, and the villagers have a warm hospitality that is equaled only by their surprise at the arrival of trail-weary trekkers. This area has some of the most dramatic scenery in Bhutan.

The return journey includes four passes, the highest of them just under 5,185 m (17,000 ft). The daily hikes are long and arduous, but you are rewarded with sights of a pristine wilderness dotted with crystal lakes. The trek finishes at the roadhead near Tongsa.

GANGTEY WINTER TREK (3 DAYS)

This trek goes through Phobjika Valley, one of the few glacial valleys in Bhutan and winter home of the rare black-necked cranes that migrate from the Tibetan plateau. The birds mark their arrival in late October by circling the Gangtey monastery clockwise three times before landing. You make your way through forests of juniper, magnolia, bamboo, and rhododendron, stopping to visit the villages of Gogona and Khotokha. The people of Gogona speak Bjopkha, the language of nomads. Their life in this isolated valley has protected this ancient dialect. This is one of the finest low-level treks in Bhutan.

When to Tour Bhutan

The peak seasons in Bhutan occur at festival times, during months that also happen to offer the best weather, March–May and September–November. The best times to trek are also autumn, when days are crisp and sunny, and spring, when the forests come alive with blooming rhododendrons. Most tour operators will incorporate local festival celebrations in their trekking itineraries. During the winter (late Nov.–Feb.) it tends to be cold at night, but the days are warmer, with clear blue skies and good visibility. Snow can be expected by the end of December, causing transportation delays and road closings. Most of the trekking routes are also closed during the winter. Spring (Mar.–May) is a lovely time of year in Bhutan. The flowers are in full bloom, the bird life is abundant, and there are usually clear views of the snow-capped peaks. The monsoon season occurs during the summer months of June, July, and August, sometimes causing road closings and flight delays or cancellations.

Despite potential weather problems, a visit to Bhutan during the off-season is highly recommended. The tariff rate is lower, and there are fewer crowds. During this time, you will probably get a reservation at the hotel of your choice and are more likely to get your preferred flight dates on Druk Air. Since there are fewer people, the hotel proprietors can provide much better service and spend more time with you.

PARO

As your plane begins its final descent into Paro Valley, you get your first glimpse of this Land of the Thunder Dragon: beautifully terraced, cast in shades of green, clusters of prayer flags blowing in the distance. The beautiful landscapes, scenic villages, and historic buildings of the land have a certain peacefulness. Some of the country's oldest temples and monasteries are here. Since the nation's only airstrip is also here, most trips to Bhutan begin and end in Paro. It's an unusually enchanting place of welcome, and one you will always remember.

The valley of Paro has many interesting sites and requires a few days to be properly explored. The ruins of **Drukgyel Dzong,** at the end of the valley, is a magnificent place to view the towering peak of Mount Chomolhari. Also of interest is the **National Museum,** which is in a converted 17th-century watchtower. The museum has an extensive collection of Bhutanese artifacts. Situated in a commanding viewpoint at the eastern end of the Paro Valley, the Paro Dzong, also called "the fortress of the heap of jewels, is an architectural wonder.

One of the country's most sacred pilgrimage sites, Taktsang Lhakhang, or the "Tiger's Nest," clings to sheer cliffs high above the valley. The trek uphill to the monastery is exhilarating, and the views are breathtaking. In 1998, a fire destroyed the Taktsang's medieval wall paintings and all the inner temples. Reconstruction of this landmark is under way.

Exploring Paro

The valley of Paro extends from Mount Chomolhari on the Tibetan border, all the way to Chuzom, the confluence of Paro Chhu and Thimphu Chhu. In the center of Paro, near the village, the valley is divided in half. One valley is called Dopchari, and runs to the north for approximately 15 km (9 mi), while the main valley of Paro, with the paved road, continues northwest. In Paro Valley, the roads are lined with willow trees, and brilliant white dzongs dot the landscape, shadowed by the green and brown hues from the fields. The town of Paro is in the southeast region of the valley. The airport is farther south, and the ruins of Drukgyel Dzong are in the northwest.

To fully appreciate the beauty and splendor of this magnificent valley, a walk on foot through the village and its surrounding areas is suggested. Your tour operator will arrange private transportation to many of the historic sites. There streets are not named in Paro, including the main road, which is affectionately referred to as "Main Street," which is how it is listed here.

Paro Village

The village of Paro rests in the center of this vast valley, a short distance from the Paro Dzong. The town itself is small, since most locals live in the valley that surrounds it. Chortens (Buddhist monuments) flank the main road that takes you from the dzong's traditional cantilever bridge into Paro village. On the right is the royal palace of Ugyen Pelri, and directly adjacent on the other side is the archery field.

Built in 1985, the town consists of one wide street that runs parallel to the river. There are several small shops, as well as local eateries lined up and down the main street. A small grass town square sits at one end of town, surrounded by a few hotels, handicraft shops, the post office, and restaurants. It's worth spending some time meandering through the shops to observe the local customs and wares of this mountain town.

Numbers in the text correspond to numbers in the margin and on the Paro Valley map.

A GOOD WALK

Begin your walking tour of Paro village at the town square, and walk southeast towards the dzong. The road is wide with few cars, and you will often pass caravan drivers leading their horses, as well as fruit and vegetable sellers from the nearby villages. The are no street names in Paro, however, since it is a one-road town, you do not risk getting lost. Heading south out of the center of town, behind a row of shops and buildings, is the local Sunday market. Continue down the street. On your right will be **Druk Choeding** ①, the town temple, built in 1525. After you have passed the archery grounds, the **Ugyen Pelri Palace** ② will be on your left. Turn left and go across the traditional cantilever bridge. Once you have crossed over the river, the massive structure of the **Paro Dzong** ③ will be looming over you. Just beyond the Paro Dzong, up the hill is the **National Museum** ④, housed in an ancient watchtower, Ta Dzong, that was built in the 17th century. The museum has a large collection of paintings, postage stamps, bronzes, and intricately painted religious objects and banners. From this serene vantage point, you can take in the mountains that rise in the distance and the ice-blue river that flows just below.

Continue your journey north along the road that heads out of the museum. This winding country road takes you past Paro High School, lush green terraces, and many houses. Some of the most beautiful houses in the country, they are brightly colored and intricately carved. At the end of the road, which is a T-junction, turn left and continue past **Dumtse Lhakhang** ⑤, a temple in the shape of a chorten. If you follow this road to the end, it takes you right back to the main road in Paro village, where you can spend some time browsing in the many handicraft shops.

TIMING

This is a full morning's walk that could extend into the afternoon if you're keen on Bhutanese history and handicrafts or would like to comb through the many exhibits at the National Museum. Start early if you have afternoon plans. Keep in mind that the museum is closed on Monday and at lunchtime. If you save the handicraft shops for the end, you could complete the circuit, including a visit to the museum, in three to four hours. Be prepared to get distracted by the fascinating sites, a wooden cantilever bridge, monks in saffron-color robes, carts pulled by mules, and sun-bleached fields.

SIGHTS TO SEE

❶ Druk Choeding. This temple was built in 1525 by Ngawang Chhogyal, an ancestor of the Prince Abbotts of Ralung, in Tibet. The Abbotts, high priests of important monasteries, wielded immense political power by virtue of their religious standing. This temple is also known as Tshongdoe Naktshang. ✉ *Main St., Paro.*

NEED A BREAK?

Sonam Trophel (✉ 2nd floor, above the Bank of Bhutan, Main St., Paro, ☏ 08/2–71287) is a small café that has long been a favorite of expatriates. There is no menu, but the proprietor uses all of her own recipes and is more than happy to make suggestions. Try the momos (meat-, cheese-, or cabbage-filled dumplings), they're some of the best in Paro.

❺ Dumtse Lhakhang. Dumtse Lhakhang is an unusual temple built in the shape of a chorten. It was built in the early 1400s by Thangtong Gyalpo, a famous Tibetan lama who was also known as "the builder of iron bridges," for the eight such bridges he built before returning to Tibet. The temple was designed with three different levels representing heaven, earth, and hell. Dumtse Lhakhang has one of the most magnificent collections of religious paintings in the Himalayas. ✉ *West of Main St., Paro.*

❹ National Museum. The museum is located just above the Paro Dzong, in an ancient building that used to be a watchtower. It is also known as Ta Dzong, because the numerous religious objects inside have resulted in the museum's designation as a temple. Realizing the significance of museums in the development of national identity, His Majesty King Jigme Dorji Wangchuck ordered the renovation of the museum in 1965. It continues to be an important center for the preservation of Bhutanese artifacts, culture, and history, not only for foreign travelers, but for the Bhutanese as well. The museum plays an important role in the education of Bhutanese children; many school groups and villagers travel here from remote areas. Because of the museum's religious significance, you must proceed through the building in a clockwise direction. A guard will show you the way.

There are six floors of galleries, surrounding a core that contains a fine collection of iconographic representations of the beliefs of Bhutanese Buddhists. In addition to containing paintings (all by Bhutanese artists), the museum houses traditional handicrafts that reflect daily life, prehistoric and medieval artifacts, ancient weapons and shields, a variety of stuffed animals, and a diverse assortment of religious costumes and ritual objects.

Overlooking the main floor, a balcony houses the *thangka* gallery, a large collection of antique and contemporary examples of these embroidered and painted religious banners. On the top floor, the gallery has an extensive collection of Bhutan's notorious philatelic stamps. Quite unusual are the holographic stamps, mini-record stamps, silk-screened stamps, and three-dimensional stamps. In the center of this gallery is the Tshogshing Lhakhang, the Temple of the Tree of Wisdom. Situated in the middle of the temple is an elaborate carving that represents the history of Buddhism. Don't forget to walk clockwise around this sacred room. Other galleries display bronze and copper teapots, jewelry,

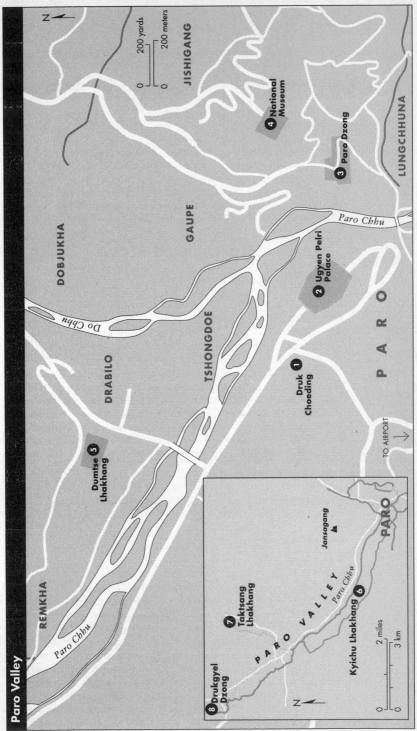

Paro Valley

N

0 ──── 200 yards
0 ──── 200 meters

JISHIGANG

DOBJUKHA

GAUPE

LUNGCHHUNA

4 National Museum

3 Paro Dzong

Paro Chhu

Do Cbhu

TSHONGDOE

2 Ugyen Pelri Palace

DRABILO

1 Druk Choeding

P A R O

P A R O

TO AIRPORT

5 Dumtse Lhakhang

REMKHA

Paro Chhu

PARO

Jansagang

PARO VALLEY

Paro Chhu

7 Taktsang Lhakhang

6 Kyichu Lhakhang

8 Drukgyel Dzong

N

0 ──── 2 miles
0 ──── 3 km

horn beer containers, and wooden objects. A natural history gallery includes an amazing display of Bhutanese butterflies. After visiting the museum, you will have a good sense of Bhutanese history and culture. ✉ *Above the Paro Dzong, Paro,* ☏ *08/2–71257.* ✆ *Nu 25.* ⊙ *Tues.– Sat. 9–4, Sun. 11–4.*

❸ **Paro Dzong.** One of the most impressive dzongs in the country, the Paro Dzong controls all secular and religious activities in the valley. The dzong's full name is Rinpung Dzong, which means "the fortress of the heap of jewels." It was constructed in 1646 by Shabdrung Ngawang Namgyal, on the foundation of a former monastery built by Padma Sambhava. For centuries, the imposing building served as the most strategic fortress against several invasion attempts by the Tibetans. Tragically, a fire in 1907 destroyed almost all its treasures, and the dzong was rebuilt by Penlop Dawa Penjor in the following year. The dzong served as the meeting hall for the National Assembly before its current home, the Tashichho Dzong, was built.

The dzong sits on a steep hill overlooking the town, a perfect command post for viewing all who enter the valley. Just above the dzong stands the ancient watchtower, which is now the National Museum. Inside the entrance is the *dochey,* a courtyard that houses the government administrative offices for the region. Built during the time of Paro Penlop in 1649, the *utse,* central tower, with its exquisite craftsmanship, is one of the most beautiful in Bhutan. A stairway leads down into the second courtyard, which holds the monastic quarters for approximately 200 monks. On the left side of the courtyard is the *Kunre,* the hall where the monks eat their meals. Many significant divinities are painted on the walls of this structure. Beneath the gallery that leads into the Kunre are mystical cosmic mandalas, images created to represent the Buddhist vision of the universe. The harmony of the color and form in these works is as vital as the actual images in Buddhist cosmology. On the right side of the courtyard is the *dukhang,* a ceremonial room. Adorning the walls of the right gallery are paintings of the many facets of the life of Milarepa, a 12th-century poet and saint. *Paro Town.*

❷ **Ugyen Pelri Palace.** Barely visible from the road, this secluded compound rests on the south side of the river, west of the dzong. The royal palace was built around 1930 by the Penlop (governor) of Paro, Tshering Penjor. An exquisite example of Bhutanese architecture, it was designed to simulate Guru Rimpoche's heavenly abode, Zangto Pelri. ✉ *Southeast end of Main St., Paro.*

Paro Valley
A GOOD TOUR

This daylong tour begins as you drive northwest down the valley. About 3 km (2 mi) out of town, just south of the road is **Kyichu Lhakhang** ⑥, built in the 8th century and one of Bhutan's most sacred shrines. Continuing down the road past Kyichu Lhakhang for about 5 km (3 mi), you will see **Taktsang Lhakhang** ⑦, the famous "Tiger's Nest" monastery, which clings to the edge of a cliff high above the valley. The walk up to the monastery was a part of every traveler's itinerary before a fire in 1998 destroyed much of the main structure. It is still worth the effort to hike to the top for the views and glimmer of historic interest. If you don't want to make the three-hour hike up the mountain, there are ponies for hire. Just be sure to have your tour operator make your reservations a few days in advance. On the way up, you cross several small streams, pass chortens with prayer wheels, walk through blue pine forests, and emerge on a bluff bristling with prayer flags. From this point, it is a short distance to a lovely log cabin restaurant where you can rest, have lunch, or buy some interesting handicrafts. Although the view from the restaurant is spectacular, many people make the strenuous walk closer to the overhang for a better view. From this vantage point, the monastery looks like it emerges from the cliffs.

Beyond Taktsang Lhakhang, the road continues down the valley through the small farming village of Drukgyel. At the end of the paved road lays the ruins of **Drukgyel Dzong** ⑧. If you are lucky, you'll get a clear view of the lofty peaks of Mount Chomolhari (24,000 ft) that tower in the distance. This is also the starting place of the Chomolhari trek.

TIMING

Even if you take the hike up to Taktsang Lhakhang, it shouldn't take more than a half day to cover these sites. Since it is quite a steep ascent, do plan on extra rest time while walking up the mountain. There is very little shade along the trail, so bring water and wear a hat to protect you from the sun. It's worth spending some extra time at the restaurant, which is a lovely place to relax while taking in the views.

SIGHTS TO SEE

⑧ **Drukgyel Dzong.** At the end of the road out of Paro, 16 km (10 mi) from the town, lies the burnt ruins of Drukgyel Dzong. Built by Shabdrung Ngawang Namgyal in 1647, on a spur above the Paro Chhu, its commanding location was chosen as a spot from which to control the route to Tibet. It was from this monastery that the Bhutanese were victorious over several invading Tibetan armies during the 17th century. In 1951, a butter lamp fell over, and a terrible fire destroyed most of the fortress, leaving only portions of its walls and roofs. Still, the remains of the dzong form a dramatic profile against the backdrop of Mount Chomolhari. In order to preserve the dzong from complete ruin, a shingled roof was added, and beams were placed throughout for support. ✉ *Drukgyel, 16 km (10 mi) from Paro, at the end of Main St.*

OFF THE
BEATEN PATH

Although it takes three hours to walk to the **Taktsang Cafeteria** (✉ Viewpoint of Taktsang Lhakhang, Paro), it is not unknown to travelers visiting Bhutan. It is definitely worth the walk to the restaurant; the charming log cabin, made of oak and blue pine, has spectacular views of the monastery. Considering that all the food and drinks have to be carried up the mountain, they have a good selection of beer. For those who have worked up quite an appetite reaching Taktsang, they serve a set lunch that includes Bhutanese and Chinese dishes.

⑥ **Kyichu Lhakhang.** Situated a short distance off the road is Kyichu Lhakhang, a monastery consisting of two temples. The first temple was built in the 7th century by the Tibetan King Songtsen Gampo. According to tradition, an ogress laid across parts of Tibet and Bhutan to stop the spread of Buddhism. The king ordered the construction of 108 temples on all the points of her body, in an effort to overcome her. One of the more well known of these temples, Kyichu Lhakhang, was built on her left foot. After the construction of these temples, there was an increasing awareness in this Buddhist region of the world of the small valley of Paro. Guru Rimpoche visited the temple to meditate.

Paintings adorning all the walls of the ancient temple depict the Twelve Acts of Buddha and all of his previous lives. Kyichu's antiquity and its role in history have made it one of the most sacred shrines in Bhutan.

A golden roof was added in 1830 and a second temple was built by Her Majesty Ashi Kesang, the Queen Mother, in 1968. The new temple is dedicated to Guru Rimpoche and contains a statue of him. It is built in the same style and stands opposite the entrance of its predecessor. ✉ *South of Main St., Paro.*

❼ Taktsang Lhakhang. Nestled in the sheer cliffs above the valley at 2,700 ft rests Taktsang Lhakhang, "Tiger's Nest," one of the most sacred pilgrimage sites of the Himalayan kingdom. The monastery gets its name from one of the many legends tied to it. According to this legend, in the 8th century Guru Rimpoche flew across the mountains on the back of a tigress, and relics of this sacred beast are held in a chorten inside the monastery.

Taktsang was built in 1648 around a cave where Guru Rimpoche is said to have meditated for three months. Here, according to another legend, Guru Rimpoche, in his wrathful form of Dorje Droloe, conquered evil demons. Later, Guru Rimpoche converted the inhabitants of Paro Valley to Buddhism. He eventually returned to Tibet in order to convey the religious teachings of the Kagye cycle to his disciples. One of Guru Rimpoche's disciples, Langchen Pelki Singye, also came to the holy site of Taktsang to meditate. Although Langchen died in Nepal, his body was brought back to Taktsang, and his relics are sealed in another chorten, deep within the cliffs.

Within the sacred walls of the complex are smaller temples—including one from which lamas are said to hurl *vajras,* thunderbolts, at malevolent forces—which surround the main shrine. Jutting from a rock above Taktsang, and built in harmony with the natural features of its precarious location, is the Zangto Pelri, Temple of Heaven, a 300-year-old spiritual retreat.

In April 1998, a fire destroyed Taktsang's medieval wall paintings and all the inner temples. However, the *pelphug,* or the holy cave in which Guru Rimpoche meditated, was found unharmed and in good condition. You can still see most of the building's structure, although the inner walls are gone. At press time, the government was overwhelmed with donations for the rebuilding of Taktsang. As soon as the construction of a bridge at Satsam Chorten and a road to Ramthangka is completed, the construction trucks will be able to reach the site and the rebuilding will begin.

The best views of Taktsang are from the restaurant, located on a ridge directly across from the monastery. You can get a closer view by ascending a steep trail for another hour. This takes you to the same level as the monastery, where the views are astounding. It looks as if Taktsang is rising from the cliffs. Due to the sanctity of the site, Taktsang is not open to visitors. ⊠ *Northwest Paro Valley.*

Dining and Lodging

Since Paro is the gateway to the Land of the Thunder Dragon, it offers a wide variety of accommodations. Bhutan is unlike any other tourist destination: most of the time you will be eating with your tour group in a hotel restaurant. However, it is worth exploring the local haunts. All the restaurants have a wide variety of dishes for you to choose from—Bhutanese, Continental, Chinese, Indian. In most cases, the food is served buffet style. If there is some special food that you would like, mention it to your tour guide; he or she can make special arrangements to fulfill your request.

$$$$ ✕⌂ **Hotel Druk.** The hotel, whose design replicates a dzong, is on 40
★   acres of land, high atop a hill overlooking the valley. The grand lobby has marble floors and chandeliers. There is a courtyard in the middle of the hotel where cultural activities, bonfires, and barbecues take place. You can stroll through the sprawling grounds and walk into the nearby orchards. A small cottage holds the hot tub, sauna, and steam room. The formal restaurant faces the river and has spectacular views

of Paro. The menu includes such Continental specialties as chicken chasseur, pepper chicken, and for dessert, crème caramel. ⊠ *Southeast of Paro town, Paro,* ☎ *08/2–71458,* FAX *08/2–71513. 52 rooms. Restaurant, hot tub, sauna, steam room, laundry service, business services. Reservations required. No credit cards.*

$$$$ ✕▥ **Kichu Resort.** Spread over an estate on the outskirts of Paro vil-
★ lage, with five beautifully manicured lawns set alongside the river, the Kichu Resort is a lovely oasis. Octagon-shape cottages are surrounded by small free-form pools filled with river stones or lilies. The rooms all have pine furniture coupled with whitewashed walls and white duvet covers, giving them a delightfully airy and fresh atmosphere. A lagoon is great for swimming or paddle boating. The restaurant is on the second floor of the main building and has an oversize stone fireplace in its center and large windows that overlook the complex. It serves an excellent selection of food, from traditional Bhutanese dishes to hot Indian curries. ⊠ *West of Paro, just off the main road in Lango, Paro* ☎ *08/2–71468,* FAX *08/2–71466. 39 rooms. Restaurant, sauna, paddle tennis, nightclub, laundry service, meeting room, travel services. Reservations essential. No credit cards.*

$$$ ✕▥ **Gangtey Palace.** Located directly across from the Paro Dzong, this hotel is housed in a 19th-century traditional palace that was once the residence of the Paro Penlop. The grounds are magnificently manicured and have outdoor seating areas that overlook the valley. The large rooms are blandly decorated with traditional carved furniture and are a bit dingy. The restaurant has a bar with a circular sitting area that's a great place to have drinks. In addition to the standard cuisines, they also serve Tibetan food. Some specialties of the house include fish balls, beef goulash, chicken à la king, and banana fritters. ⊠ *Gangtey, Paro,* ☎ *08/2–71301,* FAX *08/2–71452. 19 rooms. Restaurant, bar, laundry service, travel services. No credit cards.*

$$$ ✕▥ **Hotel Olathang.** This hotel is run by the Bhutan Tourism Corporation and was built in 1974 for guests invited to the coronation of the present king. The expansive hotel has one main building and several cottages spread over a pine-forested estate. A stuffed yak and tiger greet you in the lobby. Although the center building is in need of renovation, a stay in one of the cottages is recommended. The spacious restaurant serves Continental, Chinese, Indian, and Bhutanese cuisines. Try the chicken cordon bleu or the light fruit cocktail with cream. Also recommended are the breads and pastries, which are all baked on the premises. It's a good idea to make reservations for the restaurant. ⊠ *Olathang, Paro,* ☎ *08/2–71305,* FAX *08/2–71454. 56 rooms. Restaurant, laundry service. No credit cards.*

$$ ✕▥ **Dechen Cottages.** A very steep driveway leads you up to this lovely little hotel. Resting on a hill across the valley from Paro village, it has a nice view of Paro Dzong. The rooms are well maintained and very clean, all with traditional Bhutanese decor, including carved furniture and embroidered blankets. The dining room has a nice fireplace and a small lounge that has a view of the river. Serving the standard four cuisines (Continental, Chinese, Indian, and Bhutanese), it also offers a few hearty Western-style dishes, including club sandwiches, grilled cheese, and rice pudding. ⊠ *Gabtey, Paro,* ☎ *08/2–71392. 11 rooms. Restaurant, bar, laundry service. No credit cards.*

$$ ✕▥ **Tiger's Nest Resort.** Located at the end of the valley, this small family-run hotel is situated on a hill with a view of Taktsang Lhakhang. The rooms are in slight need of renovation, but the peaceful surroundings and friendly owners make up for the lack of ambience. The restaurant is small and cozy, with a large selection of Bhutanese handicrafts throughout. It serves mostly Continental dishes that are re-

quested by the guests. ✉ *Satsam Chorten, Paro,* ☎ *08/2–71310,* FAX
08/2–71640. 11 rooms. Restaurant, laundry service. No credit cards.

Nightlife and the Arts

Nightlife

The nightlife in Paro is very limited, with the only scheduled activities
being the cultural programs, traditional folk dances, and bonfires co-
ordinated by tour operators and hotels. The Kichu Resort (☞ Dining
and Lodging, *above*) has a discotheque on Saturday nights, however,
call first to make sure it will be open the Saturday you are visiting. It's
always worth checking out your hotel bar or lounge, since there are
bound to be some travelers who want to stay up late and create their
own pleasant, merry atmosphere.

The Arts

In March the Paro Tsechu festival takes place in honor of Padma
Sambhava, "One who was born from a lotus," also known as Guru
Rimpoche, "The Precious Teacher." Dancers perform outside the Paro
Dzong, northeast of the entrance. The Black Hat Dance is performed
annually on the second day of the five-day tsechu. Another highlight
takes place on the last day, when a *thongrol,* a huge thangka measur-
ing more than 50 sq ft, is unrolled. Guru Rimpoche is the main figure
on this magnificent thongrol. It was commissioned in the 8th century
by the eighth Desi, the secular ruler of Bhutan, Chhogyal Sherub
Wangchuck.

Shopping

Much construction took place in Paro village in 1985, and now there
are several local handicraft shops lining the main street. Many of the
shops cater to locals, carrying just the basic necessities one would expect to find in a simple town: sugar, flour, hardware supplies, and pots
and pans. However, in recent years a few new shops have opened that
carry modern goods from Thailand, India, and Nepal. Flashy sneak-
ers, sleek black handbags, colorful stuffed animals, and up-to-date gad-
gets have found their way into this small mountain village, slowly turning
the sleepy town into an urban center.

Since Paro is the main exit town for Bhutan, there are many small handicraft shops located on the main street and in the hotels for last-minute
shopping. They all have a wide range of high-quality Bhutanese textiles, wood items, thangkas, and other traditional goods. All the crafts
in Bhutan are handmade, each varying slightly in style and color. If you
are looking for something special, you will enjoy browsing in these small
shops.

Bhutanese handicrafts can be expensive, because although the demand
for them is high, the artisans are not willing to sacrifice quality for quan-
tity. Bargaining is not the custom here, and most craft shops have fixed
prices. Shops usually open around 8 AM and close around 7 PM every
day except Tuesday.

Markets

Every Sunday, villagers flock into town with fruit from local orchards,
a wide variety of vegetables, and all sorts of other spices, herbs, and
dried meats and fish. The **Sunday market** is on the southern end of the
main street, just south of the road, behind a row of shops. Every weekend, locals gather there to catch up on the latest news and purchase
fresh produce for the following week. It's a much smaller market than
the one in Thimphu, but still worth a visit. ✉ *Southern end of the main
street, Paro village.*

Paro A to Z

Arriving and Departing

If you are traveling on a tourist visa, your tour operator will arrange all of your transportation within Bhutan. The tourist tariff includes all transportation, therefore you will always have car, driver, and guide with you.

BY AIRPLANE

The inauguration of the **Paro International Airport** (☎ 08/2–71401) took place in April 1999, and it's the only airport in Bhutan. The new terminal has a restaurant with an extensive menu and delicious baked goods, a coffee/snack bar, and a comfortable lounge. The airport is southeast of Paro village, and approximately 6 km (4 mi) from the town center.

Carriers: Druk Air (☎ 02/3–22215), the Bhutanese national airline, is the only airline that serves Paro. All visitors flying into Bhutan are brought into the kingdom in its care. There are flights into Paro from Calcutta, Delhi, Bangkok, Dhaka, and Kathmandu. The flight into Paro is spectacular: Whether flying along the Himalayan range from Kathmandu or over the foothills from Calcutta, each flight has spectacular views of Everest, Kangchenjunga, and Makalu, as well as the Bhutanese peaks of Chomolhari and Gangkar Puensum.

Between the Airport and City: All transportation to and from the airport to Paro or Thimphu will be arranged prior to your arrival in Bhutan. A representative from your travel agency or your tour guide will greet you at the airport and take you to your hotel.

Contacts and Resources

CURRENCY EXCHANGE

It is best to exchange money at the currency exchange counter at the airport or at your hotel. The hotel exchange rates in Bhutan are usually the same as those at the bank, and performing the transaction at your hotel will save you hours of waiting in bank lines. Depending on the exchange counter, sometimes a small commission is charged.

EMERGENCIES

Ambulance (☎ 112), **fire** (☎ 110), **police** (☎ 113).

District Hospital Paro (✉ Gabtey, ☎ 08/2–71571, 08/2–71570 emergency after hours) has English-speaking doctors on staff. Although the Thimphu hospital has more facilities, Paro can handle emergencies 24 hours a day. The hospital has its own pharmacy on the premises.

POST OFFICE

The small **post office** (☎ 08/2–71223) is located on the east side of the town square.

THIMPHU

The city of Thimphu lies in a broad valley, on a sprawling hillside on the banks of the Thimphu River. At an altitude of 7,600 ft, Thimphu is unlike any other capital city in the world. A small rural settlement until the late 1970s, it is now home to approximately 40,000 people.

Tashichho Dzong not only houses the throne of His Majesty the King of Bhutan, the summer residence of the venerated monastic community is also Bhutan's administrative and religious center. The colossal building is set on the banks of the river, surrounded by weeping willows. Opposite the dzong, on the other side of the river, is the National Assembly Hall.

Other places of interest in Thimphu include the National Library, which houses a vast collection of historic and religious literature; the Painting School, which teaches traditional styles of thangka painting, wood carving, ceramics, papermaking, and weaving; and the Memorial Chorten, an important landmark that was built in 1974 by the mother of the third king of Bhutan, in memory of her son.

One of the delightful quirks of this capital city is its complete lack of traffic lights. Stationed at two traffic circles, traffic police stand on wooden pedestals and direct cars with graceful hand gestures, often replicating the movements of a dancer.

In order to preserve the kingdom's national identity, all new buildings in Bhutan must be designed in traditional style. The streets are spotless, there are no beggars, and prayer flags flutter in the wind, casting shadows on the intricately painted and carved buildings. The streets are dotted with monks in saffron-color robes, women in vivid *kiras* (dresses), and men in *ghos* (traditional dress for males), the Bhutanese formal dress. The town of Thimphu is, quite simply, stunning.

Exploring Thimphu

Even though Thimphu begins just beyond Lungten Zampa, a small bridge that crosses over the Thimphu River, the heart of the city lies on the west bank and slowly makes its way up the valley towards Motithang, an attractive suburb. In the central area, the small, bustling business district is filled with numerous small shops, restaurants, and bars. In the last few years, a broader range of stores and hotels has opened, thus changing the face of Thimphu forever. Despite these changes, the city retains its charm, thanks to the height and style restrictions on new architecture.

The new, modern shops and hotels are mostly situated in the area around the main intersection, at the southern traffic circle. Many of the government offices are located on the upper part of Norzin Lam, the main street in Thimphu. Just past the second traffic circle, Norzin Lam becomes Desi Lam, which continues past the Royal Thimphu Golf Course and, ultimately, Taschhoe Dzong.

Unlike many capital cities, Thimphu has no traffic jams or air pollution and is very safe, so it's a delightful place to wander around for the day. The best way to explore the city is on foot, as there are many small alleys and lanes jutting off the main road. The heart of Thimphu is very small, approximately 4 sq km (2½ sq mi). Most neighborhoods are split equally with residential homes, shops, and restaurants. One of the most enjoyable things to do while in Thimphu is to stroll along the lively, colorful streets of town, looking into many of the shops and watching the passersby.

In addition to gorgeous views of the valley from almost anywhere in Thimphu, there are several impressive buildings and historic sites. Since English is widely spoken, you will have no trouble getting around. The Bhutanese people are extremely gracious, kind, and friendly. It is common to find yourself engaged in a conversation with a local, particularly since many of the younger generation want to find out more about other cultures.

Numbers in the text correspond to numbers in the margin and on the Thimphu map.

A Good Walk

Begin your walk at the Lungten Zampa bridge at the southern end of town. Cross to the east side of the Thimphu River, turn left, and walk

| WITHOUT KODAK MAX
photos taken on 100 speed film |

Ever see someone

waiting for the sun to come out

while trying to photograph

a charging rhino?

New!
Kodak Max film:

*Now with better color,
Kodak's maximum
versatility film gives
you great pictures in
sunlight, low light,
action or still.*

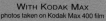

| WITH KODAK MAX
photos taken on Kodak Max 400 film |

It's all you need
to know about film.

www.kodak.com

north, parallel to the river. On your right you will pass the Riverview Hotel, and from this vantage point, there is an excellent view of the **Changlimithang Stadium** ①, the sports ground where archery competitions take place. A few minutes' further walk, on the right side of the road, is a paper factory with a small showroom. As you continue your journey north, take a look up at the hill on your right, where there is a small plaque honoring the King's Coronation Silver Jubilee. Several trees were planted by noted Bhutanese citizens to commemorate the special day.

Continue up the road for a few minutes, and take a left onto the small road that leads to the **SAARC Building** ②. Go back to the main road, backtrack for a few minutes, and turn right to cross the new Lanjupakha Zam bridge. **Tashichho Dzong** ③ will be directly in front of you, with the Royal Thimphu Golf Course alongside.

Chhophel Lam runs north–south just above the golf course. If you turn right on Chhophel Lam, then left onto Pedzoe Lam, you will reach the **National Library** ④, home to a vast collection of traditional and religious books. Farther up the road on the left is the **National School of Arts & Crafts** ⑤, followed by the **National Institute of Traditional Medicine** ⑥. To return to the main business district, walk back down to Chhophel Lam and turn right. At the end of the road, bear right, and continue until you see the northern traffic circle. That is the northern end of Norzin Lam, the main street. This will take you back into the downtown area.

TIMING

This walk will definitely take a full morning and could extend well into the afternoon if you're keen on Bhutanese history or if you decide to play a round of golf. All the national sites are closed over the weekend. You can save time by jumping in a taxi or asking your tour guide to arrange a car and driver for you. Since most of these sites are probably included in your itinerary, just let your guide know if you would like to walk rather than ride to some of them.

Sights to See

❶ **Changlimithang Stadium.** The national stadium now rests upon a field where a decisive battle took place in 1885, establishing supremacy for Bhutan's first king, Ugyen Wangchuck. This sports ground is the site of a large football stadium and is also where the national archery competitions are held. North of the main complex are squash, basketball, and tennis courts. ⊠ *Chhogyal Lam, Thimphu.*

❻ **The National Institute of Traditional Medicine.** Established in 1988, this institute is sponsored by the European Union and researches the use of medicinal herbs and plants. Bhutan's diverse terrain—land that rises from sea level to snowcapped peaks—includes many different climates and environments that support a wide range of flora. To date, more than 600 medicinal plants have been identified in Bhutan, and at least 300 are commonly used by traditional practitioners around the country. Located within the compound is the Indigenous Hospital where patients receive traditional treatments and medicines that are prepared and dispensed by the institute. A large new pharmaceutical research unit and production facility ensures quality control. At press time, a small museum and gift shop were under construction. ⊠ *Kawangjangsa,* ☎ *02/3–24647.* ☉ *Weekdays 9–3, Sat. 9–1.*

❹ **The National Library.** The library was established in 1967 to preserve the country's oldest historic and religious records. Housed within the four-story building are traditional Bhutanese and Tibetan manuscripts, xylographs, and wooden blocks used for printing books and prayer

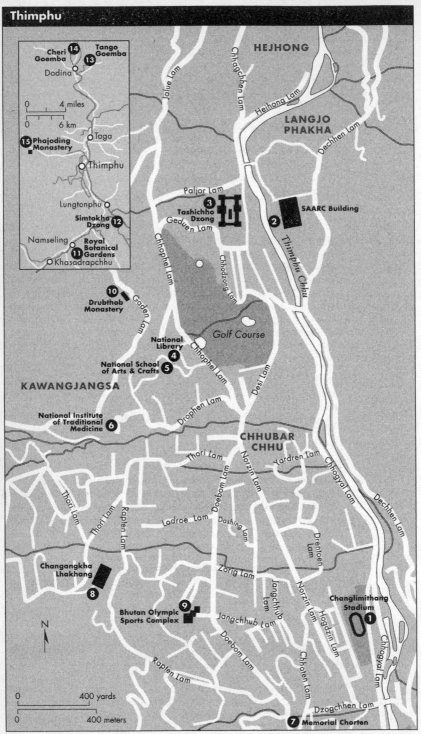

HEJHONG

LANGJO
PHAKHA

KAWANGJANGSA

CHHUBAR
CHHU

Cheri
Goemba 14   Tango
Goemba 13
Dodina

0   4 miles
0   6 km

15 Phajoding
Monastery

Taga

Thimphu

Lungtonphu

Simtokha 12
Dzong

Namseling   Royal
Botanical 11
Gardens
Khasadrapchhu

Paljor Lam

Tashichho 3
Dzong

SAARC Building
2

10 Drubthob
Monastery

National 4
Library

National School
of Arts & Crafts 5

Golf Course

National Institute
of Traditional 6
Medicine

Thori Lam   Yardren Lam

Drophen Lam

Norzin Lam

Doebom Lam

Lodroe Lam   Dashing Lam

Drenloen
Lam

Zorig Lam

Jangchhub
Lam

Changangkha
Lhakhang
8

Bhutan Olympic 9
Sports Complex

Jangchhub Lam

Changlimithang
Stadium
1

N

0   400 yards
0   400 meters

Dzogchhen Lam

7 Memorial Chorten

Chhagchhen Lam
Heihong Lam
Jalue Lam
Dechhen Lam
Thimphu Chhu
Geduen Lam
Chhodzong Lam
Chhophel Lam
Gaden Lam
Desi Lam
Chhogyal Lam
Dechhen Lam
Thori Lam
Rapten Lam
Chhoten Lam
Hodzin Lam
Rapten Lam
Doebom Lam
Chhogyal Lam

flags. If you want to learn more about Bhutan and its people, this is the place to visit. There is a collection of English-language books about the country, Buddhism, and Himalayan history, as well as reference materials and academic texts. The library houses many holy books, altars, and important historic statues depicting Guru Rimpoche, Pema Lingpa, and Shabdrung Ngawang Namgyal. Considered a holy site, many people circumambulate the building chanting mantras. ⊠ *Kawangjangsa,* ☎ *02/3–22885.* ⊙ *Weekdays 9:30–1 and 2–5.*

⑤ The National School of Arts & Crafts. Referred to as the painting school, the NSAC was established in 1971 to preserve and promote Bhutan's rich cultural heritage. The school has a comprehensive curriculum providing instruction in the traditional arts: painting, wood carving, sculpture, embroidery, slate carving, weaving, and calligraphy. Until 1999, only boys were accepted into this sought-after program; now a number of girls also attend the school.

A three-story building houses the administrative office, classrooms, hostel, prayer hall, and a small shop selling students' work at reasonable prices. If you would like to stop by, your tour guide can arrange a visit. The principal requests that visits be made in the late afternoon, when classes will not be disrupted. ⊠ *Tashi Gaypheling, Kawangjangsa, Thimphu,* ☎ *02/3–22302.* ⊙ *Daily 9–5.*

② SAARC Building. The National Assembly Hall is now situated in the South Asia Association for Regional Cooperation Building (SAARC), across the river from Tashichho Dzong. It was built in the early 1990s as a site for conferences for the heads of state and government. Bhutan's Planning and Foreign Ministries are housed here. ⊠ *Dechhen Lam, Thimphu,* ☎ *02/3–22473.* ⊙ *Daily 9–5.*

③ Tashichho Dzong. On the banks of the river lies Thimphu's most impressive structure, Tashichho Dzong. Its hundred-plus rooms house the seat of the government and the center for all religious affairs in the kingdom. The dzong also houses the throne room for His Majesty the King of Bhutan and in the warmer months, the monk body headed by His Holiness, the Je Khenpo, also makes its home here.

In 1216, a dzong called Blue Stone was built high above the Thimphu Valley, where Dechen Phodrang now stands. A few years later, the dzong changed hands and became the property of Shabdrung Ngawang Namgyal, a descendant of Lama Drigom Shigpo Phajo Drukpa Kagyu. It was then renamed Tashichho Dzong, Fortress of the Glorious Religion. Namgyal decided to house both the monk body and the civil officials within the same structure, although in a short time, he found the space to be too small. He later built another larger dzong, in the lower valley.

The original dzong burned in 1771 and all of its inhabitants, as well as the government officials, moved to the lower dzong, which was expanded. The dzong burned three more times and suffered damages from an earthquake. In 1961, King Jigme Dorji Wangchuck designated Thimphu as the capital city. Between 1962 and 1969 he authorized a complete renovation of Tashichho Dzong, following the traditional building codes. The entire dzong was built without nails or architectural plans.

Unlike most dzongs, Tashichho has two main entrances. One leads to the administrative section, the other to the monastic quarter, where the annual tsechu dances are performed. In the center of its four massive wings, stands a tall square citadel, or *utse*—one of the complex's original buildings—decorated with tantric symbols and containing many of Bhutan's finest religious paintings. ⊠ *Chhagchhen Lam, Thimphu.*

A Good Walk

Since Thimphu is situated on a hillside, in a valley, alongside a river, the scenery is breathtaking. In order to get a glimpse of the landscape at its finest, you need to ascend to a lookout point above the town. This walk takes you west, just above the main thoroughfare to a monastery perched on a ridge overlooking the valley. The views from Changangkha are superb.

Start the walk at the old clock tower in the center of town. Walk south down Wogzin Lam. At the T-junction, where the gas station is on your left, turn right onto Dzogchen Lam, and walk uphill towards the **Memorial Chorten** ⑦, built in memory of His Majesty the third king of Bhutan. Upon exiting the chorten, bear right onto Doebom Lam, take the first left onto Rapten Lam, and continue up the hill. When you get to the electrical transformer, turn left onto a narrow road, and walk to the small parking lot at its end. To the left is a small footpath that leads to a set of stone steps. Climb up to **Changangkha Lhakhang** ⑧, a temple nestled on a ridge with spectacular views of the valley. To return to town by a different route, turn right onto Rapten Lam and continue back down the hill to Doebom Lam. Once you reach the junction, turn left, and after a few hundred yards, the **Bhutan Olympic Sports Complex** ⑨ will be on your right. Continue walking all the way to the northern traffic circle. Turn right onto Norzin Lam, and you will be heading back towards the center of town.

If you are feeling a bit more adventurous and don't mind adding a few hours to your excursion, turn left out of Chagangkha Lhakhang and continue up the hill on Theghhen Lam. The road is curvy and takes a sharp bend towards the right, turning into Seriya Lam. At the top of the road is a T-junction; turn left onto Thori Lam. Follow this road for a while, past an extremely long red-and-yellow fence that encloses the home of Her Royal Highness, Ashi Dechen Wangmo Wangchuck, the king's sister. Eventually you will come to a fork in the road. Bear right onto Menri Lam, which turns into Gaden Lam, a long winding road with great views of Thimphu and the surrounding valley. On the right is **Drubthob Monastery** ⑩, which is currently inhabited by the Zilukha nunnery. The road switches back, heading you right back towards the main town.

TIMING

If you take the short route up to Changangkha Lhakhang, the walk can be done in about two hours, depending on how long you linger to take in the views along the way. If you choose the long, winding road around Thimphu, past the monastery, it will take you approximately four hours.

Sights to See

⑨ **Bhutan Olympics Sports Complex.** Thimphu's only indoor sports complex houses a swimming pool, basketball court, and gym. The pool is open to travelers. Many sporting events and tournaments take place here; check to see if anything is scheduled while you are in town. ⊠ *Doebum Lam,* ☎ *02/3–22064.* ☑ *Varies with event.* ☉ *Weekdays 4– 8, weekends 1–6.*

⑧ **Changangkha Lhakhang.** The temple is situated on a ridge high above Thimphu. Fluttering prayer flags adorn the courtyard, where the view of the valley is spectacular. Changangkha is one of the oldest temples in the valley, built in the 15th century by a descendant of Lamo Phajo Drugom Shigpo, the founder of the Drukpa school in Bhutan. Although tourists may not enter, the inner walls of the temple are said to be decorated with remarkable paintings, including a noted painting of Tsangpa Gyare Dorje, the founder of the Drukpa school in Tibet. ⊠ *Entrance at the end of Thegchhen Lam, Thimphu.*

⑩ Drubthob Monastery. This small monastery is located on the road that runs high above the dzong. The name comes from the incarnation of the saint Drubthob Thangton Gyelpo. The monastery is currently inhabited by the Zilukha nunnery. ⊠ *Gaden Lam, Thimphu.*

❼ Memorial Chorten. The Memorial Chorten is one of Thimphu's most prominent landmarks. It was built in 1974 in memory of the third king, Jigme Dorji Wangchuck, by his mother, the Royal Grandmother, Ashi Phuntsho Choegron. Within the walls of this Tibetan-style chorten are numerous tantric statues and religious paintings. Unlike other chortens, this one does not contain any remains of the king. The Memorial Chorten is a good introduction to Tantric Buddhism in all its complexity. Try to visit this religious site with a guide who can explain the principles of Tantric Buddhism and interpret the symbols found inside. ⊠ *At the junction of Chorten Lam and Doebom Lam, Thimphu.* ☉ *Daylight hours.*

NEED A BREAK?
In the heart of Thimphu is the perfect place to stop for a quick bite or linger over coffee and pastries, **Swiss Bakery** (⊠ Norzin Lam, just above the southern traffic circle, Thimphu, ☎ 02/3–22259). This eating establishment has been a favorite of expatriates for years. The closest thing in Thimphu to a fast-food restaurant, the bakery serves tasty cheese sandwiches with a secret sauce and hamburgers. The pastries here are not to be missed; a few house specialties are linzer tortes, rum balls, Swiss rolls, and sweet buns.

OFF THE BEATEN PATH
Motithang Mini Zoo. Thimphu's zoo, on the outskirts of town, has an unusually lovely story. Many years ago, the king decided that keeping animals in captivity was very much against Bhutan's moral principles, and he released the zoo animals into the wild. However, the tame takins, Bhutan's national animal, rare bovid mammals, found their way back and wandered the busy streets of Thimphu. Thus, the animals were put back into an enclosed area and are looked after by a caretaker. The "zoo," a large area enclosed by a mesh fence, is on the hill behind Motithang, and has beautiful views of the valley. It's home to about a dozen takins and a yak. ⊠ *Motithang, Thimphu.* ☉ *Daylight hours.*

Dining

Chances are you will eat the majority of your meals in hotels with your tour group. However, Thimphu has a growing number of good restaurants, so you may want to skip a few prearranged meals to see what the city has to offer. If you choose to do this, particularly in peak season, ask your guide to make reservations for you.

$$ ✕ The Blue Poppy. Opened in 1999, this spacious, airy restaurant has a relaxed atmosphere. Light-wood furniture and checkered tablecloths are juxtaposed with traditional Bhutanese paintings. The fare is Bhutanese, Indian, and Chinese, and is quite good. A few items worth sampling are chicken chili, paneer masala, and of course ema datsi, Bhutan's noted chili and cheese dish. ⊠ *2nd floor, above Bhutan Arts & Crafts Centre, Norzin Lam, Thimphu,* ☎ 02/3–22003. *No credit cards. Closed Sun.*

$$ ✕ Plum's Café. Although Plum's is a little difficult to find, it is definitely worth the search. An old favorite with expats and the Bhutanese, ★ it serves a wide variety of Asian food in a bistrolike setting. Almost everything on the menu is delicious, but the double crispy fried pork deserves special praise. Ask the owner about his secret recipe dishes that are not listed on the menu, particularly the fresh catch of the day. The kitchen's open daily, 11 AM to 10 PM. ⊠ *2nd floor, above the shops* *at the southern traffic circle, Thimphu,* ☎ *02/3–24307. Reservations essential. No credit cards.*

$$
★ ✗ **Restaurant Rabten.** This is the only restaurant in Thimphu that serves pure Bhutanese cuisine. You get the feeling that you are dining in someone's living room when you eat at this charming restaurant. Meals are served in a traditional room, decorated with beautifully carved tables, embroidered pillows, and paintings. Seating is on comfortable couches. The food is excellent and the presentation exquisite. A few of the best items on the menu are noodle dishes, some made with *puta,* a buckwheat noodle, and *phinda bjeli namchu,* a soybean noodle. Try the *paccha tsoem,* a tender cane shoot that is seasonal. Ask the proprietor to see the spice basket, where she has fine examples of Bhutanese spices, dried river weed, mushrooms, and chilies, to name a few. Outside there is a grassy area for cultural shows and bonfires. This is not a place where you can drop in; make reservations well in advance. ✉ *Thori Rd., Thimphu,* ☎ *02/3–23021. Reservations essential. No credit cards.*

$ ✗ **89 Restaurant.** Frequented by expats, this restaurant consistently serves good food at reasonable prices. Dark-wood paneling and plaid napkins and tablecloths give the place a cozy feel. Try the spaghetti Milanese, cheese momos, and potato skins. ✉ *Chorten Lam, Thimphu,* ☎ *02/3–22931. No credit cards.*

$ ✗ **Jichu Drakey Bakery.** Although it's not a restaurant, this small bakery is certainly worth mentioning. Located within the Yeedzin Guest House complex, it offers delicious pastries, cakes, and pies for takeout. The owner was trained as an apprentice pastry chef in Austria, land of the Sacher torte. A few of the scrumptious desserts are the Sacher cake, cream roll, apple pie, and eclairs. ✉ *Jangchun Lam, Thimphu,* ☎ *02/3–22980. No credit cards.*

$ ✗ **Tandin Restaurant.** The greatest draw of this restaurant is the Indian food, including tandoori chicken, fish curry, and naan bread. If you do not savor the flavors of curry and masala spices, there is also an extensive Continental menu. Be prepared (and patient): the wait staff speaks little English. ✉ *2nd floor of the Druk Shopping Complex, Norzin Lam, Thimphu,* ☎ *02/3–23380. No credit cards.*

Lodging

There is a wide variety of accommodations in Thimphu. During the last few years, a few large, modern hotels have opened, creating a new traveler's market. Excellent alternatives to the bigger hotels are the selection of small, family-run guest houses, which provide an opportunity for cultural exchange with the Bhutanese.

In most of the larger hotels, the suites and some of the deluxe rooms have televisions and VCRs available upon request. They are probably the only rooms in Thimphu that have minibars, and some even have a bidet. You will notice when traveling in Thimphu and other parts in Bhutan that you will often dine in your hotel or guest house, and the restaurants within these establishments are very good, if not better, than the other restaurants around town.

$$$$
★ ✗🏨 **Hotel Druk.** One of the biggest hotels in Thimphu, located in the heart of the business area, Hotel Druk is also considered to be one of the best. It's small in comparison to most Western hotels but offers many of their standard facilities. The rooms are reasonably sized and decorated in a luxurious yet unoriginal style, with wall-to-wall carpeting and standard contemporary hotel furniture. The modern restaurant has a small lounge that is a good place to have a drink. If you're pressed for time, the Druk is the only place that caters to a business crowd by offering a set lunch. There is also a large multicuisine menu, with an

emphasis on Indian food. The service in both the hotel and restaurant is excellent and the staff very attentive. ⊠ *Wogzin Lam, Thimphu,* ☎ *02/3–22966,* FAX *02/3–22677. 37 rooms. Restaurant, room service, beauty salon, massage, sauna, exercise room, laundry service, meeting room. No credit cards.*

$$$ ✕⊞ **Hotel Druk-Yul.** At press time, this centrally located hotel was making renovations, including the addition of a few floors and an Internet facility. Rooms are spacious, and each has a separate sitting area. The restaurant serves tasty food, with an emphasis on Continental dishes. A few specialties include the bionic Druk-Yul burger, giant vegetable club sandwich, and drums of heaven (chicken drumsticks). On Friday night, the banquet hall transforms into the Hub, a discotheque that attract both young Bhutanese and travelers alike. ⊠ *Norzin Lam, Thimphu,* ☎ *02/ 3–25714,* FAX *02/3–23592. 39 rooms. Restaurant, dance club, laundry service, meeting room, travel services. No credit cards.*

$$$ ✕⊞ **Hotel Riverview.** This large Western-style hotel on the river is one of the most luxurious in town. While not opulent by Western standards, the Riverview is very clean and comfortable. The public rooms are tastefully decorated, and there is even a gift shop, albeit overpriced. All the rooms are done in a fairly standard hotel style and have river views. The spacious restaurant has great views, so try to get a seat by the window. The menu of hearty Continental dishes includes Hungarian goulash, chicken-in-a-basket, and pork chops with apple sauce. One drawback is the slightly unfriendly front-desk staff. ⊠ *Dechhen Lam, Thimphu,* ☎ *02/3–23497,* FAX *02/3–23496. 50 rooms. Restaurant, laundry service, meeting room, business services. No credit cards.*

$$$ ✕⊞ **Hotel Taktsang.** In the midst of the shopping district, Taktsang has all the amenities of a Western hotel, including the Pelphug Arak bar, a beauty salon, and travel services. There is nothing particularly charming about this place, but it does a great job of providing large, basic, clean rooms, all with marble bathrooms. The Orchid restaurant serves good, if uninventive, Bhutanese, Chinese, Indian and Continental dishes, including pork escalope Viennoise (lightly breaded and sautéed) and beef Stroganoff. It's the only place in town that has a special Japanese menu catering to Japanese travelers. ⊠ *Doibum Lam, Thimphu,* ☎ *02/3–22102,* FAX *02/3–23284. 34 rooms. Restaurant, bar, room service, beauty salon, laundry service, travel services. AE.*

$$$ ✕⊞ **Pinewood Hotel.** One of the newer additions to Thimphu's selection
★ of accommodations, this hotel is located on a hill across the river, with a spectacular view of the valley. The creative proprietor has decorated each room in a different color, right down to the bathrooms. At night, the dining room offers a beautiful view of the lights of Thimphu. There is no set menu, since dishes vary according to the fresh ingredients that are available. There is always a fisherman's catch of the day, a seasonal vegetable, and a dessert special. House specialties include fried chicken, coconut prawn curry, and carrot cake. Richard Gere stayed here on one of his jaunts to Bhutan. ⊠ *Above Yanchenphug High School, Thimphu,* ☎ *02/3–25924,* FAX *02/3–25507. 10 rooms. Restaurant, room service, laundry service, travel services. No credit cards.*

$$ ✕⊞ **Hotel Jumolhari.** This spacious hotel, centrally located on a main street, falls somewhere between the smaller guest houses and the large new hotels of Thimphu. Rooms are tidy, with wall-to-wall carpeting and a hint of traditional Bhutanese style in their embroidered pillows and decorative paintings. The restaurant serves the ubiquitous combo of Asian standards, plus a few interesting Western dishes. Notable entrées include the grilled chicken with rosemary sauce and the fish fillet tartare. Be prepared to wait for your meal: the service tends to be on the slow side. ⊠ *Wogzin Lam,* ☎ *02/3–22747,* FAX *02/3–24412. 27 rooms. Restaurant, laundry service, meeting room. No credit cards.*

$$ ✕⊞ **Hotel Motithang.** Operated by the Bhutan Tourism Corporation Limited, this traditional Bhutanese-style hotel has clean rooms complemented by a full range of modern amenities, such as IDD telephones and abundant hot water. Wood paneling, checkered tablecloths, and a stuffed bear in the hallway give the place a rustic feel. There's a small bar with an oversized fireplace adjacent to the dining room. The restaurant serves the usual combo of Asian cuisines and has an extensive dessert menu that's worth trying. The one disadvantage to Motithang is its location, which is quite a distance from the town center. ⊠ *Motithang, Thimphu,* ☎ *02/3–23889,* FAX *02/3–23392. 15 rooms. Restaurant, bar, room service, laundry service. No credit cards.*

$$ ✕⊞ **Wangchuck Hotel.** Overlooking the stadium, this hotel has pleasant rooms with traditional Bhutanese-style decor. The helpful staff make this a comfortable place to stay, and it's frequented by expats and their guests. Bhutanese, Chinese, Continental, and Indian standards are served, and the kitchen staff knows just how to prepare them. ⊠ *Chang Lam, Thimphu,* ☎ *02/3–23532,* FAX *02/3–25174. 20 rooms. Restaurant, room service, laundry service. V.*

$ ✕⊞ **Druk Sherig Hotel.** Druk Sherig's self-proclaimed title, "Your Bhutanese Home," couldn't be more accurate. It provides a rare blend of tradition and modern comfort. The hotel has long been a favorite of expats and business travelers. All the rooms have traditional wood-carved trimmings that are exquisitely painted and adorned with Bhutanese thangkas. At press time, plans were being finalized for an upgrade of all the rooms and the construction of Thimphu's first open terrace restaurant. A small traditional Bhutanese restaurant is tucked away upstairs and serves wholesome, good food. The extended family and friends that run the hotel are very friendly and helpful. ⊠ *Wogzin Lam, Thimphu,* ☎ *02/3–23911,* FAX *02/3–22714. 12 rooms. Restaurant, room service, laundry service, business services, travel services. No credit cards.*

$ ✕⊞ **Yeedzin Guest House.** This family-run guest house makes you feel right home. Rooms are large and airy, with dark furniture and wooden floors. A few even have bathrooms with a sunken tub and a bidet. If you plan on staying for an extended amount of time, this is the place to go, since some of the rooms even have their own kitchen. Each floor has a windowed sitting area with upholstered chairs and couches, great for trading stories with other travelers. The cozy restaurant has a fireplace, cupboards, and lots of plants, including ivy growing along the rafters. An eclectic blend of dishes are served, with favorites including mushroom Mornay, fried chicken, and Singapore fried rice. ⊠ *Jangchun Lam, Thimphu,* ☎ *02/3–22932,* FAX *02/3–24995. 19 rooms. Restaurant, laundry service. No credit cards.*

Nightlife and the Arts

Nightlife

A few nightclubs pop up around the city on the weekends. Saturday nights, the hip crowd heads to Club X, a small, hole-in-the-wall club with an eclectic design and "groovy" atmosphere. The banquet hall at Hotel Druk-Yul becomes the Hub discotheque every Friday night and is very popular with both young Bhutanese and travelers. Check the *Kuensel,* the national newspaper, to see if any programs are listed, or ask your tour guide what's happening in town. Occasionally, concerts and dances take place at the high school or other public locations. Many hotel bars in Thimphu get lively during the busy season. Stop by your hotel bar or lounge, where you're bound to find other travelers who want to stay up late, and have a good time.

All Stars. This brand-new disco is aimed at the ever-growing night scene populated by Thimphu's young and well-to-do. Wednesday is Ladies

Night, with free admission for women. The only other nights the disco is open are Friday and Saturday. ⊠ *Off Wogzin Lam, near Druk Sherig, Thimphu.* ☏ *Nu 300.*

Club X. In an alley off of Wogzin Lam, this small, cramped club attracts the young, hip, affluent crowd. Open on Saturday nights only, the place doesn't get hopping until around midnight. It gets steamy and loud, with a mix of rock and disco music and a happy-go-lucky DJ's techno beat. ⊠ *Off Wogzin Lam, near Druk Sherig, Thimphu,* ☎ 02/3–25901. ☏ *Nu 150.*

Hub. By day this place is a banquet hall, but on Friday night it turns into the current hot dance spot. DJ-spun music gets the crowd going and keeps everyone dancing until the wee hours. ⊠ *In the basement of the Hotel Druk-Yul,* ☎ 02/3–23592.

The Arts

During festival time, when numerous travelers descend upon the small town of Thimphu, there are many events scheduled, including cultural programs, traditional folk dances, and bonfires arranged by tour operators and hotels. The events are held at hotels and various outdoor locations set up specifically for this purpose.

If you are traveling in a group, your tour operator can arrange a formal dance performance at the Royal Academy of Performing Arts or in the more relaxed atmosphere of the Tashi Nencha Cultural Studio. Both of these performance venues provide exposure to Bhutanese cultural through a variety of entertainment programs. Reservations for these cultural programs should be made well in advance.

The Royal Academy of Performing Arts. Run by the Special Commission for Cultural Affairs, the academy was created with the objective of preserving, promoting, and developing the performance skills that are so special to the Bhutanese tradition. The academy performs mask dances, folk songs and dances, plays, dramas, and other stage performances. Depending on the weather, afternoon shows take place in an outdoor amphitheater or in the new indoor theater completed in 1998. ⊠ *Chubachu, Thimphu,* ☎ 02/3–22569. ☏ *Nu 2,600 to be divided among all guests.* ⊙ *Daily performances at 9:30* AM.

Tashi Nencha Cultural Studio. A group of talented musicians and performers provide an evening of cultural entertainment within the Zangto Pelri compound. The program usually begins with a bonfire, followed by traditional instrumental performances and folk and tribal dances. Arrangements can be made to include a traditional Bhutanese buffet dinner with your performance. Ask your guide to make the reservations at least a week in advance. A fee of Nu 3,000–Nu 5,000 is divided among all of the guests. ⊠ *Zangto Pelri, Thimphu,* ☎ 02/3–22804.

The Artshop Gallery. This is the first modern gallery to exhibit both modern and traditional artwork by several local artists. Adorning the walls are carefully chosen watercolors and pencil drawings on handmade paper. The owner also has a small selection of textiles, wooden bowls, and art supplies. ⊠ *Town Square, Thimphu,* ☎ 02/3–25664. *Closed Wed.*

Shopping

Most Bhutanese handicrafts are not made for a tourist market, so they retain their authenticity. The prices tend to be more expensive than those of goods found in other Asian countries. Thimphu has an excellent selection of handicraft shops selling high-quality traditional paintings, textiles, jewelry, masks, and carpets. Several shops on Norzin Lam have good selections of the textiles, both ready-made and handmade kiras and khos. The philatelic shop at the post office has a fine display of stamps in vibrant colors and vivid images ranging from holographic images, to Walt Disney, to First Day Issues. Even if you're not a collector, it's still well worth the visit.

There are also many local shops carrying basic necessities and general household items. It's fun to browse in these stores and check out the local merchandise. In the last few years, many modern shops have opened, selling imported goods from Taiwan, Thailand, and India. A few kitsch items often found include Barbie-like dolls wearing traditional Bhutanese clothing, action figures, and "I Love Mom" mugs.

Some shops pay a commission to tour guides bringing in large groups. It can be more fun to venture out on your own, or with a friend. Most stores have fixed prices, and although bargaining is not the custom here, it may be worth trying if you intend to purchase several items. Note: it is illegal to export antiques.

Check out some of the smaller shops, where the owners are usually available and are very friendly and helpful. For the most part, shops in Thimphu open around 8 AM and close around 8 or 9 PM depending on the season. Shops are open on the weekends, however those located on upper Norzin Lam are closed Tuesday, and those on lower market are closed on Wednesday.

Markets

The **weekly market** takes place every Saturday and Sunday, come rain or shine. This is where local residents come to catch up on the weekly gossip and buy their fresh fruit and vegetables for the coming week. If your itinerary allows you to be in Thimphu on the weekend, the market should not be missed. Bhutanese travel from all over, including remote areas, to sell their products.

Under roofed stalls, farmers preside over piles of chilies, potatoes, red and white rice, buckwheat, flour, mushrooms, cauliflower, and a wide variety of unidentifiable roots. Fresh fruit comes from local orchards and the southern flatlands. Colorful bananas, oranges, plums, peaches, mangoes, and pineapples overflow the erected platforms. Pungent odors lurk in the air from the assortment of dried cheeses, meats, and fish. At one end of the market is the meat department, with several carcasses waiting to be split. Strips of flesh hang on hooks, while piles of innards lie nearby. At the northern corner is the handicraft section, where you will find carpets, religious items, bamboo baskets, long musical horns, brass bowls, and textiles. The folks who sell their goods here are very friendly, and don't be surprised if one of the local monks assists you with your purchase. ⊠ *Chhogyal Lam, North of Chanlimithang Stadium, Thimphu.* ۞ *6 AM–sunset.*

Specialty Stores

HANDICRAFTS

Dolkar Handicrafts (⊠ Norzin Lam, ☎ 02/3–23324), a small shop run by a lovely woman, has an unusual collection of beautiful, turquoise-encrusted, antique equestrian saddles from Tibet and Lhadakh. There is also an interesting array of old wood carvings and traditional household items.

Norling Handicrafts (⊠ Norzin Lam, ☎ 02/3–23577) has two shops in Thimphu, both on Norzin Lam, a few doors away from each other. The small one has a wide selection of high-quality jewelry set with semi-precious stones and designed by the owner's grandmother. The larger shop offers many carpets and textiles. The nontraditional colored shawls in ice-blue, pink, and green pastels are designed by the owner's mother.

Bhutan Arts & Crafts (⌧ Norzin Lam, ☏ 02/3–23861) is a large new store that seems to have been designed for the traveler who can't fit India and Nepal into his or her itinerary; many products from these country's join the Bhutanese crafts. Upscale evening bags, silk pillowcases, and pashmina shawls are just a few of the specialized items in this salonlike store.

Handicrafts Emporium (⌧ Norzin Lam, ☏ 02/3–22810) is a big, government-run store, often touted as the official tourist store. Although, the decor is a bit sterile, there is a wide variety of textiles and clothing downstairs, and a fine selection of traditional furniture, religious objects, and books upstairs. The quality here is good, but prices are slightly inflated.

Druk Trin Rural Handicrafts Center (⌧ Jangchub Lam, ☏ 02/3–24500), the brainchild of an extremely successful businesswoman, has branch stores in the lobbies of some of the most prestigious hotels in Bhutan. The store on Jangchub Lam carries an excellent selection of woven textiles and embroidered linens; there's even an antique textile display.

Handicrafts Bhutan (⌧ Chang Lam, ☏ 02/3–24469) is a part of Cottage Industries, a local development project that benefits the women who make the crafts sold here. There's a great selection of handwoven textiles made with vegetable dye, as well as masks, bamboo baskets, and small bags. There is usually a weaver in the back room.

Choki Handicrafts (⌧ Kawangjangsa, ☏ 02/3–4728), located a few minutes' drive outside the city center, employs local painters, carvers, and weavers to design and make traditional handicrafts, furniture, and paintings. A portion of the proceeds benefits the Choki Traditional Art School for underprivileged students.

ARCHERY

The Archery Shop (⌧ Choten Lam, ☏ 02/3–23323), run by a group of very experienced archers, has two service technicians on staff and a service center. Specializing in American-made fiberglass bows, they also keep a stock of traditional bows and arrows. There's an indoor practice range for those who want to test the bows before purchasing.

Side Trips from Thimphu

There are many short day trips and walks around the Thimphu Valley. A day hike to the Chari and Tango monasteries provides outstanding views of the valley. Simtokha Dzong, the kingdom's oldest dzong, is a mere 10-minute drive outside the city limits, and is home to the School for Buddhist Studies. The Royal Botanical Gardens, which were inaugurated in May 1999, are a great place to relax and admire the beautiful surroundings.

⑭ **Cheri Goemba.** Located a short distance from the Tango monastery (☞ Tango Goembo, *below*), just across a picturesque covered bridge, is the Cheri Goemba, which is built on Cheri Mountain. The monastery was built in 1619, and the first monk body was established there by Shabdrung Ngawang Namgyal. ⌧ *North of Thimphu.*

⑮ **Phajoding Monastery.** One of the nicest walks you can take around the valley is the one to Phajoding, located west of Thimphu and overlooking the whole valley. The walk is through lovely wooded areas of pine and rhododendron, followed by a steep climb up to the monastery. Phajoding was built in the 15th century by the ninth Je Khenpo, Shakya Rinchen, head of Bhutan's religious order. It takes about six hours to complete the round-trip from Thimphu. ⌧ *Phajoding, northwest of Thimphu.*

⓫ **The Royal Botanical Gardens.** Just a 20-minute drive from Thimphu,
these beautiful gardens were inaugurated in May 1999. Elaborate
flower beds welcome you, and past the entrance, up a small hill, is a
waterfall that descends onto a prayer wheel chorten and flows under
a wooden cantilever bridge. At press time the gardens were closed to
the public while areas were undergoing renovations, slated to include
500 new varieties of temperate plants, a children's park, a rock garden, and several viewing points from which to take in the fabulous views
of the river and valley. When open, the information center will sell
seedlings and saplings of ornamental plants, souvenirs, and medicines
from the medicinal plant project. If you are interested in visiting the
gardens, ask your guide to make arrangements. ⊠ *Serbithang.*

⓬ **Simtokha Dzong.** The dzong's official name is Sangak Zabdhon Phodrang, "palace of the profound meaning of secret mantras." Built in
1629 by Shabdrung Ngawang Namgyal, most Bhutanese refer to Simtokha as the oldest dzong in the kingdom. The location is excellent,
because it offers views of the whole Thimphu Valley, as well as eastward towards Dochu La. Attacked by the Tibetans in 1634, Shabdrung's
army was victorious. The damaged dzong was restored in 1671 by the
third Druk Desi (secular ruler of Bhutan), Mingyur Tenpa. Today the
dzong houses the Rigney School for monastic studies. ⊠ *Simtokha.*

⓭ **Tango Goemba.** About 12 km (7 mi) from Thimphu, the Tango
monastery is a lovely place for an afternoon excursion. The drive or
walk to reach it offers beautiful views of the countryside and the Thimphu Valley. The monastery dates back to the 13th century and was rebuilt in the 15th century by the "divine madman," Lama Drukpa
Kunley. Drukpa Kunley earned his moniker through his wanderer's
lifestyle, eccentric behavior, and style of teaching religion through
song. Plan on bringing a picnic lunch with you, because there are no
restaurants nearby. ⊠ *North of Thimphu.*

Thimphu A to Z

Arriving and Departing

If you are traveling on a tourist visa, your tour operator will arrange
all your transportation within Bhutan. The tourist tariff includes all transportation, and you will always have car, driver, and guide with you.

BY AIRPLANE

The only airport in Bhutan is the **Paro International Airport** (☞ Paro
A to Z, *above*).

Between the Airport and City: Your tour operator will arrange to have
a car transport you between the airport in Paro and Thimphu. The ride
takes approximately 1½ hours.

BY TAXI

All taxis in Thimphu are privately owned and are usually found on
Chang Lam, just above the stadium. All taxis are required by the Road
Safety & Transport Authority to use a fare meter. At press time, taxi
operators were opposing the meters and removing them from their cars,
thus using flat rates that are always open to negotiation.

Taxis in Thimphu as a whole are very affordable by Western standards.
Unfortunately since they are privately owned, you cannot call to sum-
mon a car. However, you can flag down a taxi, or go to the designated
taxi stands. Although you will probably always have a vehicle at your
disposal, you might like to get away and explore Thimphu on your
own, or visit a particular restaurant or store. If you take a taxi to your

desired location, you will have to pay the driver additional money in order to have him wait for you.

Contacts and Resources

CURRENCY EXCHANGE

Most hotels can exchange cash and traveler's checks. However, hotels occasionally run out of cash. You can also change money at the banks and at the foreign-exchange counter at the airport. There may be a small charge for check cashing at these locations, but the rates are very good. Although your trip is fully prepaid, you will need to exchange some currency in order to pay for drinks, tips, and souvenirs.

Bank of Bhutan (✉ Norzin Lam, ☎ 02/3–22266) works in conjunction with the government and the state bank of India and still uses handwritten ledgers; so don't expect a quick transaction.

Bhutan National Bank (✉ Dremton Lam, ☎ 02/3–22767), a new, modern bank, was established in 1997, is run by a computer system, and deals directly with overseas banks. The bank was recently approved to act as the official representative in Bhutan for Visa.

EMERGENCIES

Ambulance (☎ 112), **fire** (☎ 110), **police** (☎ 113).

Jigme Dorji Wangchuck National Referral Hospital (✉ Gongphel Lam, ☎ 02/3–22620) has several Western doctors on staff and is equipped to handle emergencies 24 hours a day. Among the services they provide are X rays, dentistry, ultrasound, blood screening, gynecology, and pediatric care. They have their own pharmacy.

ENGLISH-LANGUAGE BOOKSTORES

DSB Enterprises (✉ Wogzin Lam, ☎ 02/3–23123), opposite the clock tower, in the heart of the business district, has an extensive selection of English books, newspapers, magazines, and cards. They have a selection of books on Bhutan, Buddhism, and the Himalayas.

Pe Khang Enterprises (✉ Luger Theater Complex, Norzin Lam, ☎ 02/3–24777) carries English books, newspapers, and magazines, including a large selection of children's books.

POST OFFICE

Central post office (✉ Drentoen Lam, just off of Norzin Lam, ☎ 02/3–23103).

You can also receive mail through the care of American Express Travel Services. **Chhundu Travel and Tours** (✉ Box 149, Thimphu, ☎ 02/3–22592), on Norzin Lam, is an official American Express agent.

VISITOR INFORMATION

Tourism Authority of Bhutan. Popularly known as TAB, this office oversees all tourism activities in Bhutan. TAB is responsible for promoting and marketing tourism, organizing in-country programs, processing tour payments, arranging certain visas and permits, and if needed, handling tourist emergencies. Contact them if you have any questions or would like a complete listing of registered Bhutanese tour operators. ✉ *Doebom Lam,* ☎ *02/3–23251 or 02/3–23252, TAB@druknet.net.bt.* ☉ *Weekdays 9–5.*

WESTERN BHUTAN

Western Bhutan, home of the Drukpa people, is an area that begins west of Paro Valley and continues east to the Black Mountains, a natural boundary dividing the country. The region offers incredible mountain views, some of the most fertile land in the country, the oldest dzongs in the country, ethnic yak herders, and the rare black-necked cranes.

Punakha

77 km (48 mi) east of Thimphu.

The road from Simtokha, just a few miles outside Thimphu, winds into pine forests and passes by waterfalls, chortens, and prayer flags, travelling through small villages before heading up to the Dochula Pass at an altitude of 10,500 ft. On a clear day, the scenery is spectacular; you get a panoramic view of the eastern Himalayan range, including Kanchenjunga and Mount Everest. For the next two hours of the drive, the road slowly descends into the lowlands of the Punakha Valley. Due to its warmer climate, Punakha is one of the most fertile valleys in Bhutan. The vast array of vegetation changes colors from season to season, turning multitudes of beautiful browns and greens.

Just before you arrive in the village of Lobesa, you will see Chimi Lhakhang, a temple dedicated to a Tibetan mystic, Drukpa Kunley, known as the "divine madman." The temple is on a hillside in the middle of rice fields and has become a pilgrimage site for childless couples. Before Thimphu became the capital city in 1955, Punakha held the designation. Punakha Dzong is the winter home of the central monk body, which spends the warmer months in the Tashichho Dzong in Thimphu (☞ *above*), and the Je Khenpo (Head of Bhutan's religious order). If your visit coincides with the monks' migration from Punakha to Thimphu, you may be witness to the ceremonial procession.

In the 13th century, when Drukpa Kunley, "the divine madman," was destroying demons in Bhutan, he shot an arrow and said a monastery would appear where it landed. **Chimi Lhakhang** was the fulfillment of his prophecy. To destroy even more demons, Drukpa Kunley relied on more than his bow and arrow. He used his penis, which was allegedly as long as the length of his body. Those who honor him have painted phallic symbols on each side of their homes to ward off evil spirits. They also visit this monastery and worship his unusual statue, complete with his famous organ. To devotees, the penis is father heaven, who inseminated mother earth to create mankind—male energy joining with female wisdom to create the cosmic whole. ✉ *Punakha.*

The **Punakha Dzong** is the winter home of the Je Khenpo, the religious head of Bhutan. Built in 1637, it is strategically placed at the confluence of Pho Chhu (male river) and Mo Chhu (female river), on the far side of a narrow suspension bridge. The full name of the dzong is Druk Pungthang Dechhen Phodrang, "palace of great happiness." In 1639, an addition was made in celebration of the victory of the Bhutanese against the Tibetans.

To enter the dzong, you cross over the bridge to the exterior grounds. To reach the main entrance pavilion, you climb steep wooden steps that were specially designed to be lifted up in case of invasion. Two oversized prayer wheels flank each side wall, and thangkas depicting the Four Guardian Deities protect the doorway and interior structures. This entrance leads to the administrative area; the monastic quarters are in a second courtyard.

The dzong was built by the first Shabdrung of Bhutan, Ngawang Namgyal. He died while in meditation here in 1651, and his embalmed body lies in perpetual state in the Machen Lhakhang, one of the 21 sacred temples within the dzong. Only the king and two lamas who are appointed to look after the temple may enter.

Four fires during the 18th and 19th centuries ravaged the dzong, destroying numerous historic documents. In 1807, an earthquake caused more damage. The dzong has been fully restored, but now the encroaching rivers pose a new threat. The coronation of the first king of Bhutan, Ugyen Wangchuck, took place here on December 17, 1907. ⊠ *West of Mo Chu River.*

Dining and Lodging

$$$ ✕⊡ **Hotel Zangthopelri.** Set on a spectacular sprawling estate high above
★ the valley, Hotel Zangthopelri is easily one of the most luxurious hotels in Bhutan. The main hotel is surrounded by several small cabins, all with a traditional Bhutanese flavor, colorful textiles, and private balconies. One of the highlights of Zangthopelri is the only hotel swimming pool in the country. At press time, a tennis court was under construction. The restaurant here serves delicious Bhutanese, Continental, Indian, and Chinese cuisines, as well as delicious baked goods made on the premises. ⊠ *Wolakha, Punakha,* ☎ *02/5–84125,* ⨋ *02/5–84236. 45 rooms. Restaurant, bar, pool, tennis court, laundry service, meeting room. No credit cards.*

$$ ✕⊡ **Meri Puensum Resort.** Opened in 1999, this lovely, small hotel has a very homey feel, with cheerful flower boxes, a big stone patio, and a cozy dining room. The charming proprietors run the place impeccably; the spacious rooms—each with a balcony overlooking the river— are always spic-and-span. The restaurant has an extensive menu with the traditional four cuisines. A few specials of the house include vegetables au gratin, several spicy chili dishes, and a crumble custard for dessert. ⊠ *Wolakha, Punakha,* ☎ *02/5–84195,* ⨋ *02/5–84236. 8 rooms. Restaurant, bar, laundry service. No credit cards.*

Wangdue Phodrang

98 km (61 mi) east of Thimphu.

Wangdue Phodrang, a small town with a bustling market and several shops, is the last western town on the highway before you reach central Bhutan. The most visible feature of the town is **Wangdue Phodrang Dzong,** a colossal structure built high on a ridge, at the confluence of the Mo Chhu and Tang Chhu rivers. This strategic position provides excellent views of the valleys below and the routes to Trongsa, Punakha, Dagana, and Thimphu. Thus for many centuries the dzong was the seat of one of Bhutan's most powerful penlops.

Although the location is the obvious reason for the dzong's location, there are, as usual, legends surrounding its construction in 1638. The first and more religious-based legend says that the protective deity Mahakala appeared to the Shabdrung and told him that the location where the dzong was to be built would be revealed to him by four ravens flying away in different directions from the confluence of two rivers. The second legend claims the dzong's construction was inspired by Shabdrung's encounter with a small boy named Wangdu who was playing with pebbles, constructing a *phodrang* (pebble fortress). Shabdrung saw the meeting as an omen and built the Wangdue Phodrang Dzong in this location, naming it in the child's honor. ⊠ *Wangdue Phodrang.*

Dining and Lodging

$$$ ✕⊡ **Kichu Resort.** Opened in 1999, this contemporary hotel is at the
★ confluence of the Baechhu and Danchhu rivers. The architecture is simply stunning. Arched ceilings and light-wood furniture and woodwork are complemented by whitewashed walls and white linens. Surrounding the main building are small cottages whose guest rooms face the river, so the sounds of the water can lull you to sleep. The dining room

is in the central building and has a circular seating area that faces the well-manicured grounds. The chef has developed an all-vegetarian menu that includes cucumber salad, vegetables au gratin, and an array of pasta dishes. ✉ *Chuzomsa, 11 km (6½ mi) from Wangdue Phodrang,* ☎ *02/4–81319,* FAX *02/4–81360. 22 rooms. Restaurant, bar, sauna, laundry service. No credit cards.*

$$ ✕⊡ **Dragon's Nest Lodge.** This hotel, built in 1997, is situated on the banks of the Punatsangchu River. The spacious, fully carpeted, modern rooms have attached baths with large tubs. The oversize windows that flank the far walls of the restaurant overlook the river; ask for a seat with a view. Catering to a Western palate, the menu features hearty spareribs, chicken sizzler, and a delicious crème caramel. ✉ *Wangdue Phodrang,* ☎ *02/4–81366,* FAX *02/4–81274. 17 rooms. Restaurant, bar, laundry service. No credit cards.*

$ ✕⊡ **Dechen Cottages.** A very steep unpaved road leads you to these secluded cabins in the woods. Most of the rooms have a veranda with a beautiful view across the valley towards the Talo and Dalinda monasteries. Each cottage has fine wood paneling, a handwoven Bhutanese textile bedcover, and its own wood-burning stove. In the center of the complex is a stone patio, where wooden benches surround a bonfire; it gives the place a summer-camp atmosphere. If there's a large group, the proprietor will arrange traditional singing and dancing in the evenings. The rustic-style dining room has a bar, and the chef cooks Bhutanese, Chinese, and Indian dishes. ✉ *Mendegang, near Wangdue Phodrang,* ☎ *02/3–22204. 18 rooms. Restaurant, bar, laundry service. No credit cards.*

Phobjikha Valley

156 km (97 mi) east of Thimphu.

Situated south of the main highway, and about 80 km (50 mi) southeast of Wangdue Phodrang, is **Gangtey Gompa,** a 17th-century monastery. To reach it, you travel through dense forests and rich pastures dotted with grazing yaks. The monastery is perched on a ridge overlooking the beautiful Phobjikha Valley and is the only Nyingmapa monastery west of the Black Mountains. On his visit to Phobjika, the famous Nyingmapa saint Pema Lingpa, the reincarnation of Guru Rimpoche and the philosopher Longchen Rabjampa, looked up from the valley floor at the spur of land where the Gangtey Gompa now sits and predicted that one day a monastery would rest upon the site. In fact, his grandson, Gyalse Pema Thinley, founded the monastery in 1613. The religious traditions of Pema Lingpa are still taught here today. The current abbot, Kunzang Pema Namgyal, is the ninth reincarnation of the saint. Gangtey is affiliated with other Nyingmapa gompas in Bhutan, including the home of Pema Lingpa, the Tamshing Gompa in the Bumthang Valley. The complex consists of the gompa itself, the monastic quarters, a small school, and up the hill, a retreat and mediation center for the monks that was founded by the Je Khenpo in 1990. Directly opposite the main entrance is a small guest house, where visitors can stay.

Just past the gompa, on the valley floor, is the village of **Phobjikha.** The beautiful, pristine valley and village are reached by a short detour from the main east–west highway. There are no telephones or electricity in the valley. The region, which borders the Black Mountain National Park, has been designated a conservation area by the Royal Society for the Protection of Nature and is considered one of the most important wildlife preserves in Bhutan. Every year in late October, rare black-necked cranes migrate here from the Tibetan plateau. The birds spend several months in Phobjikha before flying back across the mountains in mid-February.

In 1998, Bhutan's first Crane Festival took place in Phobjikha. Although the festival was originally for the Bhutanese, there has been talk about opening it to tourists. The festival coincides with His Majesty's birthday, November 11, so there are celebrations all over the country.

Western Bhutan A to Z
Arriving and Departing
The only way to get to Western Bhutan is by car or bus. Your tour operator will make all the necessary transportation arrangements for you.

Getting Around
As in the rest of Bhutan, you will be traveling with a guide and driver. Depending on your itinerary, the drive through the area will take approximately 2–4 days.

Contacts and Resources
CURRENCY EXCHANGE
The **Bank of Bhutan** has branches in Punakha and Wangdue Phodrang. Both branches can change traveler's checks, but not without a lot of time and paperwork. Some hotels may be able to exchange currency for you, but it is strongly recommended that you change money in Thimphu before heading east.

EMERGENCIES
Ambulance (☎ 112), **fire** (☎ 110), **police** (☎ 113).

POST OFFICE
There are post office branches in Punakha (☎ 02/5–84122) and Wangdue Phodrang (☎ 02/4–81205). However, delivery from these locations is slow and unreliable, so try to send your letters from Thimphu or Paro.

CENTRAL BHUTAN

The central region of Bhutan encompasses many different ethnic groups, a variety of architecture, and vast changes in landscape. The road east of Wangdue Phodrang climbs past waterfalls, dense forests, and scurrying monkeys, leading you to Pele La at 3,301 m (10,824 ft). The breathtaking views here include sheer cliffs, sweeping valleys, clusters of prayer flags blowing in the wind, and mountains in the distance.

The route across the pass descends through the lush forests of the Longte Valley. After Chendebji Chorten, the road drops into the valley of Mangde Chhu, an area that was once protected by the massive Trongsa Dzong (☞ *below*). As you continue your journey to the east, you will see fewer cars and trucks and more pony caravans. The four valleys of Bumthang await you in all their splendor and glory, the historic and cultural heart of the kingdom. Here, old traditions prevail, and the modern age is light-years away. Ura, the easternmost valley in central Bhutan, has been the site of discoveries of prehistoric settlements. The village of Ura is the last before the climb to Bhutan's highest pass, Thumsing La (3,802 m/12,465 ft).

Trongsa
227 km (141 mi) east of Thimphu.

After passing the Nikka Chhu, the road follows the river into the Trongsa district, first leading you into the small, scenic village of Chendebji. The **Chendebji Chorten,** a large, whitewashed structure, sits beside a stream. Built in the 19th century by Lama Shida, the chorten was designed in traditional Nepalese style, with all-knowing eyes painted in each cardinal direction. A carved band of Buddhas wraps around its midsection. Nearby, an enormous mani wall, made of stones carved with the Buddhist mantra "om maani padme hum," protects the village with its inscribed prayers and images of Buddha.

On the east side of the trail sits a Bhutanese-style chorten, built in 1982, by Her Majesty the Queen Mother.

Trongsa is a four-hour drive from Wangdue Phodrang and a welcome rest to travelers. Built at the traditional key vantage point, the Trongsa Dzong sits imperiously above the valley and the neighboring countryside. From a vantage point on the opposite side of the valley, across the river, there is a clear view of the entire enormous dzong. The view is simply spectacular, as the road drops down into a steep gorge and then slowly climbs up to the commanding fortress, which towers over the nearby homes and buildings. Once you see the dzong, it is another 14 km (9 mi) around the side of the valley to the town. The approach that circles the valley clings to the sides of the mountains, while just past its edge are sheer drops straight down to the river. All the way into town you have great views of the dzong.

Trongsa is the ancestral home to the Royal family. Both His Majesty King Ugyen Wangchuck, the Penlop of Trongsa, who was the country's first hereditary monarch, and his successor, King Jigme Wangchuck, ruled from the dzong here. Traditionally, the Crown Prince of Bhutan becomes the Penlop of Trongsa before ascending the throne.

Trongsa is a charming town, comprised of traditional wooden houses lined up in a row, perched on the side of a hill. Many local women weave traditional textiles from hand-dyed wool and can often be observed practicing their craft at the looms in their shops. Trongsa is also a great place to buy carpets, since the prices in shops here are more reasonable than those in Thimphu.

Situated on a bluff, overlooking the steep Mangde Chhu River Valley, is the impregnable fortress of the **Trongsa Dzong,** the most impressive dzong in Bhutan. Ta Dzong, the watchtower that once guarded the dzong, stands just above it on a hill. The dzong itself is a maze of 23 temples, corridors, beautiful stone courtyards, and administrative offices.

The dzong was built in 1647 under the orders of Shabdrung Ngawang Namgyal. The Shabdrung also appointed Chhogyal Minjur Tenpa as the first Penlop of Trongsa. Gradually, the dzong was expanded, and in 1652 the Ta Dzong was built.

The dzong was enlarged on several occasions. Tshokey Dorji, the Penlop of Trongsa in the latter half of the 19th century, restored the dzong and built the dukhor lhakhang, a ceremonial room. Later, Penlop Jigme Namgyal, the father of Bhutan's first king, made further improvements to the structure. His son, King Ugyen Wangchuck, ordered the design of most of the existing decoration, including a large statue of Buddha of the Future that was erected in the beginning of the 20th century. In the entrance to the main hall, there is a painting of Zangtopelri, the heaven of Guru Rimpoche. Also in the main hall is a 17th-century mural depicting Swayambunath, in Nepal. ✉ *Trongsa.*

Dining and Lodging

$$ ✕▥ **Sherubling Lodge.** Sherubling is on a ridge with a beautiful view of the dzong. The courteous and pleasant management here strives to ensure that guests enjoy their stay. The small, traditionally decorated rooms have brightly colored local textiles for bedspreads and curtains. They also have IDD phones and heaters. The small lounge adjacent to the dining room has windows that face the dzong. Like other hotel restaurants in Bhutan, they serve Bhutanese, Indian, Chinese, and Continental food. ✉ *Sherubling, Trongsa,* ☎ *03/5–21116,* FAX *03/5–21107. 14 rooms. Restaurant, bar, laundry service. No credit cards.*

$ ✕ **Nida Karsum Lodge.** Situated at the southern end of town, this small, local lodge is run by a lovely woman named Tshering Dolma. If you need a quick bite, there is always some delicious Bhutanese food cooking on the stove here. If you're lucky and the place isn't too crowded, you can sit in the kitchen and chat with Tshering. Otherwise, there is a small dining room. ✉ *Trongsa,* ☎ *03/5–21133. No credit cards.*

$ ✕ **The Norling Hotel.** This nondescript cement building is right in the center of town. Good, basic Bhutanese, Chinese, and Indian food is served in a sparsely decorated dining room. ✉ *Trongsa,* ☎ *03/5– 21171. No credit cards.*

Bumthang Valley

295 km (183 mi) east of Thimphu; 68 km (42 mi) east of Tongsa.

The Yutongla Pass and a series of hold-onto-your-seat bends in the road at an elevation of 11,500 ft, separate the valley of Trongsa from the wide valleys of Bumthang. As you travel eastward, you will feel as though you have traveled further and further back in time. This region is home to Bhutan's founding and reigning dynasty, as well as its most famous saints and teachers, and is truly the spiritual heartland of the kingdom. A *bumpa* is an oblong-shaped vessel that contains holy water and *thang* means plain or field. Thus, the name Bumthang means "the field or plains shaped like a bumpa."

Bumthang is actually comprised of four valleys, Jakar (also known as Choekor), Tang, Chume, and Ura. However, Jakar contains the most important Dzongs and temples of the Bumthang region, and for that reason is often what is meant when the Bhutanese refer to the Bumthang Valley.

A Good Strategy

In the wide valley of Jakar lies the **Jakar Dzong,** Castle of the White Bird, and many other holy shrines and sacred institutions. At the far end of the valley are **Jampa Lhakhang** and the **Kurjey Monastery.** Also in this part of the valley is a rock that retains an imprint of Guru Rimpoche's body; left from his meditation there in the 8th century. You can drive or trek 17 km (10 ½ mi) from Kurjey to **Thangbi Lhakhang,** a temple founded in 1470. In the eastern part of the valley, about 5 km (3 mi) from the Jakar Dzong, is **Tamshing Lhakhang,** the most important Nyingma gompa in Bhutan.

Sights to See

Jakar Dzong. This palatial dzong, also known as Castle of the White Bird, is situated on the crest of a hill. According to legend, when the lamas were trying to decide where to build the dzong, a white bird rose into the air and landed on the spur of the hill, revealing the chosen location. The dzong was built as a monastery in the 16th century by Ngagi Wangchuck, who became the Bumthang after founding Trongsa. In the middle of the 17th century, the dzong was enlarged by the Penlop of Trongsa, Mijur Tenpa, according to the orders of Shabdrung Ngawang Namgyal. In 1897, the dzong was badly damaged by a fire and an earthquake. It was rebuilt shortly thereafter by the future first king, Ugyen Wangchuck. Additional renovations were carried out by the second king. In order to protect the dzong from invaders, an impressive wall approximately 2 km (1 mi) in circumference surrounds the fortress. In its center, a tower soars nearly 150 ft into the air. Upon entering the dzong, you pass through the administrative courtyard area. Just beyond is the utse, which contains paintings that depict the life of Milarepa. During the winter, the monk body from Trongsa moves here. ⊠ *Jakar, Bumthang.*

Jampa Lhakhang. According to legend, Jampa Lhakhang was one of the 108 temples built by King Songtsen Gampo of Tibet in order to overcome a giant ogress who laid across regions of Tibet and the Himalayas in order to prevent the spread of Buddhism. It is believed to have been built in AD 638, on the same day as Kyichu Lhakhang in Paro, and was constructed on the ogress's left knee.

The temple was visited by the Guru Rimpoche during a visit to Bumthang in the 8th century. It was on this same visit that he cured the Sindhu Raja, Sendha Gyab, an Indian who established himself as king of Bumthang, from a serious ailment and converted him to the Buddhist faith. It was renovated in the 8th century, and subsequent penlops have kept it in excellent repair. Among the many repairs and renovations was the addition of a gold-leaf roof to the central tower in the late 19th century.

The central figure in the main sanctuary is the statue of Jampa, the Buddha of the Future, which is surrounded by iron chain mail made by Pema Lingpa. Also inside the main sanctuary are three stone steps believed to represent past, present, and future. They are slowly sinking into the ground, with the first level already flush with the floor. The faithful say that when the other steps disappear the Future Buddha will arrive. Four additional temples were built in the mid-19th century, creating a closed courtyard in front of the main sanctuary.

Every October, the Jampa Lhakhang Tsechu, a religious festival, is held here. It is the only time visitors are allowed to enter. Infertile women come to get blessed by the lamas, in the hope that they will bear children. ⊠ *Jakar, Bumthang.*

Kurjey Lhakhang. At the end of the road that follows the Bumthang river sits the Kurjey Lhakhang complex. This is considered one of the most sacred sites in Bhutan. In the 8th century, the Guru Rimpoche meditated here and left his bodily imprint on a rock.

After you pass through the large gate into the complex, there are three lhakhangs (temples) situated on the right, all facing south. The first is the oldest and was built in 1652 by Minjur Tenpa when he was the penlop, before he became the Third Desi of Bhutan. The temple was built on the rock where Guru Rimpoche meditated. The second temple was built in 1900 by the first king of Bhutan, Ugyen Wangchuck. In this temple, on the upper floor, is the holiest sanctuary in the complex. The main figure here is the Guru Rimpoche, surrounded by his eight manifestations. Concealed behind this image is the site of a cave containing the rock with Guru Rimpoche's imprint. Visitors are not allowed to enter this holy area. The third lhakhang was built in 1990 by the Queen Mother, Ashi Kesang Wangchuck, who also commissioned the 108 small stone chortens that surround the entire complex. Inside the temple is the largest statue of Guru Rimpoche in Bhutan, nearly two stories high.

In June, the Kurjey Tsechu takes place here. This famous masked dance tells the story of Guru Rimpoche's victory over Shelging Karpo. The *thondrol,* a huge thangka depicting Guru Rimpoche's eight manifestations, is unrolled early in the morning before the dances begin.

The dances are performed by the monks from Trongsa, for whom Kurjey Lhakhang is a summer residence. Visitors are allowed to enter Lhakhang at this one time of year to view the dances. ⊠ *Jakar, Bumthang.*

Tamshing Lhakhang. About 5 km (3 mi) from Jakar is Tamshing Lhakhang. Founded in 1501 by Pema Lingpa, it is the most important Nyingma gompa in Bhutan. Like the Gangtey monastery in the Phobjikha Valley (☞ *above*), it is one of the only places where Pema Lingpa's religious teachings have been continued to the present. In 1959, a small monastic community from Lhalung, Tibet, came to reside here.

Inside the lhakhang, on the inner walls, are original, unrestored images that are believed to have been painted by Pema Lingpa. In each painting, there is a central figure flanked by smaller figures who make up his entourage. It is amazing that these works were never painted over, and they are of great interest to art and religious historians alike.

Tamshing was restored at the end of the 19th century, around the time of Pema Lingpa's eighth reincarnation. The temple consists of two sanctuaries, one above the other. The inner sanctuary holds a statue of Guru Rimpoche. The upper sanctuary contains an assembly hall furnished with three thrones for three of the incarnations of Pema Lingpa. A statue of Tshepamey, the Buddha of Long Life, also resides in the upper chapel. ⊠ *Jakar, Bumthang.*

Thangbi Lhakhang. Although you can drive along the unpaved road that covers the 17 km (10½ mi) between Thangbi and Kurjey, the trip also makes a lovely day hike. The Thangbi temple was founded in 1470 by the fourth Shamar Rimpoche, who came to Bumthang to establish the Karmapa religious school. It is situated across a small suspension bridge, on a beautiful plateau overlooking the river. On the ground floor are statues representing Past, Present and Future Buddhas. Two paintings of Guru Rimpoche's heaven, Zangtopelri, and the heaven of Amitabha, reside in the sanctuary. Visitors to Thangbi are not allowed inside the temple. ⊠ *Jakar, Bumthang.*

Wangduchoeling Palace. This palace was built in 1856 by the Trongsa Penlop, Jigme Namgyal. His son, the first king of Bhutan, Ugyen Wangchuck, was not only born here, but also chose this location for his main residence. The palace was used during his reign and that of the second king, Jigme Dorji Wangchuck. Wangduchoeling was also home to the third king, until he relocated the royal residence to Punakha. The palace is now private property, and is not open to the public. ⊠ *Jakar, Bumthang.*

Dining and Lodging

$$ ✕📷 **Wangdicholing Tourist Lodge.** Run by the Bhutan Tourism Corporation, this lodge is situated on the grounds of the old Wangdicholing Palace. Cottages surround a courtyard and the main dining room. Each cottage has two rooms that are connected by stone walkways that are flanked by roses and wildflowers. A few of the rooms look like they have not been touched in years, with shag carpets and corduroy upholstered couches. However, they are perfectly clean and comfortable. The restaurant is decorated in traditional style, with carved wood trimming and hand-woven carpets and upholstery, and has a large bar and seating area. The usual Bhutanese, Chinese, Continental, and Indian cuisines are served; favorite items include the roast chicken and the bread-and-butter pudding. ⊠ *Jakar, Bumthang,* ☎ *03/6–31107,* FAX *03/6–31138. 14 rooms. Restaurant, bar, laundry service. No credit cards.*

$ ✕⊞ **Kaila Guest House.** This motel-like guest house is run by Kaila who is quite an interesting character and one of the best chefs in Bumthang. The rooms here are very basic and not recommended. However, the food here is always delicious, and special requests are fulfilled. Kaila is also a great fisherman, and if you're lucky, you'll get fresh fish from the river out back with some of the best french fries in Bhutan. ⊠ *Jakar, Bumthang,* ☎ *03/6–31219,* ℻ *03/6–31247. 8 rooms. Restaurant, laundry service. No credit cards.*

$ ✕⊞ **Leki Lodge.** Owned by Ganti Tour & Travel, this family-run guest house is in a three-story, traditional Bhutanese home with several cottages in the backyard. The rooms are basic and clean, all adorned with beautifully colored textiles woven by the proprietor. There's no official restaurant, but food is prepared upon request, and you can count on the ubiquitous mix of Asian and Continental offerings. Adjacent to the dining area is a comfortable sitting area filled with lots of couches. The proprietor will arrange for a weaving demonstration on the premises. ⊠ *Dekiling, Jakar, Bumthang,* ☎ *03/6–31231. 18 rooms. Restaurant, laundry service. No credit cards.*

$ ✕⊞ **Pilgrim's Lodge.** Opened in 1999 by Yangphel Tours and Travel,
★ this rustic lodge is situated alongside a stream, right near the Kurjey Monastery. It is decorated in traditional Bhutanese style, with wood carvings and hand-woven textiles throughout, and there is a lovely pond in the central courtyard. The kitchen and a traditional bukhari heater are situated in the middle of the dining area, making you feel like you are relaxing in someone's home. The cook will take suggestions, and if you have time to teach him, he likes to learn new Western-style dishes. Check out the beautifully woven Bumthang blankets on all the beds. You might want to ask the manager if they are for sale. ⊠ *Jakar, Bumthang,* ☎ *03/6–31191,* ℻ *03/6–31176. 10 rooms. Restaurant, hot stone bath, laundry service. No credit cards.*

$ ✕⊞ **Swiss Guest House.** Located on a hill across the river from the main
★ village, this charming guest house gets its name from the nationality of its owner. Both the architecture and the decor employ a combination of natural pine and traditional carvings, giving the lodge a slight rustic touch. The rooms have a camplike feel, with traditional Bhutanese locks (wooden slat-and-hole mechanisms) and bhukari heaters. The water here is supplied by a natural rock spring, so you can drink from the taps, a rarity in Bhutan. The kitchen is big and warm and often filled with the scent of the delicious bread baked there. Other house specialties include lasagna, cheese fondue, and fresh pasta. Upstairs, there is a large balcony with outdoor seating, a great place for reading, eating, or relaxing at the end of the day. ⊠ *Kharsumphe, Bumthang,* ☎ *03/6–31145,* ℻ *03/6–31278. 13 rooms. Restaurant, laundry service. No credit cards.*

Nightlife and the Arts

One of the highlights of this valley is the **Bumthang Tsechu,** a festival in October that draws numerous visitors year after year. This tsechu is one of the liveliest and most popular in Bhutan. Unlike other tsechus, this one is held at night. The fire dancers are said to bring fertility to any woman in the audience wishing to have a baby.

The **Kurjey Tsechu,** held in June, is the famous masked dance that tells the story of Guru Rimpoche's victory over Shelging Karpo. The thondrol, a huge thangka depicting Guru Rimpoche's eight manifestations, is unrolled early in the morning before the dances begin.

Shopping

Damo Tshongkhang (⊠ Traffic circle, Jakar, Bumthang, ☎ no phone) has a sign outside that says it all: "Fulfill your wishes with all kinds of traditional gift items." The shelves are lined with basic necessities like potatoes, chilies, and dried goods, but there is also an excellent selection of traditional Bhutanese textiles, baskets, and wooden bowls. It's a great place to relax and observe the local clientele.

Dewang Paper (✉ Bumthang, ☎ 03/6–31229), a factory for traditional handmade paper, is on an unpaved road near Jambey Lhakhang. Many varieties of Bhutanese paper of different colors and sizes are sold in a small showroom. Sometimes there are a few specialty items in stock, including matching envelopes and stationery, notepads, and bags.

Traditional Gift Shop (✉ South of the traffic circle, Jakar, Bumthang, no phone) opened in 1999 and has a wide range of gift items aimed at shopping tourists. Although the place is fully stocked with postcards, books, belts, bags, textiles, and clothing, few items here are made in the Bumthang region.

Udee Wood Manufacturing and Furniture (✉ Jakar, Bumthang, ☎ 03/6–31119) is a small factory that makes modern and traditional furniture and wood carvings. A showroom in the front sells the finished products.

Vegetable Dye Project (✉ Jakar, Bumthang, ☎ 03/6–31121) is part of Cottage Industries, a project in which local women are benefitted by the sale of their handicrafts. There is a small research room where you can see all the dyes and samples of the plants from which they are derived. In the showroom you can view the finished dyed fabrics, a few of which are for sale.

Yoezer Lhamo Shop (✉ Jakar, Bumthang, no phone) is the place to go if you have a hankering for delicious, soft cheese. The gouda-like variety sold here is made right in Bumthang. There's also a wide variety of Bumthang apple juices and brandies to accompany your snack.

Around Bumthang Valley

Unequivocally, the valleys of the Bumthang region are the broadest in Bhutan, creating a feeling of spaciousness. Jakar's dzong's and temples get the most attention from visitors, but all of the valleys contain holy temples, villages where women weave on traditional pedal-driven looms, and trekking areas with magnificent views of the surrounding peaks and the pink and white carpet created by the flowering trees of apple, peach, and apricot orchards.

The first valley crossed when arriving from Western Bhutan is **Chume**, a region known for its weaving, especially *yathra*, a traditional hand-woven woolen cloth. The valley east of Jakar is **Tang**. In this remote valley, the paths are lined with mani walls, chortens, and prayer flags. The valley of Ura is southeast of Jakar. It is believed to have been home to the earliest inhabitants of Bhutan. The village of Ura is the last you encounter before entering Eastern Bhutan. Both Tang and Ura are home to herds of yak and sheep.

Chume Valley

The Chume valley begins at the village of Gyetsa, the first village you encounter in Bumthang when arriving from Trongsa or Western Bhutan. Crops grown in the valley include potatoes, wheat, barley, and buckwheat. Chumey is also known for its weaving, known as yathra. The rolls of patterned wool are produced mainly in the village of Zugney. The women there weave on pedal-driven looms, following the tradition of their ancestors. Everything, including the dyeing, is done by hand. The women make most of the dyes from plants or minerals, often using "secret ingredients." The woolen cloth, which comes in a variety of designs, is used to make blankets, cushion covers, even garments. While driving along the road through Chume, you will pass many shops selling these beautifully designed textiles. After you pass through the small town of Zugney, you reach the Kiki La Pass, with its splendid view over the Jakar Valley and Jakar Dzong.

Tang Valley

Tang is the most remote of Bumthang's valleys. Since Tang's average altitude is 2,800 m (9,185 ft), the climate doesn't support agricultural endeavors. Therefore most of the people here are yak and sheep herders. From Jakar, Tang is reached by driving 10 km (6.2 mi) along the road that follows the left bank of the river. Just beyond the Dechenpelrithang sheep farm, the road crosses a series of hills and heads north towards Tang.

A short distance off the paved road towards Tang is a small parking area from which you can follow a small path that leads to **Membartsho**, the burning lake. The lake got its name from the story of how Pema Lingpa found treasures hidden there by Guru Rimpoche in the 8th century. The legend holds that in 1475 many people saw Pema Lingpa enter the river with a torch in his hand and disappear. He re-emerged carrying a small box, with the torch still burning. The miraculous sight inspired faith in many witnesses, and Pema Lingpa's reputation spread not only within the country but also beyond its frontiers. The lake has become a great pilgrimage site.

It is also possible to reach Tang on foot from the Jakar valley, and walking is certainly the most pleasant way to discover the valley. If you choose to walk, the best place to start is a route that begins just above the Swiss farm (your guide will know the way). The walk takes you past the **Kungzandra Monastery**, founded by Pema Lingpa in the 15th century. The monastery is on a hillside that rises above the valley. It is believed to be another of the places where Guru Rimpoche meditated.

The walking route towards Tang is lined with chortens, mani walls, and prayer flags, all evidence of the importance of Buddhism in the region. The trail meanders through cultivated fields and fruit trees, and after the Phephe La Pass, drops down through a pine forest into the Tang Valley.

Ura Valley

The fourth and easternmost valley in central Bhutan before the Thumsing La Pass is the Ura Valley. The valley opens out just after the Shelthang Pass (3,600 m/11,808 ft). On a clear day, just before the pass, you get a magnificent view of Gankar Puensum, the highest peak in Bhutan (7,540 m/24,731 ft), its enormous silhouette soaring towards the sky.

The roads descends into the Ura Valley in long, winding loops. Tight clusters of shingle-roof houses, divided by cobblestone paths, give the village of Ura a medieval flair. Above the village is a new temple, founded in 1986, dedicated to Guru Rimpoche. Most residents here work raising yak and sheep, and during the harsh winters the women wear traditional sheepskin shawls that double as blankets. It is believed that Ura was home to the earliest inhabitants of Bhutan, dating back to the prehistoric period. It is the last settlement before the climb to Thumsing La, the highest road pass in Bhutan.

Royal Manas National Park

The 1,023-sq-km (634-sq-mi) Royal Manas National Park (also known as the Manas Game Sanctuary) is on the banks of the mighty Manas River in south central Bhutan, which forms the border with the Indian province of Assam. The vast tropical preserve has been protected as a wildlife sanctuary since 1966 and is home to an astounding variety of wildlife, including tigers, rhinoceros, elephants, leopards, bears, buffalo, several species of deer, and the unique golden langur, a species of money native to Bhutan. More than 300 species of birds have also been spotted in the park.

At press time, the government was enforcing travel restrictions here for travelers due to the threats posed by separatists groups occupying the border in Assam. Previously, the park was open for treks, wildlife safaris, and bird-watching groups. Check with your travel agent or tour guide for the current situation.

Central Bhutan A to Z

Arriving and Departing

The only way to get to Central Bhutan is by car or bus. Your tour operator will make all the necessary transportation arrangements for you. As in the rest of Bhutan, you will be traveling with a guide and driver. Depending on your itinerary the drive through the region will take you approximately 2–4 days.

Contacts and Resources

CURRENCY EXCHANGE

The **Bank of Bhutan** has branches in Trongsa and Bumthang. Both offices can change traveler's checks, but the process takes a lot of time and paperwork. Some hotels may be able to exchange currency for you, but the best plan is to change money in Thimphu before heading east.

EMERGENCIES

Ambulance (☏ 112), **fire** (☏ 110), **police** (☏ 113).

POST OFFICE

There are **post offices** in Trongsa (☏ 03/5–21111) and Bumthang (☏ 03/6–31128). However, service from these branches is slow and unreliable, so try to send any letters from Thimphu or Paro.

EASTERN BHUTAN

The Thumsing La Pass (3,802 m/12,465 ft) is the highest motor pass in the kingdom. The climb is breathtaking, and watch out for the descent: it's one of the most exhilarating drives in the eastern Himalayas. The road plunges in a long series of bends, through dark pine forests, wild green pastures, and a variety of fruit orchards. Farther along the descent are gushing waterfalls and sheer cliffs that drop down to the river gorge, all surrounded by a stunning blend of wildflowers and constantly changing vegetation. The journey brings you to the warmer, subtropical climate of the lower elevations of eastern Bhutan.

This is an area infrequently visited by travelers. Many Bhutanese have never been to this part of the kingdom. Yet it is rich in cultural and architectural treasures, and full of pleasant surprises. The dominant language of the eastern region is Sharchop, literally, the "language of the east," of which there are several dialects. Since Sharchop is so different from Dzongkha, the language spoken in the west, residents from the two regions often have trouble communicating with one another.

The region is rugged and sparsely populated; thus, the quality of the hotels and food here is not as high as that in other areas of the country. Be prepared for rougher conditions, basic accommodations, and a lack of hot water and Western toilets.

Mongar

486 km (302 mi) east of Thimphu; 141 km (88 mi) east of Ura.

After a long journey filled with hairpin twists and turns, reaching Mongar, the entrance to the eastern region, is a relief. The town is built on a ridge, because the valley floors are too narrow to suit development. It's a small town with just a few shops and restaurants.

The **Mongar Dzong** was built in the early 19th century and is modern in comparison to others in the kingdom. The original dzong was destroyed by fire, and its reconstruction was ordered by the third king, Jigme Dorji Wangchuck, in 1953. The original building was at a lower elevation; the current site was chosen for its better climate. The small dzong is only two stories high, with an utse and a lhakhang in its center. Above the dzong on the hill is the local high school and a hospital. The new Kurichu hydroelectric project will change the industrial emphasis of the eastern region after its completion early in the new millennium. Upon its completion, it will have the capacity to output 60 megawatts of hydroelectricity.

Dining and Lodging

$ ✕⊞ **Shongar Lodge.** Run by BTCL, the Shongar Lodge is on a hill directly across from the dzong. Built in traditional Bhutanese style, the charming guest house has simple, very clean, comfortable accommodations, with handwoven upholstery and carpets. The sitting area, furnished with lots of couches and chairs, is a great place to talk with fellow travelers, enjoy afternoon tea, or relax after a long day's drive. The dining room serves the four main cuisines, and the Bhutanese dishes are particularly excellent. Stroll around the grounds where there are beautiful gardens teeming with flowers. ⊠ *Mongar,* ☎ *04/6–41107. 7 rooms. Restaurant. No credit cards.*

Lhuentse

563 km (350 mi) east of Thimphu; 77 km (48 mi) north of Mongar.

Although it a short distance from Mongar to Lhuentse, the trip takes about three hours. When the weather turns bad, the roads can easily become blocked, making Lhuentse the most isolated district in Bhutan. However, the road follows the Kuru Chhu, and the landscape is beautiful. At times, sheer cliffs flank both the side of the road and the opposite side of the river. There are few cars in this very rural region, and you will often pass villagers eager to catch a ride.

The **Lhuentse Dzong** is perched on a rocky outcrop above the river, usually shrouded in clouds. Its hulking form dominates the small village. Pema Lingpa's son, Kunga Wangpo, established a small gompa on the spot of the dzong in the 16th century. The dzong was built in 1654, by the Penlop of Trongsa, Minjur Tenpa, after a successful military campaign against the lords of Kurtoe. The building has been restored several times over the years, and now holds the administrative offices for the district, as well as the area's monastic community.

There is very little to see and do in Lhuentse, since the town consists only of the dzong, a school, and a few food stalls and shops. The area's main claim to fame is that the Kurtoe region of Lhuentse is the ancestral home of the Royal family. The town is also known for its weavers who produce what are considered to be the finest textiles and fabrics in the country. The distinctive embroidered brocade dresses made in Lhuentse are called *kushutara*. Women come down from the hills to sell their wares. If you are interested in purchasing these beautiful handmade garments, mention it to your hotel proprietor, who will put the word out that you're looking.

Dining and Lodging

$ ╳▦ **Government Guest House.** It's almost worth making the trip all the way here just to stay in this guest house. The location is exquisite, on a hill opposite the dzong, sitting high above the river. On a clear day you can see the snowcapped peaks at the far end of the valley. Although the rooms are basic, the cook takes requests and serves delicious Bhutanese food. ⊠ *Lhuentse,* ☏ *04/5–45109. 3 rooms. Restaurant, laundry service. No credit cards.*

Trashigang and Yangtse

547 km (339 mi) east of Thimphu; 92 km (57 mi) east of Mongar.

The trip from Mongar to **Trashigang** is the easiest part of the long journey east. The three-hour drive includes crossing the Kori La Pass (2,684 m/8,800 ft) and the rapid descent through the famous Yadi loops, 10 km (6 mi) of switchbacks that weave back and forth in a series of figure eights before reaching the valley floor. The vegetation changes drastically as the climate warms, and banana groves are scattered alongside the road.

Arriving in Trashigang is eventful, as it marks the end of the long drive eastward from Thimphu. The close proximity to Samdrup Jongkhar, in the southeast Indian state of Assam, has enabled the small town to develop into an urban center for the eastern region.

The town is situated on a ridge that juts out of the mountain. The business district is at the far end of the ridge, near the dzong, while private homes, the hospital, the school, and the guest house are scattered higher along the mountain. Trashigang is a bustling marketplace with people everywhere, particularly in the main square, where an enormous prayer wheel turns incessantly. Merak and Sakteng hill tribes come to trade yak butter and other assorted provisions. The tribes are known for their traditional yak hair hats and brightly colored clothing. Merak and Sakteng are about 80 km (50 mi) east of Trashigang, near the border with India's Arunachal Pradesh. In order to protect the lifestyle of these indigenous peoples, both Merak and Sakteng have been declared restricted areas for travelers.

The **Trashigang Dzong** sits at the far end of the mountainous ridge, overlooking the Gamri River. It is protected on three sides by deep ravines. It was built in 1659 by Minjur Tenpa, the Penlop of Trongsa, and named Trashigang Dzong, the "dzong of the Auspicious Mount." The dzong governed the whole eastern region from the 17th century until the beginning of the 20th century, when it was destroyed by a fire. The dzong was enlarged by Tenzing Rabgye, the Fourth Desi of Bhutan, and restored in 1950.

Trashigang has its own festival in November, celebrated with sacred dances. The dancers are usually lamas, are almost always masked, and represent gods and demons from Buddhist mythology. It is a very exciting dance to observe, and if your trip here happens to coincide during the tsechu, you are sure to be welcomed.

About 24 km (15 mi) from Trashigang, the temple of **Gom Kora** sits alongside the road. It is another of the famous meditation sites of Guru Rimpoche. Here, it is said, he meditated to subdue a demon. An enormous boulder sits in the middle of the garden of the temple, and legend states that anyone who can climb the rock will be cleansed of sin.

Farther along the road, about 28 km (17 mi) north of Trashigang, is the small village of **Yangtse,** which developed around **Chorten Kora,** one of two chortens built in Nepalese style within the kingdom (the other is Chendebji chorten, near Trongsa). The chorten is enormous. Its location, on a plateau in the foothills, is believed to be a site where Guru Rimpoche meditated. It rests on a square base, with wide steps leading to a circular dome covered with a gold-leafed umbrella. The chorten has since become a sacred religious symbol of peace and great happiness. It is believed that the prayers made here by those with clear souls will be answered.

Just outside Yangtse, a little farther along the road, is the **Trashi Yangtse Dzong.** The original dzong was founded by Pema Lingpa, after the Drukpa conquest of 1656. Because the dzong was rather small, and its location a bit precarious, a new dzong was built in 1997, in the current site overlooking the valley. This dzong is now an administrative subdivision of Trashigang.

Dining and Lodging

$ ✕🖂 **Kelling Lodge.** Run by BTCL, the lodge is set on a hill across from the Trashigang Dzong and has breathtaking views of the valley. Built in traditional Bhutanese style, the accommodations here are basic, clean, and comfortable. There is a small, glassed-in, octagonal-shape dining room, where wholesome, tasty Bhutansese food is served. The lodge is a 20-minute walk up a winding mountain road from town. ⊠ *Trashigang,* ☎ *04/5–21145. 11 rooms. Restaurant, laundry service. No credit cards.*

Eastern Bhutan A to Z

Arriving and Departing

You will reach Eastern Bhutan by car or minivan, and as usual, the transportation will be arranged for you, including driver and guide.

Contacts and Resources

EMERGENCIES

Ambulance (☎ 112), **fire** (☎ 110), **police** (☎ 113).

CURRENCY EXCHANGE

There is no easy or reliable way to exchange money or cash traveler's checks in this region. The best idea is to take care of your finances before leaving Thimphu. If you're caught in a pinch, you may be able to find a hotel willing to cash traveler's checks.

POST OFFICE

There are **post offices** in both Mongar (☎ 04/6–41144) and Trashigang (☎ 04/5–21111). The service from these small branches is slow and unreliable, so you may want to mail any letters in Thimphu or Paro.

BHUTAN A TO Z

Arriving and Departing

By Airplane

If you are traveling to Bhutan on a tourist visa, your tour operator will arrange all of your transportation to and from Bhutan, and you will fly in and out of Paro on Druk Air.

AIRPORTS

Paro International Airport (⊠ Paro, ☎ 08/2–71401) is the main gateway into Bhutan, since it is the only airport in Bhutan. The terminal has a restaurant with an extensive menu (including delicious baked goods), a coffee/snack bar, and a comfortable lounge. The airport is southeast of Paro village, approximately 6 km (4 mi) from the town center.

CARRIERS

Druk Air (☎ 02/3–22215), the Bhutanese national airline, is the only airline that serves Bhutan. It operates flights into the Paro airport from Calcutta, Delhi, Bangkok, Dhaka, and Kathmandu. Whether flying along the Himalayan range from Kathmandu or over the foothills from Calcutta, each flight has spectacular views of Everest, Kangchenjunga, and Makalu, as well as the Bhutanese peaks of Chomolhari and Gangkar Puensum.

FLYING TIMES

Nearly all flights to Bhutan include stopovers, so the length of time you spend in the air depends on where you stop. For example, it could take from 14 to 17 hours to travel from Amsterdam to Paro, depending on whether you stop in Delhi, or Calcutta and then Kathmandu. Similarly, it can take 12 to 15 hours to reach Bhutan from Sydney, depending on whether you stop in Dhaka or Bangkok. From the United States, it also depends on your point of departure, and of course, where in Asia you stop off. On average, the trip from the United Kingdom, United States, Canada, Australia, or New Zealand takes about 14 hours.

Getting Around

By Bus

If you are traveling on a tourist visa, your tour operator will arrange all your transportation within Bhutan. The tourist tariff includes all transportation, and you will always have car, driver, and guide with you. You will not have to rely on public transportation.

By Car

If you are traveling on a tourist visa, you will have a vehicle and driver at your disposal. Driving a car yourself is not an option for travelers in Bhutan.

EMERGENCY ASSISTANCE

Since you will not be traveling on your own, your tour guide or driver will take all the appropriate measures, in the event that roadside assistance is needed. The Bhutanese are very friendly and helpful, and will stop and offer help in the case of a breakdown.

ROAD CONDITIONS

There is one main road that makes its way across the entire country, passing through forests and winding endlessly up and down the mountains. Generally, it is very well maintained. However, stretches can get blocked by landslides during the monsoon season and snowfall during the winter.

By Airplane

There is no domestic air travel within Bhutan.

Contacts and Resources

Customs and Duties

ON ARRIVAL

The tour operator in Bhutan will apply for your visa, which takes a minimum of three weeks to process. It is mandatory that visa clearance be obtained prior to departing for Bhutan. The national airline, Druk Air, will not issue your tickets without this clearance. The visa will be stamped at the port of entry upon payment of the fee of US$20. Two passport photos are required for the visa.

All visitors entering the kingdom are required to complete the Customs Form upon arrival in Paro. The following articles are exempt from customs duty: (a) personal effects; (b) 2 liters of alcohol, 400 cigarettes, 150 gm of tobacco; (c) instruments, apparatus, or appliances for professional use; (d) photographic equipment, video cameras, and other electronic goods. The articles mentioned in sections (c) and (d) must be declared on the Customs Form. If these items are disposed of in Bhutan by sale or gift, they become subject to customs duty.

Import and export of arms, ammunition, explosives, narcotics and drugs, and wildlife products is strictly prohibited.

ON DEPARTURE

Be cautious when purchasing old and used items. In order to protect Bhutan's cultural heritage, the Bhutanese Government prohibits the export of religious artifacts or antiques of any type. If you are unsure about a particular object, ask your tour guide or call the **Division of Cultural Properties** in Thimphu (☏ 02/3–22284). If you listed personal electronic equipment, cameras, or computers on the entry customs form, they will be checked upon departure. The airport departure tax is US$10.

Dining

Since travel in Bhutan is an all-inclusive package, group travel dictates where you will be eating most of your meals. Usually you will eat in a restaurant or a dining room within a hotel or guest house, in the company of your fellow travelers.

Most meals offered to tour groups are limited to a fixed menu and served buffet style. Most hotels serve Chinese, Continental, and Indian food. In the morning, the cooks usually make a standard Western breakfast (eggs, bacon, toast, orange juice). Although many restaurants have extensive menus, dishes tend to be the same from place to place. Some chefs will take requests, a new concept that seems to work well with travelers. If there is a special dish that your group would like, make sure to make your request well in advance of your scheduled mealtime.

Both lunches and dinners are always served with either a rice or noodle dish, with a variety of vegetables and meats. Since most places cater to travelers, they rarely make Bhutanese food. If you would like to try the native cuisine, which employs a delicious blend of spices, chilies, and cheeses, tell the chef you would like to sample some of the local food. If you are a vegetarian or follow a strict diet, or would prefer something off the menu, discuss this in advance with your tour guide or hotel proprietor.

PRECAUTIONS

Tap water is not safe to drink in Bhutan, and ice should not be used in any beverage. If you can, either bring a water filter with you, or bring a water bottle, and treat the water with iodine; these methods avoid the pollution of plastic bottles. If you are traveling in a group, your tour guide will probably arrange to have properly treated water available. If not, ask the guide to provide you with bottled water at all meals. Also, brush your teeth with treated, boiled, or bottled water.

It's best to steer clear of raw, unpeeled fruits and vegetables and undercooked meat. Most hotels and better restaurants soak their fruits and vegetables in iodized water. However, if you are not sure, do not eat it. It is best to avoid salads. A wise rule of thumb is to eat hot foods while they're hot.

TIPPING

In hotels and restaurants, tipping is not the norm, especially since a 10% service charge and a 10% Bhutan sales tax are added to your bill.

Of course you can always make exceptions if someone does exceptional work for you.

Embassies and Consulates

The only foreign embassies in Bhutan are the Bangladesh Embassy and the Indian Embassy. Bhutan's relations with other countries are handled through embassies in Delhi and Dhaka.

If you have an emergency, or lose your passport or other important documents, you should contact the **Tourism Authority of Bhutan.** Popularly known as TAB, this office oversees all tourism activities in Bhutan. TAB is responsible for promoting and marketing tourism, organizing in-country programs, processing tour payments, arranging certain visas and permits, and, if needed, handling tourist emergencies. Contact them if you have any questions or would like a complete listing of registered Bhutanese tour operators. ✉ *Doebom Lam,* ☎ *02/3–23251 or 02/3–23252, TAB@druknet.net.bt.* ☺ *Weekdays 9–5.*

Etiquette

In Bhutan, as in most Asian countries, there is a deep respect for elders, religion, and the monarchy. Although there are many complex Bhutanese traditions and customs, you are not expected to follow all of them. A good rule of thumb is to follow appropriate Western standards of courtesy. It is considered a sign of respect to use the word "la" at the end of a sentence.

The head is considered the most sacred part of the body, and the feet are considered unpure. Patting someone on the head is considered to be a bad omen. You should never have your feet extended in front of you. In most temples and monasteries, it is customary to remove your shoes before entering. Many people follow this practice in their homes as well. Pointing at people or beckoning them with your hand facing up is thought to be the height of rudeness.

Bhutanese people rarely say no. Usually they answer in the positive, as a way of avoiding confrontational situations. If a situation is unpleasant, most Bhutanese will remain quiet and ignore it until it passes.

If you are invited to have a meal at someone's home, it is customary to bring a small gift, perhaps a box of pastries, or a bottle of wine or liquor.

TIPPING

Throughout your stay in Bhutan, you will most likely be with the same tour guide and driver. At the end of a trip, they appreciate a tip. If you are traveling in a group, take a collection and give it to your guide in an envelope. A moderate suggestion is a few dollars a day from each person for the guide (double that for trekking guides), a little less to the driver. Trekking guides expect notably more.

WHAT TO WEAR

In general, the Bhutanese are conservative. National dress, a gho, for men and a kira for women, is mandatory in government offices and schools and for formal occasions. As in other Asian countries, travelers should know that certain Western-style dress is culturally inappropriate. Clothes that are very short, tight fitting, or revealing should be avoided.

If you have an appointment with a government official, proper dress is required. Men should wear trousers with a sweater or shirt and jacket. Women should wear dress pants, a skirt, or a dress. T-shirts and jeans are not appropriate. The more formal or sacred an occasion, the more formally dressed you should be. When attending a tsechu or festival, dress up, because the Bhutanese don their finest attire for these momentous events. If you plan on purchasing a gho or kira, you should do so before your special occasion. The Bhutanese will be flattered if you wear their national dress. They are more than happy to help you purchase one and put it on, which can be a daunting process.

Health and Safety

CRIME

Bhutan is probably one of the safest countries you can visit. By and large, the small community has managed to steer clear of begging, theft, and sexual harassment.

HEALTH

Although no inoculations are required to enter the country, you should have your tetanus vaccination updated. Also, immunizations for hepatitis A and typhoid fever are advised.

Malaria is endemic in the southern region, and as chloroquine is not totally effective, mefloquine is recommended if you're traveling to this area. Always take precautions against mosquito bites regardless. No matter where you go, it's a good idea to protect yourself from mosquito-borne illnesses with an insect repellent containing Deet.

Diarrhea is the most common illness acquired by travelers to Bhutan. Many times it is simply the result of the change of diet. Sometimes contaminated drinking water, vegetables, fresh fruit, or mishandled food is the culprit. This contamination can also cause dysentery, typhoid, hepatitis A, and parasites. Diarrhea usually lasts only a few days; if your symptoms persist or worsen, seek medical assistance.

Language

The official language of Bhutan is Dzongkha, which is similar to Tibetan, from which it was originally derived. The national newspaper, *Kuensel,* is published weekly in three languages: Dzongkha, English, and Nepali. A growing proportion of the people, especially in urban areas, speaks English. Currently, English is the language of instruction in schools, so most educated people speak it fluently. Throughout the kingdom, signs, books, menus, road signs, and even government documents are written in both Dzongkha and English.

Due to Bhutan's vast ethnic diversity, there are a number of different languages and dialects spoken throughout the kingdom. In some areas, people from different regions cannot understand one another. In the eastern parts of the country, most people speak *Sharchop;* in the southern regions, they speak *Nepali;* and in Lhuentse, *Kurtoep.*

GLOSSARY

This glossary will help you with many words and phrases that are mentioned throughout the Bhutan section. They encompass religious words, dzonkhas, and a variety of other terms.

arra—homemade local spirits
Ashi—a title given to ladies of the royal family
bukhari—traditional wood-burning stove
chhu—river
Choekey—religious language
chorten—Buddhist monument, often containing relics
churpi—small cubes of hard yak cheese
Desi—secular ruler of Bhutan
doma—betel nut and betel leaf and lime
dorje—a thunderbolt, used for rituals
druk—dragon
Drukpa Gyalpo—the King of Bhutan

Drukpa Kagyu—the official religion of Bhutan
Druk Yul—Land of the Dragon (the Dzongkha name for Bhutan)
dzong—fortress-monastery
Dzongkha—official language of Bhutan
dzongkhag—district
dzongpon—old term for lord of the dzong
gho—traditional dress for men
gompa or goemba—monastery
Guru Rimpoche—founder of Mahayana Buddhism
Je Khenpo—Head Abbot of Bhutan
kabne—ceremonial scarf for over the shoulders
kira—national dress for women
kora—circumambulation
la—mountain pass
lama—religious teacher or priest
lhakhang—temple or sanctuary
Losar—Bhutanese and Tibetan New Year
lyonpo—minister
Mahayana—school of Buddhism
mandala—mystical cosmic diagram
mani stone—stone carved with the Buddhist mantra "om maani padme hum"
mantra—prayer or chant
ngultrum—Bhutanese currency
nyingma—lineage of Himalayan Buddhism, practitioners are Nyingmapa
om maani padme hum—sacred Buddhist mantra, "hail to the jewel in the lotus"
penlop—regional governor
phajo—priest
rachu—ceremonial scarf for women
rigney—name used for a school for traditional monastic studies
rimpoche—reincarnate lama
stupa—Buddhist structure from which the chorten evolved
Taktsang—Tiger's lair, one of the most sacred monasteries in Bhutan
thangka—painted or embroidered religious banner
thondrol—huge religious banner brought out for special occasions
utse—the central tower in a dzong
yathra—woven woolen cloth from Bumthang
yeti—the abominable snowman
Zantopelri—the heaven of Guru Rimpoche

Lodging

Throughout Bhutan, hotels, guest houses, and lodges vary in style and quality. All travelers visit Bhutan through a licensed tour operator and are placed in a government-approved hotel. All hotels listed in this guide are government approved and are very clean and well maintained, ranging from plush to basic. Although many hotels do not have phones in their rooms, all hotels are equipped with telephones, fax machines, and international dialing. During the cooler months, most hotels provide guests with extra blankets and heaters. Most have private bathrooms that are reasonably modern, with 24-hour hot water.

If you are traveling to eastern Bhutan, facilities are more limited, with very basic accommodations that lack hot water and Western toilets. While trekking, campsites are set up, with sleeping and dining tents.

Mail

Post offices throughout the country all work on government hours ($\odot$ 9–5, or 9–4 in winter months; closed for lunch). It is advised to send your mail from either Thimphu or Paro, since mail coming from other cities is often held up in the transportation process to Thimphu. Generally, mail going overseas takes a minimum of three to four weeks. If you have an urgent letter, there are two companies that can expedite the process: **Bhutan Post** (☎ 02/3–22281), called EMS (Express Mail Service), and **DHL** (☎ 02/3–24730).

POSTAL RATES

The International Postage Rate for postcards, aerograms, and letters (up to.75 oz) is Nu 20.

If you make a purchase and want to send it abroad, you can either have the shop make the necessary packing and shipping arrangements, or do it yourself through EMS or DHL (☞ *above*).

RECEIVING MAIL

Though you probably won't be in the kingdom long enough to receive mail there, you can arrange to have mail sent to the post office box of either your tour operator or your hotel.

Money and Expenses

CURRENCY

Bhutan's unit of currency is the *ngultrum* (Nu), which is equivalent to one Indian rupee, which is also legal tender in the kingdom. The ngultrum is further divided into 100 cheltrum.

EXCHANGING MONEY

The money exchange counters at the airport, larger hotels, and guest houses, and the banks in Thimphu, can exchange cash and traveler's checks. Some banks in the smaller towns can exchange money for you, but be prepared for delays, since it will probably be a lengthy process. It is highly advised to change money before you travel east or leave for a trek.

FORMS OF PAYMENT

Outside of Thimphu, all purchases must be paid for in cash. The hotel proprietors, store owners, and restaurant owners will accept either Bhutanese *ngultrum* or Indian *rupees*.

At press time, Bhutan National Bank had just been granted the approval from an overseas bank to act as the Visa and MasterCard agent in Bhutan. Many hotels and shops will now be able to handle credit card transactions. In the meantime, the only establishments that accept credit cards in Thimphu are handicraft shops.

In addition, some handicraft shops will accept traveler's checks with proper identification. If you plan on paying in cash, U.S. dollars and British pounds sterling are widely accepted, although the bills must be in perfect condition, with no torn edges.

TAXES

Although this process will be taken care of by your tour operator, a 10% service charge and a 10% Bhutan sales tax will be added to all hotel and restaurant bills.

WHAT IT WILL COST

Aside from the high tariff, the cost of visiting Bhutan is very much up to you. Compared to Western standards, it is possible to live and travel quite inexpensively. The following is a list of sample prices; keep in mind that most items on the list are already included in the tourist tariff.

Sample Prices: Continental breakfast at a hotel, $3.50; a bottle of water, 40¢; coffee in your hotel, 20¢–70¢; a bottle of soda, 25¢; museum entrance, 60¢.

National Holidays

Festival dates are determined by the Bhutanese calendar. Check with the Tourism Authority of Bhutan or your tour operator for exact dates. Below are some seasonal festivals and their approximate dates.

Punakha Drupchen (February); Chorten Kora (late February–early March); Punakha Dromchoe (late February–early March); Gom Kora (March); Chukha Tsechu (March); Paro tsechu (late March–early April); Ura Yakchoe, in Bumthang (April); Kurje tsechu, in Bumthang (early June); Nimalung tsechu (July); Tamshing Phala Choepa (September); Wangdue tsechu (late September); Thimphu tsechu (late September–early October); Tangbi Mani (October); Jambay Lhakhang Drupchen (November); Prakhar tsechu (November); Nalakhang tsechu (November); Tashigang tsechu (December); Mongar tsechu (December); Trongsa tsechu (December).

Opening and Closing Times

Government offices, banks, and post offices open at 9 AM on weekdays and close at 5 PM. In the winter, government offices close at 4 PM. Most offices close for an hour for lunch. Bank transaction hours are weekdays 9–5 and Saturday 9–11.

For the most part, shops in Bhutan open around 8 AM and close around 8 or 9 PM, depending on the season. In Thimphu, shops are open on the weekends, however those located on upper Norzin Lam are closed Tuesdays, and those in the lower market are closed on Wednesdays.

Passports and Visas

There are no special passport requirements when entering Bhutan. Your tour operator will handle all your visa formalities.

All applications for tourist visas take a minimum of three weeks to process. The operator submits your application to the Tourism Authority of Bhutan. TAB will then check to see that you have paid for your trip. Upon confirmation, TAB issues an approval letter, which in turn is submitted to the Ministry of Foreign Affairs, which gives final clearance for all applicants. After all is said and done, a confirmation number is released. Druk Air will not issue you a ticket until your visa clearance has been issued from Thimphu, and you can't board the plane if you don't have a confirmation number.

Upon arrival in Bhutan, submit two photos, along with US$20, and your visa will be issued to you. You will be granted a visa for the exact period of your stay in Bhutan, up to a maximum of 15 days. Should you require additional time, an extension can be obtained by your tour operator for an additional one-time fee of Nu 510 (approximately US$12).

Telephones

LONG-DISTANCE AND INTERNATIONAL CALLS

To call Bhutan from overseas, dial the country code, 975, and then the city code, omitting the 0. The Thimphu code is 02. International calls from Bhutan are very expensive. The best way to place your call is through your hotel/guest house switchboard. It costs approximately US$3 a minute to call overseas.

Tour Operators

All foreign travelers visiting Bhutan must book through one of the 60 registered tour operators in Bhutan. You can either approach a Bhutanese tour operator directly or through a travel agent or adventure travel specialist in your own country. Dealing directly with a Bhutanese tour operator has many benefits, since they can offer you the most accurate and up-to-date information regarding travel, festival dates, new programs, and places of interest.

All tour operators in Bhutan are registered through the Tourism Authority of Bhutan (TAB), and are subject to government guidelines regarding services, standards, and rates. No matter which one you choose, you are in good hands, although some of the more established ones have more influence in obtaining hotel and plane reservations. In order to give you a broad overview of tour operators and their services, the list below includes larger agencies, specialized agencies, adventure travel agencies, and promising new agencies.

As interest in Bhutan increases, TAB and tour operators are constantly researching ideas and creating new tours to suit the growing market. Some new packages that are popping up include: Nature Walks through the rhododendron forests, Bird-Watching, Fly-Fishing, Textile Tours, Ballooning, Mushroom Hunting, Marriage Ceremonies, and Fertility Tours. For the most part, all agencies offer similar packages. If you have a special interest, mention it to your tour operator, or contact different agencies, as one may offer the exact type of tour you are looking for.

Since Bhutan went on-line in June 1999, the Internet has provided a new arena for tourism. Soon, travelers will be able to communicate directly with the tour operators with ease. Many operators now have their own websites. Contact agencies for their website address. Please note, this listing is not complete. For a listing of all registered operators, contact the **Tourism Authority of Bhutan** (☎ 02/3–23251 or 02/3–23252, FAX 02/3–23695, TAB@druknet.net.bt).

These large companies offer a wide variety of packages with an emphasis on cultural, spring flora tours, and multifaceted activity packages; they are accustomed to handling large groups. **Bhutan Tourism Corporation Ltd.** (✉ Thimphu, ☎ 02/3–24045, FAX 02/3–23392, BTCL@druknet.net.bt). **Etho Metho Tours & Treks** (✉ Lugar Complex, Norzin Lam, Thimphu, ☎ 02/3–23162, FAX 02/3–22884, ethometo@druknet.net.bt). **International Treks & Tours** (✉ Lango, Paro, ☎ 08/2–71468, FAX 08/2–71466, Bhutan@wlink.com.np).

Yangphael (✉ Chorten Lam, Thimphu, ☎ 02/3–24509, FAX 02/3–22897, yangphael@druknet.net.bt) is owned by an avid sportsman, and has an outstanding reputation for leading treks. If you like the great outdoors, Yangphael arranges fly-fishing trips and archery festivities.

In addition to mainstream tours, many operators offer specialized programs, including ballooning, religious tours, architectural tours, medicinal herb trips, and tours focused on handicrafts and textiles. For these and other specialized tours, contact: **Yeti Tours & Treks** (✉ Chorten Lam, Thimphu, ☎ 02/3–23941, FAX 02/3–23508, yeti@druknet.net.bt); **Travel Bhutan** (✉ Wogzin Lam, Thimphu, ☎ 02/3–23911, FAX 02/3–22714, travelbt@druknet.net.bt); or **Masagang Tours & Travels** (✉ Choephel Lam, Thimphu, ☎ 02/3–23206, FAX 02/3–23718, Bhutan@bhutan.net.nt).

A few other recommended companies are: **Tashi Tours & Travel** (✉ Wogzin Lam, Thimphu, ☎ 02/3–23787, FAX 02/3–23666, tasitour@druknet.net.bt); **Rainbow Tours & Treks** (✉ Thimphu, ☎ 02/3–21370, FAX 02/3–21758, rainbow@druknet.net.bt); or **Sakten Tours and Treks** (✉ Chang Lam, Thimphu, ☎ 02/3–25567, FAX 02/3–25574, sakten@druknet.net.bt).

Visitor Information

Tourism Authority of Bhutan, popularly known as TAB, oversees all tourism activities in Bhutan. Contact them if you have any questions or would like a complete listing of registered Bhutanese tour operators. ✉ *Doebom Lam, Thimphu,* ☎ *02/3–23251 or 02/3–23252,* 🖷 *02/3–23695, TAB@druknet.net.bt.*

When to Go

The peak season in Bhutan is festival time, which happens to coincide with the better weather in spring and fall. It is also the time when hordes of travelers descend upon the small, isolated kingdom, crowding the cities and taking up every hotel room.

Most travelers come to Bhutan to observe the religious festivals, trek in the Himalayas, or admire the natural beauty. In the spring, bird life is abundant, and the flowers and rhododendrons are in full bloom. It is a lovely time for botanists and nature lovers.

Winters (Dec.–Feb.) tend to be on the cool side, and poor weather conditions can cause delays, as roads get blocked because of snow. Most of the trekking routes are closed during this time of year.

During the summer months (June–Aug.), the monsoon occurs. However, you should keep in mind that weather can be unpredictable, and your visit during the off-season could surprise you with pleasant, mild weather. There are many advantages to visiting Bhutan during the off-season. The tariff is lower and there are fewer crowds. During this time, you will probably get a reservation at the hotel of your choice and are more likely to get your preferred dates on Druk Air. Since there are fewer people, the proprietors can provide much better service and spend more time with you.

CLIMATE

The lowlands that run along the Indian border are tropical and the temperature is much warmer. Generally, eastern Bhutan tends to be warmer than the western region. The central valleys of Punakha, Wangdue Phodrang, Mongar, Lhuentse, and Trashigang have a semitropical climate with cool winters. Thimphu, Trongsa, and Bumthang have a much harsher climate, with heavy monsoon rains in the summer and heavy snowfall in the winter.

Winter in Bhutan begins in mid-November and lasts until mid-March. During the winter, the climate is dry, with cool, crisp days and cold nights. The monsoon usually arrives in mid-June, with the rain falling mainly in the afternoons and evenings. Late September, after the last of the big rains, autumn suddenly arrives and is a magnificent time for trekking, with gorgeous, clear, blue skies. Views of the Himalayas are best from October through March.

What follows are average daily maximum and minimum temperatures for four locations in Bhutan.

PARO

Jan.	45F	7C	May	70F	21C	Sept.	73F	23C
	18	8		54	12		52	11
Feb.	55F	13C	June	73F	23C	Oct.	68F	20C
	37	3		55	13		48	9
Mar.	57F	14C	July	73F	23C	Nov.	57F	14C
	36	2		59	15		37	3
Apr.	59F	15C	Aug.	84F	29C	Dec.	52F	11C
	37	3		59	15		39	4

THIMPHU

Jan.	54F	12C	May	66F	19C	Sept.	70F	21C
	37	3		48	9		61	16
Feb.	63F	17C	June	75F	24C	Oct.	66F	19C
	32	0		59	15		52	11
Mar.	57F	14C	July	84F	29C	Nov.	63F	17C
	41	5		64	18		43	6
Apr.	66F	19C	Aug.	77F	25C	Dec.	59F	15C
	48	9		63	17		41	5

BUMTHANG

Jan.	46F	8C	May	66F	19C	Sept.	70F	21C
	34	1		46	8		55	13
Feb.	55F	13C	June	68F	20C	Oct.	66F	19C
	34	1		54	12		50	10
Mar.	61F	16C	July	70F	21C	Nov.	59F	15C
	41	5		55	13		36	2
Apr.	61F	16C	Aug.	72F	22C	Dec.	57F	14C
	43	6		57	14		41	5

MONGAR

Jan.	68F	20C	May	86F	30C	Sept.	86F	30C
	50	10		68	20		75	24
Feb.	77F	25C	June	88F	31C	Oct.	84F	29C
	50	10		70	21		64	18
Mar.	81F	27C	July	88F	31C	Nov.	79F	26C
	48	9		72	22		55	13
Apr.	81F	27C	Aug.	102F	39C	Dec.	75F	24C
	61	16		93	34		45	7

5 PORTRAITS OF NEPAL, TIBET, AND BHUTAN

Nepal, Tibet, and Bhutan at a Glance:
A Chronology

Abode of the Gods

Books and Videos

NEPAL, TIBET, AND BHUTAN
AT A GLANCE: A CHRONOLOGY

c. 1500– 2000 BC First evidence of human settlement discovered in Bhutan.

800 BC The Kirata (or Kiranti, or Kirati) are believed by some historians to be the aboriginal inhabitants of the Kathmandu Valley. Other scholars think they arrived from the east in this century. They are cited in the Hindu epic the Mahabharata, but beyond this, little is known about them. They carry knives and rule the Valley for more than 1,000 years. The Rai and Limbu people today claim they are descendants of the Kirata.

600 BC The Kirata develop two distinct power groups, one that controls the eastern hills, another in charge of the Kathmandu Valley. Hindus build Mithila (in Janakpur).

563 BC Siddhartha Gautama, who would later would become Buddha, the Enlightened One, is born in Lumbini.

500 BC Bönism is the prevalent religion in prehistoric Bhutan.

c. 249 BC The great Indian Emperor Ashoka visits Lumbini. He erects a stone column to commemorate the birth of Buddha. He spreads Buddhism in Northern India and Nepal. His daughter builds shrines in Chabahil, near Boudhanath.

233 BC The 28th king of Tibet receives a Buddhist scripture and introduces Buddhism to Tibet.

184 BC The Indian Mauryan Empire falls, and Hindu states spread in northern India. Hinduism begins to take hold in the Terai.

c. AD 300 The Indian Licchavi dynasty leave their capital in Bihar, move north, and rule the Kathmandu Valley for the next 300 years. They extend their scope of power by marrying a Licchavi princess to the founder of the Nepalese Gupta dynasty. The Licchavi dynasty introduces the Hindu caste system to Nepal and a halcyon period of art and architecture for both Hindu and Buddhist temples flourishes. Religious tolerance is a hallmark of this dynasty.

c. 464 An inscription is written on a pillar in Changu Narayan, the first evidence of written history in Nepal. During this period trade routes to Tibet open.

608–650 The reign of Songsten Gompo in Tibet. A time of Tibetan growth. Scholars go to India to study Sanskrit, and Tibet script is born.

640 King Srongstesen Gampo establishes the Kyichu Monastery in Paro and Jampa Lhakhang in Bumthang. Tibet occupies Nepal.

641 Songsten Gampo marries Princess Wencheng of China to unite the region. She and his other Nepalese wife instigate a spread of Buddhism. Jokhang is founded.

654–704 Tibet conquers more of central Asia, including Chinese territories.

600–750 A Licchavi princess, Bhrikuti, marries a Tibetan king. Some consider her the reincarnation of Green Tara. Diplomatic relations open with China. Chinese scholars are surprised that Nepalis have such elaborate palaces and eat with their fingers. One account claims there are "multi-story temples so tall one would take them for a crown of clouds."

707–730 Two treaties are drawn up between Tibet and China.

747 Padmasambhava, known as Guru Rimpoche, visits Bhutan and introduces Buddhism to the area.

750 Although little is known about this time, it seems this marks the beginning of more than 500 years of political and social instability.

779 Samye Monastery is founded; Tibet announces that Buddhism is the state religion.

783 Another treaty between China and Tibet is signed.

815–836 Under Ralpachen, Buddhist texts are widely translated in Tibet.

821 Another peace treaty between China and Tibet is signed. Tibet keeps its central Asian possessions.

c. 816–836 During the rule of Tibetan King Ralpachen, Mongoloid troops invade Bhutan.

830 Lam Tsangpa arrives in Bhutan to spread Buddhism.

836–1247 King Lang Darma persecutes Buddhism. He's later assassinated, and this results in a struggle for power in Tibet.

879 A new calendar is introduced. It is still used today.

978 Indian teachers are invited to Tibet, bringing about a rebirth in Buddhism.

1040 The Tibetan poet and spiritual leader, Milarepa, is born.

1182 About 100 years after the founding of Sakya Monastery, Sakya Pondit, the famous Tibetan scholar, is born.

1189 Genghis Khan becomes the leader of Mongolia.

1200 Phajo Drugom Shigpo establishes his authority in Bhutan.

1207 Tibetans send a diplomatic envoy to Mongolia. To get Mongol support, a tribute is begun.

1200 Phajo Drugom Shigpo establishes his authority in Bhutan.

c. 1200–1220 The Valley has been carved up into little empires, but Arideva takes the title Malla, which at the time is the royal title used in India.

1227 Genghis Khan dies, and the Tibetans stop paying their tribute to the Mongols.

1244 Sakya Pondit is given temporal power over central Tibet after meeting with Mongol Khan.

1252 The invasion of Tibet by the Mongols.

1254 Kublai Khan gives religious and temporal authority of Tibet to Sakya Pandit's nephew. A political/religious relationship is formed between the Mongols and the Tibetans.

1300s Jayasthiti Malla, a Hindu, marries the princess of Bhaktapur. Jayasthiti claims he is a reincarnation of Vishnu. To this day, Nepalese royalty assert their lineage to the gods. Nonetheless, the Malla government is tolerant of Buddhism and tantric practices flourish.

1349 Muslims from Bengal violently invade Nepal and pillage Hindu and Buddhist shrines.

1354 Sakya begins to lose power in Tibet.

1357 Tsongkhapa is born. He later founds the Gelugpa Order in Tibet.

mid-1300s Invasions in India drive princes to Nepal. More than 45 small states are carved out in Nepal.

1382 Jayasthiti Malla gains control of the entire Kathmandu Valley. He divides the Newaris into 64 occupational castes.

1382–1482 Jayasthiti Malla cedes the kingdom to his son Yaksha Malla who expands it to the borders of Tibet in the north, the Kali Gandaki/Gurkha area in the west, to Birtanagar and Sikkim in the east, and to the Ganges River in the south.

1387 Geduntruppa is born. Tsongkhapa's disciple is named the first Dalai Lama posthumously.

1409–19 Ganden, Drepung, and Sera Monasteries are established.

1434–1533 The Dalai Lamas of Ü and the kings of Tsang fight for temporal and spiritual power of Tibet.

1482–1767 Yaksha Malla's three sons inherit the empire. They divide the land into three kingdoms: Kathmandu, Lalitpur (Patan), and Bhadgaon (Bhaktapur). Trade with Tibet flourishes but so do arguments among the city-states over these trade rights. While the Durbar Margs (squares) become a competitive field for the grandest palace and shrine, social services like water taps, gutters, and temples are built, too.

Meanwhile, the rest of Nepal is divided into little kingdoms. The Baaisi Raja control Khasa provinces in the north and west, while the Chaubisi control Magar and Garung areas in the east.

1543 The Mongol king bestows the title of Dalai Lama on Sonam Gyantso, the third Dalai Lama.

1616 Shabdrung Ngawang Namgyal comes to Bhutan.

1617 The great Dalai Lama V is born. The Tsang kings defeat the religious leaders in Ü for control of Tibet.

1627 Some of the first Westerners come to Bhutan. Jesuit missionaries Estevão Cacella and João Cabal visit.

1641 The Mongols overthrow the Tsang kings and give temporal and spiritual control of Tibet to Dalai Lama V.

1642–60 The Gelugpa sect enforces their spiritual and political control of Tibet. Dalai Lama V bestows the title of Panchen Lama on the abbot of Tashilunpo Monastery.

1648 Tibetan troops invade Bhutan.

1652 Dalai Lama V visits China.

1670 The Chinese conquer Mongolia and occupy Lhasa.

1680 Gyalse Tenzin Rabgye becomes Deb, the ruler of Bhutan prior to monarchy.

1682 Dalai Lama V dies. His death is kept a secret by the Regent. Construction continues on Potala Palace.

1697 After 15 years of secrecy, the death of Dalai Lama V is announced. The Potala is completed. Dalai Lama VI is officially enthroned.

1705 Qosot invades Tibet.

1706 The Khan of Qosot dethrones Dalai Lama VI and banishes him to China. Dalai Lama VI dies, and the Khan enthrones his own choice for Dalai Lama VII.

1717–20   The Mongols defeat the Khan of Qosot in Lhasa. China's Manchu Emperor dethrones the Khan's Dalai Lama and officially recognizes the Tibetan choice for Dalai Lama VII.

1733   Peace agreement between Tibet and Bhutan. The Chinese place their own ruler over Tibet.

1744–66   Narayan Shah and his brother Prithvi, members of the Shah dynasty of Gurkha, a tiny state west of Kathmandu, spend a quarter of a century fighting, scheming, and negotiating their way into control of the Kathmandu Valley.

1751   After an attempted revolt against the Chinese, the Dalai Lama is again recognized as the ruler of Tibet but he receives no official temporal power.

1766   Narayan Shah dies in battle. His brother Prithvi, credited with unifying the country, extracts brutal revenge for the death of his brother. He orders that all of the conquered men above the age of 12 have their noses cut off—all but the musicians who play wind instruments, who must welcome the warriors with song.

1768   Prithvi Narayan captures Kathmandu and is honored by the Kumari (Living Goddess) placing the ceremonial tika (red dot) on his forehead.

1768–1816   The Gurkhas fight seemingly everybody around them. They attack Tibet in 1788, but are driven back and counterattack. They have to pay tributes until the early 1900s, but they conquer as far east as Sikkim and as far west as Kashmir. Prithvi throws out the missionaries, claiming that the outsiders would take over with the bible, then trade, then cannons.

1774   Anglo-Bhutanese Peace Treaty between British India and Bhutan. The British lead their first mission to Tibet.

1814   The Gurkhas attack India with 50,000 men to Nepal's 12,000.

1816   It takes two years, but the British East India Company defeats the Gurkhas. The British do not colonize Nepal, but restrictions are enforced. They reduce Nepal's land holdings. The British now control Sikkim and conduct trade with Tibet via Sikkim rather than the Kathmandu Valley. A British observer is placed in Nepal; the Nepalese give the observer malaria-infested land, but the British endure it. These observers will be among the few foreigners to see Nepal for more than 100 years. The British also begin recruiting Gurkhas to their army, so these warriors begin to see more of the outside world.

1816–46   The Shah kings of Nepal are puppets. The prime ministers are plagued by court intrigue: not one prime minister between 1769 and 1846 dies of natural causes.

1841   Annexation of the Assam Duars, Indian border state captured by Bhutan.

1846   The Kot massacre unfolds. The supreme military commander is killed. Nepalese noblemen assemble in the Kot courtyard in Kathmandu's Durbar Square to try to uncover who is the murderer. Jung Bahadur Kunwar has his men slaughter the congregated noblemen. He is left the most powerful man standing. Bahadur pronounces himself prime minister and changes his name to Rana. He then declares himself Maharaja. Hence, the beginning of a 100-year-long hereditary prime ministry system in which the Ranas retain power and the royal Shahs retain the name "king."

1846–1947 The Shah kings of Nepal are popular figureheads vested with a lineage to the gods. The Shahs and the Ranas begin to intermarry, along with strategic unions with other upper-class Nepalese. Today, the queen is a Rana, the king a Shah. Their siblings have also married one another.

The Ranas keep Nepal closed to the rest of the world; hence, the early assaults on Mt. Everest were from the Tibetan border. However, Jung Bahadur Rana traveled to Europe, which explains the Neoclassical architecture in Durbar Square and in many of the Rana palaces. The Ranas abolish sati (widow-burning) in 1920 and slavery in 1926, but they do little else for their people. Instead, they build magnificent palaces and fill them with European furnishings imported from India and carried to Nepal by porters. They own Rolls Royce cars, but have no roads.

Nepalese people need permits to leave the Kathmandu Valley. Royal Europeans are allowed into the country to hunt in the malaria-infested Terai, but very few have access to any other area. Ancient customs continue to flourish in a society where the common people live in a medieval system and are virtually untouched by the West.

Poverty and lack of education drive men to enter the Gurkha armies for the British in India. Many end up fighting in World War II, where they learn about other political ideas. Resistance to the Ranas builds.

1854 There's political conflict between Tibet and Nepal.

1865 Treaty of Sinchula, between Bhutan and British India.

1876 The Russians and British argue over privileges in Tibet.

1904 The British send a military expedition to Tibet under Colonel Younghusband. It invades Lhasa. Dalai Lama XIII flees to Mongolia.

1907 Ugyen Wangchuck elected as the hereditary King of Bhutan.

1909 The Dalai Lama returns to Tibet.

1910 The Chinese reclaim their control over eastern Tibet and send troops to Lhasa.

1911 The Chinese Republic is founded under Sun Yat-sen. There's a Tibetan uprising against the Chinese. Later the Dalai Lama continues to rule without the influence of China.

1913 The Conference of Simla takes place between the British, Chinese, and Tibetans. The Chinese refuse to sign the agreement.

1923 Conflict over the rule of Tsang continues between the Dalai Lamas and the Panchen Lamas. During a disagreement with the Dalai Lama, the ninth Panchen Lama flees to China after attempting to get Chinese backing for Tsang.

1927 Gyalse Jigme Wangchuck ascends the Golden Throne of Bhutan.

1933 Dalai Lama XIII dies.

1935 Dalai Lama XIV is born.

1940 Dalai Lama XIV is officially enthroned.

1947 Indian independence puts pressure on Nepalese politics. With support from India, the Nepali Congress is founded. While the Ranas fight with the Nepali Congress, King Tribhuvan sees an opening to regain political power for the Shah family. The British end their Tibet policy.

1949   The People's Republic of China is founded.

1950   Chinese troops invade Tibet and many Tibetans begin seeking refuge in Nepal. The Dalai Lama flees to the Sikkim border, but returns after the Chinese government assures his safety. India becomes worried that Nepal is not a strong enough buffer state. It signs the "peace and friendship" treaty with Nepal.

Meanwhile, King Tribhuvan flees into exile in India. The Ranas continue to fight the Nepali Congress. B. P. Koirala, leader of the Nepali Congress, establishes a provisional government from the eastern border town Birganj.

1951   A coalition government is set up with the Ranas and the Nepali Congress sharing rule under the king. Free elections for a parliamentary democracy are set for the next year—but never take place.

The king appears as the hero of the people. In short order, he dismisses the Rana prime minister, ending the rule of the Ranas. Because intermarrying continues and Ranas are still appointed to key power positions, the Ranas still retain a certain level of influence.

1952   King Jigme Dorji Wangchuck ascends the Golden Throne of Bhutan and introduces land reforms.

1953   Establishment of the Tshogdu, the National Assembly of Bhutan.

1954   The Dalai Lama visits Beijing. Mao Zedong tells him religion is poison.

1955   King Tribhuvan of Nepal dies, and his son, Mahendra, is crowned king.

1958   Prime Minister Nehru of India visits Bhutan. After his visit, Planned Development begins.

1959   Mahendra agrees to an election in 1959. The Nepali Congress Party win 70% of the vote. The Prime Minister B. P. Koirala begins to run the country, to the chagrin of the king. The Tibetan New Year uprising occurs in Lhasa. The Dalai Lama flees to India, where he remains in exile.

1960   Mahendra declares a state of emergency in Nepal. He dismisses the government and imprisons some of the leading politicians. Political parties are prohibited.

1962   The king establishes his own form of a panchayat system, in which village councils send a representative to the district council who in turn elect the national assembly. In theory this system is representative, but in practice it is a corrupt rubber stamp of the king who appoints 16 officials of the 35-member National Panchayat, along with the prime minister and his cabinet.

The king opens Nepal's door to the West and invites international aid groups to the country. Some argue that much of this aid enriched the royalty. Both India and China build roads in the country. Mahendra adroitly plays one superpower off the other.

1964   China officially claims Tibet as an "autonomous region"—the TAR.

1965   Establishment of the Royal Advisory Council of Bhutan, a body comprised of elected council members to act as mediator between the people and the government.

1966–76 The Cultural Revolution in China. Much Tibetan art and architecture is destroyed by Red Guards. Monks are imprisoned.

1971 Bhutan becomes a member of the United Nations.

1972 Mahendra dies, and Birendra assumes power over Nepal.

1975 After it is deemed astrologically auspicious, Birendra is crowned King of Nepal. He tightens visa restrictions, a response to the hippie invasion.

In the same year, he declares Nepal a "Zone of Peace." India is not pleased, claiming it violates the "peace and friendship" treaty of 1950, which called for mutual aid in defense. Considering Nepal is home to the Gurkhas—viewed as some of the most lethal soldiers in the world—others find humor in the idea that Nepal could be considered a Zone of Peace. Still others point to the brutal police force and corrupt political system and question the "peacefulness."

1979 Protests abound. Birendra promises a national referendum to choose between a panchayat system and democracy.

1980 Nationwide demonstrations in Nepal protest rising inflation and corruption. The national referendum calls for a panchayat system in a 55% to 45% vote. The panchayat system is instituted. To this day, some people claim the vote was fixed.

1981 King Birendra decides that the people could elect 80% of the legislature but he would retain a right to appoint 20%. Each candidate could come from one of six "government-approved" groups but the candidate would not represent any one party.

Although the constitution calls for freedom of speech, many people are imprisoned without trial for "endangering public safety."

1985 Bhutan joins SAARC, the South Asia Association for Regional Cooperation.

1989 Nepal buys antiaircraft guns from China. In response, India's Prime Minister Rajiv Gandhi imposes a trade embargo on Nepal. Gasoline and kerosene are subsequently rationed. In December of the same year, India votes in V. P. Singh, who ends the embargo. The result in Nepal, however, is popular discontent with the Nepali government due, in part, to the hardships. Death of 10th Panchen Lama. The Tiananmen Square riots occur in Beijing. Tibet is placed under martial law.

1990 Demonstrations in Nepal are met with violence from the police. This fuels more demonstrations calling for democracy and protesting corruption and police brutality. In a clash on April 6, 1990, when nearly 200,000 people march on Kathmandu's Durbar Marg, eyewitnesses say more than 200 people are killed by the police. Other estimates put overall death tolls after several protests at 300.

Under pressure from his own people and international aid organizations, the king finally lifts the ban on multiparties. He also eventually abolishes the panchayat system. The Nepali Congress Party sets up an interim government. The king accepts the role of constitutional monarch, but executive decisions are made by the prime minister and cabinet. The Parliament consists of a House of Representatives and a National Assembly directly elected by the people. Political parties are permitted.

International direct-dialing services are installed in Bhutan.

1991   Elections are held in May. The Nepali Congress Party wins 37.75% of the vote, gaining 110 seats. The Communist Party of Nepal-Unified Marxist-Leninist (CPN-UML) wins 27.98% of the vote, gaining 67 seats.

The Nepali Congress Party is more closely allied to India, while the Communist party is connected to China, causing friction on many issues. As the underdogs not in power, the Communists take the position of constantly criticizing (often fairly) the Nepali Congress Party. They organize protests, marches, and strikes that continue to this day.

1992   The kingdom of Mustang opens its borders. Organized groups are allowed to visit.

1992   On April 6, a protest in Kathmandu and Patan once again ends in security forces opening fire on unarmed protesters. Twenty-three people are killed.

The government fires more than 8,000 civil servants in an attempt to contain its corrupt bureaucratic system.

1994   Discontent grows and Prime Minister Girija Prasad Koirala (brother of the late B. P. Koirala) steps down. A midterm election is called for November. No party wins a majority of votes, but the CPN-UML party wins the most votes and forms a coalition with the Rastriya Prajatantra Party (RPP) with some support from the Nepali Congress. It becomes a democratically elected Communist government in a country with a constitutional monarchy.

1995   The government does not have a parliamentary majority and can only cautiously apply land reforms and economic plans. In September, the government is brought down when the Nepali Congress withdraws support. The Nepali Congress then forms a coalition with the RPP.

Tibet's 11th Panchen Lama is announced by the Dalai Lama. The six-year-old is then forced to go to Beijing where he's put under house arrest, while the Chinese government insists that Tibet appoints another "acceptable" Panchen Lama. Another is chosen, and the Chinese government begins grooming him to be a "politically correct" Tibetan leader.

1996   The coalition government prevails in a no-confidence vote called by the CPN-UML.

Late 1990s   In Nepal, the press appears to be freer; articles critical of government are published. There are moves to guarantee more human rights, crack down on smuggling, the skin trade, and exploitative work practices.

Nonetheless, corruption continues. Perhaps this is best understood in light of historic acceptance of it and a nation lacking in political experience because it has been so tightly controlled for centuries.

1999   His Majesty King Jigme Singye Wangchuck of Bhutan celebrates the 25th Anniversary of his coronation. Television and the Internet are launched in the kingdom. The 14-year-old 17th Karmapa of Tibet flees to Dharamsala to join the Dalai Lama, who is still in exile.

ABODE OF THE GODS

Nepal is the world's only Hindu kingdom. Bhutan, on the other hand, is the last remaining Himalayan Buddhist state. And Tibet still houses a wealth of Buddhist history, despite radical attempts to secularize the country.

The fact is, in the brutal Himalayas where nature can be so cruel, faith is an integral part of everyday life. And thus the differences between Nepal's Hinduism and Bhutan's Buddhism are narrowed by the common thread of the importance of religion.

In Nepal, the very fabric of the country is the intricate tapestry woven between Hinduism and Buddhism. Hindus and Buddhists worship each other's deities and observe similar festivals, customs, and rites. For example, the Kumari, the virgin Hindu goddess, is selected from a Buddhist clan. Maya Deva, Buddha's mother, is worshipped as a Hindu figure. And Buddha is considered the ninth incarnation of the Hindu god, Vishnu, the preserver of the universe.

Religion is the cornerstone of these countries.

Buddhism

Siddhartha Gautama was born in about 563 BC. Raised as a prince in Lumbini, along the Indian and Nepalese border, he had all the material goods a man could desire at the time. One day, he ventured outside his palace and for the very first time, he encountered suffering. He decided to renounce his privileged status—an act called the Great Renunciation—to live as an ascetic and seek Enlightenment, which would end the everlasting cycle of death and rebirth. After practicing yoga and strict asceticism, he entered a lengthy meditation that led to his Great Enlightenment, in Bodhgaya under the bodhi tree. He called it the Middle Way to Enlightenment.

Transformed, Siddhartha went to Sarnath, near Varanasi in India, and preached his revolutionary sermon on the dharma (truth), also called "The Setting in Motion of the Wheel of Truth or Law." His discourse set forth his Four Noble Truths, which define the essence of Buddhism: (1) Life is suffering, (2) a suffering that arises from insatiable desires and a self-centered nature; (3) once one understands the cause of his suffering, he or she can overcome it by following (4) the Eightfold Path.

The Eightfold Path includes right views and right aspirations, which lead to wisdom. Right speech, right behavior, right means of livelihood, and right efforts to follow the path to salvation relate to proper and intelligent conduct. Right meditation and right contemplation bring wisdom and, ultimately, nirvana (supreme bliss).

Siddhartha Gautama became the Buddha (Enlightened One), or Sakyamuni (Sage of the Sakya clan). His faith became Theravada Buddhism, a religion of compassion and reason in which images were not worshipped, the existence of a permanent soul (atman in Hinduism) was denied, and the authority of the Hindu Vedas was rejected.

In the first century AD, a second school, Mahayana Buddhism, was formed that introduced the concept of the bodhisattva—the enlightened being who postpones his own nirvana to help others. Unlike Theravadans, who meditated only before symbols, such as the Buddha's empty throne or his footprints, Mahayanists also worshipped before depictions of the various Buddhas, other gods and goddesses, and revered bodhisattvas. Over time, Mahayana Buddhism divided into subsects, based on differences in philosophical systems or ritual practices. These subsects include Nyingmapa, Kargyu, Sakya, and Gelug. The Gelug achieved spiritual preeminence in Tibet. Their leader, His Holiness the Dalai Lama, is considered the God King of Tibet and is currently living in exile in Dharamsala, India.

Buddhist Pantheon

Once you know the symbols that identify the more popular members of the pantheon, they're easy to recognize.

BUDDHAS

Adibuddha (Original or Supreme Buddha) is considered infinite or abstract: without beginning or end. Still, he is often depicted in human form, sitting in the lotus (cross-legged) position with his arms crossed. One hand holds a vajra (thunderbolt: symbol of Ultimate Reality); the other hand holds the ghanta (bell: symbol of Wisdom). His body is usually blue.

The Five Dhyani (Cosmic) Buddhas, which emanated from the Adibuddha, represent the top tier of the Mahayana pantheon and embody the five elements of the cosmos: earth, water, fire, air, and ether. They are always shown in a meditation pose. They often appear on stupas, facing their respective directions. You might note them at the stupa in Swayambhunath, in the Kathmandu Valley in Nepal. **Vairocana** (Buddha of Resplendent Light or the Buddha Supreme and Eternal) is also known as Buddha in the Center. Both hands appear in front of his chest in an image of a preacher who is "Turning the Wheel of Truth." His color is white, his symbol is the wheel, his element is ether, and his vehicle is the lion. **Amitabha** (Buddha of Boundless Light) is also known as Buddha of the West. Both hands usually rest on his lap. His color is red, his symbol is the lotus, his element is water, and his vehicle is the peacock. **Aksobhya** (Undisturbed Buddha) is also known as Buddha of the East. The fingers of his right hand usually touch the earth. His color is blue, his symbol is the thunderbolt, his element is air, and his vehicle is the elephant. **Ratansambhava** (Jewel Being or Buddha of Precious Birth) is also known as Buddha of the South. His right hand is held low, palm open. His color is yellow, his symbol is the jewel, his element is fire, and his vehicle is the horse. **Amoghasiddhi** (Buddha of Infallible Power) is also known as the Buddha of the North. He holds his right hand up in a gesture of fearlessness, which also offers a blessing of confidence. His color is green, his symbol is the double thunderbolt (dorgee), his element is earth, and his vehicle is Garuda (half-man and half-bird).

Sakyamuni (Historic Buddha) has a third eye symbolizing wisdom and usually sits on a lotus throne. His body is gold, his earlobes are long, a protuberance atop his head is a symbol of his enlightenment, and he wears monastic garb. His hands gesture one of three ways: His right hand may touch the earth signifying his realization of spiritual discovery; both hands may be in his lap, palms turned upward as in meditation; or both hands may be near his chest, symbolic of the delivery of his sermon, "The Wheel of Truth."

BODHISATTVAS

Maitreya. (Future Buddha) usually appears with one hand held to his chest in the gesture of a preacher delivering "The Wheel of Truth," while the other hand holds a jug of water. His color is yellow, and he usually sits with his feet resting on a flowering lotus.

Avalokitesvara (Buddha of Compassion) has up to 11 heads and 1,000 arms and signifies compassion and wisdom. When he is portrayed with four heads, he is seated in the lotus position; when he appears with his 11 heads, he is standing. One hand holds a mala (rosary beads) and another carries a lotus. All Dalai Lamas are considered his incarnation.

Manjushri (Buddha of Transcendent Wisdom) appears with a sword held high in one hand, symbolizing his power to cut through ignorance. His other hand carries a book on a lotus, symbolic of wisdom.

Vajrapani (Buddha of Rain or Power) is blue, appears either seated or standing, and wears a serpent around his neck. In his most ferocious aspect, he carries a thunderbolt; in other depictions, he also holds a lotus.

Amitayus (Buddha of Eternal Life) is bright red, appears seated in meditation in the lotus position, and carries a vase of ambrosia, symbolic of long life.

THE BUDDHA SAKTIS

Green Tara (Green Savioress) is the patron goddess of Tibet and Avalokitesvra's consort. She sits on a lotus throne and holds a lotus in each hand.

White Tara (White Savioress) is also Avalokitesvra's consort. She usually sits in the lotus position, with her right hand outstretched in a gesture of charity, her left hand holding a lotus in full bloom.

NAGARJUNA AND PADMASAMBHAVA

Nagarjuna, the founder of the Mahayana School of Buddhism, usually wears a crown with seven snakes, monastic garb, and looks like the Buddha with long earlobes. His hands are normally held palm to palm to his breast.

Padmasambhava (Guru Rinpoche or Lotus Born) appears in royal robes, including the red cap of the Nyingma sect, and sits on an open lotus. His right hand carries the thunderbolt; his left hand holds a patra (begging bowl), and tucked in his arm is his khatvanga (magic tantric stick), which cuts through evil and ignorance.

Important Symbols

"Om Mani Padme Hum" is a mantra (invocation), which means "hail to the jewel in the lotus," reminding the devotee of the Four Noble Truths. The lotus, usually shown as the throne of the enlightened, grows out of mud to reveal its purity and beauty above water. Reciting the mantra helps the devotee rise above imperfection and end the cycle of rebirths.

Mani Walls are low stone walls, inscribed with "Om Mani Padme Hum," that guard Buddhist villages in the spiritual sense and protect them and nearby crops by diverting the runoff from heavy rains. You should always keep the wall to your right when you are walking by a mani wall. You may encounter them hiking in the Himalayas.

Stupas, or "receptacles of offerings," are tall hemispheres made of stone and clay, built near monasteries or villages. Eight early stupas are said to contain the divided ashes of the Buddha. Subsequent stupas hold the remains of sacred lamas (monks) or commemorate an event in the Buddha's life. If you see five steps built into the central mound, they stand for the elements that form the cosmos (earth, water, fire, air, and ether). The 13 rings depict the Path to Enlightenment.

Prayer Wheels are prayer-inscribed cylinders that contain the inscription, "Om Mani Padme Hum." Rotating the prayer wheel clockwise sends the mantra to heaven.

The Wheel of Life, which the Buddha traced for his disciples, appears in most monasteries and represents a visual microcosm of Buddhism. The central image is a large circle or wheel divided into six sections, with a small interior circle and a large circle around the rim. Often the wheel is held by Shindje, the Lord of Death, whose presence is a reminder of mortality. The interior circle shows the symbols of the root of suffering: a cock (lust), a pig (ignorance), and a snake (lack of compassion). The six sections inside the large circle describe the stations of life that come with rebirth. The bottom half portrays the three lowest forms: animals, ghosts, and the tormented in purgatory. The upper half reveals the inhabitants of the three worthiest realms: the deities, the ashuruas (fallen deities) who long to rejoin the deities, and the mortals who hope for ascension. The band around this circle depicts allegories of human faults or conditions that man must overcome. A blind woman represents ignorance, the monkey is consciousness, and a woman in labor represents birth, to name a few.

Thangkas, religious scrolls, appear in monasteries or private shrines as aids to meditation. These detailed paintings on cloth show deities, the mandala (☞ *below*), or the Wheel of Life. The entire painting is often enclosed in a silk brocade border, called its door.

Mandalas, created in sand paintings or thangkas, are geometric renderings of the dwelling of the god who resides within a circle that is set inside a square with four entrances, one on each side. During meditation, Buddhists gaze at the mandala to help acquire union with the divine.

THE EIGHT AUSPICIOUS SIGNS

The **Jeweled Parasol** protects the mind from evil influences. The **Golden Fish** represents man's rescue from the ocean of misery and is a symbol of spiritual happiness and wealth. The **Conch Shell** proclaims the glory of those who have achieved Enlightenment. (Before the Historic Buddha preached his first sermon, he blew on a conch shell.) The **Holy Vase** represents spiritual wealth and eternal bliss. The **Sacred Lotus** reaffirms the pledge to attain purity and salvation. The **Knot of Eternity,** which has no beginning or end, stands for the Four Noble Truths and eternity. The **Banner of Victory,** which is used in rituals and processions, proclaims the victory of the Four Noble Truths over evil. The **Eight-Spoked Wheel of Truth** symbolizes the Eightfold Path that leads to nirvana.

Hinduism

Hinduism, with its megafamily of gods and goddesses, extends back at least three millennia. Like Buddhists, Hindus believe in reincarnation. Hindus also share the Buddhist goal: liberation from the endless cycle of rebirth and the attainment of nirvana. Hinduism also espouses a similar relationship between dharma (truth) and karma (action). If one fulfills one's assigned duty and moral obligations to society, one will be rewarded in the next life.

Sacrifice is an essential part of dharma. An offering to a god blesses the worshipper in return. Sacrifice also calls for the relinquishment of one's individuality, which the Hindu believes frees the atman (universal consciousness) and allows the realization of nirvana. This theory explains the important ritual attached to cremation: The head of the deceased is ignited first to free the atman for the journey that will, it is hoped, end in heaven.

Devout Hindus also practice yoga, which they consider an indispensable expression of faith. Yoga, which literally means "union," is a series of complex mental and physical exercises that rid the practitioner of all thought to experience a sense of detachment from the realities of the physical world.

Strictures underlying dharma and karma also help to explain the tolerance of the caste system that divides all Hindus into four segregated rankings: Brahmans (priests), Ksatriyas (nobles and warriors), Vaisya (tradesmen), and Shudras (menial laborers). Panchamas (the filth), more commonly known as "Untouchables," fell outside the system, and now prefer to be called Dalits, or the "oppressed." A member of one of the castes who accidently touched a Panchama was considered polluted until he went through purification rites.

To most Westerners, the caste system seems like fuel for revolution, but it was a complex way of ordering society. Still, for the lowest categories, the system was doubtless very cruel. While it is said that they accepted their fate, seeing it as a direct result of their karma in previous births, poetry by lower-caste devotees from as early as the 12th century explicitly rejects caste. Centuries passed before the Untouchables found a way to come back from exclusion. The catalysts were Mahatma Gandhi and Bhimrao Ramji Ambedkar, a Dalit leader in India who was one of the principal authors of the Indian Constitution. Despite their frequent disagreements, Gandhi's and Ambedkar's efforts changed the way modern India (and the rest of the Hindu world) think about caste and saw to it that discrimination based on caste was legally abolished in 1947. Practically speaking, though, it still regulates much of Hindu behavior, such as marriage practices, despite matchmaking advertisements in major Indian newspapers that proclaim "Caste no bar."

Hindu Temple

As in Buddhism, the Hindu temple is filled with symbols of belief. Before the structure is built, a priest traces a mandala, which represents the cosmos, and determines the placement of all rooms and icons. The center of the temple, called the inner sanctum, represents the egg or womb from which all life originates. This is where the sacred deity resides. The vimana (spire) is directly over the inner sanctum. It draws the attention of the devout to the heavenly realm and its connection with the sacred deity.

Many festivals take place in the temple's mandapa (a front porch that may be an elaborate pillared pavilion or a simple overhang). Devotees congregate in the mandapa until the deity is revealed. Water is the agent of purification. Ideally, a temple is constructed by a river or lake, but if no natural water source is available, a large tank is built with steps around it. Before the devout Hindu worships, he takes a ritual dip to rid himself of impurities. Daily worship—usually performed at sunrise, noon, sunset, and midnight— is imbued with sacred traditions. Ancient rituals combine into an elaborate pageantry, with a touching gentleness toward the god's idol.

Hindu Pantheon

The Hindu pantheon is dominated by three gods—**Brahma, Shiva,** and **Vishnu**— along with their numerous avatars (incarnations). **Brahma,** the Creator of the World and the Progenitor of All Living Things, has four heads and four arms, each one holding sway over a quarter of the universe. The four heads also signify the four Vedas, the most sacred Hindu holy books, which put forth the concept of rebirth. Brahma is the god of wisdom; the rosary that he counts in one hand represents time, and his lotus seat represents the earth. Brahma's vehicle is the swan, a symbol of the freedom that comes with knowledge. His consort is **Sarasvati,** the goddess of learning. Unlike Shiva and Vishnu, Brahma has no avatars.

Shiva is the God of Destruction—destruction that gives rise to creation, just as the seedling tears apart the seed. This is why Shiva is also called the God of Creation and Sexual Powers and is often worshiped in the form of a lingam (phallic symbol). Images of Shiva have distinctive elements, like the third eye in the middle of his forehead, the tiger skins wrapped around his loins, and the serpents coiled around his body. Shiva often carries a weapon, a trident, or bow, fashioned from a human skull. **Cosmic Shiva,** a common manifestation of Shiva, shows him as a dancer, with four hands poised and surrounded by a ring that represents the earth. Since one foot holds down Apasmara, the demon of ignorance, his dance ensures perpetual creation. His mount, **Nandi,** the sacred bull, usually guards the entrance to a Shiva temple. Priests who pray to Shiva have three horizontal stripes painted on their forehead. Vishnu priests have three vertical stripes.

Shiva's consort is the most powerful Hindu goddess. With each avatar she assumes, her name and image change. When she is benevolent **Parvati,** wife of Shiva, she's beautiful and sexy. As **Durga,** the goddess of battle, she holds weapons of retribution in each of 10 hands. As **Kali,** the terrible black goddess who conquered time, she wears a necklace of skulls and dangles her red tongue. Devotees must appease her with sacrifices, formerly humans. Now, she accepts considerably less.

Ganesh, Shiva and Parvati's son, is the popular god of wealth and good fortune. He has the head of an elephant because, one legend claims, Shiva, unaware he was a father, returned from a trip just after Parvati told Ganesh to guard the house while she slept. When Shiva approached, Ganesh blocked the entrance. Shiva lopped off his head. When he discovered Ganesh was his son, he ordered the servants into the forest to take the head of the first creature they saw—an elephant.

The preserver of the universe, **Vishnu,** has nine known avatars; a 10th is prophesied. Each successive avatar reflects a step up the evolutionary cycle, beginning with the fish and moving up to the ninth, Buddha, accepted by the all-embracing Hindus as a figure within their own pantheon. Vishnu's most popular incarnations are **Rama** and **Krishna,** the sixth and seventh, respectively, who are the two gods embodying humanity.

Vishnu appears with four arms that signify the four cardinal directions and his command over the realms they encompass. In one hand, he carries the lotus, the symbol of the universe. The conch shell held in a second hand represents the evolutionary nature of all existence. A wheel in the third hand refers to the rotation of the earth, with each spoke honoring a specific season of the year. In his fourth hand, Vishnu often holds a weapon to protect him from demons. A common image of Vishnu has him lying on a bed of coils formed by his serpent **Ananta,** who symbolizes time. Creation will begin when Vishnu wakes up. Vishnu has two consorts: **Bhudevi,** the goddess of earth, and **Lakshmi,** the goddess of wealth and prosperity, who rose from the foam of the ocean like Venus. Lakshmi assumes a different name with each of Vishnu's avatars. When he's Rama, she's **Sita;** when he's Krishna, she's **Radha.**

Rama, the hero of the Hindu epic, Ramayana, slew the 10-headed demon **Ravana,** who had kidnapped Sita. This episode, including her rescue by **Hanuman,** the monkey god and Rama's faithful servant, is celebrated at Dussehra, one of India's most festive holidays. **Krishna,** a central figure in another great Hindu epic, Mahabharata, is a playful boy god. He plays the flute, has a weakness for teasing young girls, and is colored blue. An embodiment of a human love that has the power to destroy all pain, Krishna represents the ideal man and lover.

Other Faiths

Although Hinduism and Buddhism are the primary religions in the Himalaya (they comprise 95% of the population in Nepal and allegedly 100% of the Bhutanese population), there are some people of other faiths living in the region.

Islam

"There is no God but Allah, and Mohammed is his Prophet." This, the shahadah (religious creed) and the most important pillar of the Islamic faith, originated with the merchant **Mohammed** (his name means "highly praised") who was born about AD 570 in the Arabian town of Mecca. A series of revelations from Allah, passed on through the Angel Gabriel, instructed Mohammed to preach against the paganism practiced by the Meccans. Initially, Mohammed saw himself as a social reformer who advocated virtuous life in a city where virtue had vanished. The Meccans, however, saw him as a menace and a threat and forced him to flee to Yathrib (present-day Medina).

This move in AD 622, which Muslims now call hijra, marks the beginning of the Islamic era—an era in which Mohammed established the concept of Islam, which means "submission," as a way of life that dictated the proper behavior of the individual. By the time Mohammed died in AD 632, an expanse stretching from the Punjab in India to the Pyrenees in Europe, and from Samarkand (in Uzbekistan) to the Sahara, had converted to Islam.

The next ruler, called caliph (successor of the Prophet), was **Abu Bakr**, Mohammed's father-in-law. However, some Moslems favored, **Ali**, the Prophet's nephew, husband of his daughter Fatima and the first convert to Islam. After Ali finally succeeded to the caliphate in AD 656, civil war broke out. Ali moved his capital to Mesopotamia, where he was murdered by Moslem dissidents.

Ali's death signaled the beginning of a period of religious dissension between the traditionalists, Sunnis who followed the orthodox teaching and example of the Prophet, and Ali's supporters, who claimed Ali's right to the caliphate based on his descent from the Prophet. In time, Ali's supporters formed a sect known as the Shias or Shiites (the party of Ali.)

Originally political in nature, the differences between the Sunnis and Shiites took on theological overtones. Though the Sunnis retained the doctrine of leadership by consensus, after Syrians massacred Hussain, Ali's grandson, at Karbala in Iraq, the Shiites strengthened their resolve that only Mohammed's rightful heirs should rule. They modified the shahadah: "There is no God but Allah; Mohammed is the Prophet of God and Ali is the Saint of God."

Islam demands submission to God—a God who is invisible yet omnipresent. To represent him in any form is a sin, which explains the absence of icons in mosques and tombs. Every bit of decoration, often fashioned out of myriad tiny gems, is limited to inscriptions of the holy scripture, the Quran, and the names of Mohammed and his important followers.

Moslems believe Allah (God) existed throughout time, but men had strayed from his true teaching until Mohammed set them straight. Islam has concepts similar to those of Judaism or Christianity: guardian angels, the Day of Judgment, the general resurrection, heaven and hell, and the eternal life of the soul.

The duties of the Moslem form the five pillars of the faith. These are the recitation of the shahadah, salat (daily prayer), zagat (almsgiving), siyam (fasting), and haj (pilgrimage). The believer must pray to Allah five times daily, with each occasion preceded by a ritual washing of hands, feet, neck, and head. Every aspect of salat, during which one always faces Mecca, is predetermined by the Quran: the genuflections, prostrations, the actual prayer recited. Whenever possible, men pray at a mosque under a prayer leader. This is obligatory on Fridays. Women may also attend public worship but are segregated from the men.

The ninth month of the Moslem calendar, Ramadan, when Mohammed received his revelations, is a month of obligatory fasting from sunrise to sunset for all but the weak, pregnant women, and very small children. During this period of abstinence smoking and sexual intercourse are also forbidden.

During his life, a Moslem is supposed to make the haj to the Great Mosque in Mecca to participate in 10 days of special rites held during the 12th month of the lunar calendar. The returning pilgrim is entitled to the honorific "jaji" before his name and a turban carved on his tombstone.

The permanent struggle for the triumph of the word of God on earth, the jihad, is used to justify wars. However, most Moslems see it in a broader context of a code of ethical conduct that encourages generosity, fairness, honesty, and respect and forbids adultery, gambling, usury, and the consumption of pork and alcohol.

Mosque, or masjid, means "a place of prostration." It is generally square in shape; is constructed from stone, clay, or brick; and has an open courtyard surrounded with madrasas (cloisters) for students who are studying the Quran. After the muezzin (crier) sings the call for prayer from the minaret, the faithful line up in rows behind the imam (one who has studied the Quran). The imam stands in the sacred part of the masjid facing the mihrab (a niche in a wall that indicates the direction of Mecca). When the imam prays, the mihrab— an ingenious amplifier—bounces his voice back to the devotees. Only prayers are heard and prostrations are made; ceremonies connected with birth, marriage, and death occur elsewhere. You won't hear any music or singing either. For the Moslem, the human voice in prayer creates the sweetest sound to Allah.

Sikhism

Guru Nanak, the founder of Sikhism, was born into a Hindu family in 1469 when the Lodi sultanate, a Moslem dynasty from Afghanistan, ruled over his north Indian homeland. From an early age, he railed against the caste system, the corruption of Hindu priests, their superstitious beliefs, their unwieldy family of gods. His anger led to his new theology, which believed in one God, and his title of guru (gu: one who drives away darkness and preaches enlightenment: ru. In his poems and teachings, Guru Nanak urged egalitarianism based on love and devotion to a single, non-incarnate divinity called the Wahi Guru and conceived as the embodiment of truth, goodness, and uniqueness (these three words are the translation of the common Sikh greeting "Sat Sri Akal."

Nanak's view of Sikhism, recorded in the Adi Granth (Sikh Holy Book), subscribed to the Islamic belief that the goal of religion was the union with God, who dwelled within the soul. Through meditation and dharma (Hindu concepts), he believed the devotee could rid himself of impurities, free himself from the endless cycle of rebirth, and attain eternal bliss. For Hindus at the bottom of society, Sikhism offered equality and tolerance. They gladly converted and became Sikhs (disciples).

During the early years of the Mogul Empire, Sikhism flourished without interference until Emperor Jahangir assumed the throne. Jahangir resented the Sikh view of Islam and ultimately tortured and murdered the fifth guru. When Aurangzeb, an 18th-century conqueror, revealed his own ruthless intolerance, Gobind Singh, the 10th and final guru, forged the Sikhs into a martial community that he called the khalsa, which means "the pure." Gobind Singh instructed every Sikh man to observe and wear the five kakkari (visible symbols): kesh (uncut hair and beard); kachh (boxer shorts); kara (a steel bangle); kanga (a wooden comb); and kirpan (a dagger). All Sikh men also assumed the surname Singh, meaning "lion" (though not all Singhs are Sikh), and Sikh women adopted the name Kaur, meaning "lioness" or "princess." Members of the khalsa were to follow a strict code of conduct that forbade the use of alcohol and tobacco and advocated a life of meditation and courage.

Popular Beliefs

In Nepal, in particular, popular beliefs are as ingrained and often as important as Hinduism and Buddhism. Local spirits (deuta) are believed to live in lakes, rivers, trees, and stones; and worshipping these spirits appeases them.

Nagas, or serpent deities, live in lakes and rivers. Because they shed their skin, they are often hailed as symbols of rebirth. Trees such as the banyan, pipal (or bodhi), and nim are all considered auspicious. Buddha was said to have attained enlightenment under the bodhi tree. The spirit of the nim tree is said to help alleviate skin diseases.

To this day, a despised neighbor may be deemed a witch or boksi. In 1999, there were several reported stonings in small villages where one neighbor decided the other was a witch and should be killed. Often, such occurrences happen after the boksi is said to have cast an evil eye on something or someone.

Shamans are still popularly called on to recognize or appease the spirits. Shamans or jhankri are said to have an innate talent for mediating between the spirits and the others.

BOOKS AND VIDEOS

Books

The Himalayas

The Ascent of Rum Doodle, by W. E. Bowman, is a spoof on mountaineering in the Himalayas.

Don't Fall Off The Mountain, by Shirley MacLaine, is a personal account of her journeys through the Himalayan region.

Himalayan Flowers & Trees, by Dorothy Mierow & Tirtha Bahadur Shrestha, is a useful field guide pocket book with color pictures of the plants of Nepal.

The Snow Leopard, by Peter Matthiessen, is the masterfully written account of searching for the elusive cat in the Dolpo region of the Himal, but it is also a Zen search for inner peace.

Stones of Silence: Journeys in the Himalaya, by George Schaller, is a book to read if you didn't want *The Snow Leopard* to end because you were so absorbed in the flora and fauna. It was written by the wildlife biologist who accompanied Matthiessen in his pursuit of the snow leopard.

Video Night in Kathmandu, by Pico Iyer, is a delightful collection of essays on the *Time* correspondent's travels through Asia.

Nepal

Annapurna, by Maurice Herzog, a chilling account of the first successful climb of an 8,000-m (26,240-ft) peak.

Annapurna: A Woman's Place, by Arlene Blum, is a wonderfully told, inspiring, yet tragic story about the first women's expedition to Annapurna in 1978.

Birds of Nepal, by Robert Fleming, Sr., Robert Fleming, Jr., and Lain Singh Bangdel, is a field guide to Nepal's birds.

The Climb, by Anatoli Boukreev, is his version of what happened on Everest in May 1996 when eight climbers died attempting the ascent. Read it in conjunction with *Into Thin Air.*

Everest South West Face, by Chris Bonington, tells the story of how an expedition on a Himalayan mountain is planned and recounts the unsuccessful climb of the difficult mountain face. Other Bonnington books include *The Everest Years* and *Mountaineering.*

High Exposure: An Enduring Passion for Everest and Unforgiving Places, by David Breashears, traces his fascination with mountaineering and his introduction to the world of cinematography. (He's won four Emmy awards for cinematography, and is behind the stunning IMAX documentary of Everest.)

Into Thin Air, by Jon Krakauer, is a chilling account of the deadliest season in the history of Everest: the 1996 accidents.

Muna Madan, by Laxmi Prasad Devkota, a famous Nepali poet, tells the tale of a trader who leaves his young wife to travel to Lhasa.

Nepal: The Kingdom in the Himalaya, by Toni Hagen, is a look at Nepal before tourism. Hagen, a Swiss geologist, first visited Nepal in 1950, when it was still "forbidden" to outsiders.

People of Nepal, by Dor Bahadur Bista, is an excellent description of the various ethnic groups of Nepal.

Portrait of Nepal, by Kevin Bubriski, a coffee-table book featuring portraits of local Nepali faces.

Vignettes of Nepal, by Harka Gurung, shows Nepal as seen through the eyes of a Nepali.

White Water Nepal, by Peter Knowles and Dave Allardice, is an excellent guide to river rafting in Nepal.

Tibet

The Art of Happiness: A Handbook for Living is a book in which the Dalai Lama discusses (with psychiatrist Howard Cutler) the way to live a happy, meaningful life.

The Autobiography of a Tibetan Monk, by Palden Gyatso and Tsering Shakya (translator), is a gripping story of a Tibetan monk and his experiences in a Chinese prison until 1992.

Circling the Sacred Mountain: A Spiritual Adventure Through the Himalayas, by Robert Thurman and Tad Wise, recounts Thurman's trip to Mt. Kailash. For Thurman, with his Buddhist background, and Wise, who undergoes a spiritual transition here, the kora is a sacred journey.

The Dragon in the Land of Snows: A History of Modern Tibet since 1947, by Tsering Shakya, was published at the end of 1999 and discusses the modern history of Tibet and the complex political relationship between China and Tibet. Tsering Shakya succeeds at objectively viewing the issue from both sides of the fence.

Everest, by Walt Unsworth, is 700 pages of Everest and the stories surrounding the conquering of its peak.

Freedom in Exile: The Autobiography of the Dalai Lama, contains the story of the Dalai Lama's exile and his hopes for Tibet.

A History of Modern Tibet, 1913–1951: The Demise of the Lamaist State, by Melvyn Goldstein. In this book, one of the most prolific Tibet historians discusses what led to China's rule of Tibet.

In Exile from the Land of Snows: The Definitive Account of the Dalai Lama and Tibet Since the Chinese Conquest, by John Avedon, is considered a classic must-read that chronicles the Dalai Lama's exile from Tibet under Chinese rule.

A Mountain in Tibet, by Charles Allen, is a great read about Mt. Kailash and its history.

Seven Years in Tibet, by Heinrich Harrer, is the personal account of Harrer's incredible adventures in Tibet before the Chinese invaded.

Tears of Blood: A Cry for Tibet, by Mary Craig, tells a tragic story of Tibet under Chinese rule.

Yak Butter & Black Tea: A Journey into Tibet, by Wade Brackenbury, is the an account of how an American chiropractor/mountaineer and a photojournalist battle Chinese travel restrictions to find the Drung people, a remote tribe living in an area of Tibet where no Westerner had been for at least a century.

Bhutan

Beyond the Sky and Earth, by Jamie Zeppa, is an account of her stay in Bhutan as a volunteer.

Bhutan and the British, by Peter Collister, is a history of the more than 200 years of Anglo-Bhutanese relations.

Bhutan Mountain Fortress of the Gods, by Christian Schicklgruber and Francoise Pommaret, is a detailed history of this last surviving Mahayana Buddhist Kingdom.

From the Land of the Thunder Dragon: Textile Arts of Bhutan, by Diana K. Myers and Susan B. Bean, is a beautifully illustrated book on Bhutanese textiles.

An Introduction to Bird Watching in Bhutan, by Carol and Tim Inskipp, is an illustrated guide to Bhutan's birds.

In The Kingdom of the Thunder Dragon, by Joanna Lumley, is a personal account of one family's fascination with the Kingdom of Bhutan. Captivated by her grandparents' journey across Bhutan in 1931, Joanna retraces their steps.

The Raven Crown—The Origins of Buddhist Monarchy in Bhutan, by Michael Aris, combines unfolding narrative with rare historical photographs recounting the turbulent career of the Black Regent, followed by the lives and achievements of the first two kings.

Videos

Everest IMAX movie, by David Breashears, follows an international team of climbers as they scale the tallest Himalayan peak through skin-blistering cold, angry blizzards, and dizzying altitudes. Filmed during the infamous 1996 storm that claimed eight lives.

Everest: The Death Zone, Video from Nova, this film followed in the wake of the 1996 disaster. Scientists follow a team of hikers to measure, for the first time ever, the toll that high-altitude climbing takes on the heart, lungs, blood, and brain.

From the Land of the Thunder Dragon, Textile Arts from Bhutan, was made in 1994 by the Peabody Museum in Massachusetts.

Kundun, the Martin Scorsese film, is a cinematographic masterpiece about the life of the Dalai Lama.

Little Buddha, starring Keanu Reeves and Chris Isaak, includes much footage shot at the Paro Dzong in Bhutan.

Red River Valley is a Chinese film that shows the British invasion of Tibet from the perspective of Chinese government propaganda.

Seven Years in Tibet. They say the book is better, but Brad Pitt and David Thewlis appear in some beautiful shots chronicling Heinrich Harrer and Peter Aufschnaiter's amazing trek over the peak of Nanga Parbat into Tibet. There they're changed by the Tibetan people and their friendship with the young Dalai Lama.

Xiu Xiu: The Sent Down Girl. Joan Chen's directorial debut tells the over-the-top tragic tale of a girl who loses her innocence after being sent to the countryside of Tibet during the Cultural Revolution.

INDEX

Icons and Symbols

★ Our special recommendations

✕ Restaurant

🏠 Lodging establishment

✕🏠 Lodging establishment whose restaurant warrants a special trip

🦆 Good for kids (rubber duck)

☞ Sends you to another section of the guide for more information

✉ Address

☎ Telephone number

🕐 Opening and closing times

💳 Admission prices

Numbers in white and black circles ③ ❸ that appear on the maps, in the margins, and within the tours correspond to one another.

A

Acute Mountain Sickness (AMS), *109, 113–114, 161, 170*
Agnipura temple, *51*
Airports and transfers, *xii*
Air travel, *x–xii*
Bhutan, 224–225
bikes as luggage, xiii
booking your flight, x
carriers, x–xi
check-in and boarding, xi
with children, xiv
complaints, xii
cutting costs, xi
for disabled travelers, xvii
discount reservations, xviii
enjoying the flight, xi
flying times, xii
Kathmandu, 40–41
luggage limits, xxiv
Nepal, 110–111, 112
Paro, 195
Pokhara, 82
reconfirming, xii
Terai region, 98
Thimphu, 208
Tibet, 167
to trekking areas, 108
Akash Bhairav Temple, *26*
Aksobhya Buddha, *50*
Altitude sickness. ☞ Acute Mountain Sickness
Amitabha Buddha, *50*
Amoghasiddhi Buddha, *50*
Anantaupural shikhara, *51*
Ani Tshamkung, *133*
Annapurna region, *103–106*

Annapurna Temple, *27*
Antiques, *xxv*
Archery, *179*
Archery shops, *207*
Art galleries and museums
Bhaktapur, 65
Kathmandu, 39
Patan, 60
Swayambhunath, 51
Thimphu, 205
Art of Tibet, *127*
Arts and crafts schools, *199*
Artshop Gallery, *205*

B

Baha Bahi, *61*
Ballooning, *39–40*
Basantapur Tower, *21*
Basant Panchami, *9*
Bas-relief of Kalo (black) Bhairav, *21*
Baths, *61*
Besisahar, *105*
Bhadgaon. ☞ Bhaktapur
Bhai Dega Temple, *58*
Bhairabanath Temple, *65*
Bhaktapur
contacts and resources, 73
dining, 66–67
exploring, 64–66
festivals, 9
getting around, 73
Bhaktapur Art Gallery, *65*
Bhimsen Temple (Patan), *59*
Bhimsen Temple (Pokhara), *76*
Bhote Koshi River, *19*
Bhutan, *3, 174–175.* ☞ Paro; Thimphu
arriving and departing, 224–225
central region, 213–221
contacts and resources, 225–234
dining, 175, 177, 226–227
eastern region, 221–224
festivals, 178, 218, 231
getting around, 225
itineraries, 182–183
lodging, 178–179, 229
new and noteworthy, 5
outdoor activities and sports, 179–180
tourism policy, 181–182
trekking, 183–185
western region, 209–213
when to tour, 186, 233–234
Bhutan Olympics Sports Complex, *200*
Bicycling, *xiii*
Kathmandu, 41, 45
Lhasa, 144
mountain biking, 180
Pokhara, 82
Pokhara Valley, 86

Binde Basini Temple, *76*
Bird-watching, *179–180, 212–213*
Birenthanti, *104*
Birth of Sakyamuni celebration, *10*
Bishwakarma Temple, *62*
Bisket Jatra, *9*
Black Hat Dance, *178*
Boating, *81*
Books on Nepal, Tibet, and Bhutan, *251–252*
Boudhanath
contacts and resources, 73, 74
dining, 55
exploring, 52–55
festivals, 9
getting around, 73
lodging, 55–56
shopping, 56
Brass and Bronze Museum, *65*
Buddha Jayanti, *9*
Buddha's Enlightenment Day, *128*
Buddhism, *244–246*
Bumthang trek, *185*
Bumthang Tsechu, *218*
Bumthang Valley, *215–220, 234*
Burial mounds, *151*
Bus travel, *xiii*
Kathmandu, 41–42
Lhasa, 144
Nepal, 110, 111
Pokhara, 82
Terai region, 97
Tibet, 168
to trekking areas, 108
Tsang Province, 162
Ü Province, 151–152

C

Cable car rides, *86*
Cameras, *xiii*
Camping, *xxi*
on treks, 100
Canoeing, *90*
Carpet shops, *39*
Car travel (hired cars), *xiv*
Bhutan, 225
Kathmandu, 42
Nepal, 111–112
Pokhara, 82
Pokhara Valley, 86–87
Terai region, 97, 98
Tibet, 167–168
to trekking areas, 108
Tsang Province, 162
Ü Province, 152
Casinos, *38*
Caves
Mahendra Gupha, 85
Pharping, 68

Looking for a different kind of vacation?

Fodor's makes it easy with a full line of specialty guidebooks to suit a variety of interests—from adventure to romance to language help.

Fodor's. For the world of ways you travel.